BUDDHIST LEGENDS

BUDDHIST LEGENDS

EUGENE WATSON BURLINGAME

Published by

FacsiMile Publisher
12 Pragati Market
Ashok Vihar, Ph-2
Delhi - 110052, India
Phone: 011-47034999
Email: www.facsimilepublishers.com
info@facsimilepublishers.com

Distribution Network
gyanbooks.com
India, USA, Canada, UK, Australia

ISBN: 978-93-7073-637-5 (PB)
First Published, 1921

2nd Impression 2025

Printed at: Gyan Press, Delhi.

BUDDHIST LEGENDS
Author: EUGENE WATSON BURLINGAME

THE HARVARD ORIENTAL SERIES

VOLUME TWENTY-EIGHT

THE volumes of the HARVARD ORIENTAL SERIES are printed at the expense of funds given to Harvard University by Henry Clarke Warren (1854-1899), of Cambridge, Massachusetts. The third volume, Warren's *Buddhism,* is a noble monument to his courage in adversity and to his scholarship. The Series, as a contribution to the work of enabling the Occident to understand the Orient, is the fruit of an enlightened liberality which now seems to have been an almost prophetic anticipation on his part of a great political need.

A brief account of Mr. Warren's life is given at the end of volume 30. Also a list of the volumes of the Series, with titles and descriptions. This is followed by a partial list of Public Libraries in which the Series may be found.

HARVARD ORIENTAL SERIES

EDITED

WITH THE COÖPERATION OF VARIOUS SCHOLARS

BY

CHARLES ROCKWELL LANMAN

Professor at Harvard University; Honorary Fellow of the Asiatic Society of Bengal, of France, of England, and of Germany; Corresponding Member of the Society of Sciences at Göttingen, the Russian Academy of Sciences, and the Académie des Inscriptions et Belles-Lettres of the Institute of France

Volume Twenty-Eight

CAMBRIDGE, MASSACHUSETTS

Harvard University Press

1921

BUDDHIST LEGENDS

Translated from the original Pali text of the

DHAMMAPADA COMMENTARY

BY

EUGENE WATSON BURLINGAME

Fellow of the American Academy of Arts and Sciences; sometime Harrison Fellow for Research, University of Pennsylvania, and Johnston Scholar in Sanskrit, Johns Hopkins University; Lecturer on Pāli (1917–1918) in Yale University

PART 1: INTRODUCTION; SYNOPSES; TRANSLATION OF BOOKS 1 AND 2

With a photogravure of a palm-leaf manuscript

CAMBRIDGE, MASSACHUSETTS

Harvard University Press

1921

TO MY MOTHER AND MY BROTHER

HE *whose heart is unwetted by the rain of lust,*
He whose heart is unsinged by the fire of ill-will,
He who has renounced both good and evil,
He who is vigilant, such a man has nothing to fear.

SOME *are reborn on earth, evil-doers go to hell,*
The righteous go to heaven, Arahats pass to Nibbāna.

BY *self alone is evil done, by self alone does one suffer,*
By self alone is evil left undone, by self alone does one obtain Salvation.
Salvation and Perdition depend upon self; no man can save another.

THE *shunning of all evil, the doing of good,*
The cleansing of the heart: this is the Religion of the Buddhas.

ONE *should overcome anger with kindness;*
One should overcome evil with good;
One should overcome the niggard with gifts,
And the speaker of falsehood with truth.

DHAMMAPADA 39, 126, 165, 183, 223

Palm-leaf manuscript from ...
see volum...
Given by the late Simon Hewa...

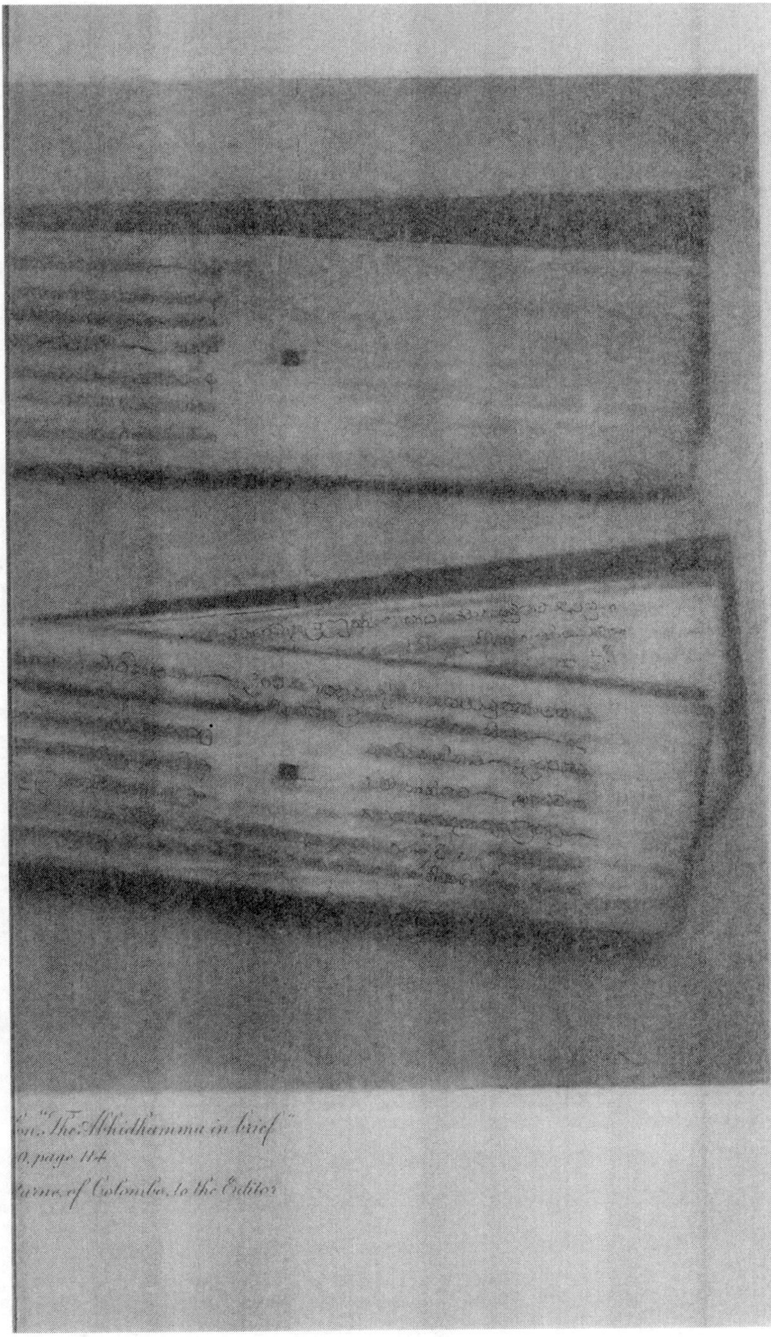

...on: "The Abhidhamma in brief"
...0, page 114
...arne, of Colombo, to the Editor

ထနံ အမ္မာတိ။ သာ ဟတ္ထပူရံ ဂဟေတွာ တဿ ဟတ္ထေသု ဌပေသိ။ တံ ဟိရညသုဝဏ္ဏမေဝ ဟောတိ။

အထ နံ သေဋ္ဌိ ကတရံ တေ အမ္မ ဂေဟန္တိ ပုစ္ဆိတွာ အသုကံ နာမာတိ ဝုတ္တေ တဿာ အသာမိကဘာဝံ ဉတွာ ဓနံ ပဋိသာမေတွာ တံ အတ္တနော ပုတ္တဿ အာနေတွာ စတ္တာလီသကောဋိဓနံ ပဋိစ္ဆာပေသိ။ တံပိ သဗ္ဗံ ဟိရညသုဝဏ္ဏမေဝ အဟောသိ။ တဿာ အပရေန သမယေန ဂဗ္ဘော ပတိဋ္ဌဟိ။ သာ ဒသမာသစ္စယေန ပုတ္တံ ဝိဇာယိ။ သော ပဒသာ ဂမနကာလေ ကာလမကာသိ။ သာ အဒိဋ္ဌပုဗ္ဗမရဏတာယ တံ ဈာပေတုံ နီဟရန္တေ ဝါရေတွာ ပုတ္တဿ မေ ဘေသဇ္ဇံ ပုစ္ဆိဿာမီတိ မတကဠေဝရံ အင်္ကေနာဒါယ အပိ နု မေ ပုတ္တဿ ဘေသဇ္ဇံ ဇာနာထာတိ ပုစ္ဆန္တီ ဃရပဋိပါဋိယာ ဝိစရတိ။ အထ နံ မနုဿာ အမ္မ တွံ ဥမ္မတ္တိကာ ဇာတာ မတကပုတ္တဿ ဘေသဇ္ဇံ ပုစ္ဆန္တီ ဝိစရသီတိ ဝဒန္တိ။ သာ အဝဿံ မမ ပုတ္တဿ ဘေသဇ္ဇံ ဇာနနကံ လဘိဿာမီတိ မညမာနာ ဝိစရတိ။ အထ နံ ဧကော ပဏ္ဍိတပုရိသော ဒိသွာ အယံ မမ ဓီတာ ပဌမံ ပုတ္တကံ ဝိဇာတာ ဘဝိဿတိ၊ အဒိဋ္ဌပုဗ္ဗမရဏာ တိ မယာ ဣမိဿာ အဝဿယေန ဘဝိတုံ ဝဋ္ဋတီတိ စိန္တေတွာ အာဟ။ အမ္မ အဟံ ဘေသဇ္ဇံ န ဇာနာမိ၊ ဘေသဇ္ဇဇာနနကံ ပန ဇာနာမီတိ။ ကော ဇာနာတိ တာတာတိ။ သတ္ထာ အမ္မ ဇာနာတိ။ ဂစ္ဆ တံ ပုစ္ဆာဟီတိ။ သာ ဂမိဿာမိ တာတ ပုစ္ဆိဿာမိ တာတာတိ ဝတွာ သတ္ထာရံ ဥပသင်္ကမိတွာ ဝန္ဒိတွာ ဧကမန္တံ ဌိတာ ပုစ္ဆိ။ တုမှေ ကိရ မေ ပုတ္တဿ ဘေသဇ္ဇံ ဇာနာထ ဘန္တေတိ။ အာမ ဇာနာမီတိ။ ကိံ လဒ္ဓုံ ဝဋ္ဋတီတိ။ အစ္ဆရဂ္ဂဟဏမတ္တံ သိဒ္ဓတ္ထကံ လဒ္ဓုံ ဝဋ္ဋတီတိ။ လဘိဿာမိ ဘန္တေ၊ ကဿ ပန ဂေဟေ လဒ္ဓုံ ဝဋ္ဋတီတိ။ ယဿ ဂေဟေ ပုတ္တော ဝါ ဓီတာ ဝါ န ကောစိ မတပုဗ္ဗောတိ။ သာ သာဓု ဘန္တေတိ သတ္ထာရံ ဝန္ဒိတွာ မတပုတ္တကံ အင်္ကေနာဒါယ ဂါမံ ပဝိသိတွာ ပဌမဂေဟဿ ဒွါရေ ဌတွာ အတ္ထိ နု ခေါ ဣမသ္မိံ ဂေဟေ သိဒ္ဓတ္ထကော၊ ပုတ္တဿ ကိရ မေ ဘေသဇ္ဇံ ဧတန္တိ ဝတွာ အတ္ထီတိ ဝုတ္တေ တေန ဟိ ဒေထာတိ။ တေဟိ အာဟရိတွာ သိဒ္ဓတ္ထကေသု ဒိယျမာနေသု ဣမသ္မိံ ဂေဟေ ပုတ္တော ဝါ ဓီတာ ဝါ မတပုဗ္ဗော ကစ္စိ နတ္ထိ အမ္မာတိ ပုစ္ဆိတွာ ကိံ ဝဒေသိ အမ္မ၊ ဇီဝမာနာ ဟိ ကတိပယာ၊ မတကာ ဧဝ ဗဟုကာတိ

Kisā Gotamī seeks mustard-seed to cure her dead child

Pāli text, in Burmese letters, of Story 13, Book 8, Volume 29

Page 485 of the Burmese edition, described below, page 67

For the same in Roman letters, see Norman's edition, 2.272.12–

—oo—

ඨමපුත්තකං විජාතා භවිස්සතී'ති අදිට්ඨපුබ්බමරණතාය මයා ඉමිස්සා
අවස්සයෙන භවිතුං වට්ටතී'ති චින්තෙත්වා ආහ අහං අම්ම භෙසජ්ජං
න ජානාමි භෙසජ්ජජානනකං පන ජානාමී'ති කො ජානාති තාතා'ති
සත්ථා අම්ම ජානාති ගච්ඡ තං පුච්ඡා'ති සා ගමිස්සාමි තාත පුච්ඡිස්සා
මී'ති වත්වා සත්ථාරං උපසඞ්කමිත්වා වන්දිත්වා එකමන්තං ඨිතා පුච්ඡි
තුම්හෙ කිර මෙ පුත්තස්ස භෙසජ්ජං ජානාථ භන්තෙ'ති ආම ජානා
මී'ති කිං ලද්ධුං වට්ටතී'ති අච්ඡරගහණමත්තං සිද්ධත්ථකෙ ලද්ධුං වට්ට
තී'ති ලභිස්සාමි භන්තෙ කස්ස පන ගෙහෙ ලද්ධුං වට්ටතී'ති යස්ස
ගෙහෙ පුත්තො වා ධීතා වා න කොචි මතපුබ්බො'ති සා සාධු භ
න්තෙ'ති සත්ථාරං වන්දිත්වා මතපුත්තකං අඞ්කෙනාදාය අන්තොගා
මං පවිසිත්වා පඨමගෙහස්ස ද්වාරෙ ඨත්වා අත්ථි නු ඛො ඉමස්මිං ගෙ
හෙ සිද්ධත්ථකො පුත්තස්ස කිර මෙ භෙසජ්ජං එතං'ති වත්වා අත්ථී'ති
වුත්තෙ තෙනහි දෙථා'ති තෙහි ආහරිත්වා සිද්ධත්ථකෙසු දීයමානෙ
සු ඉමස්මිං ගෙහෙ පුත්තො වා ධීතා වා මතපුබ්බො කච්චි නත්ථි අ
ම්මා'ති පුච්ඡිත්වා කිං වදෙසි අම්ම ජීවමානා හි කතිපයා මතකා එ
ව බහුකා'ති වුත්තෙ තෙනහි ගණ්හථ වො සිද්ධත්ථකෙ න තං මම පු
ත්තස්ස භෙසජ්ජ'න්ති පටික්ඛිපි සා ඉමිනා නියාමෙන ආදිතො පට්ඨා
ය පුච්ඡන්ති විචරි සා එකගෙහෙ'පි සිද්ධත්ථකෙ අගහෙත්වා සායණ්හ
සමයෙ චින්තෙසි අහො භාරියං කම්මං අහං මමෙව පුත්තො මතො
'ති සඤ්ඤමකාසිං සකලගාමෙ හි පන ජීවන්තෙහි මතකාව බහුතරා
ති තස්සා එවං චින්තයමානාය පුත්තසිනෙහං මුදුකහදයං ථද්ධභා
වං අගමාසි සා පුත්තං අරඤ්ඤෙ ඡඩ්ඩෙත්වා සත්ථුසන්තිකං ගන්ත්වා
වන්දිත්වා එකමන්තං අට්ඨාසි අථ නං සත්ථා ලද්ධා තෙ එකච්ඡරමත්තා
සිද්ධත්ථකා'ති ආහ න ලද්ධා භන්තෙ'ති සකලගාමෙ'පි ජීවන්තෙහි ම
තකායෙව බහුතරා'ති අථ නං සත්ථා ත්වං මමෙව පුත්තො මතො
'ති සල්ලක්ඛෙසි ධුවධම්මො එස සත්තානං මච්චුරාජා හි සබ්බස
ත්තෙ අපරිපුණ්ණජ්ඣාසයෙ එව මහොඝො විය පරිකඩ්ඩමානො
යෙව අපායසමුද්දෙ පක්ඛිපතී'ති වත්වා ධම්මං දෙසෙන්තො ඉමං ගා
ථමාහ:—

තං පුත්තපසුසම්මත්තං බ්‍යාසත්තමනසං නරං,
සුත්තං ගාමං මහොඝොව මච්චු ආදාය ගච්ඡතී'ති.

ගාථාපරියොසානෙ කිසාගොතමී සොතාපත්තිඵලෙ පතිට්ඨහි අ
ඤ්ඤෙපි බහූ සොතාපත්තිඵලාදීනි පාපුණිංසූ'ති සා පන සත්ථාරං
පබ්බජ්ජං යාචි සත්ථා භික්ඛුණීනං සන්තිකං පෙසෙත්වා පබ්බාජෙසි
සා ලද්ධූපසම්පදා කිසාගොතමීථෙරී'ති පඤ්ඤායි සා එකදිවසං උ
පොසථාගාරෙ වාරං පත්වා දීපං ජාලෙත්වා නිසින්නා දීපජාලා උප්ප
ජ්ජන්තියො ච උප්පජ්ජන්තියො ච දිස්වා එවමෙවම්පිමෙ සත්තා උ
ප්පජ්ජන්තිචෙව නිරුජ්ඣන්තිච නිබ්බාණප්පත්තා එව න පඤ්ඤායු

Kisā Gotamī seeks mustard-seed to cure her dead child

Pāli text, in Cingalese letters, of Story 13, Book 8, Volume 29

Page 346 of the Cingalese edition, described below, page 67

For the same in Roman letters, see Norman's edition, 2.273.6–

PREFATORY NOTE

I wish to thank Professor Morris Jastrow, Jr., Librarian of the University of Pennsylvania, and his assistants, and Dr. M. L. Raney, Librarian of the Johns Hopkins University, for generous facilities afforded me in the loan of books. I am greatly indebted also to Mr. Albert J. Edmunds of Philadelphia, author of *Buddhist and Christian Gospels*, and of a translation of the Dhammapada, for the loan of many rare and valuable books from his private collection, at present deposited in the Library of Bryn Mawr College. I have also to thank Mrs. C. A. F. Rhys Davids, Honorary Secretary of the Pāli Text Society, for her kindness in sending to me, as fast as issued, the advance sheets of the Society's edition of the text of the Dhammapada Commentary.

During the progress of the work, more particularly during my years of residence at the Johns Hopkins University as Johnston Scholar in Sanskrit, Professor Maurice Bloomfield has greatly assisted me with hints and suggestions of the highest value with reference to correct philological method as applied to the interpretation of Indic texts. I am especially indebted to Professor Bloomfield for assistance in solving many difficult problems in the comparative grammar of Sanskrit and Pāli, in Pāli lexicography, and in the history of the religions of India; and for innumerable suggestions relating to the handling of Hindu legends and folk-tales and to the analytical study of psychic motifs recurring in Hindu fiction. For this generous assistance I wish to express to him my most grateful thanks.

NOTE FOR LIBRARIANS AND CATALOGUERS

Dhámma-pada, or Way of Righteousness, is the name of one of the canonical books of the Buddhist Sacred Scriptures. It is written in the Pāli language. It consists of 423 stanzas. These are reputed to be the very words of the Buddha.

The Dhámmapada Commentary (in Pāli, Dhammapad-Aṭṭha-kathā) is ascribed to Buddhaghosa, the greatest of all the Buddhist scholastics. This ascription is without due warrant, as appears from the translator's Introduction, page 60. The Commentary purports to tell us "where, when, why, for what purpose, with reference to what situation, with reference to what person or persons" Buddha uttered each one of these stanzas — see page 27. In so doing, the author of the Commentary narrates 299 legends or stories. These stories are the preponderating element of the Commentary, and it is these which are here translated.

The Library of Congress issues printed catalogue-cards made to follow rules now generally approved by the best experts. The cards for this work bear the serial number 20–27590, and the main entry is Dhammapadaṭṭhakathā. Complete sets of these cards may be had (at a nominal price of 12 cents for each set of 8) upon application to "The Library of Congress — Card Division, Washington, D. C." But (to foreign librarians, at least) the suggestion may be welcome that this work be recorded in Library Catalogues under the following eight entries:

Burlingame, Eugene Watson	Buddhist Legends
Dhammapad-Aṭṭha-kathā	Dhammapada Commentary
Buddhaghosa	Warren, Henry Clarke, 1854–1899 (as subject of Memorial)
Harvard Oriental Series	Lanman, C. R., 1850– (as editor, and as author of Memorial)

MEANING OF REFERENCES IN THE HEAD-LINES

The references in square brackets at the inside upper corners of the Translation are intended to be read across from the left-hand page to the right-hand page. They show the portions of the original Pāli text (in the edition of H. C. Norman: hence the "N.") the translation of which is contained upon any two pages that face each other, — that is, contained between the first line of a left-hand page of the Translation and the last line of the next right-hand page. Thus, in this volume, pages 194 and 195 contain the translation of that portion of the Pāli text which begins in Norman's edition at volume 1, page 83, line 14, and ends at page 85, line 24. — In numbering the lines of the pages of the original, the Vagga-headings (in capitals) and story-headings (in capitals and small capitals), added by the Editor, have not been counted, and of course not the head-lines of the pages.

NOTE AS TO PRONOUNCING THE PALI NAMES

Short *a*, as in *organ*, or like the *u* in *but*. The other vowels, as in the key-words *fār*, *pin*, *pīque*, *pull*, *rūle*, (and roughly) *they*, *so*. Pronounce *c* like *ch* in *church*, and *j* as in *judge*. The "aspirates" are true aspirates: thus, *th*, *dh*, *ph*, as in *hothouse*, *madhouse*, *uphill*. They are not spirants, as in *thin*, *graphic*. The underdotted *ṭ*, *ḍ*, *ṇ*, etc. are pronounced (by the Hindus, at least) with the tip of the tongue turned up and drawn back. Dotted *ṁ* indicates nasalization of the preceding vowel.

The completed manuscript of this translation was delivered by the author, January 10, 1917

CONTENTS

INTRODUCTION

SYNOPSES OF THE LEGENDS OR STORIES

The synopses occupy pages 71 to 141 of Volume 28
A detailed Table of Contents of this portion of the work is uncalled for
The page at which the synopsis of any given story begins is given below, with a capital letter S and in parentheses

TRANSLATION OF THE LEGENDS OR STORIES

The Table of Contents of this portion of the work may advantageously be made to serve also as a finding-index:

1. For the place of the Synopsis of a given story (see above);
2. For the Dhammapada-Stanza [numbers in brackets] to which the story relates;
3. For the place of the text of the story in Norman's edition (N); and
4. For the same in the Rangoon or Burmese edition (B); and
5. For the same in the Colombo or Cingalese edition (C). — Accordingly,

For each Story, there is given, in each *odd* line,

1. The number of the Story in the Book,
2. An English title,
3. The page (in parentheses and with an S prefixed) of the Synopsis, and
4. The page at which the Translation begins. — And

For each Story, there is given, in each *even* line,

1. Its Pāli title,
2. The number [in brackets] of the stanza to which the Story relates,
2 *a*. As counted from the beginning of the Book concerned, and
2 *b*. As counted from the beginning of the Dhammapada (so Fausböll),
3. The volume and page (with N prefixed) of the Pāli text in Norman's edition,
4. The page (with B prefixed) of the Pāli text in the Burmese edition, and
5. The page (with C prefixed) of the Pāli text in the Cingalese edition.

Book I. Pairs, Yamaka Vagga. Volume 28

Book II. Heedfulness, Appamāda Vagga. Volume 28

Book III. Thoughts, Citta Vagga. Volume 29

Book IV. Flowers, Puppha Vagga. Volume 29

Book V. The Simpleton, Bāla Vagga. Volume 29

Book IX. Evil, Pāpa Vagga. Volume 29

Book X. The Rod or Punishment, Daṇḍa Vagga. Volume 29

Book XI. Old Age, Jarā Vagga. Volume 29

Book XII. Self, Atta Vagga. Volume 29

Book XIII. The World, Loka Vagga. Volume 30

Book XIV. The Enlightened, Buddha Vagga. Volume 30

Book XV. Happiness, Sukha Vagga. Volume 30

Book XVI. Objects of Affection, Piya Vagga. Volume 30

Book XVII. Anger, Kodha Vagga. Volume 30

Book XVIII. Blemishes, Mala Vagga. Volume 30

Book XIX. The Righteous, Dhammaṭṭha Vagga. Volume 30

* In C, pages 522–529 are misnumbered as 122–129.

Book XX. The Path, Magga Vagga. Volume 30

Book XXI. Miscellaneous, Pakiṇṇaka Vagga. Volume 30

* In C, pages 522–529 are misnumbered as 122–129.

Book XXII. Hell, Niraya Vagga. Volume 30

Book XXIII. The Elephant, Nāga Vagga. Volume 30

Book XXIV. Thirst or Craving, Taṇhā Vagga. Volume 30

Book XXV. The Monk, Bhikkhu Vagga. Volume 30

Book XXVI. The Brahman, Brāhmaṇa Vagga. Volume 30

* In C, pages 642–673 are misnumbered as 624–655.

* In C, pages 642–673 are misnumbered as 624–655.

INTRODUCTION

§ 1. Legendary life of the Buddha

§ 1 a. **Birth amid rejoicing of angels.** The legends and stories of this collection assume a knowledge on the part of the reader of at least the principal facts and legends of the life of the Buddha as set forth in the Sacred Scriptures.[1] The Buddha was born in 563 B.C. and died in 483.[2] His father was Suddhodana, king of the Sākiya clan in Kapilavatthu, and his mother was Queen Māyā, daughter of the king of the neighboring Koliya clan. He was born in the Lumbini Garden near Kapilavatthu, his mother standing upright at his birth and supporting herself by a branch of a Sāl-tree.[3] In the Nālaka Sutta of the Sutta Nipāta,[4] one of the oldest of old Buddhist books, we read that at his birth the angels rejoiced and sang. The aged seer Asita asked them, "Why doth the company of angels rejoice?" They replied, "He that shall become Buddha is born in the village of the Sākiyas for the welfare and happiness of mankind; therefore are we joyful and exceeding glad."

[1] For a brief account of the divisions, contents, and date of the Sacred Scriptures of the Buddhists, see T. W. Rhys Davids's article *Buddhism* in *Encyclopaedia Britannica*, 11th ed. Cf. also Introduction, § 4. For a more comprehensive account, see M. Winternitz, *Geschichte der Indischen Litteratur:* ii. 1, *Die Buddhistische Litteratur*, pp. 1–139. Winternitz gives a useful bibliography of the subject at p. 1, note 1. Rhys Davids holds that the Four Greater Nikāyas and the greater part of such books of the Lesser Nikāya as *Itivuttaka* and *Sutta Nipāta* are as old as 400 B.C., and that of the *Vinaya*, *Mahā Vagga* and *Culla Vagga*, i–x, are as old as 300 B.C. Most scholars consider these dates too early, but there are the best of reasons for believing the greater part of these books to be anterior to the Inscriptions of Asoka; that is to say, older than 250 B.C. The *Jātaka Book* represented by Fausböll's text is a recension made in Ceylon in the early part of the fifth century A.D., but contains a vast amount of material many centuries older. For translations of the Sacred Books, see Introduction, § 17, paragraph 3.

[2] On the date of the Buddha, see J. F. Fleet, *Inscriptions (Indian)*, in *Encyclopaedia Britannica*, vol. xiv. p. 624, col. 1, and bibliography in Winternitz, p. 2, note 1.

[3] On the birth of the Buddha, see *Dīgha*, 14: i. 16–30; *Majjhima*, 123; *Aṅguttara*, ii. 130^{17}–131^{26}; *Nidānakathā*, *Jātaka*, i. 47^{21}–53^{32}: translated by Rhys Davids, *Buddhist Birth Stories*, pp. 58–68; by Warren, *Buddhism in Translations*, pp. 38–48. On the subject in general, see E. Windisch, *Buddhas Geburt*.

[4] *Sutta Nipāta*, iii. 11, part 1 (Stanzas 679–698).

§ **1 b. The Buddhist Simeon.**[1] Asita went to Suddhodana's residence and said, "Where is the child? I too wish to see him." The Sākiyas showed him the child. When Asita saw the child, he rejoiced and was exceeding glad. And he took him in his arms and said, "Incomparable is he! preëminent among men!" But remembering his own departure, he became sorrowful and wept tears. Said the Sākiyas, "Is any adversity in store for the child?" "No," replied Asita, "this child shall attain Supreme Enlightenment; he shall behold Nibbāna; out of love and compassion for the multitude he shall set in motion the Wheel of the Law; far and wide shall his Religion be dispersed. But as for me, I have not long to live in this world; ere these things shall come to pass, death will be upon me. I shall not hear the Law from the Peerless Champion. Therefore am I stricken with woe, overwhelmed with sorrow, afflicted with grief."

§ **1 c. Youth and marriage.**[2] When the child was five days old, he was named Siddhattha. Seven Brahmans prophesied that he would become either a Universal Monarch or a Buddha. But the eighth, Koṇḍañña, perceiving that the child possessed the Infallible Signs of a Future Buddha, prophesied that he would become a Buddha. On the same day each of eighty thousand kinsmen dedicated a son to his service. Seven days after his birth his mother died, and he was reared by his aunt and stepmother, Mahā Pajāpatī Gotamī. In his nineteenth year he was married to his own cousin Yasodharā, daughter of Suddhodana. He passed his youth amid luxury and splendor, in three mansions appropriate to the three seasons, surrounded by forty thousand nautch-girls, like a very god surrounded by troops of celestial nymphs. In his twenty-ninth year he beheld the Four Ominous Sights: an Old Man, a Sick Man, a Corpse, and a Monk. Thereupon he resolved to become a monk.

§ **1 d. Resolve to seek after Nibbāna.**[3] At this time word was brought to him that his wife had given birth to a son. "Rāhula is born!" he exclaimed, "a Bond is born!" Therefore his son was named Rāhula. As he entered the city in state, Kisā Gotamī, a

[1] *Sutta Nipâta*, iii. 11, part 1. Derived from the same source is *Nidānakathā*, *Jātaka*, i. 54^{11}–55^{29}: translated by Rhys Davids, *Buddhist Birth Stories*, pp. 68–71; by Warren, *Buddhism in Translations*, pp. 48–51.

[2] *Nidānakathā*, *Jātaka*, i. 55^{29}–59^{32}: translated, *Buddhist Birth Stories*, pp. 71–78; *Buddhism in Translations*, pp. 51–57. See also *Dīgha*, 14: ii. 16–30; *Aṅguttara*, i. 145–146; *Majjhima*, 26: i. 163.

[3] *Nidānakathā*, *Jātaka*, i. 60^{20}–61^{14}: translated, *Buddhist Birth Stories*, pp. 79–80; *Buddhism in Translations*, pp. 58–60.

maiden of the Warrior caste, cried out, "Happy the mother, happy the father, happy the wife, of such as he!" Thought the Future Buddha, "She says that the heart is thus made happy (*nibbāyati*). Now what must be extinguished (*nibbuta*) that the heart may be happy (*nibbuta*)?" Then the answer came to him, "When the Fire of Lust, Hatred, and Delusion is extinguished (*nibbuta*), then only is the heart truly happy (*nibbuta*). She has taught me a good lesson. For I am in search of happiness (*nibbāna*). This very day I must renounce the house-life, retire from the world, become a monk, and seek after True Happiness (*Nibbāna*).

§ 1 e. **The Great Retirement.**[1] Returning to his palace, he lay down on his bed, and troops of nautch-girls came in and began to dance and sing. But the Future Buddha no more took pleasure in them and fell asleep. Waking in the night, he beheld those nautch-girls asleep, and disgusted by their loathsome appearance, resolved to make the Great Retirement immediately. So rising from his bed, he called his charioteer Channa and ordered him to saddle his horse Kanthaka. "I will just take a look at my son," thought the Future Buddha, and opened the door of his wife's apartment. But fearing that, if he woke his wife, he might be prevented from carrying out his resolution, he closed the door again and departed without seeing his son.

Mounted on his horse Kanthaka and accompanied by his charioteer Channa, he passed out of the city gate, an angel opening the gate. Māra the Evil One offered him Universal Sovereignty if he would abandon his purpose, but the Future Buddha rebuked the Tempter and passed on. But the Evil One ever followed him, watching his opportunity. The Future Buddha proceeded to the river Anomā, where he received the Eight Requisites of a monk from an angel and dismissed Channa and Kanthaka. Channa returned sorrowfully to the city, but Kanthaka died of a broken heart. The Future Buddha spent the next seven days in Anūpiya Mango Grove in the enjoyment of the bliss of monkhood.

§ 1 f. **The Great Struggle.**[2] From Anūpiya Mango Grove the

[1] *Nidānakathā*, *Jātaka*, i. 61^{14}–65, end: translated, *Buddhist Birth Stories*, pp. 80–87; *Buddhism in Translations*, pp. 60–67. See also *Majjhima*, 26: i. 163.

[2] *Nidānakathā*, *Jātaka*, i. 66^{1}–68^{5}: translated, *Buddhist Birth Stories*, pp. 87–91; *Buddhism in Translations*, pp. 67–71. The story of the Buddha's visit to Rājagaha and interview with Bimbisāra is derived from *Sutta Nipāta*, iii. 1, *Pabbajjā Sutta*, and *Commentary*, as is expressly stated at *Jātaka*, i. 66^{31-33}. For the story of the Buddha's student-days under Āḷāra Kālāma and Uddaka, see *Majjhima*, 26: i. 163–166. For the story of the Great Struggle, see *Majjhima*, 36, and *Majjhima*, 12 (last half): i.

Future Buddha went on foot to Rājāgaha, the capital of King Bimbisāra, and made his round for alms from door to door. Bimbisāra, pleased with his deportment, offered him his kingdon. But the Future Buddha refused his offer, declaring that he had renounced all for the sake of attaining Supreme Enlightenment. Bimbisāra then requested him, so soon as he should become a Buddha, to visit his kingdom first, and the Future Buddha gave him his promise so to do. The Future Buddha then attached himself to Āḷāra Kālāma and Uddaka Rāmaputta, teachers of the Yoga philosophy. But becoming convinced that the Yoga discipline was not the Way of Salvation, he abandoned the practice of it. The Future Buddha then proceeded to Uruvelā, and attended by Koṇḍañña and four other monks, entered upon the Great Struggle.

For six years he engaged in prolonged fasts and other austerities, hoping thus to win mastery over self and Supreme Enlightenment. While thus engaged, he was approached and tempted to abandon the Great Struggle by Māra the Evil One, accompanied by his Nine Hosts, namely, Lust, Discontent, Hunger and Thirst, Craving, Sloth and Laziness, Cowardice, Doubt, Hypocrisy and Stupidity, Gain, Fame, Honor, and Glory Falsely Obtained, Exaltation of Self, and Contempt of Others. But the Future Buddha rebuked the Evil One, and he departed. One day, while absorbed in trance induced by suspension of the breath, he became utterly exhausted and fell in a swoon. His five companions believed him to be dead, and certain deities went to his father, King Suddhodana, and so informed him. But the king refused to believe this, declaring that his son could not die before attaining Enlightenment. The Future Buddha, convinced that fasting and other forms of self-mortification were not the Way of Salvation, abandoned the Great Struggle. Thereupon his five companions, regarding him as a backslider, deserted him and went to the Deer-park near Benāres.

§ 1 g. **The Enlightenment.**[1] One night the Future Buddha beheld

77^{23}–81. For the story of the Temptation by Māra, see *Sutta Nipāta*, iii. 2, *Padhāna Sutta*.

[1] The first two paragraphs are derived from *Nidānakathā*, *Jātaka*, i. 68^{5}–81^{14}: translated, *Buddhist Birth Stories*, pp. 91–111; the story of the Enlightenment is also translated in *Buddhism in Translations*, pp. 71–83. For much simpler accounts of the Enlightenment, see *Dīgha*, 14: ii. 30–35, and *Majjhima*, 26: i. 167. The story of the Temptation of the Buddha by the Daughters of Māra is derived from *Saṁyutta*, iv. 3. 5. This story is alluded to in *Sutta Nipāta*, Stanza 835. A connected account of the Buddha's life from the Enlightenment to the reception of Sāriputta and Mog-

five visions. After considering their purport, he came to the following conclusion, "This very day I shall attain Enlightenment." So on the evening of the following day he seated himself under a banyan-tree and formed the following resolution, "Let my skin, my nerves, and my bones dry up, and likewise my flesh and blood; but until I attain Supreme Enlightenment, I will not leave this seat!" Māra the Evil One endeavored to drive him from his seat with the Nine Rains, namely, wind, rain, rocks, weapons, blazing coals, hot ashes, sand, mud, and darkness. But the Future Buddha sat unmoved. Māra then approached the Future Buddha and commanded him to leave his seat. But the Future Buddha refused and rebuked him. Thereupon the Evil One left him, and troops of angels came and honored him. In the first watch of the night the Future Buddha obtained Knowledge of Previous Existences; in the middle watch, Supernatural Vision; and in the last watch, Knowledge of the Causes of Craving, Rebirth, and Suffering. Thus did he attain Supreme Enlightenment and become a Buddha. Thereupon he breathed forth the Song of Triumph of all the Buddhas.

For seven days the Buddha sat motionless on the Throne of Enlightenment, experiencing the Bliss of Deliverance. After spending four weeks in earnest thought near the Tree of Wisdom (the Bo-tree), he spent the fifth week at the Goatherd's Banyan-tree. Here he was tempted by the three daughters of Māra the Evil One, namely, Craving, Discontent, and Lust. But he repulsed their advances, saying to them, "Begone! The Exalted One has put away Lust, Ill-will, and Delusion." The sixth and seventh weeks were spent at the Mucalinda-tree and the Rājāyatana-tree respectively. On the last day of the seventh week he received his first converts, two merchants named Tapussa and Bhallika. He then returned to the Goatherd's Banyan-tree.

Here, according to the Mahā-Parinibbāna Sutta,[1] Māra the Evil One tempted him to accomplish his decease, saying, "Let the Exalted One now pass into Supreme Nibbāna." But the Buddha resisted the temptation, declaring that he should not accomplish his decease until his Religion had been preached far and wide.[2] But according to the

gallāna into the Order is given in the *Vinaya, Mahā Vagga*, i. 1–24. The *Nidānakathā* follows this account in the main.

[1] *Dīgha*, 16: ii. 112–114.

[2] Cf. *Dīgha*, 16: ii. 104–106; *Saṁyutta*, li. 10: v. 260–262; *Udāna*, vi. 1: 63–64.

Vinaya,[1] the Mahāpadāna Sutta,[2] the Ariyapariyesana Sutta,[3] and the Nidānakathā,[4] the Buddha was assailed by doubt as to the wisdom of preaching a Religion so profound and difficult of comprehension to a race in the bondage of desire. The more he considered the matter, the more his heart inclined to a life of inaction and the less to the preaching of the Law. Thereupon Brahmā, fearing that the world would be lost, approached him and besought him to make known what he had himself received. Out of compassion for mankind the Buddha granted his request.

§ 1 h. **Ministry and death.**[5] Thought the Buddha, "To whom shall I first preach the Law?" Immediately he thought of his former teacher Āḷāra Kālāma. But a deity told him that Āḷāra Kālāma had been dead for seven days. Then he thought of Uddaka Rāmaputta. But a deity told him that Uddaka Rāmaputta had died that very evening. Then he thought of the five monks who had been his companions, and perceiving by the power of Supernatural Vision that they were residing in the Deer-park near Benāres, he resolved to go thither and set in motion the Wheel of the Law. On his way thither he met Upaka the Naked Ascetic. "Who are you?" inquired Upaka. "I am the Supreme Buddha." Upaka expressed neither approval nor disapproval. "It may be," he remarked, and walked away shaking his head and wagging his tongue.[6]

When the five monks saw him approaching, they exclaimed, "Here comes the backslider! Pay no attention to him!" But the Buddha so completely suffused the hearts of those monks with love that they arose from their seats and prostrated themselves before his feet. To these five monks the Buddha then preached his first sermon, the Discourse on the Four Noble Truths; to wit, the Nature of Suffering, the Origin of Suffering, the Cessation of Suffering, and the Noble Eightfold Path as the Way thereto. The five monks perceived that whatsoever comes into existence, that must also cease to be, and requested the Buddha to receive them into his Order. Thereupon the Buddha founded his Order of Monks by saying in a formal manner to the five,

[1] *Vinaya, Mahā Vagga*, i. 5.

[2] *Dīgha*, 14: ii. 35–40.

[3] *Majjhima*, 26: i. 167–169.

[4] *Jātaka*, i. 81.

[5] *Nidānakathā, Jātaka*, i. 81^{14}–94, end: translated, *Buddhist Birth Stories*, pp. 111–133. The *Nidānakathā* follows closely *Vinaya, Mahā Vagga*, i. 6–24, and *Culla Vagga*, vi. 4. For the death of the Buddha, see *Dīgha*, 16.

[6] Cf. story xxiv. 9.

"Come, monks! lead the Holy Life, to the utter extinction of Suffering." The Buddha then preached to the five monks the Discourse on Unreality. Through this sermon they were freed from the Contaminations, that is to say, lust, desire for existence, and ignorance of the Truths, and thus attained Arahatship.

At that time there lived in Benāres a rich young man named Yasa. He possessed three mansions appropriate to the three seasons and lived amid luxury and splendor, with a large retinue of nautch-girls. One night he beheld those nautch-girls asleep, and disgusted by their loathsome appearance, resolved to abandon the house-life for the houseless life of a monk. So leaving his house, he came to the Buddha by night and said, "How distressing! how oppressing!" Said the Buddha, "Here is naught that distresses or oppresses. Come, Yasa, sit down; let me teach you the Law." So saying, the Buddha preached the Law of Morality to the rich young man, discoursing on the duty of almsgiving, the Moral Precepts, the folly of gratifying the lusts of the flesh, and the benefits to be gained by renouncing the same. Then, perceiving that the rich young man possessed the dispositions of mind and heart requisite to the understanding of the Law of Deliverance, he preached to him the Sublime Discourse of all the Buddhas, namely, Suffering, the Origin and Cessation thereof, and the Way of Salvation. Yasa and his fifty-four companions were established in Arahatship. There were thus, exclusive of the Buddha, Sixty Arahats in the world.

And the Buddha said to the Sixty, "I am freed from all fetters, both divine and human. Ye also are freed from all fetters, both divine and human. Go forth and journey from place to place, for the welfare of many, for the happiness of many, out of compassion for the world, for the benefit and welfare and happiness of angels and men. Go no two of you together. Preach the Law, sound in the beginning, sound in the middle, sound in the end, in the spirit and in the letter. Proclaim the Holy Life in all its fullness and purity." So saying, he sent the Sixty into all the world. He himself set out for Uruvelā. On the way thither he halted in a forest, and meeting thirty young nobles who were seeking a woman, he converted them and received them into the Order. In Uruvelā he converted the three brothers Kassapa, members of the Order of Jaṭilas, together with their thousand followers. Passing on to Gayāsīsa, where he established his new converts in Arahatship by means of the Discourse on Fire, he proceeded to Rājagaha in order to redeem his promise to King Bimbisāra.

The king received the Buddha with every mark of courtesy and reverence, hearkened to the Law, and together with his retinue obtained the Fruit of Conversion. The king formally presented to the Buddha his own pleasure garden, Bamboo Grove, and the Buddha and the Congregation of Monks there entered upon residence. While the Buddha was in residence at Bamboo Grove, there came to him two monks who had for some time been disciples of Sañjaya, but who had recently obtained the Fruit of Conversion through the preaching of Assaji. These two monks were elevated by the Buddha to the rank of his two Chief Disciples and were thereafter known as Sāriputta and Moggallāna.[1] From Bamboo Grove the Buddha went to his father's city, Kapilavatthu, and there received into the Order his own son Rāhula and his own half-brother Nanda.[2] From Kapilavatthu he returned to Rājagaha, tarrying by the way at Anūpiya Mango Grove and there receiving many converts, among others the Six Princes. At Rājagaha he converted the rich merchant Anāthapiṇḍika, who thereupon purchased the Jetavana Grove, paying for it as many gold pieces as were required to cover the ground, and presented it to him. The Buddha accepted the gift and entered upon residence at the Jetavana. With this event closes the second year of his ministry.

For forty-five years the Buddha journeyed from place to place in this manner, preaching and teaching. The three months of the rains he always spent at the Jetavana or at Bamboo Grove or in some other one place. His missionary journeys took him up and down the valley of the Ganges, throughout the old kingdoms of Magadha and Kosala in the eastern part of North India. At no time did he go farther than 250 miles from Benāres. To this period of his life belong the great majority of the acts and discourses, both real and fictitious, attributed to him, not only in the Sacred Scriptures, but also in this and other later collections of legends and stories.

Among the more interesting legends and stories of this collection relating to this particular period of his life are the following: i. 5, Quarrel among the monks of Kosambi and residence in Protected Forest with a noble elephant; i. 12 *b*, Intrigues of Devadatta against the Buddha and King Bimbisāra; iv. 3, Annihilation of the Sākiyas by Viḍūḍabha; xiii. 6, Conversion of the robber Finger-garland (Añgulimāla); xiii. 9 and xxii. 1, Confutation of false charges brought against the Buddha by suborned nuns; xiv. 2, Twin Miracle, Ascent to Heaven, and Descent from Heaven; xv. 1, Abatement of

[1] Story i. 8 contains a brief outline of the entire *Nidānakathā* to this point.

[2] Cf. story i. 9.

quarrel between the Sākiyas and the Koliyas; xxi. 1, Abatement of the Three Plagues at Vesāli; and xxiii. 8, which tells how, while the Buddha was residing in a forest-hut in the Himālaya, he was tempted by Māra the Evil One to exercise sovereignty and to transmute the Himālaya mountains into gold. The Buddha died in 483 B.C. near the city of Kusinārā, his end being hastened by a meal consisting of truffles. His body was cremated with pomp and ceremony, and the relics were divided among princes and nobles.

§ 1 i. **Buddhist-Christian parallels.** The many striking parallels between passages in the Buddhist Scriptures and passages in the New Testament have for many years attracted the attention of Indologists and students of the History of Religions.[1] The theory of Buddhist loans in the New Testament has been advocated by several scholars, notably R. Seydel,[2] G. A. van den Bergh van Eysinga,[3] and A. J. Edmunds.[4] In one form or another it has won the acceptance of many distinguished scholars, among others O. Pfleiderer,[5] E. Kuhn,[6] R. Pischel,[7] and R. Garbe.[8] M. Winternitz admits the possibility of such

[1] For a bibliography of this interesting and important subject, see M. Winternitz, *History of Buddhist Literature*, p. 280, note 1. Since Winternitz's book was written Garbe has announced his adhesion to Edmunds's loan theory. See note 8.

[2] R. Seydel, *Das Evangelium von Jesu in seinen Verhältnissen zu Buddha-Sage und Buddha-Lehre*, Leipzig, 1882. *Die Buddha-Legende und das Leben Jesu nach den Evangelien*, erneute Prüfung ihres gegenseitigen Verhältnisses, Leipzig, 1884; 2 Auflage, mit ergänzenden Anmerkungen von Martin Seydel, Weimar, 1897. Cf. Winternitz, l. c., p. 278.

[3] G. A. van den Bergh van Eysinga, *Indische Einflüsse auf evangelische Erzählungen*, Göttingen, 1904; 2 Auflage, 1909. Cf. Winternitz, l. c., p. 279.

[4] A. J. Edmunds, *Buddhist and Christian Gospels*, now first compared from the originals, 4th ed., edited by M. Anesaki, Philadelphia, 1908–09. Cf. Winternitz, l. c., pp. 279 ff. See also the following papers by Edmunds: *Buddhist Loans to Christianity*, in *Monist*, 22. 1912, pp. 129–138; *The Progress of Buddhist Research*, in *Monist*, 22. 1912, pp. 633–635; *The Accessibility of Buddhist Lore to the Christian Evangelists*, in *Monist*, 23. 1913, pp. 517–522; *The Buddhist Origin of Luke's Penitent Thief*, in *Open Court*, 28. 1914, pp. 287–291.

[5] O. Pfleiderer, *Religion und Religionen*, München, 1906. *Die Entstehung des Christentums*, 2 Auflage, München, 1907.

[6] E. Kuhn, in *Nachwort* to Bergh van Eysinga's work, pp. 102 ff.

[7] R. Pischel, *Deutsche Literaturzeitung*, 1904, col. 2938 ff. Pischel here says: "Die Frage, ob sich überhaupt indische Einflüsse in der evangelischen Erzählungslitteratur finden, kann heute nicht mehr verneint werden." See also Pischel, *Leben und Lehre des Buddha*, in the Series *Aus Natur und Geisteswelt*, 2 Auflage, Leipzig, 1910, pp. 17–19. At p. 18, referring to the story of Simeon, Pischel says: "Eine Entlehnung ist hier sehr wahrscheinlich, und der Weg ist jetzt nicht mehr so schwer nachzuweisen wie früher." He then discusses at some length the bearings of recent discoveries in Turkestan on the subject.

[8] R. Garbe, *Indien und das Christentum*, Tübingen, 1914, chap. i, pp. 47 ff.

loans,[1] and H. Oldenberg, who formerly rejected the theory, now holds that the theory can neither be proved nor disproved.[2] Of the opponents of the theory, E. Windisch presents the strongest arguments.[3]

The most striking of these parallels are the following:

1. Infancy legends

a. Rejoicing of angels at nativity.
b. Asita-Simeon.

Sutta Nipāta, iii. 11, part 1 (679–698); translated, Introduction, § 1 *a–b*.	*St. Luke* ii. 8–14, 25–35.

See Edmunds, *BCG.*, i. 77–89, 181–191; *Monist*, 22. 1912, pp. 129–131. Edmunds translates *manussaloke hitasukhatāya jāto*, "is born for weal and welfare in the world of men." The correct translation is, "is born for the weal and welfare of mankind." Cf. *Dīgha*, ii. 104^{1-4}; *Saṁyutta*, v. 259^{28-30}; *Udāna*, p. 62, last two lines; *Itivuttaka*, p. 11, last two lines. On the locative construction involved, see Whitney's *Sanskrit Grammar*, § 303 *a*.

The loan theory is accepted by Pischel, *Leben und Lehre des Buddha*, pp. 17–19; Winternitz, *History of Buddhist Literature*, p. 281; Garbe, *Indien und das Christentum*, chap. i, pp. 47 ff. (translated, *Monist*, 24. 1914, pp. 481 ff.).

2. Mission of Sixty (Seventy)

Vinaya, Mahā Vagga, i. 11; translated, Introduction, § 1 *h*, paragraph 4. Cf. *Nidānakathā*, *Jātaka*, i. 82^{24-26}.	*St. Luke*, x. 1.

See Edmunds, *BCG.*, i. 224–229.

(translated, *Monist*, 24. 1914, pp. 481 ff.). Garbe expresses himself as follows: "Ich wende mich nunmehr zu den Fällen — es sind vier an der Zahl —, bei denen ich mich nach langer Ueberlegung davon überzeugt habe, dass buddhistischer Einfluss in den Erzählungen der Evangelien nicht zu leugnen ist. Diese Ueberzeugung fusst im ersten und zweiten Fall wesentlich auf deren neuester Darstellung aus Edmunds' Feder." The "four cases" are: 1. The Asita-Simeon legend; 2. Temptations by the Evil One; 3. Peter's walking on the water; 4. Multiplication of the loaves. The paper by Edmunds referred to is his paper in the *Monist*, 22. 1912, pp. 129–138.

[1] M. Winternitz, *History of Buddhist Literature*, pp. 281 f.

[2] H. Oldenberg, *Die Indische Religion*, in *Die Religionen des Orients*, Teil i, Abteilung iii. 1, of *Die Kultur der Gegenwart*. At p. 80 Oldenberg refers to the loan theory as follows: ". . . das Eindringen buddhistischer Elemente in die Evangelien — eine weder zu erweisende noch zu widerlegende Hypothese, die ich meinerseits eher unwahrscheinlich finden möchte."

[3] E. Windisch, *Māra und Buddha*, chap. ix; *Buddhas Geburt*, chap. xii.

3. Conversion of robber

Majjhima, 86; translated, Story xiii. 6. — *St. Luke*, xxiii. 39–43.

See Edmunds, *The Buddhist Origin of Luke's Penitent Thief*, in *Open Court*, 28. 1914, pp. 287–291.

4. Feeding of five hundred (five thousand)

Introduction to *Jātaka* 78: i. 345–349; translated, Story iv. 5.

St. Matthew xiv. 15–21.
St. Mark vi. 35–44.
St. Luke ix. 13–17.
St. John vi. 5–14.

The loan theory is accepted by Garbe, *Indien und das Christentum*, chap. i (translated, *Monist*, 24. 1914, pp. 491–492).

5. Walking on the sea

Introduction to *Jātaka* 190: i. 111; cf. the Act of Truth in Story vi. 4.

St. Matthew xiv. 28–31;
cf. *St. Matthew* xiv. 22–27,
St. Mark vi. 45–54,
St. John vi. 15–21.

The loan theory is accepted by Garbe, *Indien und das Christentum*, chap. i (translated, *Monist*, 24. 1914, pp. 488–491).

6. Temptations by the Evil One

a. As the Future Buddha is about to make the Great Retirement, the Evil One urges him to abandon his purpose, assuring him that in such case he will attain Universal Sovereignty.

Nidānakathā, *Jātaka*, i. 63^{17-25}; cf. Introduction, § 1 *e*, paragraph 2. This legend is from a late source and is probably derived from the first of the two legends marked *g*.

b. While the Future Buddha is engaged in the prolonged fasts and austerities of the Great Struggle, he is tempted to abandon the Struggle by the Evil One, accompanied by his Nine Hosts, namely, Lust, Discontent, Hunger and Thirst, Craving, Sloth and Laziness, Cowardice, Doubt, Hypocrisy and Stupidity, Gain, Fame, Honor, and Glory Falsely Obtained, Exaltation of Self, and Contempt of Others.

Sutta Nipāta, iii. 2; cf. Introduction, § 1 *f*, paragraph 2. Cf. also *Lalitavistara*, xviii. This legend is from an early source, as is also its sequel *d*. See Windisch, *Māra und Buddha*, chap. i, pp. 1–32, also pp. 304–315.

c. Immediately before the Enlightenment, the Evil One attempts to drive the Future Buddha from his seat with the Nine Rains, namely, wind, rain, rocks, weapons, blazing coals, hot ashes, sand, mud, and darkness.

Nidānakathā, Jātaka, i. 71^{27}–72^{7}; cf. Introduction, § 1 *g*, paragraph 1. Cf. also *Lalitavistara,* xxi. This legend is from a late source and is probably derived from *b.*

d. In the fifth week after the Enlightenment, the Buddha is tempted by the three daughters of the Evil One, namely, Craving, Discontent, and Lust.

Saṁyutta, iv. 3. 5; cf. Introduction, § 1 *g*, paragraph 2. Cf. also *Sutta Nipāta,* Stanza 835. This legend is from an early source and forms a sequel to *b.* Craving, Discontent, and Lust are numbered among the Nine Hosts of Māra in *b.* See Windisch, *Māra und Buddha,* pp. 119–124.

e. In the eighth week after the Enlightenment, the Buddha is assailed by doubt as to the wisdom of preaching a Religion so profound and difficult of comprehension to a race in the bondage of desire. The more he considers the matter, the more his heart inclines to a life of inaction.

Vinaya, Mahā Vagga, i. 5; *Dīgha,* 14: ii. 35–40; *Majjhima,* 26: i. 167–169; *Nidānakathā, Jātaka,* i. 81; cf. Introduction, § 1 *g*, paragraph 3. This legend is from an early source and is probably the original of *f.* Doubt and Sloth-and-Laziness are numbered among the Nine Hosts of Māra in *b.*

f. According to other accounts, the Buddha is at this time tempted by the Evil One to accomplish his decease.

Dīgha, 16: ii. 112–114; cf. Introduction, § 1 *g*, paragraph 3. Cf. also *Lalitavistara,* xxiv: p. 489; *Divyāvadāna,* xvii: p. 202. This legend is probably a later form of *e.* See Windisch, *Māra und Buddha,* chap. ii, especially pp. 35, 46, 66, 67; also p. 213. Windisch proves that the order of development of this temptation is as follows: *Lalitavistara,* xxiv; *Udāna,* vi. 1; *Dīgha,* 16; *Divyāvadāna,* xvii.

g. While the Buddha is residing in a forest-hut in the Himālaya, he is tempted by the Evil One to exercise sovereignty and to transmute the Himālaya mountains into gold.

Saṁyutta, iv. 2. 10; translated, Story xxiii. 8. This legend is from an early source and is probably the original of *a.* See Windisch, *Māra und Buddha,* pp. 107–109.

h. Three months before his death, the Buddha is tempted by the Evil One to accomplish his decease immediately.

Dīgha, 16: ii. 104–106. Cf. *Saṁyutta,* li. 10: v. 260–262, and *Udāna,* vi. 1: 63–64. Cf. also *Divyāvadāna,* xvii: p. 202. As Windisch remarks (*Māra und Buddha,* p. 67), this temptation at the end of the Buddha's life is meaningless. It is of course a duplicate of *f.*

The following is a brief outline of Edmunds's theory:[1]

Both religions are independent in the main, but out of eighty-nine chapters in the Gospels, the equivalent of one, mostly in the Gospel according to St. Luke, is colored by a knowledge of Buddhism. The sections thus colored especially are:

a. The rejoicing of angels at the nativity, and the Simeon episode. (See 1. *Infancy legends.*)

b. The three temptations in *St. Luke* iv. 1–13 and *St. Matthew* iv. 1–11. Edmunds calls these: *a*, temptation to assume empire; *b*, temptation to transmute matter; *c*, temptation to commit suicide. (See the last two of the eight legends outlined in 6. *Temptations by the Evil One.*)

c. The seventy missionaries. (See 2. *Mission of Sixty.*)

d. The penitent thief. (See 3. *Conversion of robber.*)

At the beginning of the Christian era there were four great powers: the Chinese, the Hindus, the Parthians, and the Romans. Between the Chinese and the Parthians, and extending into parts of India, was a fifth power: the Indo-Scythian empire. This was the seat of an aggressive missionary Buddhism, at that time the most powerful religion in the world. Coins of these Indo-Scythian Buddhist kings, especially those of Kanishka, have come down to our own time, some of them bearing the image of the Buddha, together with his name in Greek letters. The Gentile Evangelist St. Luke was a physician of Antioch, a great international metropolis and the terminus of the Chinese silk-trade. There is every reason to believe that he had seen these coins and that he was familiar with the principal legends of the Buddha's life. India, Bactria, and the eastern part of the Parthian empire were covered with his temples. On these temples were sculptured scenes of the Buddha's life, and one of the characters portrayed was a converted robber. Recent finds in Central Asia prove that at the beginning of the Christian era the Buddhist Scriptures were being translated into Sogdian and Tokharish, vernaculars of the Parthian empire, the buffer state between Palestine and India. Parthians were present at Pentecost.

While Edmunds's argument lacks the element of finality, the following conclusions, in the main favorable to his theory, seem to be warranted by the evidence:

The Christian Evangelists, more particularly the Gentile Evangelist St. Luke, probably had access to the principal legends of the Buddha's life. The legend of the rejoicing of angels at the nativity and the story of Simeon are probably colored by Buddhist influence. The assumption that St. Luke was acquainted with the Buddhist legend of the conversion of a robber is a not unlikely explanation of the discrepancy between St. Mark xv. 32 and St. Luke xxiii. 39–43.

[1] See *Buddhist and Christian Gospels*, i. 111–164; also *Monist*, 22. 1912, pp. 633–635; *Monist*, 23. 1913, pp. 517–522; *Open Court*, 28. 1914, pp. 287–291. On trade-relations between India and the West at the Christian era, see W. H. Schoff, *The Periplus of the Erythraean Sea*, New York, 1912. See also Schoff's papers in *Monist*, 22. 1912, pp. 138–149, 638; *JAOS.*, 35. 1915, pp. 31–41. A good introduction to the recent explorations in Central Asia is Sir M. Aurel Stein's *Ruins of Desert Cathay*, 2 vols., London, 1912.

It seems probable that the accounts of the temptations are to some extent colored by Buddhist influence.[1]

§ 2. Teachings of the Buddha

§ 2 a. The Beginningless Round of Existences. The primary mission of the Buddha was to deliver mankind from the frightful jungle or ocean of the Round of Existences. In the Anamatagga Saṁyutta[2] he is represented as saying: Without conceivable beginning is this Round of Existences; unknown is a starting-point in the past of beings impeded by the Impediment of Ignorance, fettered by the Fetter of Craving, passing, coursing, from birth to birth. The ancestors of a man are more numerous than all the blades of grass and sticks and branches and leaves in India; more numerous than all the particles of dust that compose the earth. The tears shed, the mother's milk drunk by a man in his previous states of existence, are more abundant than all the water contained in the four great oceans.

How long is a cycle of time? Longer than it would take a range of mountains a league in length, a league in breadth, a league in height, of solid rock, without a cleft, without a crack, to waste and wear away, were it to be wiped once a century with a silken cloth; longer than it would take a heap of mustard-seed of the same dimensions to disappear were a single seed to be removed once a century. Of cycles of time as long as this there have elapsed many hundreds of cycles, many thousands of cycles, many hundreds of thousands of cycles. Indeed, it is impossible to count them in terms of cycles or hundreds of cycles or thousands of cycles or hundreds of thousands of cycles. For example, were each of four centenarians to call to mind a hundred thousand

[1] Edmunds deals only with the legends marked *g* and *h* in the table of parallels given above. Edmunds calls the third temptation a temptation "to commit suicide." Neither *h* nor its original *f*, however, is a temptation to commit suicide, in the strict sense of the word. Moreover, *f* is probably a later form of *e*, which is a temptation to sloth, pure and simple. On the Christian side the temptation to leap from a pinnacle of the temple is in no sense a temptation to suicide, but rather to pride and vanity. The Buddhist parallels are not *g* and *h*, but *b* and *g*. In *b* the Buddha, emaciated and hungry, is assailed by the Evil One, accompanied by his Nine Hosts, the Third being Hunger and Thirst and the Ninth being Gain, Fame, Honor, and Glory Falsely Obtained, Exaltation of Self, and Contempt of Others. The correspondence between this temptation and the temptations recorded by St. Luke and St. Matthew hardly needs to be pointed out. Yet Edmunds does not even mention it.

[2] *Saṁyutta*, xv.

cycles of time every day of his life, all four would die or ever they could count them all.

The cycles of time that have elapsed are more numerous than all the sands that lie between the source and the mouth of the Ganges. The bones left by a single individual in his passage from birth to birth during a single cycle of time would form a pile so huge that were all the mountains of Vepulla-range to be gathered up and piled in a heap, that heap of mountains would appear as naught beside it. The head of every man has been cut off so many times in his previous states of existence, either as a human being or as an animal, as to cause him to shed blood more abundant than all the water contained in the four great oceans. For so long a time as this, concludes the Buddha, you have endured suffering, you have endured agony, you have endured calamity. In view of this, you have every reason to feel disgust and aversion for all existing things and to free yourselves from them.

§ 2 b. **The motive of the Religious Life.** The motive of the Religious Life is expressly declared to be the hope of obtaining deliverance from this frightful Round of Existences, the hope of attaining Nibbāna. In the Rathavinīta Sutta,[1] Sāriputta is represented as asking Puṇṇa Mantāṇiputta, "What is the motive of the Religious Life? Do we live the Religious Life for the sake of purity of conduct?" "No." "For the sake of purity of heart?" "No." "Of purity of belief?" "No." "Of purity of certitude?" "No." "Of purity of insight through knowledge of what is the Way and what is not the Way?" "No." "Of purity of insight through knowledge of the Path?" "No." "For the sake of purity of insight through knowledge?" "No." All these things are necessary, but they are only the means to an end. "For the sake of what, then, do we live the Religious Life?" "That we may, through detachment from the things of this world, attain Supreme Nibbāna."

§ 2 c. **Impermanence, Suffering, Unreality.** For, according to the Buddha, the things of this world, and the things of heaven as well, possess the following Three Characteristics: Impermanence, Suffering, and Unreality. All things are transitory. In all things inheres suffering. There is no soul. Moreover, the Supreme Being is a fiction of the imagination. There are few finer bits of humor in all literature than the famous passage in the Kevaddha Sutta[2] in which is related the journey of a monk to the World of Brahmā to obtain an answer to

[1] *Majjhima*, 24.

[2] *Dīgha*, 11. Cf. also *Dīgha*, 1; *Majjhima*, 49; *Saṁyutta*, vi. 1. 4; *Jātaka* 405.

a question which troubled him. The monk first put his question to the gods of the retinue of the Four Great Kings. They replied, "Neither do we know. But there are Four Great Kings who are more powerful and mighty than we. They might know." The monk next put his question to the Four Great Kings. They referred him to the Thirty-three Gods. They referred him to their king, Sakka. The monk, after visiting six heavens in vain, finally went to the seventh heaven, the highest of all, the World of Brahmā. And having put his question to the gods of the retinue of Brahmā, he received the following reply, "Neither do we know. But there is Brahmā, Great Brahmā, the Supreme Being, the Invincible, the All-Seeing, the Subduer, the Lord, the Maker, the Creator, the Ancient of Days, the Conqueror, the Ruler, the Father of all that are and are to be. He is more powerful and mighty than we. He might know." So the monk waited for the glory of Brahmā to appear and then put his question. Brahmā replied, "I am Brahmā, Great Brahmā, the Supreme Being, the Invincible, the All-Seeing, the Subduer, the Lord, the Maker, the Creator, the Ancient of Days, the Conqueror, the Ruler, the Father of all that are and are to be." Said the monk, "I did not ask you this question. I asked you that other." Then Brahmā took that monk by the arm, led him aside, and said this to him, "Monk, the gods of my retinue imagine that there is nothing I do not know, nothing I do not see. Therefore I did not give you a direct answer to your question in their presence. But, monk, neither do I know the answer to your question. Go to the Buddha, and whatever answer he gives you, that you may safely believe."

§ 2 d. **The Four Noble Truths regarding Suffering.** There are two extremes, declares the Buddha in his first sermon,[1] which the monk should not pursue: devotion to the pleasures of sense, and the practice of self-mortification. A Middle Way, which avoids both of these extremes, has been discovered by the Tathāgata. It makes for insight, for knowledge; it conduces to tranquillity, to higher wisdom, to enlightenment, to Nibbāna. It is the Noble Eightfold Path, to wit: Right Views (the Four Noble Truths), Right Resolution (to renounce the lusts of the flesh, to bear malice towards none, and to injure no living creature), Right Speech, Right Conduct, Right Means of Livelihood, Right Exertion, Right Mindfulness (Heedfulness), Right Concentration (the Practice of Meditation).

[1] *Vinaya, Mahā Vagga*, i. 6. 17–22.

The Noble Truth regarding Suffering is this: Birth is Suffering, the Decrepitude of Old Age is Suffering, Disease is Suffering, Death is Suffering, Association with Enemies is Suffering, Separation from Friends is Suffering, Failure to Obtain What One Desires is Suffering; in brief, the Five Elements of Being Which Spring from Attachment are involved in Suffering. The Noble Truth regarding the Origin of Suffering is this: It is Craving that leads to Rebirth; Craving for Sensual Pleasure, Craving for Existence, Craving for Wealth. The Noble Truth regarding the Cessation of Suffering is this: It ceases when Craving ceases. The Noble Truth regarding the Way to the Cessation of Suffering is this: It is the Noble Eightfold Path.

§ 2 e. **The Noble Eightfold Path to Nibbāna.** Ridiculing the idea of a Supreme Being, denying the existence of the soul, declaring that men ought not to be satisfied merely with a life of good works leading to rebirth in heaven, the Buddha urged his hearers to renounce the house-life, the life of the laity, and to adopt the houseless life, the life of the monk and nun. He taught that every living being had passed through states of existence as impossible to number as the sands of the sea; that in each of these states of existence he had endured the sufferings of birth, old age, disease, death, association with enemies, separation from friends, and failure to obtain what he desired; that the cause of rebirth and of the sufferings connected therewith was Craving; that rebirth and the sufferings of repeated existences would come to an end only when Craving had been plucked up by the root and utterly destroyed; that the Way of Escape from the Round of Existences and the sufferings thereof was the Noble Eightfold Path.

The Noble Eightfold Path may briefly be described as follows: Since a correct diagnosis of maladies and the application of proper remedies are essential to the cure of spiritual and physical ills, the seeker after Salvation, which is of course Escape from the Round of Existences, Nibbāna, must first accept the Four Noble Truths.[1] He must resolve to renounce the lusts of the flesh, to bear malice towards none, to refrain from injuring a single living creature, and to cherish love for all living creatures without respect of kind or person. He must observe the Moral Precepts in thought, word, and deed, walking in the Way of Righteousness with Energy and Heedfulness. He must finally, by the Practice of Meditation, so grasp, fix in mind, and com-

[1] The Buddha expressly says (*Vinaya, Mahā Vagga*, vi. 29): "It is because both I and you did not understand and comprehend these Four Noble Truths that we have run this long and weary course of the Round of Existences."

prehend, the Three Characteristics of all existing things, Impermanence, Suffering, and Unreality, as to eradicate utterly the cause of rebirth and suffering, namely, Craving. By so doing he becomes what is called an Arahat, obtains Supernatural Knowledge and the Supernatural Powers, and attains the Nibbāna of the Living. At death the Five Elements of Being of which he is composed are utterly destroyed. His Past Deeds, by the power of which, under other circumstances, a new individual would immediately come into existence, are likewise utterly destroyed. He has at last attained the Summum Bonum, Deliverance from the Round of Existences, Supreme Nibbāna.

Not the Practice of Meditation in and by itself, it will be observed, nor yet the Practice of Morality in and by itself, is the Buddha's Way of Salvation. The Way of Salvation is the Practice of Meditation based upon Morality. There is no other Way to Nibbāna. On neither of these two points, of course, is the Buddha's teaching wholly original. The Buddha, like all other religious teachers, built on the foundations of the past, selecting, rejecting, adding, and combining. The faith and practice of Buddhism have much in common with other Indian systems of philosophy and religion, not to speak of extra-Indian systems. Nevertheless the system of meditation and the code of morality which the Buddha gave his followers contain at least two original contributions to the development of the religious thought of India of the highest importance. They are the Doctrine of the Middle Way between extremes and the Doctrine of Love for all living creatures (Mettā).

For example, the Jains taught the Doctrine of Non-Injury; the doctrine, namely, that it is a wicked thing to injure man, animal, or plant. But this doctrine, noble as it is, they carried to what was perhaps a logical, but for all that, quite absurd extreme. The Buddha also taught the Doctrine of Non-Injury, but took pains to confine it within reasonable limits.[1] He condemned the killing of animals even

[1] What may be the genesis of this holy horror of injuring and killing we do not know for certain. But we know what it was not. It was not, as has frequently been asserted by uninformed persons, fear of injuring a deceased relative in animal form and thus incurring his vengeance. There is not a word in all the Sacred Scriptures of the Buddhists which would afford the slightest justification for such a theory. It is quite probable that fundamentally and essentially there is nothing moral or religious about it at all. Even a European or an American shrinks from treading on a caterpillar. In a country like India the sight and smell of death in revolting and horrible forms, the ever-present spectacle, for example, of insects and creeping things trodden underfoot, carcasses of animals in various stages of decay, and exposed corpses, cannot but arouse physical repulsion for death and horror of death-dealing acts. What may be in

for food, but did not altogether forbid the eating of flesh and fish. But he was not satisfied merely to condemn the injuring and killing of living creatures; he taught no such merely negative doctrine. Instead he taught the most sublime doctrine that ever fell from the lips of a human being; the doctrine, namely, of love for all living creatures without respect of kind or person and for the whole visible creation. A man must love his fellow-man as himself, returning good for evil and love for hatred. But this is not all. He must extend his love to the fishes of the sea and the beasts of the field and the fowls of the air, to the plants and the trees, to the rivers and the mountains. A man must not kill his fellow-man even in self-defense. All war is unholy.

The Doctrine of the Middle Way between the two extremes of self-indulgence and self-mortification, which was preached for the first time in India by the Buddha, illustrates in a most striking manner, not only the spirit of moderation which pervades his teaching, but also the points of contact between his own teachings and the teachings of his predecessors and contemporaries. Pischel has shown that the Buddha derived the materials for his system of meditation from the Yoga system of philosophy and self-discipline. The ascetic practices of the Yoga system, however, many of which were as horrible methods of self-torture as can well be imagined, the Buddha rejected in their entirety, as having no spiritual value whatever.[1] But again the Yoga system emphasized the importance of Right Conduct, while the related Sāṁkhya system emphasized the importance of Right Knowledge to the exclusion of all else. The Buddha emphasized the importance of both. Now the beginning of the Noble Eightfold Path is Right Knowledge, the middle is Right Conduct and Right Meditation, and the end is Nibbāna. Not one of these elements is new. Yet the Noble Eightfold Path is new.

§ 3. Practice of Meditation

Since the Religion of the Buddha knows no God, prayer forms no part of the religious life and is not even mentioned. Frequent mention is made of the Earnest Wish, which is simply the formal expres-

origin merely squeamishness and disgust would easily and quickly take on a moral and religious character. Disgust is indeed one of the most powerful motives of the Religious Life in Buddhism.

[1] For a brief account of Hindu Asceticism, see A. S. Geden, in Hastings, *Encyclopaedia of Religion and Ethics*, ii. 87-96.

sion of an intense desire for advantage of some kind in a later existence. But this Earnest Wish is not in any sense a prayer, for it is not addressed to any deity, much less to a Supreme Being. The Earnest Wish sometimes takes on high religious character. For example, in i. 8 the Future Buddha is said to have attained Enlightenment as the fruit of an Earnest Wish made under twenty-four previous Buddhas, and many other examples are given.

However, the Earnest Wish as a religious act always accompanies a work of merit, and is thus analogous to the Intention with which a Catholic performs a work of merit, as when a priest celebrates Mass or a lay person hears Mass or gives alms for a certain Intention. The Earnest Wish also plays an interesting role in the avenging of murder. In i. 4, v. 7, and viii. 2 the victim of a brutal murder, in each case a woman, utters at the moment of death the Earnest Wish that she may be reborn as an ogress, able to wreak vengeance on her murderer. Here again the Earnest Wish is religious in character, for the Wish becomes the instrument, and the maker of the Wish the agent, of the Power of Past Deeds by which, in a later existence, the murderer reaps the fruit of his sin.

For the ordinary purposes of everyday life the Act of Truth supplies, to some extent at least, the place of prayer. An Act of Truth is simply a formal declaration of fact, accompanied by a command that the purpose of the agent shall be accomplished. For example, in xvii. 3 *b* a jealous woman throws boiling oil on Uttarā. Uttarā makes the following Act of Truth, "If I cherish anger towards her, may this oil burn me; if not, may it not burn me." The boiling oil becomes to her like cold water. Other examples are given in vi. 4 *b* and xiii. 6. Frequent mention is made also of prayers and vows to deities and spirits, for the purpose of obtaining temporal blessings or averting disaster of some kind. But neither the Earnest Wish nor the Act of Truth nor yet prayers and vows to deities and spirits have any part in the religious life strictly so called. The place of Prayer is supplied by the Practice of Meditation.

Meditation, in the Buddhist sense of the word, is not mere desultory reflection, but a severe exercise in attention, discipline of will and mind, and concentration of thought. The Practice of Meditation, based on Morality and leading to the Higher Wisdom, is as essential to the attainment of Nibbāna according to the Buddhist scheme of Salvation as are Mental Prayer, Meditation, and the Sacraments of Penance and the Eucharist to final perseverance according to the Catholic scheme. But whereas the Practice of Meditation is superimposed on the Catholic system, anything like methodical meditation being unknown before the fifteenth century, it is the Way of Salvation par excellence in the Buddhist scheme. It thus corresponds, although not in kind, at least in dignity and importance, to the Greater Sacraments of the Church rather than to the Spiritual Exercises of St. Ignatius Loyola and similar Catholic systems of meditation.

The system of Meditation in vogue in Ceylon in the early part of the fifth century A.D. is outlined and described in minute detail by Buddhaghosa in the Second Part of his *Visuddhi-Magga*. To this system of Meditation constant reference is made in the legends and stories of this collection. The novice is taken in hand by a preceptor, who studies his disposition and temperament and assigns him a Subject of Meditation suited to his needs, choosing one of the following

Forty Subjects of Meditation

Ten Pleasing	Ten Disgusting	Ten Reflections	Ten Higher States
The Kasiṇas			
	The Corpses:	The Triad:	Four Exalted States:
Four Elements:	11 Bloated	21 Buddha	31 Love
1 Earth	12 Purple	22 Doctrine	32 Compassion
2 Water	13 Festering	23 Order	33 Joy
3 Fire	14 Fissured		34 Indifference
4 Wind	15 Gnawed	24 Morality	
	16 Scattered	25 Generosity	Four Formless States:
Four Colors:	17 Pounded and Scattered	26 Deities and Spirits	35 Infinity of Space
5 Blue			36 Infinity of Consciousness
6 Yellow	18 Bloody	27 Death	
7 Red	19 Wormy	28 Body	37 Nothingness
8 White	20 Bony	29 In- and Out-Breathing	38 Neither Consciousness nor Unconsciousness
Light and Space:		30 Quiescence	
9 Light			
10 Glimpse of Sky			One Realization: of the
			39 Loathsomeness of Food
			One Analysis: of the
			40 Four Elements

The Ten Disgusting Subjects (11–20) and Meditation on the Thirty-two Constituent Parts of the Body (28) lead to the First Trance. The first three of the Four Exalted States (31–33) lead to the Third Trance.

The Ten Kasiṇas (1–10), the Meditation on In-and Out-Breathing (29), the last of the Four Exalted States (34), and the Four Formless States (35–38) lead to the Fourth Trance. Ten Subjects of Meditation do not lead to the Trances at all: the first seven and the last of the Ten Reflections (21–27, 30), Realization of the Loathsomeness of Food (39), and Analysis of the Four Elements (40). These Trances are of course nothing but self-induced hypnotic states. The Four Trances and the Four Formless States are counted as the Eight Attainments. The Forty Subjects of Meditation and the Four Trances lead to Detachment and to the Cessation of Craving; that is to say, to the destruction of the cause of Rebirth and Suffering, to Deliverance from the Round of Existences, to Nibbāna.

The novice retires to a quiet, secluded spot, preferably his own cell or a forest solitude, seats himself cross-legged, and begins his Meditation. More likely than not his preceptor has directed him to meditate on the Impurity of the Body, this Subject of Meditation being regarded as particularly efficacious in enabling the young to overcome the temptations of the flesh. Summoning up all the powers of his will and concentrating his attention, he begins to repeat the Formula of the Thirty-two Constituent Parts of the Body. This Formula he repeats, not once only, but hundreds and hundreds of times. Gradually the thought comes to his mind that the body, outwardly fair and beautiful, is in point of fact utterly impure and vile, a mere assemblage of decaying elements, transitory and perishable. Having obtained this mental reflex, he enters into a state of supernatural ecstasy and calm, the First Trance.

Very possibly his preceptor will next assign him the Earth-Kasiṇa. The novice drives four stakes into the ground, spreads them basketwise, and stretches a piece of cloth or a skin over them. He then kneads a disk of light-red clay, a few inches in diameter, and places it on the frame. Having so done, he seats himself cross-legged at a short distance from the frame, fixes his eyes on the disk, and begins his Meditation. He considers the worthlessness of the pleasures of sense, reflects on the virtues of the Buddha, the Law, and the Order, and concentrates his mind on the element of earth, repeating its various names and dwelling on the thought that his body is naught but earth. He gazes steadfastly at the disk, sometimes with his eyes open, sometimes with his eyes closed. As soon as the disk appears equally visible, whether his eyes are open or closed, and he has thus obtained the proper mental reflex, he rises from his seat, goes to his place of abode, and develops the reflex. Having entered into the ecstasy and calm of the First Trance, he considers and investigates his Subject of Meditation. Having so done, he abandons consideration and investigation, and thus enters into the Second Trance. Freeing himself from ecstasy, he enters into the supernatural calm of the Third Trance. From the Third Trance he passes into the Fourth Trance, becoming utterly indifferent to pleasure and pain alike.

In xx. 9 we read that the son of a goldsmith once became a monk under Elder Sāriputta. Sāriputta, desiring to enable the youth to ward off the attacks of lust, directed him to meditate on the Impurity of the Body. The youth failed miserably in his meditations. Sāriputta, not knowing what was the matter, took him to the Buddha. The Buddha surveyed the previous states of existence of the youth and perceived that in five hundred successive states of existence the youth had been reborn in the family of that same goldsmith. Knowing that in all these states of existence the youth had wrought flowers and other beautiful objects in ruddy gold, the Buddha concluded that Meditation on a Disgusting Subject was entirely unsuitable for him; that he must be assigned a Pleasant Subject.

Accordingly the Buddha created a lotus of gold, gave the lotus to the young monk, and told him to set it up on a heap of sand, to sit down cross-legged before it, and to repeat the words, "Blood-red! blood-red!" The young monk did so. He had no difficulty whatever in developing all Four Trances. The Buddha, desiring to assist the young monk to develop Specific Attainment to the uttermost, caused the lotus to wither. Immediately the young monk thought, "If things which have no attachment for the world thus decay and die, how much more will living beings who are attached to the world decay and die!" Thus he came to realize the Three Characteristics of all things, namely, Impermanence, Suffering, and Unreality.

In ii. 3 *b* the Buddha gives Little Wayman a clean cloth and directs him to face the East, rub the cloth, and repeat the words, "Removal of Impurity!" After Little Wayman has rubbed the cloth for a time, he observes that it has become soiled, and thus obtains the mental reflex of Impermanence. This was because in a previous state of existence he obtained the reflex of Impermanence by contemplating a cloth which had become soiled by the sweat of his brow. The Buddha appears to him in a vision and says, "Impurity is Lust, Hatred, Delusion. Remove these." Little Wayman immediately attains Arahatship.

In i. 6 Mahā Kāḷa obtains the mental reflex of Impermanence by contemplating the destruction by fire of the corpse of a beautiful girl. In i. 8 *d* we are told that Yasa, in a previous state of existence, acquired a sense of the Impurity of the Body by contemplating the corpse of a pregnant woman. For this reason, the moment he beheld the loathsome appearance of his sleeping nautch-girls, he became disgusted with the pleasures of sense and obtained the concept of Impurity and Impermanence. In iii. 5 we are told that Cittahattha, disgusted with the revolting appearance of his pregnant wife as she lay asleep, which reminded him of nothing so much as that of a bloated corpse, instantly obtained the mental reflex of Impermanence.

In xi. 5 and xxiv. 5 vain women obtain the mental reflex of decay and death by contemplating the decay and death of a phantom woman. In x. 10 and xxv. 10 a monk attains Arahatship by contemplating a ragged garment which he wore as a layman. In xxv. 8 we are told that some monks, while engaged in meditation, observed jasmine flowers, which had blossomed that very morning, dropping from their stems. Thereupon they thought, "So also will we obtain release from Lust, Hatred, and Delusion." Applying themselves to meditation with renewed energy, they attained Arahatship.

In ii. 8 we read of a monk who failed miserably in the Practice of Meditation. Resolving to ask the Buddha to assign him a Subject better suited to his needs, he set out to return to the Buddha. On the way he saw a forest-fire. Hastily climbing a bare mountain, he watched the fire, concentrating his mind on the following thought, "Even as this fire advances, consuming all obstacles both great and small, so also ought I to advance, consuming all obstacles both great and small by the Fire of Knowledge of the Noble Path." He immediately attained Arahatship. Under similar circumstances, in iv. 2 and xiii. 3, monks see a mirage and a waterfall and concentrate their minds on the following thoughts, "Even as this mirage appears substantial to those that are far off, but vanishes on nearer approach, so also is this existence unsubstantial by reason of birth and decay. Just as these bubbles of foam form and burst, so also is this existence formed and so also does it burst." In viii. 12 a nun obtains a mental reflex of Impermanence, Decay, and Death by contemplating vanishing drops of water, and in viii. 13 by contemplating a flickering lamp. In viii. 11 a discontented monk resolves to commit suicide and applies the razor to his throat. As he reflects on his past conduct, he perceives that it is flawless. Thereupon a thrill of joy pervades his whole body.

Suppressing the feeling of joy and developing Insight, he attains Arahatship together with the Supernatural Faculties.

§ 4. Dhammapada: its place in the Buddhist Canon

The Sacred Scriptures of the Buddhists fall into three principal divisions: Vinaya Piṭaka, Sutta Piṭaka, and Abhidhamma Piṭaka. The Vinaya Piṭaka consists of the Books of Discipline of the Order of Monks founded by the Buddha. Incidentally it contains an account of the first two years of his ministry and of many other interesting events in his career. The Abhidhamma Piṭaka contains a systematic exposition of what may be called the Buddhist psychology of sensation; with it we are not concerned. The Sutta Piṭaka, the largest of the three divisions, contains the Books of Doctrine. The Sutta Piṭaka consists of five groups, called Nikāyas, namely, Four Nikāyas the Greater and One Nikāya the Less.

The first Four Nikāyas (also called Āgamas) are as follows: (1) Dīgha, (2) Majjhima, (3) Saṁyutta, (4) Aṅguttara. The Dīgha and Majjhima contain the long and medium-length discourses of the Buddha respectively. These are cast in the form of dialogues, somewhat after the manner of the Dialogues of Plato. The Saṁyutta and Aṅguttara contain explanations of points of doctrine, arranged in catechism fashion according to topic and number respectively. The Lesser Nikāya, called the Khuddaka, consists of fifteen books, grouped in three pentads. Of these fifteen books, perhaps the most interesting and important are the Jātakas, or Buddhist Birth Stories; the Sutta Nipāta, a collection of poetical dialogues and epic pieces (probably the oldest single book in the entire Canon); the Udāna, or Solemn Utterances of the Buddha (antique verse, together with a prose commentary ranking as canonical); and the Dhammapada.

The Dhammapada is an anthology of 423 Sayings of the Buddha in verse. This anthology is divided into twenty-six parts, or books (vaggas), the arrangement of the Stanzas being by subjects. These Stanzas are for the most part taken from other books of the Pāli canon and embody, if not the very words of the Buddha's utterance, at least the actual spirit of his teaching.[1] In one recension or another the Dhammapada was dispersed throughout the Buddhist world.

[1] See the Introduction to F. Max Müller's translation of the *Dhammapada*, in *Sacred Books of the East*, vol. x; also Winternitz, *History of Buddhist Literature*, pp. 63–65.

The most noteworthy versions, in addition to the Pāli version, are the four Chinese versions from the Sanskrit, the earliest of which, an anthology of 500 Stanzas, was brought from India in 223 A.D. and, together with the rest of the Tripiṭaka, printed from blocks in 972 A.D., nearly seven centuries before Gutenberg.[1] Unfortunately this version has never been translated into any Occidental language. Next in importance is the Tibetan Udānavarga, also from the Sanskrit. The Udānavarga, which corresponds closely to the Udāna and the Dhammapada of the Pāli Tipiṭaka, was many years ago translated into English by W. W. Rockhill. Fragments of other versions of the Dhammapada are among the finds of recent explorations in Central Asia.

§ 5. Commentary: general character and structure of parts

From Vedic times Hindu commentators have delighted to introduce illustrative stories into their commentaries. The Brāhmaṇas, like the Talmud, abound in quaint and interesting tales. In the case of commentaries on Vedic and Sanskrit texts the principal purpose of the author is, as might be expected, to interpret and explain the words of the text. Since it frequently happens that a good story illustrates the meaning of a word or passage even better than a philological discussion, the author always allows himself the liberty of introducing such stories as may serve his purpose. At the same time he is careful to subordinate the element of fiction to his main purpose, namely, the exegesis of the text. He never introduces a good story merely for the sake of the story.

The tendency of commentators on the Pāli texts, however, is just the reverse. The verbal glosses begin to shrink, both in size and importance, and the stories begin to grow. Finally, as in the case of the Dhammapada Commentary, the exegesis of the text becomes a matter of secondary importance altogether and is relegated to the background. Ostensibly at least, and in name and form, the commentary remains a commentary. But in point of fact, and to all intents and purposes, what was once a commentary has become nothing more or less than a huge collection of legends and folk-tales.

Such a commentary is the Dhammapada Commentary. Ostensibly it is a commentary on the Stanzas of the Dhammapada. The author or compiler or translator says this very solemnly in the Intro-

[1] See Bunyiu Nanjio, *Catalogue of the Chinese Translation of the Buddhist Tripiṭaka.* (There is a copy of this valuable and important work in the Library of the Peabody Institute, Baltimore.)

ductory and Concluding Stanzas. There exists, he says, in the Island of Ceylon, an erudite Commentary on the Dhammapada which has been handed down from time immemorial. But it is in the Cingalese language, and is therefore of use only to the few. The suggestion has been made to him by Elder Kumāra Kassapa that, were it to be translated into Pāli, it would conduce to the welfare of the whole world. The suggestion seems to him to be a good one, and he purposes to carry it into effect. It is his intention, therefore, to translate this Cingalese Commentary into Pāli. He will thus make clear everything that has not been made clear in the Stanzas themselves, whether in letter or in word. The rest he will also tell in Pāli, but more freely, *in accordance with the spirit* of the Stanzas.

Just what he means by the last statement is not at once apparent. But a study of the Commentary as a whole, in its relation to the Sacred Scriptures and to other Commentaries, makes his meaning abundantly plain. The reader will wish to know, first of all, who uttered the Stanza. He must be told that every one of the Stanzas is the very Word of the Buddha himself. But this will not satisfy his curiosity. He will ask many other questions about the Stanza; such, for example, as the following: Where was it uttered? when? why? for what purpose? with reference to what situation? with reference to what person or persons? The commentator will satisfy the reader's curiosity on all of these points. He is thoroughly familiar with the Sacred Scriptures, and the Sacred Scriptures tell him that the Stanza was uttered either on one certain occasion or on any number of different occasions. He is familiar also with voluminous Commentaries, both in Pāli and in Cingalese. Moreover, he has at his command the immense storehouse of Hindu legend.

If a legend or story which he finds in the Sacred Scriptures or Commentaries can be improved on by alteration or expansion or compression, he makes such changes in it as suit his purpose. If a story will do very well just as it stands, he copies it word for word, sometimes telling where he got it, but more often not. Or it may suit his purpose better to tell the story in his own words, introducing original touches here and there. Or he may have heard a good story from a traveler or a sailor or a villager or a fellow-monk. No matter where he read the story, no matter where he heard it, no matter what its character, it becomes grist for his mill.[1] Some of the stories he tells sound as though

[1] For a detailed discussion of the author's methods of handling motifs and story material generally, see Story v. 1, note 1.

they had come out of drinking-taverns, and it is quite possible that they did. Like Kipling's Homer, "Wot 'e thought 'e might require, 'e went and took." Not only does he display good judgment in selecting stories, and consummate skill in adapting them to his purpose, but he is also a first-rate story-teller on his own account. Many of the best stories cannot be traced to other sources, and of these at least a considerable number are doubtless original.

It will be observed that he does not claim to be the author of the verbal glosses. It is well for his reputation that he does not. Semi-occasionally a gloss is of some assistance in the interpretation of the text. But more often than not the glosses are not only of no assistance whatever, but are positively misleading. Words and expressions from eight to ten centuries old, whose meaning and history are perfectly well known to us, the glossographer, whoever he may be, interprets after the manner of the scholastics of the fifth century A.D. Such etymologies as he gives are, like all other Hindu etymologies, the merest puns and utterly valueless. The problem of really difficult words, he generally evades, either by not noticing the words at all, or by the familiar expedient of including the term defined in the definition. There are only two glosses of any real interest or value in the entire collection: the long glosses on Stanzas 324 and 354 (end of Stories xxiii. 3 and xxiv. 10 respectively). These have been translated in full. As an illustration of the glossographer's stupid handling of difficult words, the short gloss on Stanza 415 (near the end of Story xxvi. 32) has been translated. All other glosses have been omitted from the translation.

The author or redactor or compiler of these legends and stories appears to have used as his models chiefly the prose-and-verse Udāna and the prose-and-verse Jātaka Book. In most cases there is no organic connection between the prose and the verse of the Udāna, and the same remark applies to the Dhammapada Commentary. So far as the stories of this collection conform to the type of the prose-and-verse Udāna, and a very large number do, no more need be said of them than that they consist of a Stanza and an illustrative tale. The structure of such stories as conform to the prose-and-verse Jātaka type, which form the bulk of the collection, is much more complex. Ordinarily each story of this type consists of eight subdivisions, as follows: (1) citation of the stanza (gāthā) to which the story relates; (2) mention of the person or persons with reference to whom the story was told; (3) story proper; or, more strictly, Story of the Present (paccuppanna-vatthu), closing with the utterance of the (4) stanza or stanzas; (5) word-for-word commentary or gloss on the stanza; (6) brief statement of the spiritual benefits which accrued to the hearer or hearers;[1] (7) Story of the Past; or, more accurately, Story of Previous Existences (atīta-vatthu); (8) identification of the personages of the Story of the Past with those of the Story of the Present. Sometimes the Story of the Past precedes the Story of the Present, and not infrequently more than one Story of the Past is given.

§ 6. Subject-matter and motifs of the stories

§ 6 a. Fruit of Past Deeds and Rebirth as motifs. As in other collections of Hindu tales, the psychic motif and literary device most frequently employed is the Fruit of Past Deeds and Rebirth. It is no exaggeration to say that in each and every story it is at least the ostensible purpose of the writer to illustrate the truth of the maxim, "Whatsoever a man soweth, that shall he also reap." Every story is in a very strict, although by no means narrow, sense a "moral tale." Sometimes, it is true, the obligation to point a moral weighs so heavily upon the writer that he deliberately spoils a good story for the sake of the moral. But this is infrequently the case. Ordinarily he selects, remodels, and invents, with the utmost freedom, stories of all sorts and kinds, ranging all the way from stories of heroic virtue and sanctity to stories of unspeakable villainy and unbelievable wickedness, moved apparently by one and only one consideration, namely, that of telling the best story he can think of.

The earth is always ready to yawn and swallow up a sinner, and the Avīci hell to envelop him with its flames. The troubles and woes of a sinner are frequently more amusing and picturesque than the evil deeds that brought them upon him. A sinner is certain to be punished sooner or later. If retribution does not overtake him in one state of existence, it surely will in a later state. The worse a man behaves in one state of existence, the better the chance to tell a good story about him in a later state. It will thus be apparent that the requirement that each story shall be a "moral tale," far from hampering or restricting

[1] This enumeration of spiritual benefits generally takes the following form: "At the conclusion of the stanza (or discourse), that monk (or layman) was established in the Fruit of Conversion, and many others in the Fruits of the Second and Third Paths. The company present also profited thereby." Since this formula adds nothing to the story, and the repetition of it becomes very wearisome, it has been omitted in the translation.

the story-teller, opens up to him a field of immense possibilities. Sometimes even the temporary discomfiture of a sinner or the conversion of a sinner from his evil ways is a more effective device in the hands of the story-teller than his punishment. There are few more effective dénouements in the world's fiction than the disproof of the false accusation brought against the Buddha by the wandering nun Ciñcā (xiii. 9) and the conversion of the robber Aṅgulimāla (xiii. 6).

A correct understanding of the Buddhist doctrine of the Fruit of Past Deeds is essential to a just appreciation of its importance and effectiveness as a psychic motif and literary device. Good deeds, works of merit, a life of righteousness conformed to the ethical teachings of the Buddha, lead to happiness and prosperity in this life, and at death to rebirth either in a happier human estate or in one of the heavens. To be sure, this is not Salvation, for Salvation is Escape from the Round of Existences, Attainment of Nibbāna. Not Morality, but the Practice of Meditation, is the Way of Salvation, although of course Morality is the indispensable prerequisite to the Practice of Meditation. The merely moral man, however, will forever remain in the Round of Existences, and is therefore in a very real sense as far from Salvation as the sinner. But the Practice of Meditation, leading to Attainment of Nibbāna, while not without value as a literary motif, is of slight importance as compared with the Fruit of Past Deeds, more particularly the Fruit of Evil Deeds, and with it we are not chiefly concerned.

Just as good deeds lead to happiness, both here and hereafter, so evil deeds lead to sorrow and pain and adversity in this life, and at death to rebirth in one of the hells, in the animal kingdom, in the world of ghosts, or in the world of the fallen deities. The power of past deeds (kammabala), whether of the accumulated merit of good deeds (puñña) or of the accumulated merit of evil deeds (apuñña), is superior to all other powers spiritual or physical, human or superhuman. No man or deity or devil can stay the operation of the power of past deeds; there is no forgiveness of sins; every evil deed must be wiped out with the blood and tears of the evildoer. Moreover, as the Buddha makes abundantly clear in the Fifteenth Saṁyutta, the Round of Existences is without conceivable beginning; of it no starting-point in the past is known. Nor will there ever be an end of it for any human being unless by the Practice of Meditation, pursued with Energy and Heedfulness, he tear up by the roots and utterly destroy Craving, the cause of it. Now it is the burden of the Buddha's complaint that most men walk in ways of wickedness, few in the way of righteousness, and fewer still in the Way of Salvation. It is therefore not surprising that in Buddhist works of fiction, as in Hindu fiction in general, such extensive use should be made of this motif of the Fruit of Past Deeds; there is simply no limit to its possibilities as an instrument in the hands of the story-teller. A glance at a few of the most interesting instances of its employment in the legends and stories of this collection will make this abundantly clear.

In ii. 7 we are told that Sakka (Indra), King of the Thirty-three Gods, was at one time a Brahman youth named Magha, and that Magha obtained rebirth as Sakka by fulfilling Seven Vows. The rest of the Thirty-three Gods were in their human estate associated with Magha in the performance of works of merit. Vissakamma (the Indian Vulcan) was a common carpenter. Likewise three virtuous women of Magha's household, by the performance of works of merit, obtained rebirth as wives of Sakka. The fourth, thinking it a sufficient distinction to be a cousin of Magha, did nothing but adorn herself and was therefore reborn as a crane. However, by observing the Five Precepts even to the point of abstaining from the eating of live fish, she obtained rebirth as a potter's daughter; by persevering in the observance of the Five Precepts, she obtained rebirth as an Asura maiden and eventually became one of Sakka's wives.

The story of the seven marvelous escapes from death of the luck-child Ghosaka (ii. 1. 2) well illustrates, often in a most amusing way, the great variety of ways in which this motif is frequently employed within the limits of a single story. Ghosaka, in a previous existence as Kotūhalaka, cast his young son away in time of famine and was reborn as a dog. Dying of a broken heart for love of a Private Buddha, because of his straightforwardness and lack of deceit (which, the writer remarks, distinguish dogs from human beings), he was reborn as a god in the Heaven of the Thirty-three. In consequence of indulging in the pleasures of sense, he was reborn as the son of a courtezan. Because in his existence as Kotūhalaka he cast his own son away, he was himself cast away seven times. Because in his existence as a dog he made friends with a Private Buddha, he was miraculously preserved from death. The daughter of a rich man, because in his existence as Kotūhalaka she was his wife, fell in love with him at first sight and married him.

In xxvi. 33 *d* we are told that one day a monk who was an Arahat stopped at the house of a goldsmith to solicit gold for the erection of the shrine of the Buddha Kassapa. At that moment the goldsmith was engaged in a quarrel with his wife. Irritated at the sight of the monk, he said angrily to his wife, "Throw your Teacher into the water!" As the fruit of this sin, in seven successive existences he was cast into the water on the day of his birth. But because he made reparation for the insult by offering three vessels of golden flowers at the shrine of the Buddha, a mountain of gold uprose for him in his seventh existence as Jaṭila.

The power of habit is considered to be the fruit of past deeds. In xxvi. 25 we are told that the monks once complained to the Buddha that one of their fellows was in the habit of accosting everybody he met with the epithet commonly applied to outcasts. The Buddha, after surveying the previous existences of the accused monk, informed his accusers that in five hundred successive existences the monk had been reborn as a Brahman, and that he used the epithet, not out of ill-will, but simply from the force of habit. There is a similar explanation in xviii. 9 of the various attitudes of five laymen while the Buddha was preaching. In five hundred successive existences the first had been a dragon, and therefore fell asleep; the second had been an earthworm, and therefore dug the earth with his finger; the third had been a monkey, and therefore shook a tree; the fourth had been an astrologer, and therefore gazed at the sky; the fifth had been a repeater of the Veda, and therefore listened attentively.

All manner of physical disabilities are looked upon as the fruit of past deeds. In xvii. 1 we read of a maiden who suffered from an eruption of the skin because in a previous existence as a queen, in a fit of jealousy and anger, she had ruined the complexion of a nautch-girl. In iii. 7 a monk suffers from an eruption of the skin because in a previous existence as a fowler he had been guilty of cruelty to birds. In v. 7 we are told that a youth once spat upon a Private Buddha. Moreover, in company with three other youths, he once murdered a courtezan for her jewels. At the moment of death the courtezan made the Earnest Wish that she might be reborn as an ogress, able to kill her murderers. The youth, because he spat upon a Private Buddha, was reborn as a leper. One day, shortly after he had obtained the Fruit of Conversion, he was set upon by a heifer and kicked in the head. As a matter of fact, the heifer was none other than the courtezan, who had been reborn as an ogress and who had disguised herself as a heifer to get revenge.

In i. 1 *a* a wicked physician blinds a woman who attempts to cheat him out of his fee for curing her of an affection of the eyes. In his next existence as a monk he attains Arahatship and loses his eyesight at one and the same moment. In ix. 9 a wicked physician who was seeking employment for his services would have allowed a snake to bite some small boys. But one of the boys threw the snake on the physician's head, and he was bitten to death. In his next existence as a hunter he tormented a monk and was devoured by his own dogs. In v. 3 a niggard is reborn as a monstrosity and is forced to beg his food from door to door. In xxiv. 1 an insolent monk is reborn as a fish with a bad breath. In vii. 9 *c* Sīvali remained in the womb of his mother for seven days and seven months and seven years for no other reason than that in a previous existence he once blockaded a city and reduced the inhabitants to starvation.

The killing of animals, no less than the murder of human beings, brings down upon the guilty person's head the direst forms of retribution. In v. 1 *c* a queen once killed a ewe for food, and was reborn in hell. Afterwards, since the fruit of her wicked deed was not yet exhausted, her own head was cut off just as many times as there were hairs in the ewe's fleece. In i. 10 a pig-killer goes stark mad and for seven days crawls about his house, squealing and grunting like a pig. Dying, he is reborn in the Avīci hell. In xviii. 1 a cow-killer cuts off the tongue of a live ox, has it cooked, and sits down to eat. The moment he places a piece of ox-tongue in his mouth, his own tongue is cleft in twain and falls out of his mouth. Going stark mad, he crawls about on his hands and knees, bellowing like an ox. Dying, he is reborn in the Avīci hell. In xii. 1 *c* we are told that because in a previous state of existence Prince Bodhi ate some bird's eggs he was destined to remain childless all his life. In xxiv. 11 a rich man remains childless because he once killed his nephew for his money.

In x. 7 Moggallāna the Great, one of the Two Chief Disciples of the Buddha, is torn limb from limb by brigands and his bones ground into powder because in a previous existence he killed his mother and father. In xii. 5 Mahā Kāla, a faithful layman, is beaten to death because in a previous existence he beat a traveler to death in order to obtain possession of his wife. In ix. 11 a crow is burned to a crisp in mid-air because in a previous existence as a farmer he burned a lazy ox to death; the wife of a sea-captain is cast overboard as a Jonah because in a previous existence she drowned her dog; and seven monks are imprisoned in a cave for seven days because in a previous existence as young cowherds they thoughtlessly allowed a lizard to remain imprisoned in an ant-hill for seven days. Revenge pursued through successive existences, the motive power being supplied by the Earnest Wish, is the theme of i. 4 and xxi. 2. In iii. 9, in consequence of expressing a wicked wish, a man is transformed into a woman, and thus is created the extraordinary situation of one and the same person being both the father and the mother of children. The writer remarks in the most matter-of-fact sort of way that there are no men who have not been women at some time or other, and no women who have not, at some time or other, been men.

§ 6 b. **Other motifs.**[1] Among the motifs found in this collection which are most frequently repeated in both Hindu and European fiction are the following:

Act of Truth:[2] curse, i. 3 *a*; to cross rivers on dry foot, vi. 4 *b*; to ease childbirth, xiii. 6 (cf. xxvi. 31); to cool boiling oil, xvii. 3 *b*.
Arrow pierces five hundred warriors at once; on removing armor, they fall dead, iv. 3.
Arrow turns back, ii. 1. 6.

Bad company mars manners, xxv. 5 *a*.
Baling out the ocean, xx. 8 *a*.
Beauty fades, xi. 5, xxiv. 5.
Braggart, but of humble origin, xviii. 8.
Bow requiring a thousand men to string, ii. 1. 6, iv. 3.

Captive king and captor's daughter, ii. 1. 4.
Change of sex, iii. 9.
Charm inadvertently recited, disperses robbers and saves king's life, ii. 3 *c*.
Charm to attract and banish elephants, ii. 1. 1, ii. 1. 4.
Charmed life borne by luck-child, ii. 1. 2.
Child's query, "Have we no relatives?" ii. 3 *a*, iv. 3.
Conflict between Devas and Asuras, ii. 7 *b*.
Cure for death, viii. 13 *b*.
Cure for gluttony, xv. 6, xxiii. 4.
Cure for love, xi. 2.

Daughter her father's senior, i. 13.
Daughter of rich man falls in love with her inferior: with hunter, ix. 8; with slave, ii. 3 *a*, viii. 12; with thief, viii. 3.
David and Uriah, v. 1.
Death-warrant borne by self, ii. 1. 2.

[1] On the subject of repeated motifs in Hindu fiction, see the following papers by Professor Maurice Bloomfield: *On Recurring Psychic Motifs in Hindu Fiction, and the Laugh and Cry Motif*, in *Journal of the American Oriental Society*, 36. 1916, pp. 54–89; *On Talking Birds in Hindu Fiction*, in *Festschrift für Ernst Windisch*, pp. 349–361; *The Character and Adventures of Mūladeva*, in *Proceedings of the American Philosophical Society*, 52. 1913, pp. 616–650.

[2] For a discussion of this motif, see E. W. Burlingame, *The Act of Truth* (Saccakiriyā); *a Hindu Spell and its Employment as a Psychic Motif in Hindu Fiction*, in *Journal of the Royal Asiatic Society*, 1917.

Delayed pursuit, ii. 1. 4.
Destroyer of friendships, xx. 6 *a*.
Disloyal children: daughters, viii. 14; sons, xxiii. 3.
"Don't count your chickens before they 're hatched," iii. 4.
Drunkenness: drunken Asuras, ii. 7 *b*; drunken prince, x. 9, xiii. 4; drunken asses, vi. 8; drunken women, xi. 1; drunkenness of Suppabuddha, ix. 12.

Earnest Wish, i. 4 (xxi. 2), i. 8, iv. 8 *a*, v. 7, viii. 2.
Enchanted hunter, ix. 8.

Fakirs: bat-wing, xxvi. 11; with radiance from navel, xxvi. 30 *b*; skull-tapper, xxvi. 37.
False accusation of Buddha by suborned nuns, xiii. 9, xxii. 1.
Fruit of Past Deeds, see Introduction, § 6 *a*.

Golden maiden, xvi. 5.

Haunted forest, i. 1, iii. 6.
Haunted pool, x. 8 *a*.
Head splitting into seven pieces, i. 1, i. 3, xiii. 10.
Heir in disguise, ii. 2.
Homesickness, iv. 3 *a*, xxi. 6.
Hunger-strike (*āhāra-upacchcda*), viii. 3, xv. 3, xvi. 6.

"I have conquered!" iii. 5, ix. 1.
Identification: by footprint, ii. 1. 5 (cf. xiv. 1), ix. 8; by ring and mantle, ii. 1. 1; by the voice, ii. 2.

Jealous woman maltreats rival, xvii. 1 *b*, xxii. 6.
Jonah, v. 3, ix. 9, ix. 11 *b*.
Joseph and Potiphar's wife, xiii. 9 *a*.

King in disguise eavesdropping, ii. 3 *c*.

Laugh, ii. 1. 2 (p. 265), xvii. 3 *b*.
Laugh and cry, v. 1 *b c*.
Cf. also Smile.
Lioness mother of a human being, xxv. 9.
Longing of pregnancy, iv. 3.

Magic bird, xii. 1 *a*.
Mind-reading, iii. 2, ii. 1. 6.
Moses in the bulrushes, xxvi. 33 *c*.
Multiplication of food by miracle, iv. 5, xviii. 10.
Multiplication of men by miracle, ii. 3 *b*.

Niggardliness, i. 2, iv. 5.

Oath to wash bench with human blood, iv. 3.

Pious fraud, ii. 7 *b*, iv. 10.
Pride goeth before a fall, i. 3, i. 14, v. 5, vi. 3, xviii. 4, xviii. 8.

Rebirth, see Introduction, § 6 *a*.
Reflection in jeweled walls frightens warriors, xxvi. 34.
Removed, yet unremoved, xxvi. 23.
Riddling charm, ii. 3 *c*.
Riddling injunctions, iv. 8, xxi. 8.
Riddling phrases, ix. 8, i. 13.
Riddling questions, xiii. 7.
Riddling song, xiv. 3.

Slip of tongue, ii. 1. 2, xi. 7.
Smile of Buddha, x. 9, xi. 9, xxiv. 2, xxvi. 32.
Smile of Moggallāna, v. 12, v. 13, x. 6, xx. 6, xxii. 2.
Sounds of evil omen, v. 1.
Spit-fire monk and dragon, xiv. 6.
"Strike, but hear!" ix. 10.
Substitution of live cocks for dead cocks, ii. 1. 6.
Substitution of letter, ii. 1. 2.
Sword breaks, viii. 9 *a*.
Sycophants and rich youth, xi. 9.

Talkative tortoise, xxv. 3 *a*.
Talkativeness cured by tossing pellets of dung into the mouth, v. 13 *a*.
Transmutation of baser substances into gold, viii. 13 *a*, xvii. 3 *a*, xxiii. 8.
Treacherous wife, xxiv. 7 *a*.

Vow to spirits, i. 1, v. 1 *b*, viii. 3, viii. 9.

"We were three, we were two, I alone am left," ii. 1. 3.
Women and monks: former wives, i. 6; innocent monk beaten by husband, xxvi. 22; phantom woman, x. 4; St. Antony motif, vii. 10, xxvi. 32.
Wooden elephant filled with warriors, ii. 1. 4.

§ 6 c. **Humorous stories.** The book abounds in humorous stories and amusing situations. Niggardliness, drunkenness, pride, and the temptations of women are favorite themes. In i. 2 we read of a Brahman, very appropriately named Never-Gave, of disposition so niggardly that when he wished to have a pair of ear-rings made for his son, he beat out the gold himself to save the expense of employing a goldsmith; when his son was attacked by jaundice, he refused the request of his wife that a physician be called, for fear of having to pay him his fee, but inquiring of various physicians what remedies they were accustomed to prescribe for such and such ailments, prescribed for his son himself; and when, as the result of his treatment, his son grew steadily worse and was about to die, he carried him out of the house and laid him down on the terrace, fearing that persons who called to see his dying son might get a glimpse of the wealth the house contained. When his son died, he had the body burned, and went daily to the burning-ground and wept and lamented. The son, reborn as a deity, decided to teach the father a lesson, and resuming human form, went to the burning-ground and wept and lamented also. "Why are you weeping?" inquired the father. "I want the sun and the moon," replied the son. "You are a fool." "But which of us is the bigger fool, I who weep for what exists, or you who weep for what does not exist?"

In iv. 5 we read of another miser, a rich man named Niggardly. One day he saw a half-starved countryman eating a round cake stuffed with sour gruel. The sight made him hungry; but for fear that, if he said anything to his wife, many others might wish to eat with him and his substance might thus be wasted, he walked about all day long, enduring the pangs of hunger as best he could, until finally he was forced to take to his bed. His wife begged him to tell her what was the matter with him, suggesting that perhaps the king or some member of his household might be the cause of his woe. "Nothing of the sort." "Then perhaps you have a craving for something." When Niggardly heard this, he was struck dumb. Finally he admitted that he should like a round cake to eat. "Why did n't you tell me so before? I will bake enough cakes for all the residents of the street." "Why for them?" "Then enough for you and your children and your wife." "Why for them?" "Then enough for you and me." "Why for you?" "Very well, I will bake just enough for you." But for fear others might get wind of the fact that there was cooking going on in the house, Niggardly compelled his wife to bake the cake on the top floor of the house. By direction of the Buddha, Elder Moggallāna flew through the air to Niggardly's house and stood poised in the air outside of the window. When Niggardly saw the Elder, knowing very well that he had come for food, he sputtered and blustered, declaring that, for all the Elder's pains, he should get nothing. Finally the Elder began to belch forth smoke, whereupon Niggardly said to his wife, "Cook one tiny little cake for him and let's get rid of him. But each cake his wife baked grew bigger than the previous one, and when his wife tried to take a single cake from the basket, the cakes all stuck together. In despair Niggardly presented cakes, basket, and all to the Elder.

We are told in ii. 7 *b* that when Magha and his thirty-two companions were reborn in the World of the Thirty-three as Sakka and the Devas, the Asuras prepared strong drink to welcome the new deities. Sakka and his companions would not touch it, but the Asuras got very drunk. Then Sakka gave the signal, and his companions picked up the Asuras by the heels and flung them into the abyss. We read in x. 9 that King Pasenadi, pleased with his Prime Minister Santati, turned over his kingdom to him for seven days and gave him a nautch-girl. For seven days Santati steeped himself in liquor, and on the seventh day, magnificently adorned, seated on the back of the state elephant, set out for the bathing-place on the river. Even the Buddha smiled when he saw him, for he knew that he was destined on that very day to pass into Nibbāna. Returning from the river, Santati seated himself in his drinking-hall, and his nautch-girl stepped on the stage and began to dance and sing. Now the nautch-girl had fasted for seven days to improve her figure, and suddenly dropped dead of heart-failure. "Look to the lady!" cried Santati. "She is dead." Instantly, says the text, all the liquor he had drunk during the preceding week vanished away like drops of water in a red-hot potsherd.

In xi. 1 we read that on a certain drinking festival five hundred men of Sāvatthi intrusted their wives to Visākhā and went on a spree for seven days. On the eighth day the drum announced resumption of work, and the men obeyed. But their wives, discovering that a great quantity of liquor remained, drank it surreptitiously and became uproariously drunk. In order to escape punishment at the hands of their husbands, they took to their beds and pretended to be sick. But their husbands discovered what was the matter with them and beat them well. At a subsequent drinking festival they accompanied Visākhā to the monastery, carrying jugs of liquor under their cloaks. After drinking the liquor, they seated themselves in the Hall of Truth in the presence of the Buddha. Visākhā requested the Buddha to preach the Law to them. But those same women were so drunk that their bodies swayed back and forth, and suddenly they took it into their heads to dance and sing. An evil spirit, seeing his opportunity, took possession of them. Immediately some of them clapped their hands and laughed, while others began to dance. The Buddha sent forth a ray of light from his eyebrow, and straightway there was black darkness. So terribly were those women frightened, says the text, that instantly the strong drink within their bellies dried up. In ix. 12 we are told that the Buddha's father-in-law, Suppabuddha, because of a fancied grievance, intoxicated himself, sprawled in the street, and refused to allow the Buddha to pass. Seven days later, because of this insult, Suppabuddha fell down seven flights of stairs, was swallowed up by the earth, and was reborn in the Avīci hell.

Amusing stories of pride, insolence, and obstinacy are i. 3, i. 14, v. 5, vi. 3, xviii. 4, and xviii. 8. In i. 3 we have an account of the haughty behavior of Elder Tissa, a cousin of the Buddha, towards some monks who came to pay their respects to him. Even when the Buddha directed Tissa to apologize to the monks, he refused to do so; whereupon the Buddha, remarking that this was not the first time Tissa had proved intractable, related the story of Devala and Nārada (i. 3 *a*). This story, one of the most entertaining and interesting in the entire collection, begins with a quarrel between two monks, culminates in curse and counter-curse, and ends with the avoidance of the consequences of the curse by the guilty monk by means of a trick. In xviii. 4 a proud monk is driven away with sticks and stones and falls into a cesspool. In xviii. 8 we have the age-long story of the youth of humble origin, who, when away from home, finds fault with everything and everybody and boasts and brags about how much better things are at home.

In i. 6 we read of the attempts of the former wives of two brothers who had become monks to recover their husbands. The two wives of the younger brother made their husband the butt of their ridicule, tore off his monastic robes, clothed him in white robes, and thus succeeded in their purpose. Now while the younger brother had only two wives, the older brother had eight, and the monks therefore expressed the opinion that the older brother would immediately succumb to their wiles. The Buddha, however, assured them that they were wrong. And so they were. For when the eight wives of the older brother sought to strip him of his monastic robes, he put forth his supernatural power, flew up into the air, and thus escaped from their clutches.

One of the most delightful stories in the entire collection is i. 9, the story of Nanda. Nanda became a monk in spite of himself, became dissatisfied with the Religious Life, and was won to complete obedience by the promise of a retinue of celestial nymphs, just as in a previous existence as a recalcitrant donkey he was won to obedience by the promise of a beautiful mate. Another good story is iii. 2, which turns on mind-reading. A monk is entertained in the house of a female lay disciple, who, as an Arahat, has the power of reading the thoughts of others. The monk has but to think of his needs, and his host immediately supplies them. But suddenly the thought occurs to him, "If I should entertain a single sinful thought, my host would doubtless seize me by the topknot and treat me like a criminal. I had best leave this house." And this he does, returning to the Buddha.

The Buddha, however, sends him back, admonishing him to control his thoughts. In no long time the monk attains Arahatship. One day, curious to know what may have been the relations between him and his host in previous existences, he calls up before his mind ninety-nine previous existences, and to his horror perceives that in each of these existences his host murdered him. "Oh, what a sinner she has been!" thinks the monk. "Call up one more existence," replies his host from her own chamber. The monk obeys. Calling up before his mind the hundredth existence, he perceives that in that existence she spared his life. Thereat he rejoices greatly and immediately passes into Nibbāna. The St. Antony motif is effectively employed in vii. 10 and xxvi. 32.

Common stupidity is, as might be expected, the theme of several ludicrous stories. In iv. 4 we are told that a hundred of our years are equal to a night and a day in the World of the Thirty-three Gods. One day Garland-wearer, a deity resident in the World of the Thirty-three, is informed that although men live only a hundred years, they are ever heedless and given to wicked ways. "Can it be possible that men are so stupid!" he exclaims. In i. 8 *b* Upatissa and Kolita invite their former teacher Sañjaya to accompany them to the Buddha. "No," replies Sañjaya, "I am too old to become anybody's pupil. Let the wise men go to the wise monk Gotama, and let the stupid come to stupid me." In xi. 7 *a* a young farmer spends an entire year learning a single stanza which he is to recite by way of petition to the king. The stanza closes with the words, "Pray give me another ox." When, however, the young farmer recites the stanza before the king, following his usual habit of saying the wrong thing instead of the right thing, he closes his petition as follows, "Pray take my other ox."

In ii. 3 *c* we read of another young man who was so stupid that his teacher despaired of ever teaching him anything. But wishing to provide him with some means of earning his living, his teacher taught him a charm, impressing upon him the importance of repeating it constantly, to avoid forgetting it. And this was the charm, "You 're rubbing! you 're rubbing! why are you rubbing? I know too!" By this charm, recited inadvertently, the young man frightens robbers out of his house, and the king is saved from death at the hands of his barber. Out of gratitude the king appoints the young man Prime Minister. In ii. 1. 4 we read of another charm which did not work so well. King Udena had an elephant-charm which had always worked admirably until one day he tried it on what turned out to be a wooden elephant, posted on his frontier to entrap him. The wooden elephant was fitted with mechanical appliances worked from the inside by sixty men and could move very rapidly. Moreover, its belly contained also a quantity of elephant-dung, which the men inside dumped at regular intervals. King Udena suddenly found himself the captive of his rival, King Caṇḍa Pajjota, who, it appears, had resorted to this ruse to get possession of Udena's elephant-charm. Udena refused to teach him the charm unless he would pay him homage, but agreed to teach it to another. Caṇḍa Pajjota seated Udena on one side of a curtain and his own daughter on the other side, first telling Udena that his pupil was a hunchback and telling his daughter that her teacher was a leper. But Caṇḍa Pajjota lost both charm and daughter when Udena, in a fit of impatience, cried out, "Dunce of a hunchback!" and his pupil in indignation asked him to look and see for himself that she was no such thing.

In iv. 12 we are told that a disciple of the Buddha, angered by the repeated assertions of a friend that the Jain ascetics knew all about the past, the present, and the future, and could tell unerringly just what was going to happen and just what was not going to happen, resolved to teach those same ascetics a good lesson. So first preparing a trap for them, he invited them to his house. Suddenly they were all tipped over backwards and flung heels over head into a ditch filled with filth. In v. 13 *a* a cripple, seated behind a curtain, cures a house-priest of talkativeness by tossing pellets of goat's dung into his mouth. In iii. 4 a discontented young monk, who has resolved to return to the life of a layman, muses on ways and means of earning a living as he stands and fans his uncle. Roused to a high pitch of anger at the thought that his future wife may disobey him, he swings his fan vigorously and brings it down on the head of the older monk. The older monk, who happens to be his uncle, knowing the thoughts that are passing through the mind of his nephew, calmly remarks, "Nephew, you did n't succeed in hitting your wife; but why should an old monk suffer for it?" In viii. 10 a monk enters into a state of trance. A pack of thieves mistake him for the trunk of a tree, pile their sacks on his head and body, and lie down to sleep. In the morning they discover their mistake, beg the monk's pardon, and are converted.

There is grim humor in the ruse by which, in ii. 1. 6, King Udena makes Māgandiyā confess her guilt to the crime of causing the death by fire of Sāmāvatī. "Whoever did this deed must have loved me greatly." "It was I." "I am delighted! Send for your relatives, and I will reward you all properly." Thereupon many persons in no way related to Māgandiyā come forward and claim relationship. When the king has them all in his power, he causes them to be tortured and put to death. Grim humor attaches also to the device by which, in xi. 2, the Buddha cures a monk of love. It appears that a monk once fell in love with the female lay disciple Sirimā, a former courtezan. Sirimā sickened and died. By order of the Buddha the corpse was exposed for four days and then offered to the highest bidder. No one would take her, even as a gift. "See," said the Buddha, "this woman used to bring a thousand pieces of money a night; but now there is no one who will take her, even as a gift." The monk was cured of love.

Many amusing stories are told about Sakka, the king of the gods. In xxvi. 23 Sakka, disguised as an old Brahman, finds himself an unwelcome guest in the house of another Brahman. "Put him out!" cries the Brahman's wife. The Brahman tries to, but Sakka refuses to stir from where he sits. Then the Brahman's wife suggests, "You take hold of one arm and I 'll take hold of the other." The Brahman and his wife manage to drag him out of the house. But as soon as they turn around, they see Sakka sitting just where he sat before, waving his hands back and forth! In xvii. 1 *c* four deities quarrel over the possession of a celestial nymph and refer the decision to Sakka. The moment Sakka looks upon the nymph he desires her for himself. So he says to the four deities, "What manner of thoughts have arisen within you since you saw this nymph?" The first replies that his thoughts have been as restless as a battle-drum; the second, that his thoughts have run wild like a mountain torrent; the third, that his eyes have popped out like the eyes of a crab; the fourth, that his thoughts have been as restless as the banner on a shrine. Says Sakka, "Friends, I see that your thoughts are all on fire. My decision is that I will take her for myself."

§ 6 d. **Animal stories.** The elephant appears more frequently in the stories of this collection than any other animal. Perhaps the best elephant-story in the book is i. 5 *b*, in which are related at length the ministrations of the noble elephant Pārileyyaka to the Buddha during the residence of the latter in Protected Forest. A monkey attempts to imitate the elephant, but comes to grief. When the Buddha takes leave of the elephant, the elephant dies of a broken heart, just as does the dog in ii. 1. 2 and the horse Kanthaka in the Nidānakathā. In i. 7 *a* a noble elephant, instead of crushing a hunter, rebukes him. Trained elephants appear in ii. 1. 1, ii. 7 *b*, and xiii. 10. In vi. 1 *a* we read of an elephant who presented his son to some carpenters to show his gratitude to them for removing a thorn from his foot. In xxiii. 3 *a* the homesick elephant Dhanapāla will not eat for love of his mother. In xxv. 5 *a* we read of the elephant Damsel-face, who behaved very well with the well-behaved, but very badly with the ill-behaved. In xxiii. 6 we read of a warrior-elephant who stuck fast in the mud. His keeper arrayed himself as for battle and caused the battle-drum to be beaten. The moment the warrior-elephant heard the battle-call he made a tremendous effort and pulled himself out of the mud. In xiii. 10 a rogue elephant, holding a parasol in his trunk, is led up to the monk Aṅgulimāla. Now Aṅgulimāla, before his conversion, was a notorious brigand and murderer. When, therefore, the rogue elephant is led up to the former brigand, he is immediately cowed. He thrusts his tail between his legs, drops both his ears, closes his eyes, and stands motionless. "What a way for a rogue elephant to behave!" remarks the king. In ii. 7 *b* an elephant refuses to trample the virtuous. Similarly in ii. 1. 2 a bull and draft-oxen refuse to trample the child Ghosaka, and a she-goat gives him suck. In ii. 1. 1 and viii. 12 birds mistake human beings for pieces of meat and carry them off. Perhaps the most entertaining animal stories in the collection are i. 9 *c*, the story of the recalcitrant donkey; xii. 2 *a*, the story of the otters and the jackal; and xxvi. 11 *a*, the story of the ascetic and the lizard. The wail of a louse is the theme of xviii. 3.

§ 6 e. **Legends of the Saints.** Especially noteworthy among the many legends of heroic sanctity found in the collection are the following: iv. 8, Visākhā; viii. 12, Paṭācārā; viii. 13 *b*, Kisā Gotamī; xiii. 6, Aṅgulimāla; and xiii. 7, The Weaver's Daughter. Visākhā, a young woman of remarkable beauty, profound wisdom, and noble character, daughter of the wealthy Dhanañjaya and a disciple of the Buddha, is married to Puṇṇavaddhana, son of the wealthy Migāra, an adherent of the Jains. The story turns in a measure on the interpretation by Visākhā of Ten Riddling Injunctions given her by her father within the hearing of her father-in-law. Visākhā's whole life is devoted to good works, and she lives to be a hundred and twenty years old. Paṭācārā, daughter of a wealthy merchant, runs away from home with her lover and in the course of time gives birth to two children. Her husband is bitten to death by a snake, one of her children is carried off by a hawk and the other swept away by a river, and her mother and father and brother perish in a whirlwind. Driven mad by her sufferings, she is restored to sanity by the Buddha and attains Arahatship. Kisā Gotamī, daughter of a poverty-stricken house, loses her child by death and asks the Buddha for medicine wherewith to cure him. The Buddha tells her to obtain a pinch of mustard-seed in some house wherein no one has ever died. By degrees it dawns upon her that she has undertaken a futile task. When she returns to the Buddha and tells him that her quest has been in vain, the Buddha comforts her, admonishing her that death is common to all living beings. She too attains Arahatship. Añgulimāla, a notorious brigand and murderer, was converted by the Buddha and became a model disciple. The Weaver's Daughter meditated on death for three years, answered correctly Four Riddling Questions asked her by the Buddha, and died on the same day.

§ 6 f. **Stories of seven-year-old novices.** One of the finest groups of stories in the collection is a group of six stories relating to seven-year-old novices. In v. 15 we read of a seven-year-old novice who acquired four names: Tissa, Food-giver, Blanket-giver, and Forest-dweller. Tissa won all hearts, received gifts in profusion, and walked with the Buddha. In vi. 5 we read of a novice named Wiseman and in x. 11 *b* of a novice named Happy, these names being given to them by reason of the fact that, from the day they were born, wisdom and happiness prevailed in their respective households. The two stories are closely similar and turn on the motif of the Practice of Meditation. The story of Spearman, viii. 9, a story of unusual interest for a variety of reasons, tells of the miraculous birth and miraculous preservation from death of another seven-year-old novice. In xxv. 12 *c* we read of the adventures of the novice Flower with a dragon. The story of the Four Novices, xxvi. 23, is one of the most amusing stories in the collection.

§ 6 g. **Stories of good and evil spirits.** Stories of benevolent and kindly tree-spirits, who, however, sometimes show resentment to the monks for intruding into their forest solitudes, are the following: i. 1, ii. 1. 6, iii. 6, vii. 9, xvii. 2, xix. 3. Allusions to the offering of human sacrifice to spirits of forest and mountain are contained in v. 1 *b*, viii. 3, and viii. 9 *a*. Man-eating ogres and ogresses appear in i. 4 (cf. xxi. 2) and x. 8 *a*. Instances of demoniacal possession are xi. 1, xv. 2, xxiii. 5, and xxvi. 21. The last two are plain cases of epileptic seizure. Stories of ghosts are the following: v. 12, v. 13, x. 6, xx. 6, xxii. 2.

§ 7. Literary relations of the Dhammapada Commentary

§ 7 a. Relation to the Four Āgamas. The Dhammapada Commentary derives only a few stories from the Dīgha, Majjhima, and Aṅguttara Nikāyas. The story of the visit of Subhadda to the Buddha on his deathbed (xviii. 12) is derived from the Mahā-Parinibbāna Sutta of the Dīgha (16. 23–30), and the story of the entertainment of the Buddha by Bodhi-rājakumāra (xii. 1) is derived either from the Sutta of the same name in the Majjhima (85) or from the Vinaya (Culla Vagga, v. 21). From the Aṅguttara are derived the following stories: iii. 1, Meghiya; iv. 9, Ānandathera-pañha (almost word for word); vii. 6, Sāriputta; and (through the medium of Jātaka 40) the first page of ix. 4, Anāthapiṇḍika.

From the Saṁyutta are derived seventeen stories, fifteen of them almost word for word. Brief outlines of Saṁyutta stories are: xv. 2, Māra, and xxii. 2, Aṭṭhisaṁkhalikapetādayo. Verbally identical with the Saṁyutta, or nearly so, are the following: Introduction to ii. 7, Mahālipañha; iv. 11, Godhika; Introduction to v. 12, Ahipeta; Introduction to v. 13, Saṭṭhikūṭapeta; Introduction to x. 6, Ajagarapeta; xv. 6, Pasenadi Kosala; Introduction to xx. 6, Sūkarapeta; xxi. 6, Vajjiputtaka; xxiii. 3, Parijiṇṇabrāhmaṇaputtā; xxiii. 5, Sāṇu sāmaṇera; xxiii. 8, Māra; xxiv. 11, Aputtaka seṭṭhi; xxv. 11, Vakkali; xxvi. 16, Akkosaka; and xxvi. 40, Devahita. Five of these stories are stories about petas and are taken from the Lakkhaṇa Saṁyutta. It is possible that this group of stories forms the connecting link between the Lakkhaṇa Saṁyutta and the prose stories of the Petavatthu Commentary.

Synoptical Table A

A star means that the correspondence is close

Saṁyutta Nikāya	Dhammapada Commentary
i. 4. 3. 7, last stanza	*iii. 221^{18-21} = iv. 81^{4-7}
iii. 1. 9. 2–3: i. 75–76	*ii. 7^{6-13}
iii. 2. 3: i. 81-82	*xv. 6: iii. 264–267
	*xxiii. 4: iv. 15–17 (brief)
iii. 2. 10: i. 91–92	*xxiv. 11: iv. 76–79
iv. 2. 8: i. 113–114	*xv. 2: iii. 257-259
iv. 2. 10: i. 116–117	*xxiii. 8: iv. 31–33
iv. 3. 3: i. 120–122	*iv. 11: i. 431–433
vi. 1. 10: i. 149–153	iv. 91^{4-6} (reference)
vii. 1. 1: i. 160–161	*xxvi. 16: iv. 161–163

Saṁyutta Nikāya	Dhammapada Commentary
vii. 2. 3: i. 174–175	*xxvi. 40: iv. 233
vii. 2. 4: i. 175–177	*xxiii. 3: iv. 7–13
viii. 12, last stanza	*iv. 127^{18-19}
ix. 9: i. 201–202	*xxi. 6: iii. 460–462
x. 5: i. 208–209	*xxiii. 5: iv. 18–25
xi. 2. 3: i. 230–231	*ii. 7 *a*: i. 263^{13}–265^{15}
xv: ii. 178–193	*ii. 32^{14-15} (reference)
xix: ii. 254–262	*v. 12: ii. 64
	*v. 13: ii. 68^{20}–69^{8}
	*x. 6: iii. 60^{13}–61^{11}
	*xx. 6: iii. 410^{11}–411^{17}
	*xxii. 2: iii. 479
xxii. 84: iii. 106–109	i. 37^{15-18} (reference)
xxii. 87: iii. 119–124	*xxv. 11: iv. 117–119

§ 7 b. **Relation to the Vinaya.** From the Vinaya are derived the following seventeen stories of the Dhammapada Commentary: i. 5, Kosambakā bhikkhū; the story of Sāriputta and Moggallāna in i. 8; the story of Rāhula in i. 9; i. 12, Devadatta; v. 14, Citta and Sudhamma; vi. 2, Assajipunabbasukā; vi. 3, Channa; vi. 8, Disorderly monks; vii. 3, Monk stores food; ix. 2, Seyyasaka; x. 1, Chabbaggiyā; x. 2, Chabbaggiyā; xii. 1, Bodhi-rājakumāra; xii. 7, Devadatta; the story of Piṇḍola in xiv. 2; xvii. 2, Monk and tree-spirit; xvii. 8, Chabbaggiyā; and xviii. 10, Meṇḍaka the Magician. The story of the monks' quarrel in i. 5 is almost word for word the same as Jātaka 428, which in turn is derived from the Vinaya; the account of the Buddha's sojourn in the forest in the same story is derived immediately from the Vinaya. The story of Rāhula in i. 9 is almost word for word the same as the corresponding story in the Nidānakathā, which in turn is derived from the Vinaya.

Synoptical Table B

Mahā Vagga, Vinaya	Dhammapada Commentary
i. 6. 7–9: i. 8	xxiv. 9: iv. 71–72
i. 14: i. 23–24	ii. 32^{11-12} (reference)
i. 23–24.4: i. 39^{23}–43^{7}	i. 8 *b*: i. 88^{15}–96^{21}
i. 54. 1–2, 4–5: i. 82^{8-17}, 82^{30}–83^{5}	i. 116^{15}–118^{1} (through Jātaka, i. 91^{17}–92^{18})
v. 6: i. 188^{9}–189^{3}	xvii. 8: iii. 330
v. 8. 1: i. 190^{1-6}	iii. 451^{16-22} (quotation)
v. 34: i. 240^{6}–245^{7}	xviii. 10: iii. 363–375
vi. 23. 1–9: i. 216–218	i. 411^{1-10}
viii. 1: i. 268–281	ii. 164^{6} (reference)

Mahā Vagga, Vinaya	Dhammapada Commentary
viii. 15: i. 290–294	i. 408^{2}
x. 1–5: i. 337–357	i. 5: i. 53–65 (pp. 53–56 through Jātaka, iii. 486–587)
Culla Vagga, Vinaya	
i. 13: ii. 9^{29}–13^{22}	vi. 2: ii. 108–109
i. 18: ii. 15^{29}–18^{30}	v. 14: ii. 74–83
v. 8: ii. 110–112	iii. 199^{12}–203^{22}
v. 21: ii. 127–129	xii. 1 *b*: iii. 136–137
vi. 11: ii. 166–167	x. 1: iii. 48–49
vii. 1–4: ii. 180–203	i. 12: i. 133–150
vii. 2. 5, stanza	iii. 156^{22-23}
vii. 3. 17: ii. 198^{17-35}	xii. 7: iii. 154
xi. 1. 12–16: ii. 290^{9}–292^{24}	vi. 3: ii. 110–112
Pārājika, Vinaya	
i. 1–4: iii. 1–11	vi. 8: ii. 153–155
iv. 1: iii. 87–91	xxii. 3: iii. 480–481
Saṁghādisesa, Vinaya	
i. 1: iii. 110–112	ix. 2: iii. 5
Pācittiya, Vinaya	
xi. 1: iv. 34	xvii. 2: iii. 299–302
xxxiv. 1: iv. 78–79	ii. 149^{10} (reference)
xxxviii. 1: iv. 86–87	vii. 3: ii. 170–173
lxxiv. 1: iv. 145–146	x. 1: iii. 48–49
lxxv. 1: iv. 146–147	x. 2: iii. 49–50

§ 7 c. Relation to the Udāna. The Udāna is the source of twelve stories of the Dhammapada Commentary and contains parallels to three more. Two stories, i. 9, Nanda, and xxvi. 31, Sīvali, are almost word for word the same as the Udāna. In three stories, ii. 1. 6, Sāmāvatī, iv. 10, Mahā Kassapa, and v. 7, Suppabuddha kuṭṭhī, the Udāna is referred to by name and the prose of the Udāna is quoted. The following six stories are free versions of Udāna stories: iii. 8, Nanda gopāla; viii. 2, Bāhiya Dārucīriya; xvi. 3, Visākhā; xxiv. 1, Kapilamaccha; xxv. 7, Soṇa Koṭikaṇṇa; and xxvi. 25, Pilindavaccha. The story of Sundarī, xxii. 1, is almost word for word the same as the Introduction to Jātaka 285, which in turn is derived from the Udāna. Parallel to stories of the Udāna are the story of Buddha and the elephant in i. 5, derived from the Vinaya (Mahā Vagga, x. 4. 6–7); the story of Devadatta's schism in i. 12, also derived from the Vinaya (Culla Vagga, vii. 3. 17); and the story of Meghiya, iii. 1, derived from the Aṅguttara. About one third of the Udāna is embodied in the Dhammapada Commentary.

Synoptical Table C

Udāna	Dhammapada Commentary
i. 10: 6–9 Bāhiya Dārucīriya	viii. 2: ii. 209–217
ii. 8: 15–18 Suppavāsā	xxvi. 31: iv. 192–194 Sīvali
iii. 2: 21–24 Nanda	i. 9: i. 115–125
iii. 3: 24–27 Yasoja	xxiv. 1: iv. 37–46 Kapilamaccha
iii. 6: 28–29 Pilindavaccha	xxvi. 25: iv. 181–182
iii. 7: 29–30 Mahā Kassapa	iv. 10: i. 423–430
iv. 1: 34–37 Meghiya	iii. 1: i. 287–289
iv. 3: 38–39 gopālaka	iii. 8: i. 322–325 Nanda gopāla
iv. 5: 41–42 Pālileyyaka	(i. 5): i. 56^{14}–59^{16} Pārileyyaka
iv. 8: 43–45 Sundarī	xxii. 1: iii. 474–478
v. 3: 48–50 Suppabuddha kuṭṭhī	v. 7: ii. 33–37
v. 6: 57–59 Soṇa Koṭikaṇṇa	xxv. 7: iv. 101–112
v. 8: 60–61 Devadatta	(i. 12): i. 141–142
vii. 10: 79 Sāmāvatī	(ii. 1. 6): i. 221–222
viii. 8: 91–92 Visākhā	xvi. 3: iii. 278–279

§ 7 d. Relation to the Works of Buddhaghosa. So little of Buddhaghosa's work has been published that no more than a brief sketch of the relation of the Dhammapada Commentary to his writings is here possible. The principal works of Buddhaghosa are the Visuddhi-Magga and the Commentaries on the Dīgha, Majjhima, Saṁyutta, and Aṅguttara Nikāyas. The approximate date of the Visuddhi-Magga is 410 A.D. The rest of his works are later, for they presuppose the existence of the Visuddhi-Magga and frequently refer to it.

The Dhammapada Commentary is demonstrably later than the works of Buddhaghosa, for much the same reason that the Commentaries on the four greater Nikāyas are later than the Visuddhi-Magga. Nothing is more certain than that the Jātaka Book is earlier than the Dhammapada Commentary. The Dhammapada Commentary refers frequently to the Jātaka and contains from forty to fifty stories derived from it, nearly one half of them being verbally identical with Jātaka stories. If, therefore, references occur in the Jātaka Book to the Commentaries of Buddhaghosa, the priority of the latter both to the Jātaka Book and to the Dhammapada Commentary is clearly established. The Jātaka Book refers at least twice to Commentaries of Buddhaghosa: at i. 131^{23-24} to Aṅguttara Commentary and at v. 38^{4-5} to Saṁyutta Commentary.

Moreover, there is evidence in the Dhammapada Commentary itself of the existence of Buddhaghosa's Commentaries. The story of Sāṇu the novice, xxiii. 5: iv. 18-25, is almost word for word the same as the story of Sāṇu in the Commentary on Saṁyutta x. 5 (see Dhammapada Commentary, iv. 255, note 1). At iv. 91^{4-6} Dhammapada Commentary refers to the Kokālika Sutta and to the Commentary thereon; that is to say, either to Saṁyutta vi. 1. 10 and Commentary or to Sutta-Nipāta iii. 10 and Commentary. The Dhammapada Commentary makes such extensive use of Saṁyutta material, taking over more than a dozen stories of the Saṁyutta word for word, that the reference is probably to the Saṁyutta and to the Saṁyutta Commentary. The balance of probability in favor of the Saṁyutta is still further increased by the fact that the form of the name given as the title of the Sutta is Kokālika in the Dhammapada Commentary and in the Saṁyutta, but Kokāliya in the Sutta-Nipāta.

Synoptical Table D 1

The Commentaries on the Dhammapada, Therī-Gāthā, and Aṅguttara have the following stories in common:

	Dhammapada Commentary	Therī-Gāthā Commentary	Aṅguttara Commentary
1 Kuṇḍalakesī	viii. 3: ii. 217–227	xlvi. 99–102	*JRAS.*, 1893, pp. 771–785
2 Paṭācārā	viii. 12: ii. 260–270	xlvii. 108–112	" " " 552–560
3 Kisā Gotamī	viii. 13: ii. 270–275	lxiii. 174–176	" " " 791–796
4 Nandā	xi. 5: iii. 113–119	xli. 80–86	" " " 763–766
5 Khemā	xxiv. 5: iv. 57–59	lii. 126–128	" " " 527–532
6 Dhammadinnā	xxvi. 38: iv. 229–231	xii. 15–16	" " " 560–566

A comparison of the text of the Therī-Gāthā Commentary with the text of the Dhammapada Commentary and of the Aṅguttara Commentary reveals the fact that in the case of Stories 1, 3, 5, and 6 the Therī-Gāthā Commentary follows the Aṅguttara Commentary, frequently word for word; but that in the case of Stories 2 and 4 the compiler of the Therī-Gāthā Commentary uses both the Aṅguttara Commentary and the Dhammapada Commentary as authorities.

In Story 2, Paṭācārā, Th. 2. cm. 108^{8}–109^{4} follows A. cm. almost word for word; but Th. 2. cm. 109^{8}–112^{28} is almost word for word the same as Dh. cm. ii. 262^{21}–270^{11}. In Story 4, Nandā, Th. 2. cm. 80^{31}–81^{12} follows A. cm. almost word for word; but Th. 2. cm. 81^{13}–82^{6}, although much briefer than Dh. cm., is almost word for word the same as Dh. cm. iii. 113^{5}–118^{11}. Nandā is called Janapada-Kalyāṇī Rūpa-Nandā in Dh. cm. and A. cm., and Sundarī Nandā Janapada-Kalyāṇī in Th. 2. cm. Abhirūpa-Nandā (Th. 2. cm. xix) is her double, just as Vāsitthī (Th. 2. cm. li) is Paṭācārā's double. Story 5, Khemā, is similar to Story 4, Nandā.

A comparison of the text of the Dhammapada Commentary with the text of the Aṅguttara Commentary tends to show that in every case the Dhammapada Commentary version and the Aṅguttara Commentary version are derived independently of each other from a common original. The Story of the Past, a prominent feature of the Aṅguttara Commentary versions, is entirely lacking in the Dhammapada Commentary version of Stories 1, 3, 4, and 5, and is only briefly referred to in the same version of Stories 2 and 6.

Synoptical Table D 2

Dhammapada Commentary	Title	Aṅguttara Commentary [1]
i. 8 b g: i. 96–97, 104–112	Aggasāvakā	i. 2–3: 91–100
i. 8 c: i. 97–99	Aññā-Koṇḍañña	i. 1: 84–88
i. 9: i. 115–125	Nanda	iv. 8: 190–192
ii. 1: i. 169–191, 199–231	Udena (Parts 2, 3, 5, 6)	vii. 3–4: 249–264
ii. 3: i. 239–255	Culla Panthaka	ii. 1–2: 129–135
iv. 8: i. 384–420	Visākhā	vii. 2: 241–249
v. 14: ii. 74–83	Citta-Sudhamma	vi. 3: 229–231
vi. 4: ii. 112–127	Mahā Kappina	iv. 9: 192–196
vii. 9: ii. 188–200 (cf. xxvi. 31)	Khadiravaniya Revata	ii. 5: 137–141
viii. 2: ii. 209–217	Bāhiya Dārucīriya	iii. 8: 170–173
viii. 3: ii. 217–227	Kuṇḍalakesī	v. 9: 220–224

[1] The references are to the native subdivisions of the Commentary on the Etadagga Vagga and to the pages of the Colombo edition of 1904.

Dhammapada Commentary	Title	Aṅguttara Commentary
viii. 12: ii. 260–270	Paṭācārā	v. 4: 213–215
viii. 13: ii. 270–275	Kisā Gotamī	v. 12: 225–227
ix. 1: iii. 1–5	Culla Ekasāṭaka	i. 4: 102–104
xi. 5: iii. 113–119	Nandā (Janapada-Kalyāṇī)	v. 6: 217–218
xiv. 2: iii. 199–230	Yamaka Pāṭihāriya	Introd.: 77–79
xvii. 3: iii. 302–314	Uttarā	vii. 5: 264–268
xvii. 5: iii. 317–321	Nakulapitā	vi. 10: 238–239
xxiv. 5: iv. 57–59	Khemā	v. 2: 205–207
xxv. 7: iv. 101–112	Soṇa-Kātiyānī	vii. 8: 270–271
xxv. 11: iv. 117–119	Vakkali	ii. 10: 152–153
xxvi. 25: iv. 181–182	Pilindavaccha	iii. 7: 169–170
xxvi. 31: iv. 192–194 (cf. vii. 9)	Sīvali	ii. 9: 149–152
xxvi. 37: iv. 226–228	Vaṅgīsa	iii. 4: 163–165
xxvi. 38: iv. 229–231	Dhammadinnā	v. 5: 215–217

In every case the two versions appear to be derived independently of each other from a common original. It is perhaps worthy of note that the first three and last three pages of the Cullaseṭṭhi Jātaka are verbally identical with Buddhaghosa's version of the story of Culla Panthaka.[1]

Versions of all of the six stories which go to make up the story of Udena, ii. 1: i. 161–231, occur in the writings of Buddhaghosa. For Buddhaghosa's version of Parts 2, 3, 5, and 6, see his Aṅguttara Commentary, pages 249–264, as noted above. The story of the birth and youthful career of Udena (cf. ii. 1. 1) and the story of the winning of Vāsuladattā by Udena (cf. ii. 1. 4) are related briefly in the Commentary on Majjhima 85 (see F. Lacôte, *Essai sur Guṇāḍhya et la Bṛhatkathā*, p. 251). The story of the compassing of Sāmāvatī's death by Māgandiyā (cf. ii. 1. 6: i. 210–231) is related briefly in Visuddhi-Magga, xii. 169 ff. Visuddhi-Magga, xii. 149 ff., contains a brief outline of the story of the death of Moggallāna (cf. x. 7: iii. 65–71). These stories of Buddhaghosa and the parallel stories in the Dhammapada Commentary are undoubtedly drawn from a common source.

The Khuddaka-Pāṭha Commentary is the only work of Buddhaghosa which has been published in its entirety. Buddhaghosa is undoubtedly the author of it, for it closely resembles, in language and

[1] Compare Jātaka 4 (i. 114–123) with Aṅguttara Commentary 129–135. That the redactor of the Jātaka Book has borrowed most of his story from the Aṅguttara Commentary is plain from the reference to the Aṅguttara Commentary at Jātaka i. 131[23]. The compiler of the Dhammapada Commentary has in turn borrowed the story of Culla Panthaka (ii. 3 *a b*) from the Jātaka Book, and while still retaining the Jātaka stanza, has substituted an entirely different Story of the Past.

style, Buddhaghosa's better known writings and frequently quotes from the Visuddhi-Magga and from the principal Commentaries of Buddhaghosa. Three stories of the Dhammapada Commentary are derived from the Khuddaka-Pāṭha Commentary. The story of Sāriputta and Moggallāna, i. 100^{17}–104^{21}, is substantially the same story as Khuddaka-Pāṭha Commentary, 202^{4}–206^{6}. The story of the monks and the tree-spirits, iii. 6: i. 313–316, is a much abbreviated version of Khuddaka-Pāṭha Commentary, 232^{7}–235^{23}, 251^{25}–252^{20}. The story of the Buddha's visit to Vesāli, xxi. 1: iii. 436–439, is almost word for word the same as Khuddaka-Pāṭha Commentary, 160^{22}–165^{10}, 196^{22}–201^{6}. At 129^{16-21} Buddhaghosa refers to the stories of Sumana the gardener, Mallikā, and others as instances of benefits received for rendering honor to whom honor is due, and at 129^{21}–130^{24} he gives an outline of the story of Sumana referred to. It is in all respects the same as Dhammapada Commentary, v. 9: ii. 40–47, save only that the latter version lacks the cliché of the Buddha's smile. Here again Buddhaghosa and the compiler of the Dhammapada Commentary have drawn from the same source.

§ 7 e. **Relation to the Jātaka Book.** The Dhammapada Commentary is more intimately related to the Jātaka Book than to any other book, canonical or uncanonical, and derives a greater amount of material from the Jātaka than from all other known sources combined. Over fifty stories of the Dhammapada Commentary, representing from one fifth to one quarter of its bulk, are either derivatives of Jātaka stories or close parallels. In addition many other Jātaka stories are referred to and many Jātaka stanzas are quoted. For example, in i. 12, fourteen Jātakas are referred to and twelve stanzas are quoted.

Verbally identical with Jātaka stories, or nearly so, are the following: story of the monks' quarrel in i. 5; story of Rāhula in i. 9; story of Culla Panthaka in ii. 3 (Story of the Past entirely different); story of Sakka and the parrot in ii. 9; iv. 3, Viḍūḍabha; iv. 5, Macchariyakosiya; ix. 4, Anāthapiṇḍika (brief); x. 8, Bahubhaṇḍika; xiii. 9, Ciñcā; xv. 1, Ñātikalahavūpasamana (brief); xvii. 5, Sāketa brāhmaṇa; xx. 8, Sambahulā mahallakā; xxii. 1, Sundarī; xxiv. 4, Bandhanāgāra; xxv. 2, Haṁsaghātaka; and story of tortoise and geese in xxv. 3. Closely following the Jātaka versions, but yet not word for word, are the following: v. 2, Kassapa's companion; story of the stone-thrower in v. 13; ix. 9 *a*, Physician, boys, and snake; xii. 4, Birth of Kumāra Kassapa; xxvi. 32, Sundarasamudda.

Free versions of Jātaka stories are the following: i. 2, Maṭṭhakuṇḍali; i. 7, Devadatta (more detailed); i. 12, Devadatta (very free); story of Magha in ii. 7; iii. 5, Cittahattha; iv. 3 *a*, Kesava; story of Hell-Pot in v. 1; vi. 7, Mother of Kāṇā; vi. 8, Pack of vagabonds; vii. 9 *c*, Sīvali's previous states of existence; x. 7, Death of Moggallāna; xi. 1, Visākhā's companions (very free); xi. 7, Lāḷudāyi; xii. 2, Upananda; xii. 3, Padhānikatissa (very free); xiv. 2, Twin Miracle (much longer and more detailed); xvi. 5, Anitthigandha; xviii. 5, Discontented monk; xviii. 8, Tissadahara; xx. 5, Padhānakammika; xxiv. 7, Culla Dhanuggaha; xxiv. 11, Aputtaka seṭṭhi; xxv. 1, Pañca bhikkhū; xxv. 5, Vipakkhasevaka; xxvi. 11, Kuhaka brāhmaṇa; xxvi. 31, Sīvali. Similar stories: i. 3 *a*, Devala and Nārada, is similar to the story of Jātimanta and the Bodhisatta in Jātaka 497; v. 1 *c*, Woman and ewe, is similar to Jātaka 18; viii. 3, Kuṇḍalakesī, is similar to Jātaka 419, Sulasā; xvi. 2, Loss of a son, is similar to Introduction to Jātaka 354.

Synoptical Table E

The letter I signifies that the correspondence is with the Introduction to the Jātaka (Story of the Present); the letter J that the correspondence is with the Jātaka proper (Story of the Past). An asterisk (*) signifies that the correspondence is close. References are to the number of the story and to the volume and page of the text.

Jātaka Book		Dhammapada Commentary
4: i. 114–120 Cullaka Seṭṭhi	(I*)	ii. 3: i. 239–250 Culla Panthaka
6: i. 126–133 Devadhamma	(I* J*)	x. 8: iii. 72–78 Bahubhaṇḍika
12: i. 145–149 Nigrodhamiga	(I*)	xii. 4: iii. 144–149 Kumāra Kassapa
14: i. 156–159 Vātamiga	(I*)	xxvi. 32: iv. 194–199 Sundarasamudda
18: i. 166–168 Matakabhatta	(J)	v. 1 *c*: ii. 17[14]–18[14] Woman and ewe
26: i. 185–188 Mahilāmukha	(I)	xxv. 5: iv. 95–97 Vipakkhasevaka
31: i. 198–206 Kulāvaka	(J)	ii. 7: i. 263–281 Magha
40: i. 226–231 Khadirañgāra	(I)	ix. 4: iii. 9–15 Anāthapiṇḍika
65: i. 301–302 Anabhirati	(I J)	xviii. 5: iii. 348–351 Aññatara kulaputta
68: i. 308–310 Sāketa	(I* J*)	xvii. 5: iii. 317–321 Sāketa
70: i. 311–315 Kuddāla	(I J)	iii. 5: i. 305–313 Cittahattha

Jātaka Book		Dhammapada Commentary
71: i. 316–319 Varaṇa	(I)	xx. 5: iii. 407–410 Padhānakammika Tissa
78: i. 345–349 Illīsa	(I*)	iv. 5: i. 366–376 Macchariya Kosiya
80: i. 355–356 Bhīmasena	(I)	xviii. 8: iii. 357–359 Tissa dahara
96: i. 393–401 Telapatta	(J)	xxv. 1: iv. 83–86 Pañca bhikkhū
100: i. 407–408 Asātarūpa	(I)	xxvi. 31: iv. 192–194 Sīvali
	(J)	vii. 9 *c*: ii. 196–200
107: i. 418–420 Sālittaka	(J*)	v. 13 *a*: ii. 68–73 Saṭṭhikūṭapeta
	(I*)	xxv. 2: iv. 86–88 Haṁsaghātaka
119: i. 435 Akālarāvi	(I)	xii. 3: iii. 142–144 Padhānika Tissa
137: i. 477–480 Babbu	(I J)	vi. 7: ii. 149–153 Kāṇā-mātā
138: i. 480–482 Godha	(J)	xxvi. 11: iv. 152–156 Kuhaka
146: i. 497–499 Kāka	(I J*)	xx. 8: iii. 421–425 Sambahulā mahallakā
182: ii. 92–94 Saṁgāmāvacara	(I*)	i. 9: i. 115–122 Nanda
183: ii. 95–97 Vālodaka	(I J)	vi. 8: ii. 153–157 Pack of vagabonds
201: ii. 139–141 Bandhanāgāra	(I* J*)	xxiv. 4: iv. 53–57 Bandhanāgāra
211: ii. 164–167 Somadatta	(I J)	xi. 7: iii. 123–127 Lāḷudāyi
215: ii. 175–178 Kacchapa	(I J*)	xxv. 3: iv. 91–93 Kokālika
221: ii. 196–199 Kāsāva	(I J)	i. 7: i. 77–83 Devadatta
263: ii. 328 Culla Palobhana	(J)	xvi. 5: iii. 281–284 Anitthigandha
276: ii. 365–381 Kurudhamma	(I* J)	xxv. 2: iv. 86–90 Haṁsaghātaka
285: ii. 415–417 Maṇisūkara	(I*)	xxii. 1: iii. 474–478 Sundarī
314: iii. 43–48 Story of the Hell-Pot	(I J)	v. 1: ii. 1–19
321: iii. 71–74 Kuṭidūsaka	(I* J)	v. 2: ii. 19–25 Kassapa's pupil

Jātaka Book		Dhammapada Commentary
325: iii. 84–86 Godha	(J)	xxvi. 11: iv. 152–156 Kuhaka brāhmaṇa
328: iii. 93–94 Ananusociya	(J)	xvi. 5: iii. 281–284 Anitthigandha
346: iii. 142–145 Kesava	(J)	iv. 3 *a*: i. 342–345 Kesava
354: iii. 162–168 Uraga	(I)	xvi. 2: iii. 276–278 Aññatara kuṭumbika
367: iii. 202–203 Sāliya	(J*)	ix. 9 *a*: iii. 33 Physician, boys, and snake
374: iii. 219–224 Culla Dhanuggaha	(I J)	xxiv. 7: iv. 65–69 Culla Dhanuggaha
390: iii. 299–303 Mayhaka	(I J)	xxiv. 11: iv. 76–80 Aputtaka seṭṭhi
400: iii. 332–336 Dabbhapuppha	(I J)	xii. 2: iii. 139–142 Upananda
419: iii. 435–438 Sulasā	(J)	viii. 3: ii. 217–227 Kuṇḍalakesī
428: iii. 486–490 Quarrel of the monks at Kosambi	(I*)	i. 5: i. 53–66
429: iii. 491–494 Mahāsuka	(J*)	ii. 9: i. 283–286 Nigamavāsī Tissa
449: iv. 59–62 Maṭṭakuṇḍali	(I J)	i. 2: i. 25–37 Maṭṭhakuṇḍali
454: iv. 79–87 Ghata	(J)	i. 2: i. 25–37 Maṭṭhakuṇḍali
455: iv. 90–95 Mātiposaka	(J)	xxiii. 3: iv. 13–15 Verbal gloss
465: iv. 144–153 Bhaddasāla	(I*)	iv. 3: i. 337–362 Viḍūḍabha
466: iv. 158–159 Samuddavāṇija	(I)	i. 12: i. 133–150 Devadatta
472: iv. 187–196 Mahā Paduma	(I* J)	xiii. 9: iii. 178–183 Ciñcā
483: iv. 263–267 Sarabhamiga	(I)	xiv. 2: iii. 199–230 Yamaka Pāṭihāriya
497: iv. 388–389 Jātimanta	(J)	i. 3 *a*: i. 39–43 Devala
507: iv. 469 Mahā Palobhana	(J)	xvi. 5: iii. 281–284 Anitthigandha
512: v. 11 Kumbha	(I)	xi. 1: iii. 100–103 Drunken women
522: v. 125–127 Sarabhaṅga	(I)	x. 7: iii. 65–71 Mahā Moggallāna
531: v. 282–285 Kusa	(J)	xvi. 5: iii. 281–284 Anitthigandha

Jātaka Book		Dhammapada Commentary
533: v. 333–337 Culla haṁsa	(I)	i. 12: i. 133–150 Devadatta
536: v. 412–416 Kuṇāla	(I*)	xv. 1: iii. 254–257 Ñātikalahavūpasamana
536: v. 433^{28}–434^{8} Kuṇāla	(J*)	xxvi. 32: iv. 194–199 Sundarasamudda
542: vi. 129–131 Khaṇḍahāla	(I)	i. 12: i. 133–150 Devadatta

§ 7 f. **Relation to the Commentaries of Dhammapāla.** Internal evidence proves conclusively that the Commentaries of Dhammapāla on the Thera-Gāthā, Therī-Gāthā, Vimānavatthu, and Petavatthu are later than the Dhammapada Commentary. Dhammapāla refers to the Dhammapada Commentary four times in Thera-Gāthā Commentary (cxc, ccv, ccxxx, ccxl) and once in Vimānavatthu Commentary (iii. 8). Thera-Gāthā Commentary refers (xxvi) to Therī-Gāthā Commentary as yet to come, and Vimānavatthu Commentary is referred to four times by Petavatthu Commentary.[1] Internal evidence further proves that between twenty-five and thirty stories contained in these four Commentaries are derived from the Dhammapada Commentary.

From the Dhammapada Commentary are derived most of the following stories of the Thera-Gāthā Commentary: lx, Sīvali; lxii, Vajjiputta; lxvi, Meghiya; lxviii, Ekudāniya; lxix, Channa; xcv, Cakkhupāla; cxxxvi, Mahā Kāḷa; cxxxix, Nanda; clxxviii, Yasoja; cxc, Jambuka; ccv, Vakkali; ccxv, Sappadāsa; ccxix, Sumana; ccxxiv, Sundarasamudda; ccxxxv, Mahā Kappina; ccxl, Saṁkicca; cclix, Sāriputta; and cclxiv, Vaṅgīsa. Dhammapāla names the Dhammapada Commentary as the source of stories cxc and ccxl, and Aṅguttara Commentary and Dhammapada Commentary as the sources of story ccv.

In two stories of the Therī-Gāthā Commentary, xli and xlvii, Dhammapāla employs both Aṅguttara Commentary and Dhammapada Commentary as authorities. In the case of story xli, Nandā, the first fourteen lines are almost word for word the same as Aṅguttara Commentary; the rest of the story, although briefer than the original, is almost word for word the same as Dhammapada Commentary. Similarly in the story of Paṭācārā, xlvii, the first page is almost word for word the same as Aṅguttara Commentary; but the last four pages

[1] See *Petavatthu Commentary*, 71^{30-32}, 92^{17-29}, 244^{6-10}, 257^{5-11}.

are almost word for word the same as Dhammapada Commentary. For further details, see Introduction, § 7 *d.*

Four stories of the Vimānavatthu Commentary are derived from the Dhammapada Commentary. vii. 9, Maṭṭhakuṇḍali, is a free version of Dhammapada Commentary, i. 2. Verbally identical with Dhammapada Commentary are stories i. 15, Uttarā (= Dh. cm. xvii. 3); i. 16, Sirimā (= Dh. cm. xi. 2); and v. 2, Revatī (= Dh. cm. xvi. 9, Nandiya). Three stories of the Petavatthu Commentary are derived from the Dhammapada Commentary: i. 3, Pūtimukha (from Dh. cm. xx. 6); iv. 15 (cf. iv. 1), story of the Hell-Pot (from Dh. cm. v. 1); iv. 16, Saṭṭhikūṭa (from Dh. cm. v. 13).

Synoptical Table F

Psalms of the Brethren		Dhammapada Commentary
xxxix. 43–44	Tissa	i. 3: i. 37–45
xliv. 48–49	Sānu	xxiii. 5: iv. 18–25
lx. 60–62	Sīvali	xxvi. 31: iv. 192–194
		(vii. 9 *b*): ii. 192–195
lxii. 63	Vajjiputta	xxi. 6: iii. 460–463
lxvi. 67	Meghiya	iii. 1: i. 287–289
lxviii. 68–69	Ekudāniya	xix. 3: iii. 384–386
xcv. 88–89	Cakkhupāla	i. 1: i. 3–24
cxxxvi. 123–124	Mahā Kāḷa	i. 6: i. 66–77
cxxxix. 126–127	Nanda	i. 9: i. 115–125
clxxviii. 166–167	Yasoja	xxiv. 1: iv. 37–46
cxc. 179–180	Jambuka	v. 11: ii. 52–63
ccv. 197–200	Vakkali	xxv. 11: iv. 117–119
ccxv. 214–215	Sappadāsa	viii. 11: ii. 256–260
ccxix. 220–221	Sumana	(xxv. 12): iv. 129–137
ccxxiv. 228–230	Sundarasamudda	xxvi. 32: iv. 194–198
ccxxx. 241 refers to		iv. 12: i. 434–447
ccxxxv. 254–257	Mahā Kappina	vi. 4: ii. 112–127
ccxl. 266–268	Saṁkicca	viii. 9: ii. 240–253
cclix. 340–342	Sāriputta	(i. 8): i. 88–96
cclxiv. 395–397	Vaṅgīsa	xxvi. 37: iv. 226–228

§ 8. Date of the Dhammapada Commentary: 450 A.D.

The facts brought out in the preceding discussion of the relation of the Dhammapada Commentary to the works of Buddhaghosa, to the Jātaka Book, and to the Commentaries of Dhammapāla make it abundantly clear that the works with which we are chiefly concerned must be arranged in the following chronological order:

1. Buddhaghosa's Visuddhi-Magga and Commentaries, 410–432 A.D.[1]
2. Jātaka Book (Jātaka-Aṭṭhavaṇṇanā); redactor unknown.[2]
3. Dhammapada Commentary (Dhammapada-Aṭṭhakathā); compiler unknown.[3]
4. Dhammapāla's Commentaries, latter part of fifth century A.D.[4]

An apparently naïve remark by the compiler of the Dhammapada Commentary in the story of the Hell-Pot, v. 1, gives us a possible clew to the date of the work. At the end of the story of the four adulterers, ii. 11^{13-16}, he remarks, "Although the four wicked wights have been sinking in the Pot ever since King Pasenadi Kosala heard those sounds, not even yet (*ajjāpi*) have a thousand years elapsed."

If Pasenadi is the king so often referred to as warring with Ajātasattu, we may set 500 B.C. as his approximate date.[5] The remark referred to would then be good evidence that the Dhammapada Commentary was composed between 450 and 500 A.D. Moreover, the particle *api* would seem to indicate that at the time of writing the period of a thousand years was not quite up, but nearly so.

The evidence furnished by this remark agrees perfectly with the evidence we find in the Dhammapada Commentary regarding the chronological order of Buddhaghosa's works, Jātaka Book, Dhammapada Commentary, and Dhammapāla's Commentaries. It is certain that the Dhammapada Commentary is later than the Jātaka Book, and that the Jātaka Book is later than the works of Buddhaghosa. Now the date of Buddhaghosa's literary activity is approximately 410–432 A.D. Therefore we shall probably be not far from right if we fix 440 A.D. as the approximate date of the redaction of the Jātaka Book and 450 A.D. as the approximate date of the Dhammapada Commentary.

[1] For Buddhaghosa's life and work, see Rhys Davids's articles in the *Encyclopaedia Britannica* and in Hastings, *Encyclopaedia of Religion and Ethics*. Cf. also Winternitz, *History of Buddhist Literature*, pp. 152–154, 157–161, 164–166.

[2] On the *Jātaka Book*, see Rhys Davids, *Buddhist India*, chap. xi, pp. 189–209; Winternitz, *History of Buddhist Literature*, pp. 89–127, 153–154; and Winternitz's article in Hastings, *Encyclopaedia*.

[3] On the *Dhammapada Commentary*, cf. Winternitz, *History of Buddhist Literature*, pp. 153–157, and his article on the *Jātaka*, in Hastings, *Encyclopaedia*.

[4] On Dhammapāla, see Winternitz, *History of Buddhist Literature*, pp. 161–164, and Rhys Davids's article in Hastings, *Encyclopaedia*. According to Rhys Davids, Dhammapāla flourished in the last quarter of the fifth century A.D.

[5] On Pasenadi, see Rhys Davids, *Buddhist India*, pp. 8–11. Vincent A. Smith, *Early History of India*, 2d ed., p. 44, puts Ajātasattu at 500–475 B.C.

§ 9. Authorship of the Dhammapada Commentary

The authorship of the Dhammapada Commentary is ascribed in the colophon to Buddhaghosa. This colophon, however, is the only evidence the four volumes of text contain that such is the case. The question is one which affects not only the Dhammapada Commentary, but the Jātaka Commentary as well. Indeed, so closely does the Dhammapada Commentary resemble the Jātaka Commentary, both in form and content, and so dependent on the Jātaka Commentary is the Dhammapada Commentary, that the problem of their authorship is a single problem, not to be divided, and best approached from the side of the Jātaka.

Buddhaghosa expressly names himself as the author of the Visuddhi-Magga, the Commentary on the Vinaya Piṭaka, and the Commentaries on the four greater Nikāyas in the introductory stanzas to these works. In the Gandhavaṁsa, a Burmese work of the seventeenth century A.D., he is also named as the author of the Commentaries on the Pātimokkhas, Abhidhamma Piṭaka, Khuddaka-Pāṭha, Dhammapada, Sutta-Nipāta, Jātaka, and Apadāna.[1] In the second part of chapter xxxvii of the Mahāvaṁsa, which contains an account of Buddhaghosa's literary career, the yet more sweeping statement is made that Buddhaghosa "translated all the Cingalese Commentaries into Pāli." [2]

Rhys Davids, in discussing the authorship of the Jātaka Commentary, argues that this statement by no means implies that Buddhaghosa is the author of all the Commentaries we possess.[3] In his opinion Buddhaghosa would certainly not have begun work on the Jātaka Commentary before completing Visuddhi-Magga, Vinaya Commentary, and the Commentaries on the four greater Nikāyas. Yet this is practically what we are asked to believe. Otherwise we should expect to find in the introductory stanzas to the Jātaka Commentary at least a reference to Buddhaghosa's principal works. As a matter of fact, while three elders are there mentioned with respect, there are no references to Buddhaghosa's teachers in India and Ceylon and no allusions to his conversion, journey from India, or previous writings. The argument from silence seems to Rhys Davids to be convincing.

1 *Gandhavaṁsa*, *JPTS.*, 1886, p. 59.

2 Text in Andersen's *Pāli Reader*, part 1, pp. 113–114 (114^{27-28}).

3 See Rhys Davids, *Buddhist Birth Stories*, pp. lxiii–lxvi.

Fausböll, referring to the statement of the Gandhavaṁsa that Buddhaghosa is the author of the Jātaka Commentary, argues that while it is certain that Buddhaghosa is the author of the Visuddhi-Magga, the Commentary on the Vinaya, and the Commentaries on the four greater Nikāyas, it is incredible that he should have written six others equally long, especially if he remained only three years in Ceylon and was not only a translator, but also an independent writer.[1]

The arguments of Rhys Davids and Fausböll are convincing and apply also to the Dhammapada Commentary.[2] Indeed, on account of the dependent relation of the Dhammapada Commentary to the Jātaka Commentary, they apply with even greater force to the Dhammapada Commentary. But the strongest argument of all is this: The Jātaka Commentary and the Dhammapada Commentary differ so widely in language and style from the genuine works of Buddhaghosa as to make it in the highest degree improbable that he is the author of either of them.[3] The cumulative force of these three arguments is irresistible.

Buddhaghosa is not the author of the Jātaka Commentary or of the Dhammapada Commentary. Their authors are unknown.

§ 10. References to Dhammapada Commentary stories in Milindapañha iv and vi

It has long been the opinion of scholars that, while Books ii and iii of the Milindapañha date from the beginning of the Christian era, Books iv–vii and parts of Book i are as late as the fifth century A.D.[4] Books iv–vii are full of references to the Jātaka Book, and Books iv and vi refer to many stories and legends found only in fifth century Commentaries. The publication of the Dhammapada Commentary

[1] See the *Postscriptum* to Fausböll's edition of the *Jātaka*, vol. vii. pp. viii–ix.

[2] Cf. Winternitz, *History of Buddhist Literature*, pp. 152–154.

[3] In Hastings, *Encyclopaedia of Religion and Ethics*, vol. ii. p. 886, col. 2, Rhys Davids says of the *Jātaka Commentary* and the *Dhammapada Commentary:* "In both style and matter each of these books differs from the other, and from such portions of the works of Buddhaghosa as are accessible to us." The last half of this statement is quite correct, but the first half is utterly wrong. The *Jātaka Book* and the *Dhammapada Commentary* are so similar in language and style and subject-matter as to arouse the suspicion that they are by the same author. There is no absolute proof that this is the case, however. See Introduction, § 7 *e*. For a comparative study of the *Dhammapada Commentary* and *Aṅguttara Commentary* versions of a typical story, see E. Hardy, *Story of the Merchant Ghosaka*, in *JRAS.*, 1898, pp. 741–794.

[4] See Schrader, *Fragen des Königs Menandros*, Einleitung, pp. vii–xxxv; also Winternitz, *History of Buddhist Literature*, pp. 139–146.

enables us to identify a considerable number of these stories. Book iv, at p. 115 of the text and p. 291, refers to a group of seven stories, and Book vi, at p. 350, to a group of ten additional stories, all of which (with a single exception) occur either in the Dhammapada Commentary or in the Jātaka Book or in the Vimānavatthu Commentary. *Most of these stories, however, occur in the Dhammapada Commentary and nowhere else.*

The Dhammapada Commentary stories referred to are as follows: i. 2, Maṭṭhakuṇḍali; (possibly) iv. 8, Suppiyā; iv. 12, Garahadinna; v. 3, Ānanda seṭṭhi; v. 9, Sumana mālākāra; v. 11, Jambuka ājīvaka; ix. 1, Ekasāṭaka brāhmaṇa; xi. 2, Sirimā nagarasobhinī; xiii. 7, Pesakāradhītā; xvii. 3, Puṇṇa bhataka; xvii. 5, Sāketa-brāhmaṇassa āḷāhanadassana; xvii. 6, Puṇṇā dāsī; xxi. 8, Cūḷā Subhaddā. In addition Milindapañha at 349^{21}, 350^{3}, and 350^{4} refers respectively to the three principal legends of the Dhammapada Commentary version of the Twin Miracle, xiv. 2; namely, 1. Twin Miracle, 2. Preaching of the Abhidhamma in the World of the Thirty-three, 3. Descent to earth of the Buddha and attendant deities. Most of the references at Milindapañha 349 appear to be to the Commentary on the Sutta-Nipāta.

These references are of little assistance in fixing the date of the Dhammapada Commentary, but tend to prove that Books iv–vii of Milindapañha are as late as the beginning of the sixth century A.D.

Synoptical Table G

I Milindapañha 115^{12-16}	Dhammapada Commentary	Other Commentaries	Milindapañha
1* Sumana mālākāra	v. 9: ii. 40–47		291^{19-21}
2* Ekasāṭaka brāhmaṇa	ix. 1: iii. 1–5	A. cm. 102–104	291^{21-23}
3* Puṇṇa bhataka	xvii. 3: iii. 302–307		291^{9-11}
4 Mallikā devī		Jā. cm. iii. 405–406	291^{17-19}
5 Gopālamātā			291^{11-14}
6 Suppiyā upāsikā	(iv. 8): i. 411^{6-10}	(Cf. Vin. 1. 217^{10}–218^{10})	291^{14-17}
7* Puṇṇā dāsī	xvii. 6: iii. 321–325	Jā. cm. ii. 286–287	

II Milindapañha 350^{9-15}		
1* Sumana mālākāra	v. 9: ii. 40–47 (47^{13})	See Story 1 above
2* Garahadinna	iv. 12: i. 434–447 (446^{14})	
3* Ānanda seṭṭhi	v. 3: ii. 25–29 (29^{7})	
4* Jambuka ājīvaka	v. 11: ii. 52–63 (63^{19})	
5 Maṇḍūka devaputta		Vv. cm. 216–219 (219^{26})
6* Maṭṭakuṇḍali "	i. 2: i. 25–37 (37^{7})	Vv. cm. 322–330 (330^{33}); Jā. cm. iv. 59–62

II Milindapañha 350^{9-15}	Dhammapada Commentary	Other Commentaries
7 Sulasā nagarasobhinī		Jā. cm. iii. 435–439
8* Sirimā "	xi. 2: iii. 104–109 (109^{17})	
9* Pesakāradhītā	xiii. 7: iii. 170–176 (175^{15})	
10* Cūlā Subhaddā	xxi. 8: iii. 465–471 (471^{5})	
11* Sāketa-brāhmaṇassa āḷāhanadassana	xvii. 5: iii. 317–321 (320^{10})	Jā. cm. i. 308–310

§ 11. Parallels to Story-Cycle of Udena [1]

The story of Udena is the longest, and in many respects the most interesting, of all the stories of the Dhammapada Commentary. It is in reality a cycle of six stories of diverse origin and character, dealing with the fortunes of Udena, his principal treasurer, and his three queen-consorts. Only two of the stories are mainly concerned with the fortunes of Udena, the rest being introduced by simple and familiar literary devices. The story of the fortunes of Udena in the Dhammapada Commentary stands in much the same relation to the embedded stories as the frame-story of Udena in the Kathāsaritsāgara to the rest of the collection. Parallels to one or more of the stories are found in Buddhaghosa's Visuddhi-Magga, Buddhaghosa's Commentaries on the Majjhima and Aṅguttara, the Divyāvadāna, Kathāsaritsāgara, and other Sanskrit collections, and the Tibetan Kandjur. The kernel of two of the stories is derived from the Sutta-Nipāta and the Udāna.

Story ii. 1. 1: i. 161–169 relates the circumstances of the birth and youthful career of Udena. The same story is related briefly by Buddhaghosa in his Commentary on Majjhima 85 (see Lacôte, p. 251). A somewhat different version of the story is found in chapter ix of the Kathāsaritsāgara.

Story ii. 1. 2: i. 169–187 relates the seven marvelous escapes from death of the luck-child Ghosaka, and is preceded by an account of Ghosaka's previous kamma. The same story is related in detail by Buddhaghosa in his Commentary on the Etadagga Sutta of the Aṅguttara.[2] For a comparative study of the two versions, see E. Hardy, *JRAS.*, 1898, pp. 741–794. Parallels occur in many Sanskrit collections, and in fact in almost all of the literatures of the world. For a comparative study of the Oriental versions, see J. Schick, *Das Glückskind mit dem Todesbrief.*[3]

[1] See F. Lacôte, *Essai sur Guṇāḍhya et la Bṛhatkathā*, pp. 247–273.

[2] See footnote number 1 on next page.

[3] J. Schick, *Corpus Hamleticum* (Berlin, 1912): 1 Abteilung, 1 Band, *Das Glückskind mit dem Todesbrief, Orientalische Fassungen.*

Story ii. 1. 3: i. 187–191 relates the circumstances under which Sāmāvatī became one of the queen-consorts of Udena.[1] Similar in all respects is the story of Pradyota and Çāntā (Sāmāvatī) in the Kandjur. See A. Schiefner, *Mahākātjājana und König Tshanḍa-Pradjota:*[2] v, Epidemie zu Udshdshajinī (pp. 14–17).

Story ii. 1. 4: i. 191–199 relates the capture of Udena by Caṇḍa-Pajjota and the winning of Vāsuladattā by Udena. Close parallels to this story occur in the Kathāsaritsāgara and Kandjur. See Kathāsaritsāgara, frame-story of chapters xi–xiv; and Schiefner, *Mahākatjājana*, xv, Udajana's Gefangennehmung und Rettung (pp. 35–40). The same story is related very briefly by Buddhaghosa in his Commentary on Majjhima 85 (see Lacôte, p. 251).

Story ii. 1. 5: i. 199–203 (cf. xiv. 1: iii. 193–199) relates the Buddha's rejection of Māgandiya's offer of his daughter in marriage. The source of this story is Sutta-Nipāta, iv. 9, or some derivative thereof.[1] A close parallel is Divyāvadāna, xxxvi, part 1, pp. 515–529. For a Sanskrit parallel from Eastern Turkestan, see A. F. R. Hoernle, *JRAS.*, 1916, pp. 709 ff.

Story ii. 1. 6: i. 208–231 relates the compassing of Sāmāvatī's death by Māgandiyā, and is preceded by the stories of the three treasurers, the monks and the tree-spirit, and Khujjuttarā.[1] A close parallel to this story is Divyāvadāna, xxxvi, part 2, pp. 529–544. Brief outlines of the story occur in Buddhaghosa's Visuddhi-Magga, xii. 169 ff., and in Schiefner, *Lebensbeschreibung Çākjamuni's* (from the Kandjur), p. 47 (247). The burning of Sāmāvatī and her five hundred women is the subject of Udāna, vii. 10. The Dhammapada Commentary quotes the Udāna-passage word for word.

§ 12. Parallels to Dhammapada Commentary stories in Sanskrit (Divyāvadāna) and Tibetan (Kandjur)

The Divyāvadāna contains four parallels to stories of the Dhammapada Commentary. The story of Meṇḍhaka, chaps. ix–x, pp. 123–135, is a close parallel to the Dhammapada Commentary story of Meṇḍaka, xviii. 10: iii. 363–376. The story of the Twin Miracle in Divyāvadāna, chap. xii, pp. 143–166, is closer to Jātaka 483: iv. 263–267, than to

[1] Buddhaghosa's version of Parts 2, 3, 5, and 6 of the Udena-cycle is found in his Aṅguttara Commentary at pages 249–264, as stated above at p. 50, Synoptical Table D 2.—Postscript footnote.

[2] *Mémoires de l'académie impériale des sciences de St.-Pétersbourg*, viic série, tome xxii, No. 7.

Dhammapada Commentary, xiv. 2: iii. 199–230. The Divyāvadāna version of the story of Culla Panthaka, Cūḍāpaksha, chap. xxxv, pp. 483–515, differs materially from the version common to Jātaka 4: i. 114–120, and Dhammapada Commentary, ii. 3: i. 239–250. The Story of the Past is the story of the mouse-merchant, as in the Jātaka. Part 1 of the story of Mākandika, chap. xxxvi, pp. 515–529, is a close parallel to the story of Māgandiyā in Dhammapada Commentary, xiv. 1: iii. 193–199 (cf. ii. 1. 5: i. 199–203). Part 2 of the story of Mākandika, chap. xxxvi, pp. 529–544, is a close parallel to the story of the compassing of Sāmāvatī's death by Māgandiyā in Dhammapada Commentary, ii. 1. 6: i. 213–231. In Divyāvadāna, Māgandiyā's motive is jealousy; in Dhammapada Commentary, it is hatred of the Buddha. On Divyāvadāna, xxxvi, see Lacôte, pp. 258–262.

The Tibetan Kandjur exhibits parallels to stories of our collection. Thus three stories in Schiefner, *Mahākātjājana und König Tshaṇḍa-Pradjota*, are strikingly similar to stories of the Dhammapada Commentary. Stories v and xv, corresponding respectively to Dhammapada Commentary, ii. 1. 3 and ii. 1. 4, have been discussed above. The third story, xix, Pradjota's Träume und deren Deutung durch Mahākātjājana, relates Mahā Kātyāyana's interpretation of twelve words heard and eight visions seen in a dream by King Pradyota. It is a striking parallel to the story in Dhammapada Commentary, v. 1: ii. 1–12, and Jātaka 314: iii. 43–48, of the Buddha's interpretation of four syllables heard by King Pasenadi; to the story in Jātaka 418: iii. 428–434, of the Bodhisatta's interpretation of eight sounds heard by the King of Benares; and to the Buddha's interpretation of the sixteen dreams of King Pasenadi in Jātaka 77: i. 334–346. Stories xix–xx form a striking parallel to the story of the king's dreams in Bidpai's Fables. See Keith-Falconer, Introduction, pp. xxxi–xxxiii, and translation, pp. 219–247; also Knatchbull's translation, pp. 314–338.

§ 13. Hardy's Legends of Gotama Buddha (Cingalese)

Chapter vii of Robert Spence Hardy's *Manual of Buddhism* contains fifty-two legends of Gotama Buddha, representing in bulk nearly one half of the work. Most of these legends are derived from a Cingalese translation of the Jātaka Book or from medieval Cingalese collections of legends and stories. From a comparison of the contents of the Dhammapada Commentary with the contents of this chapter it appears likely that nearly one half of Hardy's Legends are indirectly, through the medium of medieval Cingalese collections, derived from the Dhammapada Commentary. The correspondences are indicated in the following table:

Hardy's Legends of Gotama Buddha		Subject	Dhammapada Commentary	
Number	Page (Ed. 2)		Book	Story
10	200–203	Sāriputta and Moggallāna	i	8 *b*
[11	203–210	Buddha visits Kapila	i	9 *a*]
12	210–212	Nanda and Rāhula	i	9 *a–b*
17	226–234	Visākhā	iv	8
18	234–242	Anuruddha-Sumana	xxv	12
19	242–244]	Buddha visits Vesāli	xxi	1
21	257–261	Aṅgulimāla	xiii	6
29	284–286	Ciñcā	xiii	9
30	287–290	Mind-reading	iii	2
31	290–292	Bandhula	iv	3
32	292–294	Vāsabhakhattiyā	iv	3
35	296–297	Chattapāṇi	iv	7
36	297–298	Asadisadāna	xiii	10
38	300–308	Yamakapāṭihāriya	xiv	2 *a–d*
39	308–313	"	xiv	2 *e–f*
40	313–314	Aggidatta	xiv	6
41	314–317	Sounds of evil omen	v	1
42	317–320	Sākiyas and Koliyas	xv	1
43	326–333	Devadatta and Ajātasattu	i	12
45	337–340	Death of Devadatta	i	12
49	349–351	Death of Moggallāna	x	7
50	351–352	Suppabuddha	ix	12

§ 14. Rogers's Buddhaghosha's Parables (Burmese)

In 1870 Captain T. Rogers published under the title *Buddhaghosha's Parables* an English translation of twenty-nine Burmese legends and stories. Of these, fifteen are late Burmese versions of legends and stories of the Dhammapada Commentary. The correspondences are indicated in the following table:

Buddhaghosha's Parables		Title	Dhammapada Commentary	
Chapter	Page		Book	Story
1	1–11	Cakkhupāla	i	1
2	12–17	Maddhakuṇḍali	i	2
3	18–24	Tissa Thera	i	3
4	25–31	Culla Kāla and Mahā Kāla	i	6
5	32–60	Udena [1]	ii	1

[1] The story of Ghosaka is omitted and the story of Sāmāvatī is compressed into one paragraph.

Buddhaghosha's Parables		Title	Dhammapada Commentary	
Chapter	Page		Book	Story
6	61–71	Culla Panthaka	ii	3
7	72–77	Probationer Tissa	v	15
8	78–86	Mahā Kappina Thera	vi	4
9	87–97	Probationer Paṇḍita	vi	5
10	98–102	Kisā Gotamī	viii	13
11	103–104	Girl and Hen	xxi	2
12	105–106	Hen and Little Sow	xxiv	2
13	107–119	Culla Sumana	xxv	12
15	125–135	Hell-Pot	v	1
24	160–163	Dhammadāna	xxiv	10

§ 15. Previous translations of Dhammapada and of parts of Commentary

The *Dhammapada* has been translated many times. The following list contains the titles and names of authors of all the complete translations: *Pāli into Latin: Dhammapadam,* V. Fausböll, Hauniae, 1855. Revision of the same: *The Dhammapada,* V. Fausböll, London, 1900. *Pāli into English: Buddha's Dhammapada, or Path of Virtue,* F. Max Müller (in the Introduction to Captain T. Rogers, *Buddhaghosha's Parables*), London, 1870. Also the following revisions of the same: *The Dhammapada,* F. Max Müller, forming part 1 of volume x of the *Sacred Books of the East,* 1st ed., Oxford, 1881; 2d ed., Oxford, 1898. *Dhammapada,* James Gray, 1st ed., Rangoon, 1881; 2d ed., Calcutta, 1887. *Hymns of the Faith (Dhammapada),* Albert J. Edmunds, Chicago, 1902. *The Buddha's Way of Virtue,* in the *Wisdom of the East Series,* W. D. C. Wagiswara and K. J. Saunders, New York, 1912. *Pāli into German: Das Dhammapadaṁ,* A. Weber, in *ZDMG.,* 14. 1860; reprinted in *Indische Streifen,* 1. 1868. *Worte der Wahrheit,* L. v. Schroeder, Leipzig, 1892. *Der Wahrheitspfad,* K. E. Neumann, Leipzig, 1893. *Pāli into French: Le Dhammapada,* Fernand Hû, Paris, 1878. *Pāli into Italian: Il Dhammapada,* P. E. Pavolini, Mailand, 1908. *Sanskrit into Chinese into English: Texts from the Buddhist Canon, commonly known as Dhammapada,* Samuel Beal, London, 1878. *Sanskrit into Tibetan into English: Udānavarga,* W. W. Rockhill, London, 1883.

Only a few of the stories of the *Dhammapada Commentary* have ever been translated. The first four stories are translated by C. Duroiselle in volume ii of the review *Buddhism,* Rangoon, 1905–08. The first two stories are translated by Godefroy de Blonay and Louis de la

Vallée Poussin in the *Revue de l'Histoire des Religions*, 26. 1892. Stories i. 5 and iv. 3 are translated by the same scholars in the same *Revue*, 29. 1894. Warren, *Buddhism in Translations*, contains iv. 4 (pp. 264–267), iv. 8 (pp. 451–481), iv. 11 (pp. 380–383), x. 7 (pp. 221–226), xvii. 2 (pp. 430–431), and xxv. 2 (pp. 432–433). A translation of the story of Ghosaka (ii. 1. 2, Story of the Present) by E. Hardy is given in *JRAS.*, 1898, pp. 741–794. For an analysis of the stories of Books i–iv, see my paper, *Buddhaghosa's Dhammapada Commentary*, in *Proceedings of the American Academy of Arts and Sciences*, 45, pp. 467–550. For translations of parallel stories in the *Jātaka Book*, see the Cambridge translation into English, or J. Dutoit's translation into German. The German version is vastly superior to the English.

§ 16. Editions of the text of the Dhammapada Commentary

In 1855 extracts from the Commentary were published by V. Fausböll in his edition of the *Dhammapada*. These extracts form the basis of the admirable translations by H. C. Warren in *Buddhism in Translations* (see Introduction, § 15, paragraph 2). In 1906 the Pāli Text Society began the publication of a complete edition of the text, under the editorship of H. C. Norman of Benāres. The contents and date of publication of the several installments are as follows: Vol. i, part 1, containing Book i, 1906. Vol. i, part 2, containing Books ii–iv, 1909. Vol. ii, containing Books v–viii, 1911. Vol. iii, containing Books ix–xxii, 1912. Vol. iv, containing Books xxiii–xxvi, 1914. Vol. v, Indexes, 1915. Much to the regret of all students of Pāli literature, Professor Norman died on April 11, 1913, before the publication of the fourth and last volume of the text. The revision of the last three or four sheets of the text and the copying and revision of the Indexes was completed by a pupil of Norman's, Pandit Lakshman Shastri Tailang. There are two excellent native editions of the Commentary: a Burmese edition by Ū Yan, Rangoon, 1903, and a Cingalese edition by W. Dhammānanda Mahā Thera and M. Ñāṇissara Thera, Colombo, 1898–1908. The Pāli Text Society edition of the Commentary contains so many errors, the result not only of careless proof-reading, but of failure to exercise good judgment and common sense in the choice of readings, that the translator has been obliged to rely mainly on the Burmese native edition. The readings of this edition are generally given (although not always correctly) in the footnotes of the London edition.

§ 17. Brief list of books on the life and teachings of the Buddha

Many books have been written about the Buddha, but not many good ones. **Bibliography:** *Buddhism*, a list of references in the New York Public Library. Compiled by Ida A. Pratt, New York Public Library, 1916. **On the life of the Buddha,** see T. W. Rhys Davids's article *Buddha* in the *Encyclopaedia Britannica*, 11th ed., and A. S. Geden's article *Buddha* in Hastings, *Encyclopaedia of Religion and Ethics.* **On the teachings of the Buddha,** see Rhys Davids's article *Buddhism* in the *Britannica.* The best handbook of the life and teachings of the Buddha is R. Pischel, *Leben und Lehre des Buddha,* in the Series *Aus Natur und Geisteswelt,* Band 109, 2 Auflage, Leipzig, 1910. The following books will also be found useful: T. W. Rhys Davids, *Buddhism: its History and Literature,* in *American Lectures on the History of Religions,* New York and London, 1904. Edmund Hardy, *Der Buddhismus nach älteren Pāli-Werken dargestellt,* Münster, 1890. Edmund Hardy's brief manual *Buddha* in the *Sammlung Göschen,* Leipzig, 1905. Hermann Oldenberg, *Buddha: Sein Leben, seine Lehre, seine Gemeinde,* 6 Auflage, Stuttgart und Berlin, 1914. Reginald S. Copleston, *Buddhism, Primitive and Present, in Magadha and Ceylon,* 2d ed., London, 1908. H. Kern, *Manual of Indian Buddhism,* in the *Grundriss der Indo-Arischen Philologie,* Strassburg, 1896.

On Primitive Buddhism in its relation to other Indian religions, see G. F. Moore, *History of Religions,* vol. i, chap. ii, and H. Oldenberg, *Die Indische Religion,* in *Die Religionen des Orients,* Teil i, Abteilung iii. 1, of *Die Kultur der Gegenwart.* **For a comprehensive sketch of Buddhism as a world-religion,** see H. Hackmann, *Buddhism as a Religion,* in *Probsthain's Oriental Series,* vol. ii, London, 1910. **On the early history of Buddhism in India,** see T. W. Rhys Davids, *Buddhist India,* in *The Story of the Nations,* London and New York, 1911. **On the history of the Buddhist sects,** see Rhys Davids's article *Hīnayāna* in Hastings, *Encyclopaedia of Religion and Ethics.* **On the Buddhist literature,** see M. Winternitz, *Die Buddhistische Litteratur,* in *Geschichte der Indischen Litteratur,* Zweiter Band, Erste Hälfte, Leipzig, 1913; also A. A. Macdonell's article *Literature (Buddhist)* in Hastings, *Encyclopaedia of Religion and Ethics,* and Rhys Davids's article *Buddhism* in the *Britannica.*

Translations of Selections: H. C. Warren, *Buddhism in Translations,* in *Harvard Oriental Series,* vol. iii, Cambridge, Massachusetts, Sixth Issue, 1915; J. Dutoit, *Das Leben des Buddha,* Leipzig, 1906; K. Seidenstücker, *Pāli-Buddhismus in Übersetzungen,* Breslau, 1911; M. Winternitz, *Buddhismus,* in A. Bertholet, *Religionsgeschichtliches*

Lesebuch, Tübingen, 1908. **Complete Translations of Texts:** Of the *Vinaya*, *Pātimokkha*, *Mahā Vagga*, and *Culla Vagga* have been translated by T. W. Rhys Davids and H. Oldenberg in *Sacred Books of the East*, vols. xiii, xvii, and xx. Of the *Dīgha*, Suttas 1–13 (vol. i) have been translated by K. E. Neumann, *Die Reden Gotamo Buddhos aus der längeren Sammlung Dīghanikāyo des Pāli-Kanons*, I Band, München, 1907; Suttas 1–23 (vols. i–ii) by T. W. Rhys Davids, *Dialogues of the Buddha*, vols. i–ii (vols. ii–iii of the *Sacred Books of the Buddhists*), London, 1899, 1910. The entire *Majjhima* has been translated by K. E. Neumann, *Die Reden Gotamo Buddhos aus der mittleren Sammlung Majjhimanikāyo des Pāli-Kanons*, 3 Bde., Leipzig, 1896–1902; Suttas 1–50 have been translated into English by the Bhikkhu Sīlācāra, *Discourses of Gotama the Buddha*, vols. i–ii, London, 1912, 1913. Of the *Aṅguttara*, *Nipātas* 1–3 (vol. i) have been translated by E. R. J. Gooneratne, Galle, Ceylon, 1913. For translations of the *Dhammapada*, see Introduction, § 15. The *Udāna* has been translated by D. M. Strong, London, 1902. The *Itivuttaka* has been translated by J. H. Moore, *Sayings of the Buddha*, New York, 1908. The *Sutta Nipāta* has been translated by V. Fausböll, part 2 of volume x of the *Sacred Books of the East*, 1st ed., Oxford, 1881; 2d ed., Oxford, 1898; also by K. E. Neumann, *Die Reden Gotamo Buddhos aus der Sammlung der Bruchstücke Suttanipāto des Pāli-Kanons*, Leipzig, 1905, 2 Auflage, 1911. The *Thera-Gāthā and Therī-Gāthā* have been translated by K. E. Neumann, *Die Lieder der Mönche und Nonnen Gotamo Buddhos*, Berlin, 1899; also, together with the greater part of the stories in prose from the *Commentaries of Dhammapāla*, by Mrs. C. A. F. Rhys Davids, *Psalms of the Early Buddhists:* i, *Psalms of the Sisters* (*Therī-Gāthā Commentary*), London, 1909; ii, *Psalms of the Brethren* (*Thera-Gāthā Commentary*), London, 1913. Of the *Jātaka Book* there are two complete translations: the Cambridge translation into English and the far superior translation into German of J. Dutoit. The *Nidānakathā* has been translated by T. W. Rhys Davids, *Buddhist Birth Stories*, London, 1880. The *Milindapañha* has been translated by T. W. Rhys Davids in *Sacred Books of the East*, vols. xxxv, xxxvi. — **Addendum.** *Dīghanikāya in Auswahl übersetzt* by R. Otto Franke, Göttingen, 1913. Suttas 1–5, 8, 9, 11, 13, 16, 21, 26, 27.

SYNOPSES OF THE LEGENDS OF THE DHAMMAPADA COMMENTARY

Book I. Pairs, Yamaka Vagga

1. "If thine eye offend thee, pluck it out" [i. 1 = 1]. A householder of Sāvatthi makes a vow to a tree-spirit, whereby he becomes the father of two sons. Because the tree was protected (pālita) by him, he names his sons Mahā Pāla and Culla Pāla. When the sons reach manhood, their parents set them up in households of their own. At this time the Buddha takes up his residence at Jetavana, and establishes the multitude in the Way to Heaven and the Way to Deliverance. The Noble Disciples perform two duties daily: before breakfast, they give alms; after breakfast, bearing offerings, they go to Jetavana monastery to hear the Law. One day Mahā Pāla accompanies them to the monastery, and is so impressed by the Buddha's sermon that he decides to retire from the world and become a monk. Taking leave of his younger brother, he retires from the world and is admitted to the Order.

After five years have passed, he comes to the Buddha and asks him how many are the Burdens of the Religious Life. On being told that there are two: the Burden of Study of the Scriptures, and the Burden of the Practice of Meditation, he chooses the latter as being better suited to his advanced years. The Buddha gives him a Subject of Meditation, and accompanied by sixty monks, he retires to a distant village and enters upon residence for the season of the rains. The villagers obtain the privilege of entertaining them, and a physician offers them his services. Mahā Pāla, on learning that the monks intend to avail themselves of all of the Four Postures (walking, standing, sitting, lying), takes a vow not to lie down. After encouraging each other to observe Heedfulness, the monks devote themselves to the Practice of Meditation.

At the end of the first month, Mahā Pāla's eyes begin to trouble him. The physician treats him, but as he never lies down to rest, the treatment does him no good. However, he resolutely keeps his vow, and one night, at one and the same moment, loses his eyesight and attains Arahatship. At the end of the rainy season the monks attain Arahatship, and express a desire to see the Teacher. Mahā Pāla, knowing that there is a forest on the way haunted by evil spirits, and fearing that he may be a hindrance to them, sends them on ahead, directing them to ask his brother Culla Pāla to send some one to lead him, and to greet the Buddha and the Eighty Chief Elders in his name. Culla Pāla sends his nephew Pālita. As Pālita is leading his blind uncle through the forest, he hears the voice of a woman singing. Pālita excuses himself, goes to her, and breaks his vow of chastity. Mahā Pāla dismisses him. Sakka king of gods sees Mahā Pāla's plight, disguises himself as a wayfarer, and leads the blind Elder to Sāvatthi. One night after a heavy rain, the blind Elder takes a walk in the cloister and tramples many insects to death. Visiting monks report the matter to the Buddha, who replies that as the Elder did not see the insects, he is innocent of offense. The monks then ask how it happened that the Elder, although predestined to Arahatship, lost the sight of his eyes. The Buddha relates the following

1 a. Story of the Past: The wicked physician and the woman. A woman of Benāres promises to become the slave of a physician if he will cure her of an affection of the eyes. The physician cures her; but the woman, repenting of her bargain, attempts to deceive him by telling him that her eyes are worse than ever. In revenge the physician gives her an ointment that makes her blind. That physician was Mahā Pāla.

2. **Why cry for the moon?** [i. 2 = 2]. A niggardly Brahman named Never-Gave has an only son, whom he dearly loves. Desiring to give his son a pair of ear-rings, but at the same time to avoid unnecessary expense, he beats out the gold himself and makes him a pair, wherefore the people call the boy Burnished-Ear-rings, Maṭṭhakuṇḍali. When the boy is sixteen years of age, he has an attack of jaundice. The mother wishes to have a physician called, but the father demurs at the thought of paying him his fee, inquires of various physicians what remedies they are accustomed to prescribe for such and such ailments, and prescribes for him himself. The boy grows steadily worse, and is soon at the point of death. Realizing this, and fearing that those who come to see his son may also see the wealth the house contains, the Brahman carries his son outside and lays him down on the terrace.

The Exalted One, arising from a Trance of Great Compassion, and surveying the world with the Eye of a Buddha, beholds Maṭṭhakuṇḍali. Foreseeing that the sick youth, and through him, many others, will attain the Fruit of Conversion, the Buddha visits him. After making an Act of Faith in the Buddha, the youth dies and is reborn in the World of the Thirty-three. The father has the body of his son burned, and goes daily to the burning-ground and weeps and laments. Maṭṭhakuṇḍali, desiring to convert his father, resumes human form, goes to the burning-ground, and weeps and laments also. The Brahman asks the youth why he weeps. The youth replies, "I want the sun and the moon." The Brahman tells him that he is a simpleton. "But which of us is the bigger simpleton," asks the youth, "I, who weep for what exists, or you, who weep for what does not exist?" The youth then reveals his identity, and tells his father that he attained his present glory by making an Act of Faith in the Buddha. The Brahman is immediately converted. The Brahman invites the Buddha and his monks to take a meal with him. The Buddha accepts. The Brahman asks the Buddha whether it is possible to obtain rebirth in Heaven by a mere Act of Faith. The Buddha replies in the affirmative, and to convince the bystanders, summons Maṭṭhakuṇḍali, who appears in all his glory and confirms the Buddha's statement.

3. **Tissa the Fat** [i. 3–4 = 3–4]. Tissa, a kinsman of the Buddha, lives on the food of the Buddhas, and grows to be fat and well-liking. One day he so far presumes on his kinship with the Buddha as to snub some monks who come to pay their respects. When the monks show their resentment of his treatment of them, he tells them who he is, and threatens to extirpate their whole race. The monks complain to the Buddha, who directs Tissa to apologize. This Tissa refuses to do. The monks remark that Tissa is obstinate and intractable, whereupon the Buddha tells them that it is not the first time Tissa has shown himself obstinate and intractable. So saying, he relates the following

3 a. **Story of the Past: Devala and Nārada.** Two ascetics, Devala and Nārada, obtain lodging for the night in the same rest-house. After Nārada has lain down, Devala, in order to start a quarrel by causing Nārada to stumble over him in the dark, lies down in the doorway. Nārada, having occasion to go out during the night, treads on Devala's matted locks. Devala then changes his position, turning completely around and putting his head where his feet had been. When Nārada returns, he treads on Devala's neck. Devala thereupon curses Nārada, saying, "When the sun rises to-morrow, may your head split into seven pieces!" Nārada then pronounces the following counter-curse, "When the sun rises to-morrow, may the head of the guilty man split into seven pieces!" But foreseeing that the curse will light upon

Devala, Nārada takes pity on him, and by his supernatural power prevents the sun from rising.

By reason of the darkness, the people are unable to pursue their wonted occupations, and request the king to cause the sun to rise for them. The king, knowing that he has committed no sin, concludes that the darkness must have been caused by a quarrel of the monks. He learns the circumstances of the quarrel from Nārada, who tells him that Devala can escape the consequences of the curse by begging his pardon. This Devala refuses to do. The king, by main force, compels Devala to do so. Nārada forgives him, but tells the king that inasmuch as Devala did not beg his pardon of his own free will, the king must take Devala to a certain pond, put a lump of clay on top of his head, and make him stand in the water up to his neck. The king does so. Nārada then tells Devala that he is about to put forth his magical power and cause the sun to rise; that the moment the sun rises, he must duck in the water, rise in a different place, and go his way. As soon as the sun's rays touch the lump of clay, it splits into seven pieces, whereupon Devala ducks in the water, rises in a different place, and goes his way. Devala was the obstinate monk.

4. **"Not hatred for hatred"** [i. 5 = 5]. A barren wife, knowing that her rival wife, if she bears a child, will become sole mistress of the household, mixes a drug in her rival's food, and causes two successive abortions. On the third attempt, she kills both mother and child. Just before the mother dies, she utters the prayer that she may be reborn as an ogress, able to devour the children of her persecutor. Thereafter, in three successive states of existence, the fruitful and the barren wife return hatred for hatred.

The Fruitful Wife is reborn as a Cat. The Barren Wife is reborn as a Hen. The Cat eats the eggs of the Hen, who prays that in her next existence she may be able to devour the offspring of her enemy.

The Barren Wife, at the end of her existence as a Hen, is reborn as a Leopardess. The Fruitful Wife, at the end of her existence as a Cat, is reborn as a Doe. Thrice the Doe brings forth young, and thrice the Leopardess devours the Doe's offspring. The Doe prays that in her next existence she may be able to devour the offspring of her enemy.

The Fruitful Wife, at the end of her existence as a Doe, is reborn as an Ogress. The Barren Wife, at the end of her existence as a Leopardess, is reborn in Sāvatthi as the daughter of a respectable family. The Ogress devours the first and the second child of the Young Woman. When, however, the Young Woman is about to give birth to her third child, she eludes her enemy by going to the house of her father. Here she gives birth to her child in safety. A few days later, while the mother is sitting in the grounds of the monastery, suckling the child, she sees the Ogress approaching. The terrified mother, seizing the child, flees, closely pursued by the Ogress, into the very presence of the Teacher. The Teacher, learning the circumstances of the quarrel, says to the Ogress, "Why do you return hatred for hatred? Love your enemies." The Ogress is converted. Thereafter the two live as friends.

5. **The quarrelsome monks of Kosambi** [i. 6 = 6].

5 a. **Quarrel among the monks.** A preacher of the Law is reproved by a student of the Discipline for leaving water in the bath-room. On being informed that the offense was unintentional, the student of the Discipline assures the preacher of the Law that he is guiltless. Immediately afterwards, however, he tells his own pupils that the preacher of the Law has committed sin and is without conscience in the matter. Thereupon ensues a quarrel in which monks, nuns, the unconverted, and deities from the lowest heaven to the highest, are involved. The Buddha, informed of the circumstances of the quarrel, sends word to the monks to patch up their differences. This they refuse to do. The Buddha then goes to them in person and ad-

monishes them. Still they refuse to be reconciled. Disheartened by his failure to restore harmony, he leaves them, and goes quite alone to the village of Bālaka the salt-maker, where he discourses to Elder Bhagu on the solitary life; thence to Eastern Bamboo Deer-park, where he discourses to the Three Youths on the bliss of the sweets of concord; and from there to Protected Forest. The lay brethren of Kosambi, learning the cause of the Teacher's departure, retaliate on the monks by withdrawing their support. The monks apologize to the lay brethren, but the latter refuse to accept their apology until they have made peace with the Buddha. Since, however, the rainy season is at its height, they are unable to go to the Teacher, and have a very uncomfortable time as a result. The Buddha spends the rainy season pleasantly, attended by an elephant.

5 b. **The Buddha, the elephant, and the monkey.** A noble elephant named Pārileyyaka, who has left his herd on account of the excessive annoyances to which he has been subjected, comes to Protected Forest and performs all of the major and minor duties for the Teacher. When the Teacher makes his alms-pilgrimage to the village, the elephant accompanies him to the village, and after the Teacher has made his round, accompanies him back. During the night he paces back and forth in the forest with a club in his trunk, protecting the Teacher from attacks of wild beasts. (Hence the forest came to be called Protected Forest.) The elephant's attentions to the Teacher excite in a monkey the desire to do likewise. One day the monkey finds some wild honey and presents it to the Teacher. After the monkey has removed some insects, the Teacher eats the honey. The monkey is so delighted that he leaps from branch to branch, and dances about in great glee. The branches break, down he falls on a stump, and is impaled. Dying, he is reborn in the World of the Thirty-three.

5 a. **Quarrel among the monks, concluded.** When the Teacher's residence in the forest becomes known, Anāthapiṇḍika and others request Ānanda to procure from them the privilege of hearing the Teacher. Ānanda, accompanied by five hundred monks, goes to the forest. Pārileyyaka assumes a threatening attitude, but abandons it at the command of his master. Ānanda presents Anāthapiṇḍika's petition, and the Buddha directs the monks to set out for Sāvatthi. Pārileyyaka gives forest-fruits to the monks, and seeks to delay the Teacher's departure. As the Teacher passes out of his sight, he dies of a broken heart, and is reborn in the World of the Thirty-three. When the Teacher arrives at Sāvatthi, the monks of Kosambi go thither to beg his pardon. The Teacher humiliates the quarrelsome monks by directing them to lodge apart from the rest. Thereupon they prostrate themselves at his feet and beg his pardon. The Teacher reproves them for their sinful conduct, and admonishes them on the necessity of self-restraint.

6. **Kāḷa junior and Kāḷa senior, Culla Kāḷa Mahā Kāḷa ca [i. 7–8 = 7–8].** Two caravan-drivers, Kāḷa senior and Kāḷa junior, retire from the world, the former from conviction, the latter with the intention of returning to the world and taking his brother with him. Kāḷa senior becomes a Burning-grounder and attains Arahatship by contemplating the corpse of a beautiful girl. Kāḷa junior pines for son and wife. When the Teacher visits their native town, Kāḷa junior, who has charge of the seating arrangements, is subjected to such ridicule by his two wives that he then and there leaves the Order. Since Kāḷa senior has eight wives, the monks express their opinion that he also will succumb. The Teacher assures them that they are mistaken. Kāḷa senior escapes from the clutches of his wives by soaring up into the air.

7. **Devadatta wears an unbecoming robe [i. 9–10 = 9–10].** A layman of Rājagaha, hearing Sāriputta preach on the twofold duty of giving alms and inciting others to give alms, extends an invitation to the Elder and his retinue, and enlists the assistance of the citizens. A certain householder gives a costly robe with the understanding that

if the supply of food proves insufficient, the robe may be sold and the proceeds devoted to the purchase of more food. The supply of food proves sufficient, and the layman asks his fellows to whom the robe shall be given. The question is submitted to popular vote, with the result that as between Sāriputta and Devadatta there is a majority of four in favor of the latter. But as soon as Devadatta puts on the robe, every one remarks that it is not at all becoming to him, and would have suited Sāriputta much better. When the matter is reported to the Teacher, he remarks that it is not the first time Devadatta has worn an unbecoming robe, and tells the following

7 a. Story of the Past: The elephant-hunter and the noble elephant. An elephant-hunter one day sees several thousand elephants fall on their knees before some Private Buddhas. Concluding that it is the yellow robe that inspires their reverence, he steals a yellow robe, and sits beside the elephant-trail with spear in hand and upper robe drawn over his head. By this ruse he kills the last elephant in line. Subsequently the Future Buddha is reborn as an elephant, and becomes the leader of the herd. One day the hunter throws his spear at him and darts behind a tree. The Great Being resists the temptation to crush his enemy, and contents himself with remarking that the hunter has put on robes that ill become him. The elephant-hunter was Devadatta.

8. The Chief Disciples [i. 11–12 = 11–12].

8 a. Life of the Buddha. The Future Buddha, after receiving recognition at the hands of twenty-four Buddhas beginning with Dīpaṅkara, and after fulfilling the Perfections, is reborn in the Tusita heaven. Urged by the deities to save the world, he makes the Five Great Observations, is born of Queen Māyā, passes his youth in splendor and luxury in three mansions appropriate to the three seasons, beholds the Four Ominous Sights, resolves to become a monk, renounces son and wife, is greeted by Kisā Gotamī, makes the Great Retirement and the Great Struggle, defeats the hosts of Māra, and attains Omniscience under the Bo-tree. At the request of Mahā Brahmā he sets in motion the Wheel of the Law and converts the Five Monks, Yasa and Fifty-four Companions, the Thirty Noble Youths, and the Three Brothers Kassapa; subsequently he visits King Bimbisāra and accepts from him the gift of Bamboo Grove monastery; here he enters upon residence, and here Sāriputta and Moggallāna visit him.

8 b. Life of Upatissa (Sāriputta) and Kolita (Moggallāna). Upatissa and Kolita were born on the same day, and were brought up amid great luxury. They acquired a sense of Impermanence while witnessing Mountain-top festivities, and were for a time disciples of Sañjaya. Converted to the Religion of the Buddha by Assaji, after an unsuccessful attempt to persuade Sañjaya to accompany them, they visit the Buddha, who admits them to the Order and makes them his Chief Disciples. The other disciples accuse the Buddha of favoritism in bestowing the highest dignity on new-comers and passing over what they allege to be the prior claims of the Five Monks, Yasa and Fifty-four Companions, the Thirty Noble Youths, and the Three Brothers Kassapa. The Buddha denies that he shows favoritism and declares that as is his wont, in the case of these Five Groups of persons, he bestows that for which they have made their Earnest Wish. By way of illustration he relates the following

8 c. Story of the Past: Culla Kāḷa and Mahā Kāḷa. Aññā-Koṇḍañña in his existence as Culla Kāḷa bestowed the gift of first-fruits nine times on the Buddha Vipassī and for seven days gave abundant alms to the Buddha Padumuttara, making the Earnest Wish that he might be the first to comprehend the Law.

8 d. Story of the Past: Yasa and Fifty-four Companions. Yasa and his companions performed many works of merit in the dispensation of a previous Buddha, making the Earnest Wish to attain Arahatship. In a later dispensation they acquired a sense of Impurity by contemplating the corpse of a pregnant woman. Because of this, Yasa acquired a sense of Impurity in the women's apartments, and both he and his companions developed Specific Attainment.

8 e. Story of the Past: Thirty Noble Youths. The Thirty Noble Youths made their Earnest Wish to attain Arahatship under previous Buddhas, and performed works of merit. In a later dispensation they were reborn as thirty evil-doers, but on hearing the admonition addressed to Tuṇḍila, kept the Five Precepts for sixty thousand years.

8 f. Story of the Past: Three Brothers Kassapa. Uruvela-Kassapa, Nadī-Kassapa, and Gayā-Kassapa entertained their eldest brother the Buddha Phussa, and made the Earnest Wish to attain Arahatship. After undergoing rebirth as deities during ninety-two cycles of time, they obtained the fulfillment of their Wish. The Three Ascetics of the Matted Locks, who were their serving-men, diverted to their own use the food which they had been directed to bestow in alms. In consequence of this sin, they were reborn as ghosts during four Buddha-intervals, and suffered from hunger and thirst. They came and begged food and drink of the Buddha Kakusandha, who referred them to the Buddha Koṇāgamana, who referred them to the Buddha Kassapa, who prophesied that in the dispensation of his successor Gotama, their kinsman Bimbisāra would grant them relief by making over to them the merit of alms given to the Teacher. Thus at last they obtained celestial food and drink and robes, and became deities.

8 g. Story of the Past: Sarada and Sirivaḍḍha. Sāriputta and Moggallāna were born as Sarada and Sirivaḍḍha respectively at the time when the Buddha Anomadassī appeared in the world. Sarada retired from the world with seventy-four thousand followers, entertained the Buddha, and held the flower-parasol over him for seven days, making the Earnest Wish that he might thereby become the Chief Disciple of a Buddha. Upon receiving assurance that his Wish would be fulfilled, he sent word to Sirivaḍḍha to make his Wish for the place of Second Disciple. Thereupon Sirivaḍḍha entertained the Buddha and made his Earnest Wish for the place of Second Disciple. Thus Sāriputta and Moggallāna obtained only that for which they had made their Earnest Wish under Anomadassī.

Sāriputta and Moggallāna then relate their experiences from Mountain-top festivities to their final interview with Sañjaya. The Buddha contrasts the attitude of Sañjaya with that of his own faithful followers.

9. Nanda the Elder [i. 13–14 = 13–14].

9 a. Nanda becomes a monk in spite of himself. After the events related in the preceding story, the Buddha visits his father Suddhodana and establishes him in the Fruits of the First Two Paths. On the following day, while the festivities connected with Nanda's marriage are in progress, the Buddha enters the house for alms, places his bowl in Nanda's hands, wishes him happiness, and departs without taking his bowl. So profound is Nanda's reverence for the Teacher that he dares not ask him to take his bowl, but expecting that he will ask for it sooner or later, follows him to the head of the stairs, to the foot of the stairs, and into the courtyard. Here Nanda wishes to turn back, but the Teacher goes straight ahead, and Nanda, much against his will, follows. Nanda's bride, Country-Beauty, runs after him with tears streaming down her face and hair half combed, and begs him to return. But the Teacher still gives no indication that he wishes to have his bowl returned, and Nanda follows him to the monastery. Here the Teacher asks Nanda whether he wishes to become a monk, and Nanda, in spite of himself, answers, "Yes." The Teacher then makes a monk of him.

9 b. Nanda and the celestial nymphs. After receiving his son Rāhula into the Order, and establishing his father in the Fruit of the Third Path, the Teacher enters upon residence at Jetavana. Nanda becomes dissatisfied with the Religious Life, and resolves to return to the world. The Teacher, learning that it is because of his love for Country-Beauty, takes him by the arm, leads him to a burnt field, and shows him a singed she-monkey, without ears, nose, and tail, sitting on a stump. He then conducts him to the Heaven of the Thirty-three and shows him five hundred pink-footed celestial nymphs. "Nanda, which do you consider the more beautiful, Country-Beauty or these nymphs?" "Reverend Sir, Country-Beauty is as far inferior to these nymphs as she is superior to that singed she-monkey." "Cheer up, Nanda; I guarantee that you will win these nymphs if you persevere in the Religious Life." The Teacher allows his promise to become known to the monks, whereupon they subject Nanda to such intense ridicule that he applies himself to meditation with redoubled energy, and in a short time attains Arahatship. He then goes to the Teacher and tells him that he wishes to release him from his promise. The Teacher replies that he was released from his promise the moment Nanda attained Arahatship. The Teacher remarks that this is not the first time Nanda has been won to obedience by the lure of the opposite sex, and relates the following

9 c. Story of the Past: Kappaṭa and the donkey. A merchant of Benāres named Kappaṭa makes a journey to Takkasilā with a load of pottery. While he is disposing of his wares, he lets his donkey run loose. The donkey, seeing a female of his species, makes up to her. The female donkey greets him in a friendly manner and commiserates him on his hard lot. As a result of her talk, he becomes dissatisfied with his job, and refuses to return with his master. His master, finding that threats only make the donkey more stubborn, offers to procure him a mate. By this promise the donkey is immediately won over. The donkey was Nanda.

10. Cunda the pork-butcher [i. 15 = 15]. Cunda the pork-butcher, after a course of evil conduct lasting fifty-five years, was attacked by a peculiar malady, and while he yet lived, the fire of Avīci uprose before him. For seven days he crawled about the house on his hands and knees, grunting like a pig, and on the seventh day died and was reborn in the Avīci hell.

11. The righteous lay brother [i. 16 = 16]. While a righteous lay brother, lying on his death-bed, listens to the Law, a host of deities, visible to none but him, drive up in their chariots and invite him to accompany them. The layman, wishing to hear the Law, says to the deities, "Stop!" The monks, mistaking his meaning, arise and depart. The layman's children begin to weep. The layman, to confirm their faith, performs a miracle, admonishes them, and stepping into a celestial chariot, is reborn as a deity.

12. Devadatta's career [i. 17 = 17].

12 a. Retirement from the world of the six princes. While the Future Buddha is in residence at Anūpiya Mango Grove, eighty thousand kinsmen observe on his person the Characteristics of a Tathāgata, and each dedicates a son to his service. In the course of time all of these youths become monks, with the exception of Bhaddiya, Anuruddha, Ānanda, Bhagu, Kimbila, and Devadatta. Anuruddha's brother Mahā Nāma urges Anuruddha to become a monk, promising if he will do so, to follow his example. Anuruddha, who has been brought up in such luxury that he does not even know the meaning of the word *is n't*, naturally does not know the meaning of the word *monk*, and therefore asks his brother for an explanation. Mahā Nāma explains the meaning of the word. Anuruddha replies that he is too delicate to become a monk. Mahā Nāma then suggests that he learn farming. But Anuruddha, who does not even know where boiled rice comes from, naturally does not know the meaning of the word *farming*, and therefore asks his brother to explain the word to him. Mahā Nāma explains to Anuruddha what is implied by the word. Anuruddha, aghast at the endless routine of manual labor, decides after all that he will become a monk. His mother gives her permission on condition that he persuade his friend King Bhaddiya to do the same. Bhaddiya finally consents. Thereupon the six princes, accompanied by the barber Upāli, visit the Teacher and are admitted to the Order.

12 b. **Devadatta's wicked deeds.** When the Teacher and the Congregation of Monks enter upon residence at Kosambi, the people seek out all of the Chief Disciples except Devadatta. Devadatta, knowing that neither King Bimbisāra nor King Pasenadi will have anything to do with him, makes common cause with Bimbisāra's son Ajātasattu. Overmastered by pride, he proposes to the Buddha to turn over the Congregation of Monks to him. The Buddha rejects his proposal and causes public proclamation to be made concerning him at Rājagaha. In resentment Devadatta goes to Ajātasattu and says, "You kill your father and become king, and I will kill the Exalted One and become Buddha." When Ajātasattu is established in his kingdom, Devadatta makes three attempts on the life of the Buddha. First he hires assassins to kill him, but they desert their posts and obtain the Fruit of Conversion. Then he climbs to the top of Mount Vulture Peak and hurls down a rock, but succeeds only in wounding the Teacher. Finally he despatches the elephant Nālāgiri against him, but Ānanda stands in the breach and the Teacher subdues the elephant. Devadatta then goes to the Teacher and makes the Five Demands, but is again repulsed. Finally he causes a schism in the Order by persuading five hundred monks to join him. But Sāriputta and Moggallāna convince them of the error of their course by preaching and performing miracles before them, and return with them through the air. During the Teacher's residence at Rājagaha, he relates many Jātakas about Devadatta's evil deeds in previous states of existence. Devadatta suffers from sickness for nine months, at the end of which, realizing that his end is near, he is overwhelmed with remorse, and resolves to make his peace with the Teacher. So he causes himself to be carried in a litter to Jetavana. The Teacher refuses to see him. When he raises himself from the litter and places his feet on the ground, the earth gives way and slowly swallows him up. As his jaws touch the earth, he cries out, "I seek refuge in the Buddha." Thereupon the Teacher makes a monk of Devadatta, prophesying that at the end of a hundred thousand cycles of time he will be reborn as a Private Buddha named Aṭṭhissara. After the earth has swallowed up Devadatta, he is reborn in the Avīci hell.

13. **Lady Sumanā** [i. 18 = 18]. Anāthapiṇḍika's youngest daughter Sumanā dies of grief because of her failure to obtain a husband. Just before death she addresses her father as "youngest brother." Anāthapiṇḍika, overwhelmed with grief, goes to the Buddha and tells him what has happened, dwelling on the fact that his daughter talked incoherently before she died. "Not at all," replied the Teacher, "for she had attained the Fruit of the Second Path, while you have attained only the Fruit of Conversion."

14. **Two brethren** [i. 19–20 = 19–20]. Two youths retire from the world together. The older assumes the Burden of Insight and attains Arahatship; the younger assumes the Burden of Study, acquires the Tipiṭaka, and becomes renowned as a preacher of the Law. Overmastered with pride, the younger monk resolves to seize the first opportunity to ask his senior some embarrassing questions. When the older monk comes to visit the Teacher, the latter, knowing what is in the mind of the younger monk, asks both monks several questions. The younger monk fails to answer a single question the Teacher asks him about the Paths, but the older monk answers all of the questions correctly.

Book II. Heedfulness, Appamāda Vagga

1. Story-Cycle of King Udena or Udayana [ii. 1–3 = 21–23].

Part 1. Birth and youthful career of Udena. Two kings named Allakappa and Veṭhadīpaka retire from the world and become forest-hermits. Veṭhadīpaka dies and is reborn as a deity. Desiring to see his brother, he disguises himself as a wayfarer and pays him a visit. Allakappa tells him that he is much annoyed by elephants. Veṭhadīpaka gives him a lute to charm elephants with, and teaches him the proper spells.

At this time Parantapa is King of Kosambi. One day the king and the queen are sitting in the open air, basking themselves in the sun. The queen, who is great with child, is wearing the king's scarlet blanket. As they chat together, the queen removes the king's signet-ring from his finger and slips it on her own. At that moment a monster bird, mistaking the queen for a piece of meat, swoops down, catches up the queen in his talons, carries her off to the forest, and deposits her in the fork of a banyan tree. The following morning she gives birth to a son, whom she calls Udena.

Not far from the banyan tree is the hermitage of Allakappa. The latter, discovering mother and child, escorts them to the hermitage. The mother, fearing that should the hermit leave them, they would die in the forest, seduces the hermit to violate his vow of chastity. Thereafter the two live together as husband and wife. One day the hermit observes the occultation of Parantapa's star, and informs the queen that the King of Kosambi is dead. The queen bursts into tears, reveals her identity, and expresses regret that her son should be deprived of sovereignty. The hermit promises so to arrange matters that her son shall receive his lawful inheritance.

Accordingly the hermit gives the boy the elephant-charming lute, and teaches him the proper spells. The mother tells the boy that he is son of Parantapa, King of Kosambi, and directs him to go to Kosambi and claim his kingdom, telling him that in case the citizens refuse to recognize him, he is to show them his father's blanket and signet-ring. Udena sets out with a host of warrior-elephants, invests the city, and proclaims, "Give me battle or the kingdom." Then, asserting his royal birth, he shows the blanket and the ring, whereupon the citizens open the gate of the city and confer upon him the ceremonial sprinkling of a king.

Part 2. Birth and youthful career of Ghosaka.

Story of the Past: Kotūhalaka casts his son away. There was once a famine in the kingdom of Ajita, and a man named Kotūhalaka, thinking to get a living in Kosambi, set out for that city with his young son Kāpi and his wife Kāḷi. On the way their provisions give out, and they are well nigh exhausted. Kotūhalaka proposes to cast the child away, but his wife protests, suggesting that they carry him by turns. While Kotūhalaka is carrying the child, he allows his wife to precede him, and secretly casts the child away. When the wife discovers what the husband has done, she forces him to recover the child. (In consequence of having cast his child away on this one occasion, Kotūhalaka was himself cast away seven times in a later existence.)

Continuing their journey, they arrive at the house of a herdsman. The herdsman sets abundant food before them, and then sits down to eat his own meal. Kotūhalaka watches the herdsman feed a bitch that lies under his stool, and envies the bitch her lot. During the night Kotūhalaka dies of indigestion, and is conceived in the womb of the bitch whose lot he envied. Kotūhalaka's widow bestows alms regularly on a Private Buddha. After a time the bitch gives birth to a single pup. The Private Buddha feeds the pup with his own hand, and as a result the pup becomes so fond of the Private Buddha that he performs all manner of services for him. Later on the Private Buddha takes leave of the herdsman, and flies away through the air. Thereupon the pup sets up a howl of grief and dies of a broken heart. Because of his affection for the Private Buddha, the pup is reborn as a deity named Ghosaka in the World of the Thirty-three.

Story of the Present: Ghosaka is cast away seven times and miraculously preserved from death. In consequence of having devoted himself to the pleasures of sense, Ghosaka passes from the World of the Thirty-three and is conceived in the womb of a courtezan of Kosambi.

Ghosaka is cast away the first time. When the child is born, and the courtezan learns that it is a boy, she causes him to be cast away on a refuse-heap. A passer-by takes a fancy to the child and carries him home with him.

That day there is a conjunction of a constellation, and the Treasurer of Kosambi, meeting an astrologer, asks him what the sign betokens. The astrologer replies, " A boy has been born in this city to-day who will one day become the principal treasurer of the city." Since the treasurer's wife is at that time great with child, the treasurer immediately sends word to find out whether she has been delivered or no. Learning that she has not yet been delivered, the treasurer orders a slave-woman to find the boy and fetch him to him. Having gained possession of the boy, the treasurer forms the following resolution, " If a daughter is born to me, I will marry her to this boy, and make him treasurer; but if a son is born to me, I will kill him." A few days later his wife gives birth to a son. The treasurer then sets about to carry out his plan.

Ghosaka is cast away the second time. The treasurer causes Ghosaka to be laid at the door of the cattle-pen, hoping that he will be trampled to death. But when the cattle come out, the bull halts and stands over him, allowing the cows to pass out on either side of him, and the herdsman takes him home.

Ghosaka is cast away the third time. The treasurer recovers Ghosaka, and causes him to be laid in the caravan trail, hoping that he will either be trampled by the oxen or crushed to death by the wheels of the carts. But when the oxen see the boy, they stop of their own accord. The leader picks up the boy and carries him off.

Ghosaka is cast away the fourth time. The treasurer recovers Ghosaka, and causes him to be laid under a bush in the burning-ground. Along comes a goatherd with his goats. The goatherd's suspicions are aroused by the peculiar actions of a she-goat. On making an investigation, he discovers the boy and rescues him.

Ghosaka is cast away the fifth time. The treasurer recovers Ghosaka, and causes him to be thrown down a precipice. But the boy drops into a bamboo thicket, and is rescued by a reed-maker.

Ghosaka is cast away the sixth time. In spite of the treasurer's attempts on his life, Ghosaka lives and thrives and grows to manhood. One day the treasurer goes to a potter, gives him a thousand pieces of money, tells him that he wishes to get rid of a certain base-born son, and orders the potter, when the boy comes to him on the following day with a message, to kill him, chop his body into small pieces, and throw the remains into the chatty. This the potter agrees to do. The next day the treasurer directs Ghosaka to carry the following message to the potter, " Finish the job my father gave you yesterday." As Ghosaka is on his way to the potter's, the treasurer's own son calls to him and offers to carry the message to the potter if Ghosaka will take his place in a game of marbles and make an effort to win back for him a stake he has lost. Thus Ghosaka and his foster-brother exchange places, and the treasurer's own son carries his father's message to the potter and is killed.

Ghosaka is cast away the seventh time. The treasurer, unable longer to look Ghosaka straight in the face, writes the following letter to the superintendent of his hundred villages, " This is my base-born son; kill him, and throw him into the cesspool." This letter the treasurer fastens to the hem of Ghosaka's garment and directs Ghosaka to carry to its destination. (The treasurer had never taught Ghosaka to read, for he expected sooner or later to kill him.) Ghosaka, by direction of his foster-father, stops for breakfast at the house of a certain country treasurer. The treasurer's wife takes a fancy to him, and the treasurer's beautiful daughter falls in love with him. (The treasurer's daughter was Ghosaka's wife in his former existence as Kotūhalaka.) The treasurer's daughter discovers that Ghosaka is carrying his own death-warrant, removes it, and substitutes another letter of her own composition, reading as follows, "This is my son Ghosaka. Procure presents for him from my hundred villages. Prepare a festival for him in honor of his marriage with the daughter of the country treasurer. Build him a two-storeyed house in the center of the village wherein he resides. Send me word that you have done thus and so." The superintendent, on receiving the letter, immediately does as he is told.

When the treasurer learns how miserably his last attempt has failed, he remarks, "What I would do, that I do not; what I would not do, that I do." He sickens, and is soon at the point of death. Ghosaka, accompanied by his wife, visits his foster-father in his last moments. As the treasurer is about to die, he lifts up his voice, intending to say, "I do not give my wealth to my son Ghosaka." But by a slip of the tongue he says instead, "I do give." King Udena confirms Ghosaka in his inheritance, and appoints him principal treasurer of the city. When Ghosaka learns from his wife how narrow was his escape from death, he resolves to forsake the life of Heedlessness, and to live the life of Heedfulness.

Part 3. Birth and youthful career of Sāmāvatī. Ghosaka, treasurer of Kosambi, and Bhaddavatiya, treasurer of Bhaddavati, exchange presents, and become fast friends. Subsequently a pestilence breaks out at Bhaddavati, and Bhaddavatiya, together with his wife and daughter, sets out for Kosambi, intending to ask Ghosaka for assistance. Arriving at Kosambi, they obtain lodging in a rest-house at the city-gate. On the following day the daughter goes to Ghosaka's refectory for food. "How many portions will you have?" "Three." That night her father dies. "How many portions will you have?" "Two." That night her mother dies. "How many portions will you have?" "One." A householder named Mitta, observing that she asks for less each day, remarks, "At last you know the capacity of your belly!" The whole story then comes out. Mitta takes pity on her, and adopts her as his own daughter. She renders such valuable assistance in the administration of Ghosaka's refectory as to attract the attention of Ghosaka himself, who, upon learning that she is the daughter of Bhaddavatiya, adopts her as his own daughter. One day King Udena sees her, falls in love with her, and marries her.

Part 4. Winning of Vāsuladattā. Another of Udena's queen-consorts is Vāsuladattā, daughter of Caṇḍa Pajjota, King of Ujjeni. Udena gains possession of her in the following way: Udena is a great lover of elephants. Caṇḍa Pajjota wishes to take him prisoner. He therefore has a mechanical elephant made of wood, puts sixty men inside of it, and turns the wooden elephant loose on Udena's frontier. Udena mounts his elephant and starts out in pursuit, twanging his lute and uttering spells. But the wooden elephant refuses to be charmed, and Udena is drawn into an ambuscade and captured. Caṇḍa Pajjota keeps his enemy in prison for three days, and then offers to release him if he will divulge his elephant-charm. Udena expresses willingness to do so if Caṇḍa Pajjota will pay him homage. This Caṇḍa Pajjota refuses to do. "But will you divulge the charm to another, if the other will pay you homage?" "Yes." "Well then, there is a hunchbacked woman in our house; she will sit behind a curtain; you remain outside and teach her the charm." "Very well." Caṇḍa Pajjota then says to his daughter, the beautiful Princess Vāsuladattā, "There is a leper who knows a priceless charm; you sit behind a curtain; he will remain outside and teach you the charm. Then teach it to me." (Caṇḍa Pajjota employs this stratagem for fear of their cohabiting.) Vāsuladattā learns very slowly. One day

Udena loses his patience and exclaims, "Dunce of a hunchback!" Vāsuladattā retorts angrily, "Villain of a leper, how dare you call such as I 'hunchback'?" Udena lifts the fringe of the curtain, and the secret is out. Vāsuladattā yields her chastity to Udena, and from that time on there is no more learning of charms. Udena offers to make Vāsuladattā one of his queen-consorts if she will save his life. Vāsuladattā tells her father that in order to perfect herself in the charm, it will be necessary for her to dig a certain medicinal root in the dead of night, and requests him to place a door and a riding-elephant at her disposal. Caṇḍa Pajjota places at her disposal a certain female elephant, one of Five Conveyances he came to possess as the fruit of alms bestowed on a Private Buddha in a previous existence. One day, when Caṇḍa Pajjota is away from home, Udena fills several leather sacks with gold and silver, puts them on the back of the female elephant, assists Vāsuladattā to mount, and away they go. When Caṇḍa Pajjota learns what has happened, he sends out a force in pursuit. Udena opens the sacks and scatters coins along the way. Caṇḍa Pajjota's men delay pursuit to pick them up, and Udena has no difficulty in escaping. On reaching Kosambi, Udena raises Vāsuladattā to the rank of queen-consort.

Part 5. Rejection of Māgandiyā by the Buddha. Another of Udena's queen-consorts is Māgandiyā, daughter of the Brahman Māgandiya. One day the Buddha comes to the place where the Brahman is tending the sacred fire. The Brahman is so impressed with the majestic appearance of the visitor that he then and there offers him his daughter in marriage. The Buddha makes no reply, but walks away, leaving a footprint. The Brahman goes home, and returns with his wife and daughter. The Brahman's wife, after studying the footprint, declares that it is not the footprint of one who follows the Five Lusts. The Brahman, however, seeing the Buddha, renews his offer. The Buddha then tells the Brahman that from the Great Retirement to the Session under the Banyan-tree, Māra pursued him relentlessly, only to be defeated at every point; that Māra's daughters then tempted him in various forms without exciting in him the lust of the flesh, and that nothing would induce him to touch Māgandiyā even with the sole of his foot. Māgandiyā ever after cherishes the most bitter hatred of the Buddha. The Brahman and his wife commit Māgandiyā to the care of her uncle, and retire from the world. The uncle presents her to King Udena. The king immediately falls in love with her and marries her, raising her to the rank of queen-consort.

Part 6. Death of Sāmāvatī and of Māgandiyā, and the explanation thereof.

Treasurers, monks, and tree-spirit. At this time there are living in Kosambi three treasurers, Ghosaka, Kukkuṭa, and Pāvāriya. These treasurers provide food for a company of monks during the season of the rains for several years. At the beginning of one rainy season the monks take up their abode under a huge banyan tree. The monks have but to wish for water or food, and their wish is immediately fulfilled by the tree-spirit. The monks express a wish to see the tree-spirit, whereupon the tree splits open and out he comes. The monks ask the spirit what he did to get his power. The spirit relates the following

Story of the Past: Tree-spirit's former deed. The spirit was once the servant of Anāthapiṇḍika. One Fast-day, Anāthapiṇḍika, upon learning that his servant had not been told the significance of the day, ordered a meal to be prepared for him. The servant observed that no one else was eating, learned the reason why, and followed suit. He then went out and did his day's work, was taken sick, and died that very night. "My master," said the spirit, "was devoted to the Buddha, the Law, and the Order. It was through him, and in consequence of my observance of Fast-day, that I was reborn as a powerful tree-spirit." **End of Story of the Past.**

The monks immediately seek refuge in the Buddha, the Law, and the Order. On the following day they inform the three treasurers that the Buddha, the Law, and the

Order have appeared in the world, and that they intend to visit the Teacher. The monks visit the Teacher, listen to the Law, and attain Arahatship. The three treasurers Ghosaka, Kukkuṭa, and Pāvāriya also visit the Teacher, listen to the Law, and are converted. Returning to Kosambi, they erect Ghosita, Kukkuṭa, and Pāvāriya monasteries. Here the Teacher visits them, dividing his time equally among the three. After the treasurers have entertained the Teacher for a time, their gardener Sumana asks and receives permission to entertain him for a single day.

Conversion of Sāmāvatī by Khujjuttarā. At this time King Udena is in the habit of giving Queen Sāmāvatī eight pieces of money daily to buy flowers with. This money the queen turns over to a female slave named Hunchback, Khujjuttarā, who goes regularly to the gardener Sumana's and spends four pieces on flowers, pocketing the remainder. On the day of the Teacher's visit to Sumana, Khujjuttarā is converted, and spends the entire amount on flowers. The queen asks her how she comes to return with so many flowers, and the whole story comes out. From that time on, Khujjuttarā steals no more, but becomes as it were a mother to Sāmāvatī, going regularly to hear the Law, and returning and preaching the Law to Sāmāvatī. As a result, Queen Sāmāvatī and her retinue are converted.

Māgandiyā's plot against Sāmāvatī and the Buddha. Sāmāvatī expresses a desire to see the Teacher. At the suggestion of Khujjuttarā she makes holes in the walls of the royal palace, and renders homage to the Teacher from within. Māgandiyā comes to know of this, and actuated by hatred of the Teacher, resolves to get even both with the Teacher and with Sāmāvatī. Accordingly she tells King Udena that Sāmāvatī has made holes in the walls of the palace for the purpose of killing him. The king, however, refuses to believe her. She then determines to drive the Teacher out of the city, and to this end employs ruffians to follow him about and heap abuse upon him. Ānanda proposes to the Teacher to go elsewhere, but this the Teacher declines to do, comparing himself to an elephant engaged in the fray. After seven days the uproar ceases, and Māgandiyā, realizing that she can do nothing against the Teacher, renews her determination to destroy the women who are his supporters.

Māgandiyā procures from her uncle eight live cocks and eight dead cocks, and presents the live cocks to Udena, suggesting that he ask Sāmāvatī to cook them for him. Udena does so, and Sāmāvatī sends back word that she and her followers do not take life. "Now," says Māgandiyā, "see whether she will cook them for the monk Gotama." Māgandiyā secretly substitutes the dead cocks for the live cocks, and Sāmāvatī immediately complies with the king's request. "See," says Māgandiyā, "they won't do it for the likes of you. Still you would n't believe that their inclination was towards another." The king, however, still refuses to believe her.

At this time the king divides his time equally among his three consorts, spending a week in the apartment of each. Māgandiyā, knowing that the king will go on the following day to Sāmāvatī's apartment, carrying with him as usual the lute which Allakappa gave him, procures a snake from her uncle, and puts it in the lute, stopping the opening with a bunch of flowers. She then tells the king that she has had a bad dream, and pretending to be solicitous for his safety, begs him not to go to Sāmāvatī's apartment. The king, disregarding her warning, goes to Sāmāvatī's apartment, and Māgandiyā, in spite of his protests, accompanies him. The king places the lute beside his pillow, and lies down on the bed. Māgandiyā secretly removes the flowers, and out comes the snake. At this Māgandiyā screams as if in terror, and openly accuses Sāmāvatī and her attendants of seeking to kill their sovereign. At last the king is convinced, and now believes everything Māgandiyā has told him.

Sāmāvatī urges her attendants to cherish no bitter feelings towards the king or Māgandiyā. The king takes his bow, which requires a thousand soldiers to string, and shoots a poisoned arrow at Sāmāvatī's breast. But so great is the power of

Sāmāvatī's love that the arrow turns back, and as it were penetrates the king's heart. Thereupon the king prostrates himself at Sāmāvatī's feet and cries out, "Be thou my refuge!" Sāmāvatī replies, "In whom I myself have sought refuge, in him do thou also seek refuge." The king then seeks refuge in the Buddha, the Law, and the Order, and gives generous gifts.

Burning of Sāmāvatī and punishment of Māgandiyā. Māgandiyā then instigates her uncle to set fire to Sāmāvatī's palace. Sāmāvatī and her five hundred attendants perish in the flames. The king, learning that Māgandiyā is the guilty person, causes her to be tortured and put to death, together with all her kinsfolk and friends. The Buddha then relates the following

Stories of the Past: Sāmāvatī and her attendants were burned to death because in a previous existence they attempted to burn a Private Buddha to death. Khujjuttarā became a hunchback by mocking a Private Buddha, attained the Fruit of Conversion by waiting upon some Private Buddhas, and became an errand-girl because she once asked a nun to do a menial service for her.

In conclusion the Buddha declares that the Heedless, though they live a hundred years, are yet dead; that the Heedful, whether they be dead or alive, are yet alive. Māgandiyā, while she yet lived, was dead already; Sāmāvatī and her attendants, though they be dead, yet are they alive. The Heedful never die.

2. **The voice of a rich man** [ii. 4 = 24]. The plague breaks out in Rājagaha, and the principal treasurer and his wife are attacked. Realizing that they are about to die, they bid farewell to their son Kumbhaghosaka, directing him to flee for his life and return later and dig up their treasure. The son spends twelve years in a jungle, returns, and finds the treasure undisturbed. But reflecting that since no one knows him, he may be subjected to annoyance if he digs it up and begins to spend it, he decides to make his own living, and obtains a position as a foreman. One day the king hears his voice, and exclaims, "That is the voice of some rich man." A female slave overhears the remark and offers for a consideration to make the king master of his wealth. She obtains lodging for herself and daughter in Kumbhaghosaka's house, and seduces Kumbhaghosaka to violate her daughter. She then contracts a marriage between the two, and Kumbhaghosaka is obliged to dig up some of the treasure to defray the expenses of the wedding festivities. In this way the whole story comes out. But the king, instead of confiscating Kumbhaghosaka's wealth, praises him for his wisdom, confirms him in his inheritance, and gives him his daughter in marriage.

3. **Little Wayman** [ii. 5 = 25].

3 a. **Birth of Little Wayman.** The daughter of a treasurer of Rājagaha yields her chastity to a slave, and fearing that she will be discovered, runs away with him. When the time of her delivery is at hand, she expresses a desire to return to her parents. But her lover, fearing to accompany her, puts her off from day to day, until finally she takes matters into her own hands and starts out alone. The pains of travail come upon her by the way, and she gives birth to a son, whom she therefore calls Wayman. After a time the same thing happens again. The younger son is called Little Wayman, the older Big Wayman. Big Wayman, hearing his playmates speak of their uncles and grandfathers, asks his mother whether he has any, and if so, why they do not go to see them. The mother suggests to the father that they pay her parents a visit, and the father consents to accompany her as far as the city. Her parents refuse to see her, but receive the children into their household. Big Wayman accompanies his grandfather to hear the Teacher, and one day expresses a desire to become a monk.

3 b. **Little Wayman as a monk.** Big Wayman is received into the Order, attains Arahatship, and in turn receives Little Wayman into the Order. Little Wayman, in consequence of having ridiculed a dullard monk in a previous existence, is unable to

master a single Stanza in the course of four months, and is therefore expelled from the monastery by his brother. Little Wayman, however, does not abandon the religious life. One day Jīvaka Komārabhacca invites the five hundred monks to take a meal with him. Big Wayman accepts in behalf of all but Little Wayman. Little Wayman, hearing his brother speak thus, decides to return to the world. The Teacher, aware of his intention, conducts him into the Perfumed Chamber, gives him a cloth, and directs him to face the East, rub the cloth, and say, "Removal of Impurity!" After Little Wayman has rubbed the cloth for a time, he observes that it has become soiled, and thus acquires a sense of Impermanence. The Teacher appears to him and says, "Impurity is Lust, Hatred, Delusion; remove them." Little Wayman immediately attains Arahatship.

When Jīvaka offers Water of Donation to the Teacher, the latter informs him that there are monks in the monastery. Jīvaka sends a servant to find out. At that moment Little Wayman by an exercise of supernatural power fills the Mango Grove with a thousand monks. The servant returns with the news that the Grove is full of monks. The Teacher directs him to summon Little Wayman. The servant goes to the Grove and calls out, "Little Wayman, come hither!" At this the cry goes up from a thousand throats, "Here I am!" The servant returns and makes his report to the Teacher. The Teacher directs him to take by the hand the first who says that he is Little Wayman. The rest immediately vanish, and the servant returns with his man. After the meal Little Wayman returns thanks, and the Teacher and his monks withdraw. In the evening the monks discuss the incidents of the day. The Teacher informs them that in a previous existence also Little Wayman was a dullard and won success through his assistance. So saying, he relates the following

3 c. Story of the Past: The world-renowned teacher, the young man, and the King of Benāres. A young man of Benāres once went to Takkasilā and became the pupil of a world-renowned teacher. Although faithful to duty, he was such a dullard that after a long term of residence he was unable to repeat a single Stanza. Finally he becomes discouraged and decides to go back home. His teacher, grateful to him for the assistance he has rendered him, teaches him a charm, telling him that it will insure him a living, and directing him to repeat it over and over again to avoid the possibility of forgetting it. And this is the charm: "You 're rubbing! you 're rubbing! why are you rubbing? I know too!" Shortly after the young man's return to Benāres, the King of Benāres makes an examination of his own thoughts, words, and deeds, to discover whether he has been guilty of any fault. Seeing no fault, but reflecting that one never sees his own faults, he decides to ascertain the candid opinion of his subjects, and for this purpose puts on a disguise and goes about the streets eavesdropping. The first house the king comes to is that of the young man. The king observes that some tunnel-thieves are in the act of breaking into the house. The noise awakens the young man, who begins to repeat his charm, and the thieves flee.

The king, seeing the thieves fleeing and hearing the words of the charm, makes note of the house, and on the following day sends for the young man, learns the charm from him, and gives him a thousand pieces of money. That very day the Prime Minister goes to the royal barber, gives him a thousand pieces of money, and says to him, "The next time you shave the king, cut his throat; then you shall be Prime Minister, and I shall be king." The barber agrees to the bargain. While the barber is sharpening his razor, the king begins to repeat the charm. The barber, thinking that the king is aware of his intention to kill him, throws away his razor, falls at the feet of the king in terror, and begs the king to pardon him. The king thereupon compels the barber to reveal the plot, banishes the Prime Minister, and appoints in his place the young man who taught him the charm. At that time Little Wayman was the young man, and the Buddha was the world-renowned teacher.

4. **Simpletons' Holiday** [ii. 6–7 = 26–27]. On Simpletons' Holiday it was the practice of ignorant people who knew no better to give themselves up to license for a period of seven days, uttering all manner of coarse talk, and desisting only on the payment of bribes. During this period of disorder, the Teacher and the monks remained within the monastery.

5. **Kassapa the Great** [ii. 8 = 28]. On a certain occasion Elder Kassapa the Great endeavors by the exercise of Supernatural Vision to obtain comprehension of Birth and Rebirth. The Teacher appears to him and admonishes him that only a Buddha is able to comprehend the Totality of Existences.

6. **Two brethren** [ii. 9 = 29]. Two brethren obtain a Subject of Meditation from the Teacher and retire to the forest. One of them is heedful, and attains Arahatship; the other is heedless and lazy. The Teacher praises the heedful monk and rebukes the heedless monk.

7. **How Magha became Sakka** [ii. 10 = 30].

7 a. **Story of the Present: Mahāli's question.** A Licchavi prince named Mahāli comes to the Teacher and asks him whether he has ever seen Sakka. The Teacher replies in the affirmative, tells Mahāli how Sakka came to receive his Seven Titles, and enumerates the Seven Vows by the performance of which Sakka attained Sakkaship. Mahāli desires to hear the whole story. The Teacher thereupon relates the following

7 b. **Story of the Past: How Magha became Sakka.** Once upon a time a youth named Magha went about his native village in the kingdom of Magadha doing all manner of good works, and in the course of time gathered others about him, until finally there were thirty-three persons in the village keeping the Five Precepts and doing works of merit. The village headman took a dislike to them and arraigned them before the king, alleging that they were a company of robbers. The king ordered them to be trampled by elephants. But the elephants refused to trample them. The king then summoned the youths, told them the charge the village headman had brought against them, and asked them what they had to say. On hearing their story, he asked them to pardon him, made the village headman their slave, gave them a riding-elephant, and placed the entire resources of the village at their disposal.

At this the youths rejoiced greatly, and resolved to abound yet more in good works. Summoning a carpenter, they caused him to erect a rest-house at the junction of four highways. Because they had lost all desire for women, they refused to allow women to share in the work. Now there were four women living in Magha's house, Joy, Thoughtful, Goodness, and Wellborn. Goodness bribed the carpenter to give her the chief share in the building of the rest-house. The carpenter gave her the pinnacle. The thirty-three youths built thirty-three seats. Magha planted an Ebony-tree, and under the tree set up a stone seat. Joy provided a bathing-pool, and Thoughtful a flower-garden. Wellborn, thinking it a sufficient distinction to be a cousin of Magha, did nothing but adorn herself. Magha, having fulfilled the Seven Vows, was reborn as Sakka king of gods. Magha's companions were also reborn there, the carpenter being reborn as Vissakamma.

Now at this time there were Asuras dwelling in the World of the Thirty-three, and when they learned that new gods had been reborn there, they prepared strong drink for them. Sakka forbade his companions to touch it, and they obeyed him; but the Asuras got very drunk. Then Sakka gave the signal, and his companions picked up the Asuras by the heels and flung them head-foremost into the abyss. Thereupon there sprang up at the foot of Mount Sineru the Palace of the Asuras and the Tree that is called Pied Trumpet Flower. And when the conflict between the Gods and the Asuras was over, and the Asuras had been defeated, there sprang into existence the City of the Thirty-three, crowned with a magnificent palace called the Palace of Victory. A Coral-tree sprang up to correspond with the Ebony-tree which Magha had planted, and at the foot thereof, to correspond with the stone seat he had set up, stood Sakka's Yellowstone Throne. The elephant was reborn as Erāvaṇa. Erāvaṇa created gigantic water-pots for each member of Sakka's retinue. When Goodness, Joy, and Thoughtful died, they were reborn in the World of the Thirty-three; and as the fruit of their good works there arose a mansion named Goodness, a bathing-pool named Joy, and a creeper-grove named Thoughtful.

When Wellborn died, she was reborn as a crane in a mountain cave. Sakka went to her in disguise, conducted her to the World of the Thirty-three, let her see her former companions, and assured her that she could attain equal happiness by keeping the Five Precepts. This she promised to do. After a few days Sakka, desiring to test her sincerity, lay down on the sand in the form of a fish. The crane, believing it to be dead, took it in her beak. As she was about to swallow it, the fish wriggled its tail. The crane immediately dropped it. Three times Sakka employed this stratagem, and three times the crane, discovering that the fish was alive, refused to eat it. Sakka resumed his proper form, praised the crane, and departed. At the end of her existence as a crane, Wellborn was reborn in Benāres as a potter's daughter. Sakka disguised himself as a peddler, filled a cart with jewels in the form of cucumbers, and drove into the city, offering to give his cucumbers to whoever kept the Precepts. Only the potter's daughter understands his meaning. Sakka reveals himself to her, gives her the jewels, praises her, and departs.

At the end of her existence as a potter's daughter, Wellborn is reborn in the World of the Asuras as the daughter of Vepacitti, king of the Asuras and a bitter enemy of Sakka. One day Vepacitti assembles the hosts of the Asuras and directs his daughter to choose a husband. Sakka, disguised as an aged Asura, sits down in the outer circle of the assembly. The maiden immediately throws the wreath of flowers over his head. Sakka takes her by the hand, shouts out, "I am Sakka," and flies up into the air. The Asuras cry out, "We have been fooled by old Sakka," and start up in pursuit. Sakka's charioteer Mātali brings up the chariot Victory, and Sakka, after assisting Wellborn to mount, sets out for the City of the Gods. When they reach the forest of the Silk-cotton Trees, the fledglings of the Garuḍa birds, fearing that they will be crushed, shriek aloud. Sakka thereupon commands, "Let not these creatures perish on my account; turn back the chariot." The Asuras abandon the pursuit, and Sakka bears Wellborn to the City of the Gods.

8. A monk attains Arahatship [ii. 11 = 31]. A monk who has been unsuccessful in the Practice of Meditation sees a forest-fire. Hastily climbing a bare mountain, he watches the fire, and concentrates his mind on the following thought, "Even as this fire advances, consuming all obstacles both great and small, so also ought I to advance, consuming all obstacles both great and small by the Fire of Knowledge of the Noble Path." He immediately attains Arahatship.

9. Tissa of the Market-town [ii. 12 = 32]. Tissa of the Market-town acquires the reputation of being frugal, contented, pure, resolute. The Teacher remarks that Tissa's good qualities are the result of association with himself, and relates the following

9 a. Story of the Past: Sakka and the parrot. Once upon a time many parrots lived in a grove of fig-trees. The king-parrot, when the fruits of the tree in which he lived had withered away, ate whatever he found remaining, and being very happy and contented, remained where he was. Sakka determined to put him to the test, and by his supernatural power withered up the tree. Perceiving that this made no difference at all to the Parrot, Sakka decided to grant him a boon. Accordingly, disguised as a royal goose, he went to the parrot and asked him why his heart delighted in a tree that was withered and rotten. The parrot replied, "This tree has been good to me in the past. Why should I desert it now?" Thereupon Sakka caused the tree to bloom anew and to bear ambrosial fruit.

Book III. Thoughts, Citta Vagga

1. **Elder Meghiya** [iii. 1–2 = 33–34]. By reason of attachment to the Three Evil Thoughts, Elder Meghiya is unable to practice Exertion. The Teacher admonishes him that a monk must never permit himself to be controlled by his thoughts.

2. **The mind-reader** [iii. 3 = 35]. A lay sister provides a company of monks with food and lodging during the rainy season. The monks instruct her in the Practice of Meditation, and she attains Arahatship together with the Supernatural Faculties. As she is thus able to read their thoughts, she is so successful in her ministrations that in no long time they too attain Arahatship. The monks return to the Teacher loud in their praises of the lay sister, remarking that no sooner did they wish for such and such food than she immediately supplied it. A certain monk, overhearing the remark, desires himself to enjoy so pleasant an experience. Accordingly he obtains a Subject of Meditation from the Teacher, and goes to her house. He finds everything exactly as represented, but fearing that should he entertain a single sinful thought, the lay sister might seize him by the topknot and do him harm, returns to the Teacher. The Teacher admonishes him to control his thoughts, and sends him back. In only a few days the Elder attains Arahatship. Calling up before his mind ninety-nine previous existences, he perceives that in each of these existences the lay sister murdered him. "Oh, what a sinner she has been!" thinks he. At the same moment the lay sister, sitting in her own chamber, becomes aware of what is passing through his mind. "Call up one more existence," says she. By the power of Supernatural Audition the monk immediately hears what she says. Calling up before his mind the hundredth existence, he perceives that she spared his life. Thereat he rejoices greatly, and straightway passes into Nibbāna.

3. **A discontented monk** [iii. 4 = 36]. A faithful layman becomes a monk, but soon grows discontented over the multitudinous duties imposed upon him. The Teacher admonishes him that if he will only guard his thoughts, everything else will take care of itself.

4. **Nephew Saṅgharakkhita** [iii. 5 = 37]. Nephew Saṅgharakkhita presents Uncle Saṅgharakkhita with a set of robes. The uncle, having already a complete set of robes, declines the present. The nephew is so disappointed that he resolves to return to the life of a householder. As he stands beside his uncle, fanning him, he ponders ways and means of earning a living. Finally the following thought occurs to him. "I will sell this robe and buy a she-goat. I will sell the she-goat's young and accumulate some capital. Then I will get me a wife. She will bear me a son, and I will name him after my uncle. Then I will set out with son and wife to visit my uncle. My wife will insist on carrying the child, and lacking the necessary strength, will let him fall. I will then beat her with my stick." So saying, the nephew swings his fan and brings it down on the head of his uncle. The latter rebukes him, and he starts to run away. But young monks run after him, catch him, and bring him before the Teacher. The Teacher admonishes him to control his thoughts.

5. **Elder Thought-controlled** [iii. 6–7 = 38–39]. A youth of Sāvatthi becomes a monk to obtain an easy livelihood. Tiring of the monastic life, he returns to the world. Six times he becomes a monk, and as many times returns to the world. The monks therefore call him Thought-controlled, Cittahattha. In the meantime his wife becomes pregnant. For the seventh time he decides to become a monk. As he enters his room to put on his yellow robe, he sees his wife abed and asleep. Her appearance is so repulsive to him that he then and there grasps the thought of Im-

permanence and Suffering. In a very few days he attains Arahatship. The monks express surprise that a youth predestined to Arahatship should abandon the monastic life so many times. The Teacher remarks that in a previous existence he, the Teacher, did the same thing himself, and relates the following

5 a. Story of the Past: Kuddāla and his spade. A wise man named Kuddāla once renounced the monastic life six times, all because of a blunt spade which he had used to till the ground. Finally Kuddāla made up his mind to put temptation out of his way. So taking the spade to the bank of the Ganges, he closed his eyes and threw it into the water. As he did so, he cried with a loud voice, "I have conquered!" At that moment along came the King of Benāres, returning from a successful campaign. The king heard Kuddāla's exclamation of triumph, and asked him what he meant. Kuddāla replied, "The victory you have won will have to be won again. But I have conquered the enemy Desire, and he will never conquer me again." Kuddāla preached the Law to the king, whereupon the king and his retinue retired from the world, his royal enemy shortly afterwards following his example.

6. Monks and tree-spirits [iii. 8 = 40]. Five hundred monks obtain a Subject of Meditation from the Teacher and retire to a forest to meditate. Tree-spirits, desiring to get rid of the monks, cause them to see bodiless heads and headless trunks, to hear voices of demons, and to catch all manner of diseases. The monks return to the Teacher and relate their experiences. "I will provide you with a Weapon," replies the Teacher. Thereupon he recites the Metta Sutta, and instructs the monks to return to the forest and do the same. The monks follow his instructions, the hearts of the tree-spirits are suffused with love, and the monks quickly attain Insight.

7. Cruelty a cause of boils [iii. 9 = 41]. Tissa is attacked by boils, and his condition becomes so desperate that his fellow-residents, unable to do anything for him, cast him out, and he lies on the ground without a protector. The Buddha goes to him, and bathes him with warm water, alleviating his sufferings. Then he preaches to him, and he attains Arahatship. The monks express surprise that a youth predestined to Arahatship should be visited with such an affliction. The Buddha informs them that it is the result of evil deeds committed in a previous existence, and relates the following

7 a. Story of the Past: The cruel fowler. A fowler, fearing that if he killed and kept the birds he did not sell, they would rot, and desiring to prevent his captive birds from taking flight, used to break their bones and pile the birds in a heap. One day he gave alms to a monk. The fowler was Tissa. Because of his cruelty, he suffered from boils in a later existence; because he gave alms to a monk, he attained Arahatship.

8. Nanda the herdsman [iii. 10 = 42]. Nanda the herdsman entertains the Teacher for seven days. When the Teacher departs, Nanda accompanies him on his way for a considerable distance, and then turns back. On the way back he is hit by a stray arrow and killed. The monks remark that had the Teacher not gone to visit Nanda, the latter would have escaped death. The Teacher replies that under no circumstances could Nanda have escaped death. (No one asks the Teacher about Nanda's deed in a previous existence, and therefore the Teacher says nothing about it.)

9. Mother of two and father of two [iii. 11 = 43]. A treasurer's son named Soreyya, accompanied by a friend, drives out of the city of Soreyya to bathe. Soreyya, seeing Elder Mahā Kaccāyana putting on his mantle, thinks to himself, "Oh, that this Elder might become my wife! Else may the hue of my wife's body become like the hue of his body!" Instantly Soreyya is transformed into a woman. The woman Soreyyā goes to Takkasilā, is married to the son of a treasurer of that city, and becomes the mother of two sons. (There are no men who have not been women at some time or other; and no women who have not, at some time or other, been men. Elder Ānanda once committed adultery in an existence as a blacksmith, and as a result spent many existences as a woman. Women may obtain rebirth as men by performing works of merit.) So the woman Soreyyā, who as the man Soreyya was already the father of two sons, becomes the mother of two more, making four children in all. At this time Soreyya's carriage-companion comes to Takkasilā and is entertained by the woman Soreyyā. The guest expresses surprise that his host should be so kind to him, and inquires whether she knows him. Soreyyā then tells him the whole story. The guest suggests that Soreyyā beg the Elder's pardon, assuring her that if she will do so, everything will be all right again. Soreyyā begs the Elder's pardon, and is instantly transformed into a man again. The Elder admits Soreyya to the Order. Soreyya commits the two sons of whom he is the mother to the care of their father, and returns to Sāvatthi with the Elder. When the inhabitants learn what has happened, they are much excited, and come to Soreyya and ask him, "You are the mother of two sons, and the father of two as well; for which pair of sons have you the stronger affection?" Soreyya replies, "For the sons of whom I am the mother." Subsequently he attains Arahatship. Then he replies, "My affections are set on no one." The Teacher praises him for his reply.

Book IV. Flowers, Puppha Vagga

1. **The soil of the heart** [iv. 1–2 = 44–45]. The Teacher rebukes a company of monks who are discussing different varieties of soil, telling them that they might better be occupied with tilling the soil of the heart.

2. **A monk attains Arahatship** [iv. 3 = 46]. A monk who has been unsuccessful in the Practice of Meditation, seeing a mirage, concentrates his mind on the following thought, "Even as this mirage appears substantial to those that are far off, but vanishes on nearer approach, so also is this existence unsubstantial by reason of birth and decay." Seeing a waterfall, he reflects, "Just as these bubbles of foam form and burst, so also is this existence formed and so also does it burst." He immediately attains Arahatship.

3. **Viḍūḍabha wreaks vengeance on the Sākiyas** [iv. 4 = 47]. At Sāvatthi lives Prince Pasenadi, son of the King of Kosala; at Vesāli, Prince Mahāli, of the Licchavi line; at Kusinārā, Prince Bandhula, son of the King of the Mallas. These three princes resort to a world-renowned teacher at Takkasilā for instruction, and, chancing to meet in a rest-house, become firm friends. After acquiring the various arts, they take leave of their teacher and return to their homes. The King of Kosala is so pleased with his son's attainments that he makes him king. Mahāli devotes himself to the task of educating the Licchavi princes, but over-exerts himself and loses the sight of his eyes. The princes erect a gate for him, and remain his devoted pupils. Bandhula receives a slight at the hands of the Malla princes, which makes him so angry that he determines to kill them and seize the throne. Informed by his mother and father that as the kingdom of the Mallas is an hereditary kingdom, his plan is bound to fail, he goes to Sāvatthi and takes up his residence in the household of his friend King Pasenadi. Pasenadi makes him Commander-in-chief of his army.

One day King Pasenadi sees several thousand monks pass through the street. Learning that they are on their way to breakfast at the houses of Anāthapiṇḍika, Culla Anāthapiṇḍika, Visākhā, and Suppavāsā, the king goes to the Teacher and asks for the privilege of entertaining the monks. For seven days the king gives alms to the Teacher and the Congregation of Monks; and on the seventh day asks the Teacher to come regularly to his house thereafter. The Teacher declines the invitation on the ground that many desire the Buddhas to visit them, and sends Ānanda in his place. For seven days the king serves Ānanda and his monks in person, but on the following days is so inattentive to their needs that they drop off one by one, until finally Ānanda alone is left. At this the king is much offended, and goes to the Teacher and complains. The Teacher exonerates the monks from blame, and tells the king frankly that the monks lack confidence in him. Then, addressing the monks, the Teacher explains that a family must possess Nine Distinctive Marks to be entitled to the privilege of entertaining monks. Continuing, he remarks that just so in times past wise men went to a place worthy of their confidence. So saying, he relates the following

3 a. Story of the Past: Kesava, Kappa, Nārada, and the King of Benāres. A king named Kesava once renounced his throne, and together with five hundred retainers adopted the life of an ascetic. Kappa, the keeper of his jewels, also retired from the world and became his pupil. Kesava accepted the offer of the King of Benāres to entertain him and his retinue during the season of the rains. But elephants so annoyed the monks with their cries that the monks dropped off one by one, until finally Kesava was left alone with his pupil Kappa. After a time even Kappa was unable to stand the noise any longer, and left his master. Thereupon Kesava fell sick, and begged the king to send him back to his pupils. The king immediately did so, sending Nārada and three other ministers with him. Kesava immediately recovered his health. When Nārada asked him how he liked an ascetic's fare, after eating the rich food of a king, Kesava replied that he was now completely happy, since, after all, a sense of security and confidence is the main thing. **End of Story of the Past.**

Thereupon King Pasenadi bethinks himself how best to regain the confidence of the monks. Concluding that the best way is to take to himself as wife the daughter of some kinsman of the Buddha, he sends ambassadors to the Sākiyas, requesting one of their daughters in marriage. The King of the Sākiyas sends Vāsabhakhattiyā, daughter of Mahā Nāma by a slave-woman. King Pasenadi marries her, and in the course of time she becomes the mother of a son. Pasenadi sends word to his grandmother to give the child a name. She selects the name Vallabha (Beloved); but the messenger, being a little deaf, understands her to say Viḍūḍabha, and so reports to the king. Accordingly the child is named Viḍūḍabha. When Viḍūḍabha is seven years old, he begins to ask his mother questions about her family; and one day, when he has reached the age of sixteen, he expresses the wish to visit his grandparents. Vāsabhakhattiyā reluctantly consents to let him go, taking the precaution to send ahead of him the following letter, "I am happy where I am; for the sake of my husband, say nothing to him." Viḍūḍabha sets out with a large retinue.

When the Sākiya princes learn of Viḍūḍabha's approaching visit, they decide not to render homage to him, and therefore send away all of the princes who are younger than he. When Viḍūḍabha inquires why no one renders homage to him, it is explained to him that all those about him are his seniors. One day, however, a female slave, while engaged in scrubbing Viḍūḍabha's seat, remarks contemptuously, "The seat of the son of the slave-woman Vāsabhakhattiyā!" A soldier overhears the remark, and in a short time it becomes common gossip. When it comes to the ears of Viḍūḍabha, he swears the following oath, "As these Sākiyas now wash my bench with water, so will I, when I become king, wash it with their blood!" When Viḍūḍabha returns to Sāvatthi, and King Pasenadi learns that Vāsabhakhattiyā is really the daughter of a slave-woman, he is filled with rage, and degrades Viḍūḍabha and his mother to the position of slaves. Later, however, on the strength of the Buddha's declaration that the family of the father affords the only true measure of social position, the king restores them to their former rank.

At this time Bandhula, Commander-in-chief of King Pasenadi's army, dismisses his wife Mallikā on the ground of barrenness. The Teacher bids her return to her husband, and straightway she conceives a child. One day the longing of pregnancy comes upon her, and she says to her husband, "I long to bathe in the lotus tank of Vesāli, and to drink the water thereof." Bandhula takes his bow, which requires a thousand men to string, assists Mallikā to mount the chariot, and drives to Vesāli. Driving away the guards, and tearing down the iron grating about the tank, he admits his wife to the lotus tank; and when she has bathed and drunk, drives back by the way he came. The Licchavi princes, angered by Bandhula's insolence, mount their chariots, five hundred strong, and set out to capture Bandhula. Bandhula waits until the file of chariots is so straight that but one chariot-front appears to view; and then, stringing his mighty bow, shoots an arrow. The arrow passes through the body of every one of the five hundred men. Notwithstanding, they continue the pursuit. But Bandhula stops his chariot and cries out, "You are all dead men! I will not fight with the dead." "Do we look like dead men?" "Loosen the girdle of your leader." They do so, and immediately he falls down dead. The rest return to their homes, arrange their affairs for death, and take off their armor, whereupon they all fall down dead.

Sixteen times Mallikā bears twin sons to Bandhula, and all of them become mighty men. Bandhula by his upright conduct incurs the enmity of unjust judges, who go to the king and accuse him of disloyalty. The king orders Bandhula and his sons to proceed to the frontier to put down an insurrection, and at the same time suborns men to kill them on their return. Thus Bandhula and his sons are murdered. News of the murder is brought to Mallikā on the morning of the day on which she has invited the Chief Disciples to be her guests. During the meal one of the servants drops a dish and breaks it. Sāriputta says to her, "Heed it not." Mallikā draws from a fold of her dress the letter she received that morning, and replies, "If I heed not the murder of my husband and my two and thirty sons, I am not likely to heed the breaking of a mere dish." Mallikā addresses her sons' wives, assuring them that as their husbands had lived blameless lives, their sudden end must be understood as the fruit of evil deeds committed in previous existences, and urging them to cherish no bitter feelings against the king. The king, upon learning that the charges brought against Bandhula are false, makes such amends as he can to Mallikā.

King Pasenadi appoints to the post of Commander-in-chief a nephew of Bandhula, named Dīghakārāyaṇa. Dīghakārāyaṇa does not forget that Pasenadi caused his uncle to be murdered, and bides his time for revenge. One day, while the Teacher is in residence in a neighboring village, Pasenadi sets out with a small body-guard to pay him a visit. As the king is about to enter the Perfumed Chamber, he hands the royal insignia to Dīghakārāyaṇa. The latter immediately hastens to Sāvatthi and proclaims Viḍūḍabha king. Viḍūḍabha remembers the oath he swore against the Sākiyas, and sets out with a large force, intending to kill them all. The Teacher, aware of the impending destruction of his kinsmen, seats himself under the shade of a small tree near Kapilavatthu. Thrice Viḍūḍabha sees him and turns back. The fourth time, the Teacher, knowing that because in a previous existence his kinsmen threw poison into the water, they must needs be slain, goes no more to the tree. So Viḍūḍabha goes forth to slay his enemies. The Sākiyas, as kinsmen of the Buddha, are unwilling to slay any of their enemies, and therefore make only a show of resistance. Viḍūḍabha destroys them utterly, and washes his bench with their blood.

Mahā Nāma, rather than eat with Viḍūḍabha, commits suicide. By reason of his merit he is translated to the Abode of the Nāgas, where he remains for twelve years. Viḍūḍabha searches for him in vain, and then sets out on his return journey. At nightfall Viḍūḍabha pitches camp in the bed of the river Aciravatī. During the night a violent storm arises, the bed of the river is filled with a raging torrent, and Viḍūḍabha and his retinue perish in the waters.

4. **Husband-honorer [iv. 5 = 48].** While the deity Garland-wearer is disporting

himself in the Garden of the Thirty-three, one of his wives passes from that state of existence and is reborn in Sāvatthī. Remembering her former estate, she performs many works of merit, making the Earnest Wish that she may be reborn as Garland-wearer's wife. When she marries, her devotion to her husband is so marked that she becomes known as Husband-honorer. When she dies, she is reborn as Garland-wearer's wife. When she passed from the World of the Thirty-three, it was morning, and even now it is only evening. When she tells Garland-wearer that men live only a hundred years, and that, in spite of the shortness of human life, men are ever heedless, he is greatly surprised and perturbed. The Teacher, drawing a lesson from Husband-honorer's life, warns the monks of the shortness of human life.

5. **Niggardly Kosiya** [iv. 6 = 49]. A niggardly treasurer desires to eat a cake, but for fear of having to share it with his neighbors, compels his wife to do the cooking on the seventh storey of his house. The Teacher bids Moggallāna transport the treasurer, his wife, and the cake to Jetavana. All of a sudden the treasurer sees Moggallāna, poised in the air, looking in through the window. Moggallāna indicates that he wishes to have something to eat. The treasurer blusters and threatens and refuses to give him anything. Finally, in hope of getting rid of the Elder, the treasurer bids his wife cook one little cake for him. But each cake his wife cooks grows bigger than the previous one, and when his wife tries to take a single cake from the basket, the cakes all stick together. In despair the treasurer presents cakes, basket, and all, to the Elder. The Elder preaches the Law to the treasurer and his wife, dwelling on the importance of almsgiving, and then transports the treasurer, his wife, and the cakes to Jetavana. The Teacher and his five hundred monks eat as much as they desire, and yet there is no end to the cakes that remain. After listening to the Teacher, the treasurer and his wife are established in the Fruit of Conversion, and the treasurer spends his entire wealth in the Religion of the Buddha. .The Teacher informs the monks that this is not the first time Moggallāna has converted the treasurer, and relates the Illīsa Jataka.

6. **Pāṭhika the Naked Ascetic** [iv. 7 = 50]. A Naked Ascetic seeks to prevent the wife of a certain householder from hearing the Buddha. Accordingly she decides to invite the Teacher to her house, and sends her young son to deliver the message. The Naked Ascetic discovers where the boy is going, and tells him to give the Teacher wrong directions, assuring him that if the Teacher fails to come, both he and the boy will have all the more to eat. The boy does as the Naked Ascetic tells him, but the Teacher, knowing the way of himself, comes at the appointed time. The Naked Ascetic is greatly provoked, reviles his benefactor, and leaves the house. The Teacher, observing that the mind of his hostess is agitated, urges her to pay no attention to the sins of others, but to give heed to her own shortcomings.

7. **The king and the King of Kings** [iv. 8–9 = 51–52]. When King Pasenadi Kosala comes to pay his respects to the Teacher, Chattapāṇi withholds homage. The king is provoked, but the Teacher justifies Chattapāṇi's conduct, and the king says nothing more about it. One day the king sees Chattapāṇi pass through the courtyard, and causes him to be summoned within. Chattapāṇi lays aside his parasol and sandals, and comes into the king's presence without them. The king remarks that at last Chattapāṇi seems to have found out that he is a king. Chattapāṇi replies that he always knew it. The king then asks him why he withheld homage on the day when he went to see the Teacher. Chattapāṇi replies that since he was seated in the presence of the King of Kings, it was not fitting that he should rise on seeing the king of one of his provinces. The king, satisfied by his answer, asks Chattapāṇi to preach the Law in the women's apartments. Chattapāṇi, not being a monk, declines. At the request of the king, the Teacher deputes Ānanda to preach in the palace. Mallikā learns quickly, but Vāsabhakhattiyā makes little progress.

8. Marriage of Visākhā [iv. 10 = 53]. Visākhā is the daughter of Dhanañjaya, a treasurer of the city of Bhaddiya. Dhanañjaya, at the request of King Pasenadi Kosala, removes to the kingdom of Kosala, and settles in Sāketa, not far from Sāvatthi. By this time Visākhā, who attained the Fruit of Conversion at the age of seven, has reached marriageable age. At Sāvatthi lives Puṇṇavaddhana, son of the treasurer Migāra. Puṇṇavaddhana agrees to marry a girl possessed of the Five Beauties, if such can be found. Eight Brahmans devote themselves to the task of finding such a girl, and one day, seeing Visākhā, and discovering that she is possessed of the Five Beauties, go to her father and ask her hand in marriage. Dhanañjaya consents, and the Brahmans inform Migāra. Migāra and Pasenadi, accompanied by their retinues, pay a visit to Dhanañjaya. In the meantime Dhanañjaya causes a magnificent parure to be made for his daughter, and provides her with a splendid dowry. When it is time for Visākhā to go, her father enjoins upon her the observance of the following Ten Injunctions: The indoor fire is not to be carried outside; the outdoor fire is not to be carried inside; give only to him that gives; give not to him that gives not; give both to him that gives, and to him that gives not; sit happily; eat happily; sleep happily; tend the fire; honor the household divinities. Migāra happens to be sitting in the next room, and overhears all that Dhanañjaya says. Dhanañjaya then appoints eight sponsors for Visākhā, and directs them to try her in case any charges are brought against her. He then entrusts her to the care of King Pasenadi and the treasurer, who return with her to Sāvatthi. So Visākhā, arrayed in her magnificent parure, and accompanied by a splendid retinue, enters Sāvatthi in the train of the king, and immediately wins the hearts of all the inhabitants.

That night Visākhā's thoroughbred mare gives birth to a foal, whereupon Visākhā rises from her bed, goes to the stable, and bathes the mare. At this her father-in-law is much displeased. Now Migāra is a supporter of the Naked Ascetics of the Jain Order, and when the Naked Ascetics learn that a disciple of the monk Gotama has become the wife of his son, they urge him to expel her from the house. Subsequently, at the close of a day on which Migāra has entertained the Naked Ascetics, he overhears Visākhā remark that he is eating "stale fare." Migāra then and there orders her out of the house. Visākhā, however, claims the right of being tried before her eight sponsors. Accordingly Migāra causes the sponsors to be summoned, and brings three charges against his daughter-in-law: first, that she has accused him of eating what is unclean; secondly, that she left the house at night; thirdly, that she has performed the work of menials. Visākhā clears herself of guilt on the first count by explaining that all she meant to say was that he was living on stale merit instead of acquiring fresh merit; she then explains that she left the house at night for the sole purpose of attending her mare; the third charge is dropped.

Migāra then asks Visākhā to explain the meaning of the Ten Injunctions. Visākhā explains them as follows: "The indoor fire is not to be carried outside," means that a wife must say nothing about the faults of her father-in-law or her husband. "The outdoor fire is not to be carried inside," means that a wife must not tell her father-in-law or her husband anything ill she hears of them. "Give only to him that gives," means that one should give only to those that return borrowed articles. "Give not to him that gives not," means that one should not give to those that do not return borrowed articles. "Give both to him that gives, and to him that gives not," means that when poor folk seek assistance, one should give to them, whether or not they are able to repay. "Sit happily," means that a wife must not remain sitting when she sees her husband or his parents. "Eat happily," means that a wife must not eat until she has served her husband and his parents. "Sleep happily," means that a wife must not go to bed in advance of her husband and his parents. "Tend the fire," means that a wife must reverence her husband and his parents as a flame of fire.

"Honor the household divinities," means that a wife must look upon her husband and his parents as her divinities.

Thereupon Migāra, finding no fault in Visākhā, begs her to pardon him. Visākhā does so, but tells him that now that she has been cleared of all charges, it is her intention to leave his house. She consents to stay, however, on condition that she shall be allowed to entertain the Buddha. On the occasion of the Buddha's first visit, Migāra and his wife are established in the Fruit of Conversion. Visākhā's life abounds in good works, and she lives to be a hundred and twenty years old. She endeavors to sell her magnificent parure, intending to devote the proceeds to the Order; but finding that no one else is rich enough to buy it, makes up the price herself, and erects a splendid monastery. The Teacher informs the monks that Visākhā's happiness is the result of good works performed in previous existences, and relates the following

8 a. Story of the Past: Visākhā's Earnest Wish. In the dispensations of previous Buddhas, Visākhā gave alms and made the following Earnest Wish, "May I receive the Eight Boons at the hands of some future Buddha, and may I be the foremost of the women entitled to provide him with the Four Requisites."

9. Elder Ānanda's question [iv. 11–12 = 54–55]. Elder Ānanda asks the Teacher, "Is there any perfume that goes against the wind?" The Teacher replies, "Certainly, the perfume of good works."

10. Sakka gives alms to Kassapa the Great [iv. 13 = 56]. Sakka's five hundred wives endeavor to obtain the privilege of giving alms to Kassapa the Great, but the Elder refuses their request on the ground that he prefers to allow the poor to accumulate merit by so doing. When Sakka learns this, he disguises himself as an old weaver and gives alms to the Elder. When the Elder discovers that Sakka has deceived him, he reproaches him. But Sakka explains that he hopes by the performance of this and other good works to outshine certain other deities.

11. Godhika attains Nibbāna [iv. 14 = 57]. Elder Godhika, finding himself impeded in the practice of Ecstatic Meditation by a certain disease, draws a razor and cuts his throat, passing at once to Nibbāna. Māra, in the form of a pillar of smoke, seeks his rebirth-consciousness. The Buddha informs him that he is engaged in a futile task.

12. Sirigutta and Garahadinna [iv. 15–16 = 58–59]. At Sāvatthi live two friends, Sirigutta, a disciple of the Buddha, and Garahadinna, a disciple of the Naked Ascetics of the Jain Order. Garahadinna reproaches Sirigutta for visiting the monk Gotama, and urges him to transfer his allegiance to the Naked Ascetics, principally on the ground that the Naked Ascetics know everybody's thoughts, words, and actions, and can therefore tell just what is going to happen, and just what is not going to happen. Sirigutta invites the Naked Ascetics to his house, and resolves to put them to the test. Accordingly he has a ditch dug and filled with filth, ropes stretched longitudinally over the ditch, and the seats so placed, with the front legs resting on the ground, and the back legs resting on the ropes, that the instant the heretics sit down, they will be tipped over backwards and precipitated into the ditch. When the Naked Ascetics visit him, this very thing happens. Garahadinna resolves to get revenge by humiliating the Buddha and his disciples. He employs much the same stratagem, except that instead of filling the ditch with filth, he has it filled with glowing coals. But the Buddha, by an exercise of supernatural power, causes an enormous lotus-flower to spring up from the bed of coals. And sitting thereon, surrounded by his five hundred monks, he creates an abundant supply of food, and preaches the Law. Garahadinna, Sirigutta, and many others attain the Fruit of Conversion.

Book V. The Simpleton, Bāla Vagga

1. The king and the poor man with a beautiful wife [v. 1 = 60]. King Pasenadi Kosala falls in love with the beautiful wife of a certain poor man. He determines to kill the man and take his wife. He therefore appoints the man a servant in his household, hoping that the man will commit some fault and give him a plausible excuse for killing him. Finding no fault in the man, the king orders him to go to the country of the dragons, procure water-lilies and red earth, and return to him at bathing-time. The poor man goes hastily to the country of the dragons, makes over to the dragons the merit of offerings of rice to a traveler and to the fish in the water, and implores the dragons to give him water-lilies and red earth. The king of the dragons appears to him in the guise of an old man and answers his prayer. King Pasenadi has the door of his palace closed before bathing-time, fearing that if the poor man should obtain what he sent him for, his purpose would not succeed. The poor man returns at bathing-time, and finding the door of the palace closed, places the red earth on the threshold, hangs the flowers over the door, and calls upon everybody to witness that he has executed the king's order. That night, as the king lies sleepless on his bed, consumed with passion as he thinks of the woman, he hears four terrible sounds. The Brahmans play upon his fears and persuade him to order the sacrifice of every kind of living creature. Queen Mallikā rebukes him for his credulity and conducts him to the Buddha. The Buddha informs the king that the sounds he heard were uttered by sinners in torment, and relates the following

1 a. Story of the Past: The Hell Pot. In the dispensation of the Buddha Kassapa, four sons of wealthy merchants committed adultery for twenty thousand years. When they died, they were reborn in the Avīci hell, where they suffered torment during the interval between two Buddhas. Since the fruit of their evil deeds was not yet exhausted, they were reborn in the Hell Pot. In the course of thirty thousand years they reached the bottom, and after thirty thousand years more they came to the rim. Desiring to give expression of their remorse, they opened their lips and began to speak. But after uttering one single syllable apiece, they flopped over and sank back again into the Hell Pot. The Buddha completed the stanzas which the four sinners had left uncompleted; and the king, brought to a realization of his wickedness, resolved nevermore to set his heart on another man's wife. The king ordered the release of the victims brought for the sacrifice. The Buddha informed the monks that it was not the first time Queen Mallikā had saved the lives of the innocent, and related the following

1 b. Story of the Past: The King of Benāres and Queen Dinnā. The heir apparent of the King of Benāres vowed to offer the blood of a hundred kings and a hundred queens to a tree-spirit if he came into the kingdom on the death of his father. When he became King of Benāres, he captured the hundred kings and hundred queens and prepared to fulfill his vow. Queen Dinnā, consort of King Uggasena, was great with child, and the King of Benāres therefore released her. The tree-spirit, knowing that the King of Benāres was acting on the conviction that he had captured the kings and queens with his assistance, and desiring to prevent him from carrying out his purpose, sought the advice of Sakka. Acting on Sakka's advice, the tree-spirit threatened to leave his abode on the ground that the king had violated his promise by releasing Queen Dinnā. The King of Benāres immediately summoned Queen Dinnā. Queen Dinnā refused to pay obeisance either to the King of Benāres or to the tree-spirit, and convinced the King of Benāres that the tree-spirit had had nothing to do with his success. As the Queen spoke, she first wept and then laughed. The King asked her the reason for this, and the Queen related the following

1 c. **Story of the Past: The woman who killed a ewe.** In a previous state of existence, Queen Dinnā killed a ewe for food. As a punishment for this wicked deed, she was reborn in hell. Afterwards, since the fruit of her wicked deed was not yet exhausted, her own head was cut off just as many times as there were hairs in the ewe's fleece. The thought of the suffering which she had endured made her weep, and the joy which she felt over her release made her exult. The king was thus brought to a realization of the enormity of the deed he was minded to commit, and immediately ordered the release of the hundred kings and the hundred queens.

2. **The rebellious pupil** [v. 2 = 61]. The Elder Kassapa has two pupils. One of them performs his duties faithfully, but the other shirks his duties and seeks to take credit for work really done by his brother-pupil. One day the faithless pupil obtains food from a supporter of the Elder on the plea that the Elder has sent him for it, and then eats it himself. The Elder, discovering his deceit, rebukes him. In order to show his resentment of the rebuke, the faithless pupil sets fire to the Elder's hut. The Buddha, learning of the occurrence, informs the monks that it is not the first time he has destroyed a dwelling-place, and relates the following

2 a. **Story of the Past: The monkey and the siṅgila bird, Kuṭidūsaka Jātaka.** A siṅgila bird reproached a monkey for his inconstancy. The monkey, to show his resentment of the rebuke, destroyed the bird's nest. The siṅgila bird was Kassapa, and the monkey was the rebellious pupil.

3. **A Jonah in the house** [v. 3 = 62].

3 a. **The niggardly treasurer.** Ānanda, a niggardly treasurer, admonishes his son Mūlasiri not to let the pennies slip through his fingers. Some time afterwards, he shows his son his five great stores of treasure, dies, and is reborn as a monstrosity in a community of Caṇḍālas. The king appoints Mūlasiri treasurer.

3 b. **Sequel: A Jonah in the house.** From the day the monstrosity is born, the community of Caṇḍālas receives no more wages, and has not a mouthful of rice to eat. Concluding that this is due to the presence of a Jonah among them, the Caṇḍālas make an investigation, discover the monstrosity, and expel mother and son from the community. The monstrosity is forced to beg his food from door to door. One day he enters the house in which he once lived as master. Mūlasiri's young sons take fright at the monstrosity, and the servants seize their former master, drag him out of the house, and fling him on a pile of rubbish. Just at that moment the Buddha passes the house. The Buddha informs Mūlasiri that the monstrosity is none other than his own father. Mūlasiri will not believe him. The Buddha directs the monstrosity to point out his five stores of treasure to his son. The monstrosity does so, and Mūlasiri believes and seeks refuge in the Buddha.

4. **The pickpocket** [v. 4 = 63]. Two thieves go to hear the Law. One of them is converted, and the other picks a pocket. The pickpocket calls his companion a simpleton for failing to take advantage of such a golden opportunity.

5. **The wise fool** [v. 5 = 64]. The Elder Udāyi used to sit in the Seat of the Law after the Great Elders had left the Hall of Truth. Some visiting monks, thinking that he must be a man of learning, questioned him, and discovered that he was a simpleton.

6. **From vice to virtue** [v. 6 = 65]. The Buddha meets thirty youths in a grove, where they have gone seeking a woman. They at once obey the command to follow him, and in a very short time attain Arahatship. The monks comment on the suddenness of their conversion. The Teacher remarks that it is the fruit of merit acquired in a previous existence, and relates the Tuṇḍila Jātaka.

7. **A leper is tempted to deny his faith** [v. 7 = 66]. A leper listens to the Law and attains the Fruit of Conversion. In order to test the sincerity of his conversion, Sakka promises him limitless wealth if he will deny his faith. The leper indignantly

refuses to do so. The leper approaches the Buddha, retires, and sets out for his home. When he has gone but a little way, he is kicked by a young heifer and killed.

7 a. Story of the Past: The four youths and the courtezan. Four youths, after taking their pleasure with a courtezan, plotted to rob and kill her. The courtezan overheard the plot, and when the youths were about to kill her, prayed that she might be reborn as an ogress, able to kill them even as they were killing her. One of these youths was the leper. The courtezan was the ogress, disguised as a heifer.

7 b. Story of the Past: The insolent youth. Suppabuddha was reborn as a leper because in a previous state of existence he had spat upon a Private Buddha.

8. A farmer is unjustly accused of theft [v. 8 = 67]. A pack of thieves rob a house, and divide their spoils in a field. One of the thieves drops in the field a purse which he has secreted in a fold of his garment, without noticing his loss. The Buddha goes to the field with the Elder Ānanda, and in the hearing of the farmer, makes a veiled reference to the purse. The farmer discovers the purse and buries it. The owners of the stolen property trail the thieves to the field, recover the purse, and accuse the farmer of having robbed the house. As the farmer is being led to the place of execution, he repeats the words uttered by the Buddha. The executioners take him to the king, and the truth comes out. Thus does the Buddha save an honest farmer from being convicted of theft on circumstantial evidence.

9. Sumana the gardener [v. 9 = 68]. One day Sumana, gardener to King Bimbisāra, honors the Buddha with eight measures of jasmine flowers intended for the king. The Buddha proclaims throughout the city the meritorious deed of the gardener, and the king rewards him with eightfold gifts.

10. Rape of Uppalavaṇṇā [v. 10 = 69]. A maiden of wondrous beauty rejects all of her suitors, becomes a nun, and attains Arahatship. She takes up her residence alone in a forest hermitage. A former suitor, learning her whereabouts, goes to the hermitage and assaults her. The Buddha preaches to the monks on the transitoriness of sinful pleasures. On a subsequent occasion the monks raise the question whether Arahats are to be blamed for gratifying their passions. The Buddha admonishes them that sexual passion no more adheres to the Arahat than a drop of water to a lotus-leaf. The Buddha persuades King Pasenadi Kosala to erect a convent for the nuns within the city, and forbids the nuns thenceforth to reside in the forest.

11. Jambuka the Naked Ascetic [v. 11 = 70].

11 a. Story of the Past: The jealous monk. In the dispensation of the Buddha Kassapa, a resident monk, jealous of the attentions of his supporter to a visiting monk, reviles him. He tells him that he might better eat excrement than eat food given him by the layman, that he might better tear out his hair than permit it to be shaved by the layman's barber, that he might better go naked than wear a robe given him by the layman, and that he might better lie on the ground than on the bed provided by the layman. The visiting monk departs without making a reply.

11 b. Story of the Present: Jambuka the Naked Ascetic. The jealous monk is reborn in a well-to-do household of Rājagaha. From the day he can walk, he refuses to eat ordinary food and eats only his own excrement. When he grows older, he goes naked and makes his bed on the ground. His parents decide that he is fit to live only with the Naked Ascetics. The Naked Ascetics admit him to their Order, placing him in a pit up to his neck, and tearing out his hair with a palmyra comb. Jambuka refuses to accompany the Naked Ascetics on their rounds for alms, but waits until his brethren are out of sight, and then goes to the public jakes and makes a meal of excrement. When people come to defecate, he stands on one foot, resting the other on the knee, leaning on a rock, his mouth wide open in the direction of the wind. When people ask him why he stands in this posture, he replies that he is a wind-eater practicing austerities. He steadfastly refuses to accept food. One day, however, he places on the tip of his tongue with the tip of a blade of kusa grass some butter and honey, dismissing the people with the assurance that their gift will avail to their everlasting salvation. Thus he spends fifty-five years of his life. One day the Buddha visits him, taking up his abode in a cave near by. In the night the Buddha is waited upon by the Four Great Kings, Sakka, and Brahmā. On the following morning, in reply to Jambuka's questions, the Buddha proclaims his superiority to all of these deities. The Buddha then admonishes Jambuka, establishing him in Arahatship.

12. The snake-ghost and the crow-ghost [v. 12 = 71]. As Moggallāna descends Mount Vulture-peak with Lakkhaṇa, Moggallāna smiles. Lakkhaṇa asks him why he smiles. Moggallāna replies that he will tell him as soon as they are in the presence of the Teacher. When they are in the presence of the Teacher, Lakkhaṇa repeats his question. Moggallāna tells him he saw a snake-ghost all aflame. On another occasion Moggallāna saw a crow-ghost. Moggallāna asked him about his former deed, and the crow-ghost related the following

12 a. Story of the Past: The crow-ghost. "In the dispensation of the Buddha Kassapa I was a crow. I once ate three mouthfuls of food which remained over and above to monks who had eaten. As the result of this misdeed, I was reborn in the Avīci hell. Afterwards, since the fruit of my misdeed was not yet exhausted, I was reborn as a crow-ghost." **End of Story of the crow-ghost.**

The Buddha corroborates Moggallāna's statement regarding the snake-ghost, and declares that he himself saw the same ghost as he sat on the Throne of Enlightenment. The monks ask the Buddha to tell them about his former deed, and the Buddha relates the following

12 b. Story of the Past: The snake-ghost. The leaf-hut of a Private Buddha once stood on the bank of the river near Benāres, and every morning and evening the residents of the city trooped thither with offerings. In so doing, they trampled the field of a certain farmer. The farmer protested, but without avail. Finally the farmer became so angry that he set fire to the Private Buddha's hut. The people were indignant, and taking up sticks and stones, beat the farmer to death. The farmer was reborn in the Avīci hell, and afterwards was reborn as a snake-ghost.

13. The sledge-hammer ghost [v. 13 = 72]. Under the same circumstances as in the preceding story, Moggallāna sees a ghost belabored about the head with sledgehammers. The Buddha relates the following

13 a. Story of the Past: The stone-thrower and his pupil. A cripple who was an adept at the art of throwing stones, made his living by cutting the leaves of a banyan tree in the shape of animals of various kinds. His skill attracted the attention of the king, who was troubled by a talkative house-priest. The king employed the cripple to stop the mouth of the house-priest by tossing pellets of goat's dung into the mouth of the house-priest while the latter was talking. The king was so pleased at the success of his plan, that he rewarded the cripple with eightfold gifts. The cripple's rise in the world led another man to become his pupil. The cripple admonished his pupil to hit nothing possessed of mother or father or other kin. The pupil, seeing a Private Buddha, threw a stone at him. The Private Buddha passed into Nibbāna. The indignant people beat the stone-thrower to death. He was reborn in the Avīci hell, and afterwards, as a ghost, belabored about the head with sledge-hammers.

14. Citta and Sudhamma [v. 14–15 = 73–74]. The layman Citta entertains Mahānāma and the Chief Disciples and gives generous gifts. Sudhamma, a monk resident in Citta's household, becomes jealous of the layman, and insults him. The Buddha rebukes Sudhamma and directs him to beg Citta's pardon. Sudhamma does so. Citta visits the Buddha. When he salutes the Buddha, there is a rain of flowers from heaven. Citta is honored by the Buddha, deities, and men. The Buddha relates the following

14 a. Story of the Past: Citta's deed in a former birth. In the dispensation of the Buddha Kassapa, Citta was reborn as a hunter. One day he presented offerings of food and flowers to a monk, making the Earnest Wish that his heart might be gladdened in subsequent births by presents and by flowers rained from heaven.

15. A seven-year-old novice wins all hearts [v. 16 = 75].

15 a. Story of the Past: The poor Brahman. Sāriputta visits Mahāsena, a poor Brahman. Mahāsena, having no alms to give him, hides himself. Later on he receives a portion of rice porridge and gives it all to Sāriputta, making the Earnest Wish that he may receive happiness in the next life.

15 b. Story of the Present: The novice Tissa. Mahāsena is conceived in the womb of the wife of a supporter of the Elder Sāriputta. The expectant mother longs to entertain the monks and satisfies her longing. On the day of the child's birth he presents a blanket to Sāriputta. He is named Tissa after the Elder, whose name as a layman was Upatissa. When Tissa is seven years old, he becomes a novice of the Elder Sāriputta. For seven days his parents give alms. On the eighth day the novice accompanies the monks to the city for alms. The citizens present him with five hundred cushions and five hundred portions of food. On the following day they come to the monastery and repeat their offering. Thus in two days the novice receives a thousand cushions and a thousand portions of food. These he presents to the monks, who give him the name Tissa the Food-giver.

One day the novice notices the monks warming themselves by the fire, and invites them to accompany him to the city for blankets. So monks to the number of a thousand set out under the leadership of a seven-year-old novice. He receives five hundred blankets without the city and five hundred within. A shop-keeper, warned by a niggard that a novice is collecting blankets, hides two costly blankets. But when the novice comes in sight, the shop-keeper takes a fancy to him, and straightway presents him with the two blankets. The novice returns to the monastery with a thousand blankets, and presents them all to the monks, who give him the name Tissa the Blanket-giver.

The novice receives a Subject of Meditation from the Buddha and fares forth twenty leagues into the forest. Meeting an old man at the gate of a village, he inquires of him whether there is a forest hermitage in the neighborhood. The old man answers in the affirmative, and taking a fancy to the child, escorts him to the hermitage with the most respectful attentions. The old man then goes to the village and proclaims to the villagers that Tissa the Forest-dweller has taken up his residence at the hermitage. Thus did a novice receive four names in seven years. The novice wins the hearts of all the villagers. In the third month of residence he attains Arahatship. The Chief Disciples with a retinue of forty thousand monks visit the novice. The novice preaches the Law to the multitude. There is a difference of opinion among the supporters of the novice as to the merits of his discourse. The Buddha visits the village and reconciles their differences. The novice walks with the Buddha and talks with him. They ascend a mountain together, and the Buddha asks him what thought comes into his mind as he gazes upon the Great Ocean. The novice replies that he is reminded of the tears of sorrow which he has shed in previous births. The Buddha asks him what thought most impresses him as he dwells in his cave. The novice replies that he is reminded of the times when he has died and when his body has been laid on the ground. The Buddha remarks that there is no spot on earth where men have not died, and relates the Upasāḷhaka Jātaka.

Digression: But Elder Ānanda, in order to prevent a quarrel between his supporters over the possession of his relics, passed into Nibbāna in mid-air.

Story of the Present completed: The Buddha asks the novice his impressions of the forest. The novice replies that he has come to love the forest. The Buddha returns to the Jetavana, while the novice remains in the forest. The monks express surprise that the novice should renounce gain and honor to remain in the forest.

Book VI. The Wise Man, Paṇḍita Vagga

1. A poor man wins spiritual treasure [vi. 1 = 76]. Sāriputta receives into the Order a poor man who once gave him a ladleful of his food. The poor man proves to be a model disciple. The monks comment on Sāriputta's grateful recognition of the poor man's gift. The Buddha remarks that it is not the first time Sāriputta has shown himself grateful, and relates the following

1 a. Story of the Past: The grateful elephant, Alīnacitta Jātaka. An elephant runs a thorn into his foot, and some carpenters remove it. The elephant out of gratefulness serves the carpenters and presents his son to them. The grateful elephant was Sāriputta.

2. The insolent monks [vi. 2 = 77]. Certain monks are guilty of disorderly conduct. The Buddha directs the Chief Disciples to admonish and instruct them.

3. The insolent monk [vi. 3 = 78]. Elder Channa is boastful and insolent, and the Buddha can do nothing with him. After the Buddha has passed into Nibbāna, Elder Ānanda inflicts upon Channa the punishment known as "brahmadaṇḍa." Channa is overwhelmed with remorse, and in no long time attains Arahatship.

4. Kappina the Great [vi. 4 = 79].

4 a. Story of the Past: Weavers and householders. Kappina made his Earnest Wish at the feet of the Buddha Padumuttara. In a later birth he was reborn as the senior of a community of weavers. The senior weaver and his wife, assisted by the community, once entertained a thousand Private Buddhas. In the dispensation of the Buddha Kassapa, they were reborn as householders of Benāres. One day the community of householders went to hear the Law. Just then it began to rain. Unable to find shelter in the monastery, they determined to erect a monastery. When the monastery was completed, they presented it to the monks and gave abundant alms. The wife of the senior householder presented a garment of the color of anoja flowers and a casket of anoja flowers to the Buddha, and made an Earnest Wish.

4 b. Story of the Present: King Kappina and Queen Anojā. The householders are reborn in the city of Kukkuṭavatī, the senior householder and his wife as the king and queen respectively, and the others in the households of courtiers. King Kappina and his thousand courtiers and Queen Anojā and her thousand ladies-in-waiting, hearing of the appearance in the world of the Buddha, the Law, and the Order, give splendid gifts, set out to visit the Buddha, cross three rivers on dry foot by making Acts of Truth, and retire from the world. The Elder Kappina exclaims wherever he goes, "Oh happiness!" The monks conclude that he has in mind the happiness of ruling. The Buddha informs them that the Elder refers to the happiness of Nibbāna.

5. Paṇḍita the novice [vi. 5 = 80].

5 a. Story of the Past: Sakka and the poor man. A poor man and his wife, assisted by Sakka, entertain the Buddha Kassapa. A rain of jewels falls upon his house, and urns of treasure come to light therein.

5 b. Story of the Present: Paṇḍita, the seven-year-old novice. The poor man is conceived in the womb of the wife of a supporter of Elder Sāriputta. The expectant mother longs to entertain the monks and satisfies her longing. From the child's conception, those of the household who were stupid or deaf or dumb became wise, and therefore he is given the name Wiseman, Paṇḍita. When he is seven years old, he becomes a novice of Elder Sāriputta. One day he accompanies the Elder on his rounds, sees ditch-diggers, fletchers, and carpenters at work, and asks the Elder many questions. The ease with which men control inanimate things suggests to the novice the thought of so controlling his reason as to win Arahatship. Paṇḍita takes leave of the Elder, requesting him to bring him the choicest portions of redfish, returns to his cell, and engages in meditation. At the command of Sakka, the Four Great Kings drive the noisy birds from the monastery park and keep watch over the four quarters, and the moon and the sun stand still. Sakka guards the string of the door, and the Buddha keeps watch over the gate. The Elder brings the choicest portions of redfish, and the Teacher asks him four questions. Paṇḍita overhears the Elder's answers and attains Arahatship.

6. **Unshaken as a rock [vi. 6 = 81].** Novices pull the hair and tweak the nose and ears of a dignified monk. The monk shows no resentment. The Buddha compares him to a solid rock.

7. **After the storm, calm [vi. 7 = 82].** The mother of Kāṇā is so generous to the monks that she is forced to send Kāṇā to her husband empty-handed. Kāṇā's husband puts her away, and takes to himself another wife. Kāṇā, furiously angry, reviles the monks. The Buddha talks with her and calms her. The king adopts Kāṇā, and one of his nobles marries her. The Buddha informs the monks that it is not the first time he has persuaded Kāṇā to obey him, and relates the Babbu Jātaka.

8. **A pack of vagabonds [vi. 8 = 83].** The Buddha, accompanied by five hundred monks, visits Verañjā, and at the invitation of the Brahman Verañja enters upon residence. Māra takes possession of the Brahman, and causes him to forget his obligations to the Buddha. The monks, despite the scarcity of food, live in tranquillity. The Buddha returns to Jetavana with the monks. The monks permit a pack of vagabonds to live within the monastery enclosure. The vagabonds misbehave themselves within the very shadow of the monastery. The Buddha remarks that it is not the first time these vagabonds have so conducted themselves, and relates the Vālodaka Jātaka.

9. **Husband and wife [vi. 9 = 84].** A householder asks his wife for permission to retire from the world. His wife asks him not to do so until she has given birth to her child. He waits until the child is old enough to walk, and then asks her again. She then asks him to wait until the child comes of age. Despairing of ever getting her permission, he retires from the world, and in no long time attains Arahatship. Subsequently both son and wife follow his example.

10. **"Few there be that find it" [vi. 10–11 = 85–86].** A company of people resolve to spend the night listening to the Law, but one after another falls away.

11. **Abandon the dark state [vi. 12–14 = 87–89].** The Buddha admonishes fifty visiting monks.

Book VII. The Arahat, Arahanta Vagga

1. **The Tathāgata suffers not [vii. 1 = 90].** Devadatta wounds the Buddha. Jīvaka applies an astringent, binds up the wound, and promises to return. He returns after the gate is closed, and is unable to enter. In the morning he asks the Buddha whether he did not suffer intense pain. The Buddha replies that the Tathāgata suffers not.

2. **Free from attachment [vii. 2 = 91].** While the other monks are scalding their bowls and dyeing their robes, preparatory to setting out on an alms-pilgrimage with the Buddha, Elder Kassapa washes his robes. The other monks accuse Kassapa of being attached to the households of his kinsfolk and retainers. The Buddha directs Kassapa to remain in charge of the monastery, and reproves the other monks, telling them that Kassapa is free from attachment. He then relates the story of Kassapa's Earnest Wish in a previous birth.

3. A monk stores food [vii. 3 = 92]. A certain monk stores food for future use. The Buddha forbids the practice.

4. The monk and the goddess [vii. 4 = 93]. A goddess, who in a previous state of existence was the daughter of Elder Anuruddha, gives him robes, and incites the villagers to give him food in abundance. The monks are offended, thinking that the Elder wishes to show how many relatives and retainers he has. The Buddha informs them that the Elder received these offerings through the supernatural power of a goddess.

5. Sakka honors a monk [vii. 5 = 94]. Sakka renders high honor to Elder Kaccāyana the Great. The monks are offended, and accuse Sakka of showing favoritism. The Buddha reproves the monks, and declares that those who, like Kaccāyana, keep the doors of their senses guarded, are dear alike to gods and men.

6. A fancied slight [vii. 6 = 95]. A monk takes a dislike to Elder Sāriputta because of a fancied slight. An assembly of the monks is convoked, the Elder enumerates his own virtues, and everything ends well.

7. The loss of an eye [vii. 7 = 96]. A certain Elder accidentally puts out the eye of his novice. The novice, however, shows neither anger nor resentment. The Buddha praises the novice for his self-restraint.

8. Not by the faith of another [vii. 8 = 97]. The Buddha asks Sāriputta whether he believes that faith terminates in the Deathless. Sāriputta answers that he does not go by the faith of the Exalted One in this matter. The monks misunderstand his answer and accuse him of refusing to believe the words of the Buddha. The Buddha corrects their mistake and informs them that Sāriputta has by himself realized the Paths and the Fruits.

9. Elder Revata of the acacia forest [vii. 9 = 98].

9 a. Revata becomes a monk. After all of Sāriputta's brothers and sisters, except his youngest brother Revata, have retired from the world, the mother seeks to bind Revata with the tie of marriage. Revata, however, outwits his mother, leaves his bride, and becomes a monk. He withdraws to an acacia forest and there attains Arahatship.

9 b. The Buddha visits Revata. The Buddha and Elder Sāriputta set out to visit Revata with a company of monks of whom Sīvali is one. The forest deities entertain the monks on the way, and Revata entertains them in the forest, all because of the merit of Sīvali. Two old monks resident in the forest complain that the Buddha shows favoritism to Revata. The Buddha, by an exercise of supernatural power, causes forgetfulness to overcome the old monks. The old monks wander hither and thither in the forest, and acacia thorns pierce their feet. The old monks stop at Visākhā's house for alms, and tell her that the discomforts of life in the acacia forest beggar description. Two young monks describe the forest as a place of heavenly delight. When the Buddha returns from the forest, Visākhā repeats to him the two contradictory statements. The Buddha declares that wherever Arahats reside, that spot is full of delight. Subsequently the monks ask the Buddha why Sīvali remained in his mother's womb for seven days and seven months and seven years; why he was tormented in hell; and how he came to reach the pinnacle of gain and honor. The Buddha relates the following

9 c. Story of the Past: The offering of honey and the siege of a city. In the dispensation of the Buddha Vipassī, a king and his subjects vie with one another in making offerings to the Buddha. A certain countryman buys a comb of honey for a thousand pieces of money and presents it to the Buddha. In a later existence as King of Benāres, he lays siege to a certain city for seven years and seven months. His mother, learning that he has blockaded the four principal gates of the city and left the lesser gates open, sends word to him to close the lesser gates and blockade the city completely. The king does so. On the seventh day the residents of the besieged city kill their king, and hand over the kingdom to the invader. Because Sīvali in his previous existence as a king besieged this city, he was reborn in hell, and because he closed the lesser gates he remained in the womb of his mother for seven days and seven months and seven years; because in his previous existence as a countryman he gave the comb of honey to the Buddha, he reached the pinnacle of gain and honor.

10. A courtezan tempts a monk [vii. 10 = 99]. A monk enters a garden to meditate. A courtezan goes thither to meet her lover. Her lover fails to keep his appointment. The disappointed courtezan, seeing the monk, performs indecent acts before him and arouses his passions. The Buddha appears in a vision to the monk and admonishes him. The monk attains Arahatship.

Book VIII. Thousands, Sahassa Vagga

1. A public executioner [viii. 1 = 100]. A bloodthirsty villain seeks admission to a band of thieves. The thieves refuse to admit him because of his inordinate cruelty. He ingratiates himself with a pupil of the ringleader and is finally admitted. The thieves are captured and sentenced to death. The citizens offer to spare the life of the thief who will put his brethren to death. All refuse the offer except the newest member of the band. The bloodthirsty villain puts his brethren to death, and acts as public executioner for fifty-five years. When he becomes infirm, the citizens remove him from office. Sāriputta preaches to him and converts him. When he dies, he is reborn in the heaven of the Tusita gods. The monks express surprise that so bloodthirsty a villain should be reborn in heaven. The Buddha informs them that it was because he obtained a good spiritual counselor.

2. Conversion of Bāhiya Dārucīriya [viii. 2 = 101]. Bāhiya Dārucīriya suffers shipwreck and swims to land at Suppāraka Port. Clothing himself in the bark of trees, he goes about the city and is acclaimed as an Arahat. As he ponders in his mind the meaning of the title and asks himself whether he is really one of the Arahats, a deity who was a former blood-relative of his directs him to visit the Buddha at Sāvatthi.

2 a. Digression: Story of the Past. The deity was a "former blood-relative" of Bāhiya Dārucīriya in the sense that in the dispensation of the Buddha Kassapa the two were fellow-members of a band of seven monks who climbed a mountain and attained Arahatship.

2. Conversion of Bāhiya Dārucīriya, concluded: Bāhiya Dārucīriya obeys the command of the deity, hastens to Sāvatthi, hearkens to the Law, and attains Arahatship. As he is seeking bowl and robe, an ogress in the form of a young heifer strikes him, and he passes into Nibbāna.

3. The maiden who married a thief [viii. 3-4 = 102-103]. A treasurer's daughter looks out of her window, sees a thief being led to the place of execution, and falls in love with him. She takes to her bed and informs her parents that she will starve herself to death unless she can have the thief for her husband. Her father bribes the king's officer to put another to death instead of the thief, and gives his daughter in marriage to the thief. The thief soon tires of his wife, and determines to kill her and take her jewels. He pretends to his wife that he saved his own life by vowing an offering to the deity of Robbers' Cliff, and asks her to accompany him to the top of the mountain that he may fulfill his vow. When they reach the top of the mountain, the thief tells his wife that he intends to kill her and take her jewels. The wife retains her presence of mind, and asks the thief to permit her to pay obeisance to him for the last time. When he is off his guard, she seizes him and flings him over the cliff. He is dashed to pieces against the rocks and killed.

Not daring to return home, she enters the forest, and coming to a hermitage of nuns of a sectarian Order, she retires from the world and becomes a nun. Having learned a thousand questions and answers, she goes about the country bearing in her hand a branch of the rose-apple tree, challenging all comers to match questions and answers with her. Coming to Sāvatthi, she plants her branch before the city gate, and enters the city for alms. A troop of young lads gather about the branch, waiting for something to happen. Sāriputta comes out of the city and tells the lads to trample the branch under their feet. Sāriputta answers all of the nun's questions, and then baffles her and converts her to the true faith by asking her the single question, "What is 'One'?" The monks express surprise that so few words should effect the conversion of a woman with the past of the sectarian nun.

4. **Gain and loss** [viii. 5–6 = 104–105]. A gambler asks the Buddha a question about gain and loss. The Buddha admonishes the gambler to consider spiritual gain and loss.

5. **Sāriputta's uncle** [viii. 7 = 106]. The Buddha converts Sāriputta's uncle, who has given alms to the Naked Ascetics in the hope that he may thus attain the World of Brahmā.

6. **Sāriputta's nephew** [viii. 8 = 107]. The Buddha converts Sāriputta's nephew, who has tended the sacrificial fire in the hope that he may thus attain the World of Brahmā.

7. **Sāriputta's friend** [viii. 9 = 108]. The Buddha converts Sāriputta's friend, who has tended the sacrificial fire in the hope that he may thus attain the World of Brahmā.

8. **The lad whose years increased** [viii. 10 = 109]. Vessavaṇa promises an ogre who has served him for twelve years that he shall receive the young son of a certain Brahman at the end of seven days. A sectarian monk informs the Brahman that his son is destined to die in seven days. At the monk's suggestion the Brahman asks the Buddha whether there is any way of averting his son's fate. The Buddha directs the Brahman to make preparations for the recitation of Paritta. The Brahman does so. By direction of the Buddha the monks recite Paritta for seven days and seven nights. The Buddha, having cheated the ogre of his prey, predicts that the lad will live for a hundred and twenty years. He thus receives the name Lad-Whose-Years-Increased, Āyuvaḍḍhana.

9. **Saṁkicca the novice** [viii. 11 = 110]. Thirty men of Sāvatthi become monks, receive a Subject of Meditation from the Buddha, and ask leave to retire to the forest. The Buddha reflects that they will be in danger of harm through a certain vagabond, unless they are accompanied by the novice Saṁkicca.

9 a. **Digression: How Saṁkicca got his name.** Saṁkicca was a seven-year-old novice of Elder Sāriputta. While he was yet in the womb, his mother died and her body was cremated. Her unborn child, however, was untouched by the fire. The body-burners removed the unborn child from the funeral pile, pierced it with spears, and threw it back on the coals. The flesh of the child was burned away, but there appeared on top of the coals, sitting as it were in the calyx of a lotus flower, a little boy that looked like a silver image. Because the pupil of one of his eyes had been pierced with a spear (saṁku), he received the name Saṁkicca. When Saṁkicca was seven years old, he learned of his miraculous escape from death, retired from the world, became a novice of Elder Sāriputta, and attained Arahatship.

The Buddha directs the thirty monks to see Elder Sāriputta before they leave for the forest. Sāriputta directs them to take the novice Saṁkicca with them. The monks, accompanied by the novice Saṁkicca, retire to the forest and enter upon residence. They make an agreement to spend their time in solitude, and in case any monk falls sick, to assemble on the stroke of the bell. One day the monks take pity on a vagabond and give him food. The vagabond waits upon the monks for two months, and then departs without asking leave of his hosts. As he is on his way through the forest, he is captured by a band of thieves. The thieves prepare to kill him and to make a votive offering of his flesh and blood to the forest deity. The captive begs them to spare his life, declaring that he is a mere vagabond, and suggests that they kill and sacrifice the monks in his stead. He directs them to the place of residence of the monks, and instructs them to strike the bell. The thieves strike the bell, and the monks assemble. The thieves demand a victim. Each of the monks, from the oldest to the youngest, offers himself as a willing victim. The novice Saṁkicca insists upon accompanying the thieves. The ringleader strikes the novice with his sword, and the sword bends in two. He strikes him again, and the sword splits from hilt to tip like a palm-leaf. The thief prostrates himself before the novice. The novice preaches the Law to the thieves, and one and all retire from the world. The novice, accompanied by his retinue of monks, visits his brethren, and is received with expressions of joy. He then visits the Buddha. Later on he is admitted to full membership in the Order. When Saṁkicca has been a monk for ten years, he receives his nephew Atimuttaka as a novice.

9 b. **Sequel: The novice Atimuttaka.** While the novice Atimuttaka is on his way through the forest, he is captured by thieves, who threaten to kill him and make an offering of his blood. He converts them, and they release him on condition that he shall tell no one their whereabouts. The novice sees his mother and father going straight towards the thieves, but keeps his promise to the thieves and refrains from warning his parents. His parents reproach him. The thieves praise him and become his disciples.

10. **The monk and the thieves** [viii. 12 = 111]. A certain monk enters into a state of trance. A pack of thieves mistake him for the trunk of a tree, pile their sacks on his head and body, and sleep in a circle about him all night long. In the morning they discover their mistake, beg his pardon, and are converted.

11. **On the razor's edge** [viii. 13 = 112]. A discontented monk tries to commit suicide by letting a snake bite him. The snake, however, refuses to bite. The monk then applies a razor to his throat. At that moment he attains Arahatship.

11 a. **Story of the Past: Discontented and covetous.** In a previous state of existence also this monk suffered from discontent. One day he was cured of discontent by the discovery that a brother monk was scheming to get possession of his monastic utensils.

12. **Paṭācārā is bereft of all her family** [viii. 14 = 113]. Paṭācārā, the daughter of a wealthy merchant of Sāvatthi, runs away with her page. They take up their abode in a distant village, the husband tilling the soil and the wife performing the duties of the household. Paṭācārā conceives a child, and requests her husband to take her home. The husband, fearing the vengeance of his wife's parents, puts her off from day to day. One day Paṭācārā sets out for her home alone. Her husband follows her and overtakes her. She gives birth to her child by the wayside and returns with her husband. By and by she conceives a second child, makes the same request of her husband, and receives the same answer. Again she sets out alone for her home, and again her husband follows her and overtakes her. Just as the birth-pains come upon her a fearful storm arises. She begs her husband to find her a place out of the rain. Her husband leaves her to seek materials for a shelter. He is bitten to death by a poisonous snake. Paṭācārā, alone, amid the flashes of lightning and the rumbling of thunder, gives birth to a second child. In the morning she finds the dead body of her husband. One of her children is carried off by a hawk, and the other is swept away by the river. As she proceeds to the city of Sāvatthi, she learns from a traveler that her mother and father and brother have perished in a whirlwind. Afar off she sees the

smoke of the funeral pyre. Instantly she goes mad, strips herself of her garments, and wanders hither and thither naked. Presently she comes into the presence of the Buddha. The Buddha bids her to return to her right mind. Instantly she returns to her right mind, crouches on the ground, and seeks refuge in the Buddha. A by-stander throws his cloak over her. The Buddha calms her sorrow, admonishing her that in previous states of existence she has shed tears of sorrow more abundant than the waters contained in the four oceans. Paṭācārā attains the Fruit of Conversion and becomes a nun. By meditating on vanishing drops of water, she attains Arahatship.

13. **Kisā Gotamī seeks mustard seed to cure her dead child** [viii. 15 = 114].

13 a. **Kisā Gotamī marries the son of a rich merchant.** One day all the wealth belonging to a rich merchant of Sāvatthi turns into charcoal. A friend of his directs him to expose the charcoal for sale, telling him that under certain conditions the charcoal will turn into gold and silver. The daughter of a poverty-stricken house, known by reason of the leanness of her body as Kisā Gotamī, stops at the door of his bazaar and asks him how he comes to be selling gold and silver. Taking a handful of the charcoal, she places it in the hands of the merchant, whereupon it turns into gold and silver. The merchant marries Kisā Gotamī to his son. He then gathers up his wealth, what was previously charcoal turning into gold and silver at his touch, and gives it all to her.

13 b. **Kisā Gotamī seeks mustard seed to cure her dead child.** In the course of time Kisā Gotamī gives birth to a son. The child dies as soon as he is old enough to walk. Kisā Gotamī, having never seen death before, forbids the body to be removed to the burning-ground, and taking her dead child on her hip, goes from house to house seeking medicine for her dead child. Every one thinks her crazy. A certain wise man sends her to the Buddha. Kisā Gotamī asks the Buddha whether he knows of medicine for her child. The Buddha replies that he does. The Buddha then directs her to procure a pinch of white mustard seed, cautioning her that she must procure it from a household no member of which has ever died. At every house she is told, "The living are few, but the dead are many." By degrees she comes to realize that she has taken upon herself a futile task. She returns to the Buddha without the mustard seed. The Buddha comforts her, admonishing her that death is common to all living beings. Kisā Gotamī attains the Fruit of Conversion and becomes a nun. One evening she watches a flickering lamp in the Hall of Confession. The thought is impressed upon her mind that the life of human beings flickers out precisely as does the light of the lamp. Taking this for her Subject of Meditation, she concentrates her mind on the thought and attains Arahatship.

14. **The widow Bahuputtikā and her ungrateful children** [viii. 16 = 115]. A widow with seven sons and seven daughters divides her property among her children, on the assurance of her sons that they will look after her. Her daughters and her daughters-in-law drive her from the houses of her sons. The widow thereupon becomes a nun and attains Arahatship.

Book IX. Evil, Pāpa Vagga

1. **The Brahman with a single robe** [ix. 1 = 116]. A Brahman and his wife possess a single undergarment each, and a single upper garment between them. One night the Brahman goes to hear the Law, and is seized with a desire to present the upper garment to the Teacher. Thereupon ensues a struggle between selfish and generous impulses which lasts through the three watches of the night. Finally the Brahman lays the upper garment at the feet of the Teacher, exclaiming, "I have

conquered!" King Pasenadi Kosala hears the Brahman's cry, asks him for an explanation, and upon learning what he has done, rewards him handsomely.

2. **A discontented monk** [**ix. 2 = 117**]. The Teacher rebukes a monk who allowed himself to fall into the sin of discontent many times.

3. **Goddess and monk** [**ix. 3 = 118**]. A young woman gives alms to Elder Kassapa the Great, dies of the bite of a snake, and is reborn as a goddess. For three days she secretly cares for the Elder's cell. When the Elder discovers that he has been waited upon by a goddess, he asks her to desist, that there may be no occasion for gossip. The goddess remonstrates, whereupon the Elder, losing his patience, snaps his fingers at her. The Teacher, without excusing the Elder, explains to the goddess the attitude of the Elder.

4. **Anâthapiṇḍika and the goddess** [**ix. 4–5 = 119–120**]. The treasurer Anāthapiṇḍika loses the greater part of his fortune, but keeps up his gifts to the Teacher. The goddess who resides over his gate reproaches him for his extravagant almsgiving, and urges him to abandon the Teacher and devote himself to business. The treasurer rebukes the goddess, and banishes her from his house. The goddess repents of her words, restores the treasurer's fortune, and seeks pardon from the treasurer and the Teacher.

5. **The monk who failed to keep his requisites in order** [**ix. 6 = 121**]. A monk who failed to keep his requisites in order, is summoned before the Teacher, and expresses little concern over what he has done, saying that he has committed only a slight fault. The Teacher rebukes him for regarding an evil deed as a small matter.

6. **Treasurer Catfoot** [**ix. 7 = 122**]. A layman listens to a sermon on almsgiving, invites the Teacher and his monks to a meal, and urges the people to give alms according to their means. A treasurer, believing that the layman is imposing on the people, gives him only a very small portion of alms, and on the following day goes to the layman's house intending to kill him in case he blames him for the smallness of his gift. The layman, however, prays that all who have given alms may receive a rich reward. The treasurer repents of his harsh judgment and asks pardon of the layman. The Teacher, learning of the incident, discourses on the high value of a small gift.

7. **Merchant Great-Wealth** [**ix. 8 = 123**]. A merchant sets out with his caravan, accompanied by five hundred monks, and halts for the night in a village at the entrance to the forest. A pack of thieves who are lying in wait for him send one of their number to find out his plans. The thief goes to a friend living in the village, learns from him that the merchant intends to set out on the third day, and so informs his companions. The villager tells the merchant that thieves are planning to attack him, whereupon the merchant decides to return home. The thieves learn of the merchant's decision through the villager, and immediately post themselves on the road leading in the opposite direction. The villager so informs the merchant, who then decides to remain where he is. The monks take leave of the merchant, go to the Teacher, and relate the whole story to him.

8. **The enchanted hunter** [**ix. 9 = 124**]. A rich man's daughter looks out of her window, sees a hunter pass through the street, and falls in love with him. Learning through her slave that he expects to leave the city on the following day, she leaves the house secretly, joins him on the road, and elopes with him. Seven sons are born to them, and in the course of time marry and set up households of their own. One day the Teacher, perceiving that the hunter and his sons and daughters-in-law are ripe for conversion, goes to where the nets are spread, leaves a footprint, and sits down under a bush. The hunter, having caught nothing, suspects that some one is setting the animals free; and when he sees the Teacher, draws his bow. By the power of the Teacher he is unable to release the arrow and remains rooted to the spot.

The same thing happens to his seven sons. The wife comes and exclaims, in riddling phrase, "Do not kill my father!" The hunter and his sons ask pardon of the Teacher and become his disciples. The monks complain that the wife, although a disciple of the Teacher, has assisted her husband to take life, but the Teacher assures them that such is not the case.

8 a. **Story of the Past: The city treasurer and the country treasurer.** In a previous state of existence a country treasurer bid against a city treasurer for the principal share in the building of a shrine for the relics of the Buddha Kassapa. When the city treasurer bid more than the country treasurer possessed, the latter offered to devote himself to the service of the shrine, together with his wife and his seven sons and seven daughters-in-law. The hunter was the country treasurer.

9. **The hunter who was devoured by his own dogs [ix. 10 = 125].** A hunter meets a monk, bags no game, blames the monk, and sets his dogs on him. The monk climbs a tree, and the hunter pierces the soles of his feet with the point of an arrow. The monk's cloak falls upon the hunter, completely covering him. The dogs, thinking that the monk has fallen from the tree, devour their own master. The monk, fearing that blame may attach to him, consults the Teacher. The Teacher reassures the monk and relates the following

9 a. **Story of the Past: Wicked physician, boys, and poisonous snake.** A physician seeking employment for his services would have allowed a snake to bite some little boys. But one of the boys threw the snake on the head of the physician, and he was bitten to death. The physician was the hunter.

10. **The jeweler, the monk, and the heron [ix. 11 = 126].** A jeweler's pet heron swallows a jewel before the eyes of a monk. The jeweler accuses the monk of having taken it, and when the latter denies his guilt, the jeweler beats him on the head until the blood flows. The heron drinks the blood of the monk, and the jeweler in anger kicks the heron out of the way and kills him. Then the monk tells the jeweler that the jewel was swallowed by the heron. The jeweler rips open the crop of the heron, finds the jewel, and asks the monk to pardon him for his hasty judgment. The monks ask the Teacher about the future state of the heron, the jeweler, the jeweler's wife, and the monk.

11. **Three parties of monks [ix. 12 = 127].** Three parties of monks set out to visit the Teacher, and each party meets with a strange experience by the way. **11 a.** The first party sees a crow burned to a crisp in mid-air. **11 b.** The second party sees the wife of a sea-captain cast overboard. **11 c.** Seven monks composing the third party are imprisoned in a cave for seven days. All three parties meet on the road, visit the Teacher together, and ask him to explain matters to them. The Teacher relates the following **Stories of the Past: 11 d.** The crow in a previous existence as a farmer of Benāres once burned a lazy ox to death. **11 e.** The wife of a sea-captain drowned her dog in a previous existence. **11 f.** The seven monks were once seven young cowherds who thoughtlessly allowed a lizard to remain imprisoned in an ant-hill for seven days. The monks then ask the Teacher whether there is any place where it is possible to escape from the consequences of an evil deed. The Teacher replies in the negative.

12. **Suppabuddha insults the Teacher [ix. 13 = 128].** Suppabuddha, angered at the Teacher because the latter renounced his daughter and assumed an attitude of hostility to his son, intoxicates himself, sprawls in the street, and refuses to let the Teacher pass. The Teacher utters the prediction that on the seventh day Suppabuddha will be swallowed up by the earth at the foot of his stairway. Suppabuddha learns of the Teacher's prediction, and imprisons himself on the top floor of his palace, causing the door to be barred and the stairway to be removed. On the seventh day his spirited horse breaks loose. As he starts for the door, all of the doors open of their

own accord, the stairways return to their proper places, his own guards seize him by the neck and throw him down, and when he lands at the foot of the stairway, the earth opens and swallows him up, and he is reborn in the Avīci hell.

Book X. The Rod or Punishment, Daṇḍa Vagga

1. **The Band of Six** [x. 1 = 129]. The Six Monks quarrel with the Seventeen Monks and strike them. The Teacher promulgates the precept regarding the delivering of blows.

2. **The Band of Six** [x. 2 = 130]. The Six Monks quarrel with the Seventeen Monks and strike them. Thereupon the Seventeen Monks make threatening gestures. The Teacher promulgates the precept regarding the making of threatening gestures.

3. **A company of boys** [x. 3–4 = 131–132]. The Teacher reproves some boys for beating a snake with a stick.

4. **The monk and the phantom** [x. 5–6 = 133–134]. A certain monk was accompanied wherever he went by the phantom of a woman, invisible to the monk himself, but visible to everybody else.

4 a. **Story of the Past: The goddess who took the form of a woman.** In a previous state of existence this monk was a goddess who caused a breach between two companion-monks by taking the form of a woman and making it appear that one of the monks had sinned with her. **End of Story of the Past.**

The monks ask the king to expel the monk from his kingdom. The king investigates the matter, discovers that the woman is a phantom, and out of pity for the monk provides him with shelter. The monk, reproached by his brethren, reviles them. The Teacher admonishes him to hold his tongue.

5. **Visākhā and her companions keep Fast-day** [x. 7 = 135]. Visākhā asks her companions why they keep Fast-day. The Teacher comments on their answers.

6. **The boa-constrictor ghost** [x. 8 = 136]. Moggallāna describes a ghost in the form of a boa-constrictor which he saw in torment. The Teacher relates the following

6 a. **Story of the Past: The treasurer Sumaṅgala and the thief.** A thief takes a dislike to the treasurer, and seven times burns his field, mutilates his cattle, and burns his house. Finally he burns the Perfumed Chamber. The treasurer joyfully builds another. The thief determines to kill him. The treasurer makes over to the thief the merit acquired by his almsgiving. The thief asks the treasurer for pardon. The ghost in the form of a boa-constrictor was none other than this thief.

7. **Death of Moggallāna the Great** [x. 9–12 = 137–140]. The envious sectaries hire thieves to kill Moggallāna. The Elder escapes the first time through the key-hole, the second time through the peak of the house. On their third attempt the thieves capture him, tear him limb from limb, and reduce his bones to powder. The Elder clothes himself with meditation as with a garment, takes leave of the Teacher, and passes into Nibbāna. King Ajātasattu sends spies to catch the thieves. The thieves betray themselves in a tavern, and are captured and burnt alive.

7 a. **Story of the Past: The son who killed his parents.** A wife takes a dislike to her husband's parents. The husband lures his parents into a forest and kills them. The son who killed his parents was Moggallāna.

8. **The monk of many possessions** [x. 13 = 141]. The Teacher rebukes a monk for indulging in luxuries. Angered at the rebuke, the monk strips off his outer garment and stands before the assemblage wearing only a loin-cloth. The Teacher expresses surprise at his action, and relates the following

8 a. **Story of the Past: Prince Mahiṁsāsa and the princes Moon and Sun.** The Future Buddha was reborn as Prince Mahiṁsāsa, eldest son of the King of Benāres. He had a younger brother named Prince Moon. On the death of their mother the

king takes a second wife, who gives birth to Prince Sun. The king promises the queen a boon, and she asks that her own son be given the kingdom. The king refuses, and fearing that the queen may harm his own children, sends them to the forest, telling them to return and take the kingdom when he is dead. Prince Sun accompanies them of his own accord. In the forest is a lake haunted by a water-demon who has received permission from Vessavaṇa to devour all those who cannot define the term "godlike." Princes Sun and Moon are imprisoned by the water-demon. Prince Mahiṁsāsa defines the term, converts the water-demon, and recovers his two brothers. On the death of the king, Prince Mahiṁsāsa returns to Benāres, accompanied by his two brothers and the water-demon, and takes the kingdom.

9. Santati the king's minister [x. 14 = 142]. As a reward for suppressing a rebellion, King Pasenadi gives Santati his kingdom for seven days and presents him with a nautch girl. For seven days Santati steeps himself in liquor, and on the seventh day sets out for the river, mounted on the state elephant. The Teacher predicts that Santati will attain Arahatship and pass into Nibbāna on that very day. The sectaries scoff and the orthodox rejoice. Santati returns to his drinking-hall and watches his nautch girl sing and dance. The nautch girl suddenly drops dead. Santati is at once sobered, and overwhelmed with grief goes to the Teacher. After listening to a brief discourse, Santati attains Arahatship and asks leave of the Teacher to pass into Nibbāna. The Teacher requests him first to declare to the multitude his meritorious deed in a previous birth. So Santati rises into the air to the height of seven palm-trees, and sitting cross-legged relates the following

9 a. Story of the Past: The preacher of the Law and the king. In the dispensation of the Buddha Vipassī I was reborn in the city of Bandhumatī and became a preacher of the Law. My meritorious deeds attracted the attention of the king, and he rewarded me handsomely.

Story of the Present concluded: Santati applies himself to meditation on the element of fire, enters into a state of trance, and passes into Nibbāna. Flames of fire consume his body, and his relics float to the ground. The monks ask the Teacher what title is most appropriate to Santati.

10. The Monk and the ragged garment [x. 15–16 = 143–144]. A monk overcomes discontent and attains Arahatship by contemplating a ragged garment which he wore as a layman.

11. Sukha the novice [x. 17 = 145].

11 a. Story of the Past: The treasurer Gandha, the laborer Bhattabhatika, and the Private Buddha. The treasurer Gandha resolves to spend his wealth in luxurious living before he dies. As he dines in state on the day of full moon, a poor villager asks him for his bowl of rice. Gandha refuses to give him the rice. The villager enters the treasurer's service and by working for three years earns a bowl of rice. Thus he gains the name Bhattabhatika. He presents the bowl of rice to a Private Buddha.

11 b. Story of the Present: Sukha the novice. In the dispensation of the present Buddha, Bhattabhatika is reborn in the household of a supporter of Elder Sāriputta. From the day of his conception no member of the household experiences sorrow, and therefore he is given the name Happy, Sukha. When he is seven years old, he becomes a novice of Elder Sāriputta. One day he accompanies the Elder on his rounds, sees ditch-diggers, fletchers, and carpenters at work, and asks the Elder many questions. The ease with which men control inanimate things suggests to the novice the thought of so controlling his reason as to win Arahatship. Sukha takes leave of the Elder, requesting him to bring him food of a hundred flavors, returns to his cell, and engages in meditation. At the command of Sakka, the Four Great Kings drive the noisy birds from the monastery park and keep watch over the four quarters, and the moon and the sun stand still. Sakka guards the string of the door, and the Buddha keeps watch over the gate. The Elder brings food of a hundred flavors, and the Teacher asks him four questions. Sukha overhears the Elder's answers and attains Arahatship.

Book XI. Old Age, Jarā Vagga

1. **Visākhā's companions intoxicate themselves** [xi. 1 = 146]. Five hundred clansmen entrust their wives to Visākhā, and carouse for seven days. Their wives drink the liquor which remains and become intoxicated. To escape punishment, they feign sickness, but their husbands find them out and beat them. Subsequently they accompany Visākhā to the monastery, carrying jugs of liquor concealed under their cloaks, drink the liquor secretly, become intoxicated, and commit gross improprieties in the presence of the Teacher. The Teacher subdues them with a ray of light from his eyebrow and reproves them.

2. **The Teacher cures a monk of love** [xi. 2 = 147]. The courtezan Sirimā offends against the lay disciple Uttarā, obtains pardon, and attains the Fruit of Conversion. From that time on she gives regularly the Eight Ticket-foods. A monk falls in love with her, abandons his monastic duties, and refuses to take food. Sirimā sickens and dies. By order of the Teacher the corpse is exposed for four days and offered for sale to the highest bidder. No one will take her even as a gift. The Teacher points to the corpse, and comments on the fact that her price was once a thousand pieces of money a night. The monk is cured of love.

3. **The aged nun** [xi. 3 = 148]. The Teacher addresses an aged nun who stumbles and falls.

4. **A company of over-confident monks** [xi. 4 = 149]. Five hundred over-confident monks are directed to meditate in a burning-ground. Their passions are aroused by contemplating the fresh corpses. The Teacher reproves them.

5. **The nun and the phantom** [xi. 5 = 150]. Janapada-Kalyāṇī became a nun, not because of faith, but solely out of regard for her kinsfolk, all of whom had adopted the religious life. Because of her beauty she bore the name Rūpanandā. Fearing that the Teacher might reproach her for her beauty, she avoided meeting him face to face. One day she goes to the monastery, mingling in the throng so that the Teacher will not see her. The Teacher creates the form of a beautiful woman, and causes her to pass through old age, disease, and death. Nandā is thus brought to a realization of the impermanence of all things. The Teacher compares the body to a city of bones.

6. **Queen Mallikā and her dog** [xi. 6 = 151]. Queen Mallikā goes to the bath-house with her pet dog, and commits the sin of bestiality. The king looks out of the palace window and sees her in the act. When the queen returns, the king rebukes her. The queen denies the accusation, and declares it to be a fact that whoever enters the bath-house appears double when seen from the window. To prove her statement, the queen has the king himself enter the bath-house. As soon as the king does so, the queen shouts to him from the window, asking him what he means by like misdoing with a she-goat. The king then believes the explanation given him by the queen. When Mallikā dies, she is tormented in hell for seven days as a punishment for her sin, and afterwards is reborn in the World of the Tusita Gods as a reward for her many good deeds. The king asks the Teacher where she has been reborn, and the Teacher tells him. The Teacher inspects the king's chariots, and comments on their decay.

7. **The monk who always said the wrong thing** [xi. 7 = 152]. A certain monk always says the wrong thing instead of the right thing. When the monks tell the Teacher of the mistakes he makes, the Teacher relates the following

7 a. **Story of the Past: Aggidatta, Somadatta, and the king.** A Brahman named Aggidatta had a son named Somadatta. Aggidatta tilled the soil, and Somadatta waited on the king. Aggidatta had two oxen. One day one of them died, and the

Brahman requested his son to ask the king for another. Somadatta, not wishing to presume upon the king's favor, insisted that the Brahman should go himself, and carefully instructed him how to act and what to say, teaching him a stanza ending with the words, "Pray give me another ox." The Brahman spent a year learning the stanza, but in presenting his petition to the king, said, "Pray take my other ox." The king smiled, and asked Somadatta how many oxen he had. "As many as you have given us," he replied. Pleased with the answer, the king presented the Brahman with sixteen oxen and other valuable gifts. Aggidatta was the monk who always said the wrong thing, and Somadatta was the Future Buddha.

8. Elder Ānanda's stanzas [xi. 8–9 = 153–154]. In answer to a question of Elder Ānanda, the Teacher recites the stanzas he recited on the Throne of Wisdom.

9. Great-Wealth, the treasurer's son [xi. 10–11 = 155–156]. Mahādhana falls into the hands of sycophants, and spends his fortune in riotous living. Reduced to penury in old age, he begs his food from door to door. The Teacher points him out to Elder Ānanda, and comments on his follies and wasted opportunities.

Book XII. Self, Atta Vagga

1. Prince Bodhi and the magic bird [xii. 1 = 157].

1 a. The prince, the builder, and the magic bird. A builder erects a magnificent palace for a prince. For fear he may build a similar palace for another, the prince determines to kill him. He confides his plan to a friend, who informs the builder. The builder thereupon shuts himself up in his workshop and fashions a huge wooden bird. When the bird is finished, the builder and his wife and children step inside of the bird, and the bird flies out of the window.

1 b. The prince entertains the Buddha. The prince gives a festival in honor of the completion of the palace, and invites the Buddha. Now the prince is childless, and therefore spreads mats on the floor, knowing that if he is destined to obtain children, the Buddha will tread on the mats; otherwise not. The Buddha refuses to enter the house until the prince has rolled up the mats. The prince asks the Buddha why he is destined to remain childless, and the Buddha relates the following

1 c. Story of the Past: The man who ate bird's eggs. A ship is wrecked at sea, and all on board are lost, except two persons, a man and his wife, who escape in safety to a neighboring island. The man and his wife, finding nothing else to eat, satisfy their hunger by eating bird's eggs. The man who ate bird's eggs was Prince Bodhi.

2. The greedy monk [xii. 2 = 158]. A greedy monk, skilled to teach the Law, visits one monastery after another and amasses a large number of robes and other requisites. As a fitting climax, he settles a dispute between two young monks over a fair division of two robes and a costly blanket, by awarding each of the monks a robe and himself taking the costly blanket. The monks complain to the Teacher, who relates the following

2 a. Story of the Past: The otters and the jackal. Two otters catch a redfish, and unable to effect a division satisfactory to both of them, appeal to a jackal for a decision. The jackal awards the head to one of the otters, the tail to the other, and takes the meaty portions for himself. The jackal was the greedy monk.

3. "Be ye doers of the word" [xii. 3 = 159]. A certain monk admonishes his fellows to apply themselves diligently to the practice of meditation, and himself spends the night in sleep. The monks discover his deceit and complain to the Teacher, who relates the Akālarāvi-kukkuṭa Jātaka.

4. "And hate not his father and mother" [xii. 4 = 160].

4 a. Birth of Kumāra Kassapa. A young wife, already pregnant, although she does not know it, becomes a nun of the faction of Devadatta. The nuns observe that she is pregnant and inform Devadatta, who directs that she be expelled from the Order. The nun appeals to the Buddha, a court is convened, Visākhā examines the nun, and her innocence is established. The nun gives birth to a son, who is adopted by the king. The youth is admitted to the Order, receiving the name Kumāra Kassapa, and attains Arahatship.

4 b. **"And hate not his father and mother."** For twelve years his mother grieves because of separation from her son. One day she meets him in the street and greets him affectionately. The son, fearing that if he returns her greeting it will prove her undoing, hardens his heart and speaks harshly to her. The mother uproots her affection for her son and straightway attains Arahatship. . The Teacher relates the Nigrodha Miga Jātaka.

5. **Killing of Mahā Kāla** [xii. 5 = 161]. As the layman Mahā Kāla, who has spent the night at the monastery listening to the Law, stands on the bank of the monastery pool, bathing his face, a thief runs by, and drops his spoils at the layman's feet. The pursuers of the thief, mistaking the layman for the real thief, seize him and beat him to death. Some monks find the layman's body, and report the incident to the Teacher, who thereupon relates the following

5 a. **Story of the Past: The soldier and the man with a beautiful wife.** A soldier, posted at the entrance to a forest to escort travelers back and forth, falls in love with the beautiful wife of a certain traveler. He inveigles the traveler into his house, places a precious stone in his carriage, and then accuses him of having stolen it. The traveler is convicted of the crime and is beaten to death. The soldier was the layman.

6. **Devadatta seeks to slay the Tathāgata** [xii. 6 = 162]. Devadatta seeks to slay the Tathāgata.

7. **Devadatta seeks to cause a schism in the Order** [xii. 7 = 163]. Devadatta informs Ānanda that he intends henceforth to keep Fast-day and to carry on the business of the Order apart from the Exalted One.

8. **The jealous monk** [xii. 8 = 164]. A certain monk dissuades a female lay disciple from going to hear the Teacher, fearing that if she does so, she will have no further use for him. One day the woman breaks with him, goes to the monastery, and listens to the Law. The monk follows her to the monastery, and urges the Teacher to modify his discourse to the woman. The Teacher rebukes him.

9. **Courtezans save a layman's life** [xii. 9 = 165]. As the layman Culla Kāla, who has spent the night at the monastery listening to the Law, stands on the bank of the monastery pool, bathing his face, thieves run by and drop their spoils at the layman's feet. The owners of the stolen property, mistaking the layman for one of the thieves, seize him and beat him. Passing courtezans obtain his release.

10. **By righteousness men honor the Buddha** [xii. 10 = 166]. From the day when the Teacher announces that in four months he will pass into Nibbāna, seven hundred monks spend their time in attendance upon him. And gathering in little groups, they ask each other, "What are we to do?" But a certain monk named Attadattha resolves to strive the more earnestly for the attainment of Arahatship. Accordingly Attadattha goes no more with the other monks. The monks, misunderstanding his motive, tell the Teacher that Attadattha has no affection for him. The Teacher admonishes them as follows: "Every other monk should show his affection for me just as Attadattha has done. For they that honor me with perfumes and garlands, honor me not; but they that practice the Higher and the Lower Law, they alone truly honor me."

Book XIII. The World, Loka Vagga

1. **A young girl jests with a young monk [xiii. 1 = 167].** While Visākhā's granddaughter is straining water for a young monk, she sees the reflection of her face in the water-vessel and laughs. The young monk also sees the reflection of her face and laughs. Thereupon the young girl remarks playfully, "He that laughs is a cut-head." The young monk is deeply offended, and bitter words follow. Both Visākhā and the Elder strive in vain to soothe the young monk's wounded feelings. Just then the Teacher draws near, and Visākhā relates the circumstances of the quarrel. The Teacher delivers a mild rebuke to the young girl and thus wins over the young monk.

2. **The Buddha visits Kapila [xiii. 2–3 = 168–169].** On the occasion of the Buddha's first visit to Kapila, he creates a jeweled walk in mid-air, whereon he paces back and forth preaching the Law. All his kinsfolk do reverence to him, and a shower of rain falls upon them. The Teacher relates the Vessantara Jātaka. | His kinsfolk depart without extending an invitation to him. On the following day the Teacher enters his father's city, and following the example of previous Buddhas, makes his round for alms from house to house. The king his father reproaches him, but the Teacher declares that he is but following the example of previous Buddhas.

3. **Five hundred monks attain Insight [xiii. 4 = 170].** Five hundred monks attain Insight by contemplating a mirage and bubbles of water.

4. **Prince Abhaya loses his nautch-girl [xiii. 5 = 171].** King Bimbisāra rewards his son Prince Abhaya for suppressing a rebellion by giving him a nautch-girl and conferring the kingdom on him for seven days. On the eighth day, while the nautch-girl is dancing before the prince, she suddenly drops dead. Overwhelmed with sorrow, the prince seeks consolation from the Teacher. The Teacher consoles him.

5. **The monk with a broom [xiii. 6 = 172].** A certain monk spent all of his time sweeping the rooms of the monastery. Admonished by the Elder Revata to devote a portion of his time to the practice of meditation, he obeyed the Elder's admonition and in a short time attained Arahatship.

6. **Conversion of the robber Finger-garland [xiii. 7 = 173].** A bloodthirsty robber infested the realm of King Pasenadi Kosala. He killed man after man, and wore a garland made of their fingers. One day the Buddha set out on the highway where this robber lurked. Warned that as many as forty men at a time had perished at the hands of this robber, the Buddha continued on his way in silence. When the robber saw the Buddha, he determined to kill him, and arming himself, followed close behind him. Then the Buddha effected such an exercise of supernatural power that although the robber was hurrying with all his might and the Buddha himself was walking at his ordinary gait, the robber was unable to catch up with him. Dumfounded, the robber called out, "Stand still, hermit!" Continuing his walk, the Buddha replied, "I stand still! Stand still yourself!" "What do you mean?" asked the robber. The Buddha replied, "I abide steadfast evermore, for I am merciful to all living beings. But you are merciless to living beings. Therefore I stand still, but you do not stand still." Thereupon the robber flung away his weapons and became a monk.

The king's subjects complained of the depredations of the robber and begged the king to adopt repressive measures. The king went to the Buddha, told him his troubles, and confessed that he was unable to subdue the robber. The Buddha asked the king what he would do were he to see this same robber in the robes of a monk. The king replied that he would treat him with the respect due a monk. The Buddha pointed to a monk who sat quite near him, and said, "Here he is!" The king was terror-stricken. The Buddha assured him that he had nothing to fear. The king, recovering his composure, paid his respects to the monk, and expressing to the Buddha his surprise at the conversion of the robber, took his leave.

One day, as the Elder Finger-garland was making his round, he saw a woman in the throes of childbirth. "Alas, living beings must needs suffer!" thought he, and returning to the Teacher, told him of his experience. The Teacher directed him to go and say to the woman, "From the day I was born I have never deliberately deprived living beings of life. If this be true, may health be to you, health to your unborn child." The Elder protested that this would be a deliberate falsehood. Then the Teacher told him to say, "From the day I was born of the Noble Birth." The Elder did so, and the woman was safely delivered of her child.

Shortly afterwards the Elder attained Arahatship. One day as he was making his round in Sāvatthi, he was hit by a clod of earth, a stick, and a stone. The Teacher explained to him that this was the result of his evil deeds, on account of which he might have been tormented in Hell for many thousands of years. After breathing forth many Solemn Utterances the Elder passed into Nibbāna. The monks discussed among themselves the Elder's place of rebirth, and the Teacher informed them that he had passed into Nibbāna. The monks expressed surprise that one who had committed so many murders should pass into Nibbāna.

7. The weaver's daughter [xiii. 8 = 174]. The Teacher once visited Āḷavi and urged the people to meditate upon death. With one exception, all those who heard his discourse remained absorbed in their worldly affairs as before. But a certain weaver's daughter did naught else for three years but meditate upon death. When the Teacher visited Āḷavi three years later, the people flocked to the monastery, and the weaver's daughter was all eagerness to see him. Just then her father set out for his workshop and ordered her to replenish the shuttle and bring it to him with all speed. So she sat down and replenished the shuttle. Meanwhile the Teacher waited for her to come. On her way to her father's workshop she stopped at the monastery. The Teacher asked her four questions, and she answered them all correctly. These were the four: "Whence comest thou?" "I know not." "Whither goest thou?" "I know not." "Thou knowest not?" "I know." "Thou knowest?" "I know not." When the multitude murmured, the Teacher asked her to explain her answers, which she did as follows: "I know not whence came I when I was reborn here. I know not where I shall be reborn. I know that I shall surely die. I know not at what time I shall die." The Teacher then pronounced a stanza, at the conclusion of which she was established in the Fruit of Conversion. She then took her shuttle-basket and went to her father's workshop, finding him asleep. As her father awoke, he gave the loom a pull. The tip of the loom struck the maiden in the breast and killed her. The father, overcome with grief, sought consolation of the Teacher, entered the Order, and shortly afterwards attained Arahatship.

8. Thirty monks [xiii. 9 = 175]. Thirty monks visit the Teacher, attain Arahatship, and depart through the air.

9. Ciñcā falsely accuses the Buddha [xiii. 10 = 176]. The envious sectaries conspire with a wandering nun named Ciñcā to bring a charge of incontinence against the Buddha. In the evening, when the disciples are returning from Jetavana, she walks in the direction of Jetavana. When the disciples ask her where she is going, she tells them that it is none of their business. Having spent the night at the monastery of the sectaries, she walks back in the morning when the disciples are on their way to Jetavana. When they ask her where she has spent the night, she returns the same answer. After a month or two, she declares openly that she spends the night with the Buddha in the Perfumed Chamber. After three or four months have passed, she wraps her belly about with bandages to create the impression that she is pregnant, and declares that she has conceived a child by the Buddha. When eight or nine months have passed, she fastens a disk of wood to her belly, produces swellings all over her body by pounding herself with the jaw-bone of an ox, and going to the Hall of Truth, publicly accuses the Buddha of being responsible for her condition. The Buddha replies, " Sister, whether that which you have said be true or false, that is known only to you and to me." At that moment Sakka approaches with four deities in the form of little mice. With one bite of their teeth the mice sever the cords with which the disk of wood is fastened to the belly of the woman, the disk falls upon her feet, cutting off all of her toes, the earth yawns and swallows her up, and she is reborn in the Avīci hell. On the following day the monks comment on the incident, and the Teacher relates the following

9 a. **Story of the Past: The lewd woman and the virtuous youth, Mahā Paduma Jātaka.** In a previous state of existence Ciñcā was the chief consort of the king, the fellow of the mother of the Future Buddha. She invited the Great Being to lie with her, and when he refused to do so, falsely accused him before the king. The king caused the youth to be flung from Robbers' Cliff, but the deity of the mountain saved his life, and entrusted him to the care of the King of the Dragons. Subsequently the youth retired to the Himālaya and adopted the life of a religious. The king, learning where he was, went to him and offered him his kingdom. The youth refused. The king, discovering the falsity of the charge, caused the wicked queen to be flung from Robbers' Cliff.

10. **Gifts beyond Compare [xiii. 11 = 177].** King Pasenadi Kosala and his subjects bestow alms six times in succession, each striving to outdo the other. Finally the king bestows the Gifts beyond Compare, spending thereon fourteen crores of treasure in a single day. Five hundred elephants stand beside the monks, each bearing a parasol in his trunk. A rogue elephant is placed beside Añgulimāla; the elephant behaves perfectly, and Añgulimāla shows no signs of fear. Of the king's two ministers, Kāla expresses regret that the king should expend so much money on offerings, while Juṇha is filled with joy. The Teacher refrains from pronouncing words of thanksgiving appropriate to the gifts which the king has presented, lest Kāla's head split into seven pieces. The king, grievously disappointed, asks the Teacher for an explanation. The Teacher reassures the king, and contrasts the attitudes of Kāla and Juṇha.

11. **Virtue bought and paid for [xiii. 12 = 178].** Anāthapiṇḍika has a son named Kāla who is irreligious and disobedient. He promises to give him a thousand pieces of money if he will memorize a single Sacred Stanza. Kāla goes to the Teacher, memorizes the stanza, and is established in the Fruit of Conversion. The king, pleased with the demeanor of his son, offers him the thousand pieces of money in the presence of the Teacher. The son refuses to accept the money. The Teacher comments on the high excellence of the Fruit of Conversion.

Book XIV. The Enlightened, Buddha Vagga

1. **The Buddha has naught to do with women [xiv. 1–2 = 179–180].**

1 a. **The Buddha spurns the maiden Māgandiyā.** A Brahman named Māgandiya offers to give the Buddha his beautiful daughter Māgandiyā to wife. The Buddha makes no reply, but moves away from the spot, leaving a footprint. The Brahman goes home and returns with his wife and daughter. The Brahman's wife examines the footprint and declares it to be the footprint of one who has renounced the lusts of the flesh. When the Brahman presents his daughter to the Buddha, the Buddha spurns her and tells the Brahman that he has naught to do with women. By way of illustration he tells the Brahman the story of his temptation by the daughters of Māra.

1 b. **The Buddha spurns the Daughters of Māra.** From the day of the Great Retirement, Māra pursues the Buddha relentlessly for seven years. Then Māra's three daughters assume each the forms of a hundred women of various ages, and tempt the Buddha six times. The Buddha, however, spurns them.

2. **The Twin Miracle [xiv. 3 = 181].**

2 a. **Piṇḍola Bhāradvāja performs a miracle.** A treasurer of Rājagaha finds a block of red-sandalwood in the Ganges, fashions it in the form of a bowl, suspends the bowl from a series of bamboos, and offers to give it to whoever can fly through the air and take it. Six religious teachers, of whom Nāthaputta is the most conspicuous, seek in vain to obtain the bowl. Piṇḍola Bhāradvāja flies around the city of Rājagaha, balancing on his toe a rock as big as the city itself, and wins the bowl. The Buddha rebukes Piṇḍola, and forbids his disciples to perform any more miracles.

2 b. **The Buddha promises to perform a miracle.** The sectaries rejoice, thinking that the Buddha will consider himself bound by his own precept. The Buddha assures King Bimbisāra that such is not the case, and promises the king to perform a miracle at Sāvatthi four months later. The sectaries pursue the Buddha to Sāvatthi, erect a pavilion, and proclaim their intention of performing a miracle. King Pasenadi Kosala offers to erect a pavilion for the Buddha. The Buddha informs the king that Sakka will erect a pavilion for him, and that he will perform his miracle at the foot of Gaṇḍa's mango tree. The sectaries straightway tear up by the roots all of the mango trees for a league around.

2 c. **Preliminary miracles.** By command of the Buddha, Gaṇḍa, the king's gardener, plants a mango, and straightway there springs up a mango tree fifty cubits in height. By command of Sakka the deity Wind-cloud uproots the pavilion of the sectaries, the deity Sun scorches them with his rays, and the deity Wind-cloud sprinkles them with dust and rain. Naked as they are, they flee helter-skelter; and the naked ascetic Pūraṇa Kassapa commits suicide and is reborn in the Avīci hell. The Buddha creates a jeweled walk in the sky. A multitude assembles, covering a space thirty-six leagues in extent, and many disciples, wishing to share the Teacher's burden, offer to perform miracles. Among those who offer to perform miracles are Gharaṇī, Culla Anāthapiṇḍika, Cīrā, Cunda, Uppalavaṇṇā, and Moggallāna. Moggallāna offers to swallow Mount Sineru, to roll up the earth like a mat, to spin the earth like a potter's wheel, to place the earth in his left hand and remove the inhabitants elsewhere, and to pace back and forth in the air carrying the earth balanced on Mount Sineru like an umbrella. The Buddha declines assistance, declares that he must bear his own burden, and relates the Kaṇha Usabha Jātaka and the Nandi Visāla Jātaka.

2 d. **The Buddha performs the Twin Miracle.** As the Buddha paces back and forth along the jeweled walk, preaching the Law to the multitude, he causes at one and the same time flames of fire and streams of water to proceed forth from every pore of his body. Moreover he creates a double, who exchanges question and answer with him, who sits when he stands, and stands when he sits.

2 e. **The Ascent of the Buddha to the World of the Thirty-three.** In three strides the Buddha ascends to the World of the Thirty-three, and seats himself upon the Yellowstone throne. Anuruddha informs the multitude that the Buddha has ascended to the World of the Thirty-three to expound the Abhidhamma to his mother, and that he will return in three months. The multitude accordingly pitches camp in the open air against his return. According to instructions previously received from the Buddha, Moggallāna expounds the Law to the multitude, and Culla Anāthapiṇḍika provides them with food. As the Buddha sits on the Yellowstone throne, his mother sits on his right hand, the deity Indaka on his right, and the deity Aṅkura on his left. Indaka outshines Aṅkura because, although in a previous state of existence Aṅkura set up a row of braziers twelve leagues long and gave abundant alms, Indaka once

gave a monk a spoonful of his own food. The Buddha expounds the Abhidhamma for the benefit of his mother for the space of three months without interruption, creating a double to take his place whenever he has occasion to leave. Sāriputta ascends to the World of the Thirty-three, receives the Abhidhamma from the lips of the Teacher, and returning to the world, expounds the seven books to the five hundred monks who compose his retinue. These five hundred monks are the first to receive the Abhidhamma because in a previous state of existence as little bats they listened to the recitation of the Abhidhamma by two monks.

2 f. **The Descent of the Buddha and attendant deities.** Seven days before the festival of Pavāraṇā the waiting multitude request the Elder Moggallāna to ascertain when the Buddha will descend from the World of the Thirty-three. Moggallāna ascends to the World of the Thirty-three and learns from the Buddha that he will descend with attendant deities at the gate of the city of Saṁkassa after seven days. On the festival of Pavāraṇā the Buddha, standing on the summit of Mount Sineru, performs the Twin Miracle, surveys countless thousands of worlds, and descends to earth. The Buddha himself descends on a ladder of jewels, the Thirty-three deities on a ladder of gold to the right, and Mahā Brahmā on a ladder of silver to the left. Sāriputta is the first to greet the Buddha, who pronounces the stanza "They that are devoted to meditation," establishing Sāriputta's retinue in Arahatship. The Buddha puts questions to his disciples, praises Sāriputta's answer, and relates the Parosahassa Jātaka.

3. **The king of the dragons and his daughter [xiv. 4 = 182].** A monk breaks off a blade of grass, and dying unconfessed, is reborn as a dragon. Subsequently a daughter is born to him. The dragon places his daughter within his hood and causes her to dance and sing a riddling stanza. Uttara sings in reply a stanza taught him by the Buddha. The dragon, knowing from the stanza that a Buddha has appeared in the world, visits the Buddha, and tells him his story. The Buddha discourses on the difficulty of attaining rebirth as a human being.

4. **How did the Seven Buddhas keep Fast-day? [xiv. 5–7 = 183–185].** Ānanda asks the Buddha how the Seven Buddhas observed Fast-day. The Buddha replies that their mode of keeping Fast-day was the same, and that they admonished their hearers with the same stanzas.

5. **The Buddha cures a monk of discontent [xiv. 8–9 = 186–187].** The father of a young monk dies, leaving him a hundred pieces of money. The monk becomes discontented, and decides to leave the Order. The Buddha proves to him that the money which he has inherited is insufficient to satisfy his desires, and relates the Mandhātu Jātaka.

6. **The monk and the dragon [xiv. 10–14 = 188–192].** Aggidatta, the house-priest of Mahā Kosala, retires from the world and adopts the life of a hermit. He instructs the monks of his retinue, in case they are troubled with unlawful thoughts, to fill a jar with sand and empty it in a certain place. A great heap of sand arises, and Ahicchatta king of the dragons takes possession of it. Aggidatta urges his disciples to seek refuge in mountains and forests as a means of obtaining release from suffering. The Buddha and Elder Moggallāna visit Aggidatta. Moggallāna obtains leave of Aggidatta to spend the night on the heap of sand. Moggallāna and the dragon spit fire at each other, and the dragon is put to rout. The people are amazed at Moggallāna's power. Moggallāna modestly points to the Buddha as his Teacher, and the Buddha discourses on the Refuges.

7. **Whence come men of noble birth? [xiv. 15 = 193].** Ānanda asks the Buddha from what region come men of noble birth. The Buddha replies, "The Central Region."

8. **What is the pleasantest thing in the world? [xiv. 16 = 194].** The Buddha

admonishes some monks who are discussing the question, "What is the pleasantest thing in the world?"

9. **Honor to whom honor is due** [xiv. 17–18 = 195–196]. A Brahman reverences a certain shrine, but omits to reverence the Buddha. The Buddha praises him, and admonishes the monks to render honor to whom honor is due.

Book XV. Happiness, Sukha Vagga

1. **A quarrel among brethren** [xv. 1–3 = 197–199]. The Sākiyas and the Koliyas quarrel over the diversion of the waters of the river Rohinī. The Buddha rebukes them and puts a stop to the quarrel.

2. **Māra possesses villagers** [xv. 4 = 200]. The Buddha enters the village Pañcasālā to preach the Law to five hundred maidens. Māra possesses the bodies of the villagers so that they give the Buddha no alms. The Buddha rebukes Māra.

3. **Defeat of the King of Kosala** [xv. 5 = 201]. The King of Kosala, thrice defeated in battle by his nephew Ajātasattu, takes to his bed and refuses to eat. The matter is reported to the Buddha, who comments on the evils which follow both victory and defeat.

4. **"Look not on a woman to lust after her"** [xv. 6 = 202]. The Buddha attends a wedding. The young husband, fired with lust for his bride, ignores the Buddha. The Buddha causes the bride to vanish from the sight of her husband, and admonishes the husband on the evils of the lusts of the flesh.

5. **The Buddha feeds the hungry** [xv. 7 = 203]. The Buddha goes to Āḷavi to preach the Law to a certain poor man. The poor man goes to seek his ox which was lost, and the Buddha waits for him to return. When he returns, the Buddha, observing that he is hungry, directs that food be given to him. The monks murmur, and the Buddha rebukes them.

6. **On moderation in eating** [xv. 8 = 204]. King Pasenadi Kosala visits the Buddha, suffering from over-indulgence in food. The Buddha admonishes the king on the evils of over-eating and pronounces two stanzas on the subject, which the king is unable to memorize. The Buddha therefore causes the king's nephew to memorize the stanzas and to pronounce them before the king at meal-time. The king takes the hint, diminishes his food, and improves in health. Later on the king visits the Buddha and tells him how much he has improved in health and spirits.

7. **By righteousness men honor the Buddha** [xv. 9 = 205]. From the day when the Teacher announces that in four months he will pass into Nibbāna, seven hundred monks of his retinue are overwhelmed with fear, and gather in little groups and ask each other, "What are we to do?" But a certain monk named Tissa resolves to strive the more earnestly for the attainment of Arahatship. Accordingly he adopts the Four Postures and keeps residence by himself. The monks, misunderstanding his motive, tell the Teacher that Tissa has no affection for him. The Teacher admonishes them as follows: "Only he that is like Tissa has real affection for me. For though men honor me with perfumes and garlands, they honor me not. But they that practice the Higher and the Lower Law, they alone truly honor me."

8. **Sakka ministers to the Buddha** [xv. 10–12 = 206–208]. At the close of the Buddha's life, when he is suffering from an attack of dysentery, Sakka comes and ministers to him. When the monks express surprise at Sakka's ministrations, the Buddha tells them that Sakka is merely returning favor for favor. To make the matter clear, the Buddha tells the monks the story of how Sakka once came to him terrified with the fear of death and of how he reassured him.

Book XVI. Objects of Affection, Piya Vagga

1. **Mother and father and son** [xvi. 1–3 = 209–211]. A youth retires from the world, in spite of the opposition of his parents. His father and mother follow his example. Mother and father and son, even after their retirement from the world, are unable to remain apart. The Buddha reproves them for not suppressing human affections.

2. **The Buddha comforts the afflicted** [xvi. 4 = 212]. A certain layman loses his son, and is unable to restrain his grief. The Buddha visits him and comforts him, admonishing him that death is common to all. The Buddha urges the layman to meditate upon death after the example of wise men of old, and relates the Uraga Jātaka.

3. **The Buddha comforts the afflicted** [xvi. 5 = 213]. Visākhā loses her granddaughter Dattā, and is unable to restrain her grief. The Buddha asks her to consider how many persons die daily, and convinces her that grief is unprofitable.

4. **The Licchavi princes and the courtezan** [xvi. 6 = 214]. The Licchavi princes fall to fighting over the possession of a courtezan, and are carried into the city on litters. The Buddha comments on the evils of the lusts of the flesh.

5. **The golden maiden** [xvi. 7 = 215]. A youth with a repugnance for women causes a golden image to be made in the form of a woman of surpassing beauty, offering to marry the maiden who possesses equal beauty, if such can be found. Brahmans find a maiden whose beauty far surpasses the beauty of the image, and so report to the youth's parents. The youth is all eagerness to see her. As the Brahmans are conducting her to the house of her future husband, she suddenly drops dead. The youth is inconsolable, takes to his bed, and refuses to eat. The Buddha convinces the youth that love is the cause of his grief, and establishes him in the Fruit of Conversion.

6. **Set not your heart on worldly possessions** [xvi. 8 = 216]. A Brahman promises the Buddha, in case his crop prospers, to divide with him. When he is on the point of fulfilling his promise, a severe storm ruins his crop. The Brahman, overcome with grief, takes to his bed and refuses to eat. The Buddha convinces him that desire is the cause of his grief, and establishes him in the Fruit of Conversion.

7. **Kassapa wins a basket of cakes** [xvi. 9 = 217]. Some youths carrying baskets of cakes on their shoulders pass the Buddha and his retinue without so much as offering them a cake. But when Elder Kassapa appears, they are all politeness and offer him everything they have. The Buddha comments approvingly on the delight with which men honor a monk like Kassapa.

8. **The Elder who had attained the Fruit of the Third Path** [xvi. 10 = 218]. An Elder who has attained the Fruit of the Third Path, dies without answering a question his brother monks asked him with reference to his attainment of Specific Attainment. The monks carry their grief to the Buddha, who comforts them, assuring them that their brother has been reborn in the Pure Abode.

9. **Nandiya attains heavenly glory** [xvi. 11–12 = 219–220]. Nandiya marries his uncle's daughter, inherits great wealth, and erects a dwelling for the monks. As the result of this gift, a palace of jewels arises in the World of the Thirty-three. One day Moggallāna visits the World of the Thirty-three, and is informed by celestial nymphs that the palace is the result of Nandiya's gift. Returning to the world of men, he asks the Buddha whether men may attain heavenly glory even in this life. The Buddha reminds him of what he has seen with his own eyes, and adds that when a man who has wrought works of merit goes to the next world, he is greeted by the deities as warmly as a man who has been long absent from home is greeted by his kinsfolk.

Book XVII. Anger, Kodha Vagga

1. How anger marred a maiden's looks [xvii. 1 = 221].

1 a. The maiden with blotches on her face. Elder Anuruddha once visits Kapilavatthu and is greeted by all of his kinsfolk except his sister Rohiṇī, who remains at home on account of an eruption of the skin. The Elder causes her to be summoned, and admonishes her to perform works of merit. He suggests that she build an assembly-hall. Rohiṇī follows her brother's advice, and the eruption immediately disappears. Subsequently Rohiṇī entertains the Buddha. The Buddha informs her that anger was the cause of her skin-disease, and relates the following

1 b. Story of the Past: The jealous queen and the nautch-girl. The chief consort of the King of Benāres once took a dislike to a nautch-girl, and determined to get even with her. So she reduced a number of large ripe scabs to powder, and covered the girl's body with the powder. The result was that the girl's body became covered with sores. The jealous queen was Rohiṇī.

1 c. Sequel: The celestial nymph. As the result of her gift of an assembly-hall, Rohiṇī is reborn as a celestial nymph. Four deities quarrel over her, but yield her to Sakka. She becomes Sakka's darling and delight.

2. The tree-spirit and the monk [xvii. 2 = 222]. A certain monk determines to build him a lodging, and sets about to cut down a tree. The tree-spirit begs him to desist, but he refuses to do so. The spirit, thinking that the sight of her child will touch the monk, places her child on a branch of the tree. The monk, unable to check the force of his upraised axe, cuts off the arm of the child. The tree-spirit restrains her impulse to kill the monk, and reports the matter to the Buddha. The Buddha commends her for her self-restraint, and assigns her another tree.

3. The poor man and his daughter [xvii. 3 = 223].

3 a. Puṇṇa acquires merit. A poor man named Puṇṇa worked for the treasurer Sumana, and his wife and daughter Uttarā were servants in the treasurer's household. On a certain holiday Puṇṇa directs his wife to prepare a double portion of rice, and spends the morning plowing as usual. Sāriputta goes to the field where Puṇṇa is plowing, and Puṇṇa gives him a toothstick and strains water for him. Puṇṇa's wife sets out for the field with her husband's meal, but meeting Sāriputta, gives him the rice. Returning home, she prepares a second portion of rice for her husband, takes the rice to him, and explains the reason for her delay. Puṇṇa, overjoyed at what he has heard, but utterly weary, lies down and goes to sleep.

When Puṇṇa awakens the following morning, he discovers that the field which he plowed the previous day has turned to gold. He informs the king, who orders that the gold be hauled to the palace. As the king's men gather up the gold, they say, "This is the property of the king." Immediately the gold turns to dust. The king orders them to say, "This is the property of Puṇṇa," and immediately the dust turns to gold again. The king appoints Puṇṇa treasurer, bestows all of the wealth upon him, and gives him a site for a house. Puṇṇa builds him a house, entertains the Buddha, and together with his wife and daughter Uttarā, attains the Fruit of Conversion.

3 b. Uttarā and Sirimā. Uttarā becomes the wife of the treasurer Sumana's son. Now the treasurer Sumana and all the members of his household were unbelievers; and Uttarā was unable for some time to perform any of the duties of her religion. Finally, at the suggestion of her father, she installs the courtezan Sirimā in her household as her husband's mistress, and her husband consents to the arrangement. Sirimā lives in the house for a fortnight, quite ignorant of her real position in the household, imagining herself to be the real mistress of the household. Uttarā spends her time in the kitchen, preparing food for the monks. Her husband sees her and laughs. Sirimā sees him laugh, and furiously jealous of Uttarā, enters the kitchen and throws boiling ghee on her head. Uttarā escapes injury by making an Act of Truth. The serving-women belabor Sirimā with blows, but Uttarā rescues her and bathes her with hot water and oil. Sirimā then realizes that her position in the household is that of a concubine, repents of her act, and asks Uttarā to pardon her. Uttarā promises to pardon her if the Buddha will pardon her. The Buddha admonishes Sirimā that anger should be overcome with kindness, and pronounces a stanza, establishing her in the Fruit of Conversion.

4. **Do trifling acts of merit lead to heaven? [xvii. 4 = 224].** Moggallāna goes to heaven and asks the deities to tell him through what acts of merit they attained heavenly glory. The deities mention trifling acts of merit, such as telling the truth, not getting angry, giving small gifts. Moggallāna returns to earth and asks the Buddha whether such trifling acts of merit really lead to heaven. The Buddha assures him that they do.

5. **A Brahman greets the Buddha as his son [xvii. 5 = 225].** The Buddha is entertained by an old Brahman and his wife, who greet him as their son. The monks express surprise that the Buddha should acquiesce in this form of address. The Buddha tells them that in five hundred states of existence the Brahman and his wife were his father and mother, in five hundred more his uncle and aunt, and in five hundred more his grandfather and grandmother. The old Brahman and his wife attain Arahatship and pass into Nibbāna. The Buddha follows their bodies to the burning-ground, and discourses to the monks on the bliss of Nibbāna.

6. **It is the giver that makes the gift [xvii. 6 = 226].** A female slave presents the Buddha with a cake made of rice-dust. The Buddha accepts the cake, and relates to the monks the Kuṇḍaka-sindhavapotaka Jātaka.

7. **Nothing, too much, and too little [xvii. 7–10 = 227–230].** The layman Atula blames Revata for saying nothing, Sāriputta for saying too much, and Ānanda for saying too little. The Buddha admonishes him that no one deserves unqualified blame, and no one unqualified praise.

8. **The Band of Six [xvii. 11–14 = 231–234].** The Six Monks put on wooden shoes and make a great clatter. The Buddha admonishes the monks to restrain themselves in deeds, words, and thoughts.

Book XVIII. Blemishes, Mala Vagga

1. **The cow-killer and his son [xviii. 1–4 = 235–238].** A cow-killer, angered at the failure of his wife to provide beef for his supper, cuts off the tongue of a live ox, has it cooked, and sits down to eat. The moment he places a piece of ox-tongue in his mouth, his own tongue is cleft in twain and falls out of his mouth. The cow-killer crawls about on his hands and knees, bellowing like an ox, dies shortly afterwards, and is reborn in the Avīci hell. The son flees in terror to Takkasilā, and becomes apprenticed to a goldsmith. The goldsmith so admires the young man's work that he gives him his daughter in marriage. Subsequently the cow-killer's son goes to live with his own sons, who have become disciples of the Buddha. One day his sons entertain the Buddha, who admonishes the father to make provision for his journey to the next world.

2. **Little by little [xviii. 5 = 239].** A certain Brahman clears away the grass from the place where the monks vest themselves, covers the place with sand, erects a pavilion and a hall, and gives a festival in honor of the completion of the hall. The Buddha praises the Brahman for laying up spiritual treasure little by little.

3. The louse that would have his own [xviii. 6 = 240]. A certain monk is presented with a coarse cloth eight cubits in length. From this material his sister weaves a fine cloth nine cubits in length, and the monk has a robe made of it. He dies suddenly in the night, and is reborn as a louse in his own robe. When the monks undertake to divide the robe among them, the louse runs back and forth screaming, "These monks are stealing my property." The Teacher hears his words by Supernatural Audition, and directs the robe to be laid aside for seven days. On the seventh day the louse dies, and is reborn in the World of the Tusita gods. On the eighth day the Teacher directs the robe to be divided among the monks, explains the reason for the delay, and discourses on the corroding effect of desire.

4. Pride goeth before a fall [xviii. 7 = 241]. A certain monk boasts of his ability to expound the Law, but fails miserably when put to the test. His indignant hearers drive him away with sticks and stones, and he falls into a cesspool. The Teacher tells the monks that it is not the first time he has wallowed in a cesspool, and relates the Sūkara Jātaka.

5. The wickedness of women [xviii. 8–9 = 242–243]. A young man who has been greatly embarrassed by the wicked ways of his wife, visits the Buddha. The Buddha compares women to rivers, and relates the Anabhirati Jātaka.

6. Courtesy and rudeness [xviii. 10–11 = 244–245]. A certain monk receives a portion of choice food, and offers it to an Elder. The Elder walks away without so much as thanking him. The Buddha contrasts the easy life of the shameless with the hard life of the modest.

7. All of the precepts are hard to keep [xviii. 12–14 = 246–248]. Five hundred laymen, each of whom keeps one of the precepts, fall into a dispute as to which of the precepts is the hardest to keep. The Buddha admonishes them that all of the precepts are hard to keep.

8. The fault-finding novice [xviii. 15–16 = 249–250]. A certain monk finds fault with everybody, and boasts about his kinsfolk. The monks send some novices to look up his antecedents, and the novices report that he is of humble origin. The Buddha informs the monks that it is not the first time the novice has so conducted himself, and relates the Kaṭāhaka Jātaka.

9. The inattentive laymen [xviii. 17 = 251]. Five laymen go to the monastery to hear the Law. During the Buddha's sermon the first falls asleep, the second digs the earth with his finger, the third shakes a tree, the fourth gazes at the sky; the fifth alone listens to the Law. The Buddha informs Ānanda that in five hundred successive existences the first was a dragon, the second an earthworm, the third a monkey, the fourth an astrologer, and the fifth a repeater of the Veda. What they did, they did from the force of habit.

10. Treasurer Ram [xviii. 18 = 252].

10 a. Frame-Story begun: The Buddha visits Treasurer Ram.

10 b. How did Treasurer Ram get his name? Treasurer Ram was so called because he possessed golden rams.

10 c. Story of the Past: How Treasurer Ram came to possess golden rams. In the dispensation of the Buddha Vipassī Treasurer Ram erected an elephant-stable ornamented with golden rams.

10 d. Story of the Past: How Treasurer Ram and his family came to possess magical power. In the present dispensation Treasurer Ram and his family presented a pint-pot of rice in time of famine to a Private Buddha, each member of the family making an Earnest Wish. Treasurer Ram's granaries were immediately filled to overflowing, and both he and his family were endowed with magical power.

10 e. Treasurer Ram and his family exhibit their magical power. Treasurer Ram causes his granaries to be swept, bathes his head, sits down at the door of each granary, looks up at the sky, and one after another his granaries are filled with ruddy rice. His wife adorns herself, prepares a pint-pot of boiled rice, doles out rice with a golden spoon to all who come, and the pint-pot of rice suffers no diminution. His son bathes his head, fills a purse with a thousand pieces of money, doles out money to all who come, and the thousand pieces of money suffer no diminution. His daughter-in-law adorns herself, fills a basket with seed-rice, doles out seed-rice to all who come, and the basket of seed-rice suffers no diminution. His slave adorns himself, yokes his oxen, and plows seven furrows at once.

10 a. **Frame-Story concluded: Treasurer Ram goes forth to meet the Buddha.** The sectaries find fault with the Buddha and seek to restrain Treasurer Ram from going forth to meet him. The Buddha remarks that the sectaries find in others faults which do not exist, but fail to see their own faults.

11. **The fault-finding monk [xviii. 19 = 253].** The Buddha reproves a monk who found fault with everybody.

12. **Is there a path through the air? [xviii. 20–21 = 254–255].** A wandering monk asks the Buddha three questions, all of which the Buddha answers in the negative.

Book XIX. The Righteous, Dhammaṭṭha Vagga

1. **The unjust judges [xix. 1-2 = 256–257].** Some monks see some judges taking bribes and depriving lawful owners of their property unjustly. The Buddha discourses on the true meaning of "righteous."

2. **The Band of Six [xix. 3 = 258].** The Six Monks insult some young monks and novices. The latter complain to the Buddha, who discourses on the meaning of "wise."

3. **Not therefore is a man praised for his much speaking [xix. 4 = 259].** The forest-deities applaud an Arahat who recites a single stanza, but withhold applause from two monks who recite the Law at length. The two monks complain to the Buddha, who comments on the meaning of "versed in the Law."

4. **Can a young monk be an "Elder"? [xix. 5–6 = 260–261].** Some monks express surprise that the Teacher should apply the title "Elder" to a young monk. The Teacher explains what he means by the title.

5. **What is an accomplished gentleman? [xix. 7–8 = 262–263].** The Buddha reproves some monks who pride themselves on their good address.

6. **It is not tonsure that makes the monk [xix. 9–10 = 264–265].** Whenever Hatthaka was defeated in an argument, he would invite his opponent to resume the argument at such and such a place and time. He would then go to the place before the appointed time and proclaim that his opponent's absence was a virtual confession of defeat. The Buddha reproved him and remarked that it is not tonsure that makes the monk.

7. **What is it that makes the monk? [xix. 11–12 = 266–267].** A Brahman becomes a sectarian monk, and asks the Buddha why he does not call him a monk.

8. **It is not silence that makes the sage [xix. 13–14 = 268–269].** In the first period of Enlightenment, whereas the sectarian monks express their thanks and good wishes to those who have entertained them, the orthodox monks depart with never a word of thanks. The people murmur, and the monks report the matter to the Buddha. The Buddha enjoins upon the monks the saying of thanksgivings. The sectaries complain that whereas they keep silence, as befits sages, their opponents deliver lengthy discourses. The Buddha remarks that he does not call a man a sage merely because he keeps silence.

9. **Noble is as noble does [xix. 15 = 270].** A fisherman, seeing the Buddha,

throws away his hook and line. The Buddha asks him his name, and learning that it is "Noble," reproves him for taking the lives of living creatures, and remarks that noble is as noble does.

10. **Be not puffed up** [xix. 16–17 = 271–272]. The Buddha reproves a party of monks who are puffed up because of their spiritual attainments, and admonishes them that they must be satisfied with nothing less than the attainment of Arahatship.

Book XX. The Path, Magga Vagga

1. **The Eightfold Path is the best of paths** [xx. 1–4 = 273–276]. Fifty monks engage in a conversation about the paths over which they have traveled. The Buddha admonishes them to apply themselves to the task of entering upon the Noble Eightfold Path.

2. **Impermanence** [xx. 5 = 277]. The Buddha, knowing that certain monks meditated upon Impermanence in a previous birth, directs them to meditate upon Impermanence.

3. **Suffering** [xx. 6 = 278]. The Buddha, knowing that certain monks meditated upon Suffering in a previous birth, directs them to meditate upon Suffering.

4. **Unreality** [xx. 7 = 279]. The Buddha, knowing that certain monks meditated upon Unreality in a previous birth, directs them to meditate upon Unreality.

5. **Do not postpone until to-morrow** [xx. 8 = 280]. Five hundred monks retire to the forest to meditate. One falls away, but the rest attain Arahatship. The monks return to the Teacher, who has a kind word for everybody except the monk who has fallen away. The monk renews his determination to attain Arahatship, and walks up and down the cloister all night long. Becoming drowsy, he stumbles against a stone seat and breaks his thigh. As his fellow-monks are on their way to take a meal at the house of a certain layman, they hear the groans of the unfortunate monk, and stop and minister to him. They are thus prevented from receiving promised offerings. The Teacher remarks that it is not the first time this monk has prevented his fellows from receiving promised offerings, and relates the Varaṇa Jataka. He then discourses on the evil of procrastination.

6. **The pig-ghost** [xx. 9 = 281]. As Moggallāna is descending Mount Vulture Peak with Lakkhaṇa, Moggallāna smiles. Lakkhaṇa asks him why he smiles. Moggallāna replies that he will tell him as soon as they are in the presence of the Teacher. When they are in presence of the Teacher, Lakkhaṇa repeats his question. Moggallāna tells him that he saw a ghost in the form of a pig. The Buddha corroborates his statement, and declares that he himself saw the same ghost as he sat on the Throne of Enlightenment. The monks ask the Buddha to tell them about his former deed, and the Buddha relates the following

6 a. **Story of the Past: The destroyer of friendships.** Two monks lived together in peace and harmony until a preacher of the Law destroyed their mutual friendship and confidence by telling each of them that the other had made insinuations of evil concerning him. When a hundred years had passed, the two monks discovered that the preacher of the Law had lied to them, drove him from their dwelling, and renewed their friendship. The destroyer of friendships was reborn as a ghost in the form of a pig.

7. **Poṭhila the Empty-head** [xx. 10 = 282]. The Buddha fires the determination of a certain monk to attain Arahatship by calling him "Empty-head." A seven-year-old novice tests the monk's willingness to obey by ordering him to leap into a pool of water, robes and all. The monk obeys, listens to the admonition of the novice, and after hearing a stanza uttered by an apparition of the Buddha, attains Arahatship.

8. **The old monks and the old woman** [xx. 11–12 = 283–284]. Some old monks are befriended by an old woman, the former wife of one of their number. When the old woman dies, the old monks are inconsolable. The Buddha relates the following

8 a. **Story of the Past: Kāka Jātaka.** In a previous state of existence the old monks were a flock of crows. One day the mate of one of their number got very drunk, and was swept out to sea and drowned. The crows set to work to bale out the sea with their beaks, but finally gave up the attempt.

9. **The grass withereth, the flower fadeth** [xx. 13 = 285]. A goldsmith's son, who has meditated on Impurity without success, attains Arahatship by contemplating withering leaves and fading flowers.

10. **Thou shalt surely die** [xx. 14 = 286]. A merchant sets out on a journey, but is halted by a flood. So he pitches camp by the bank of a river, and decides to remain there for a full year. The Buddha, knowing that the man is destined to die in seven days, sends Elder Ānanda to him, and afterwards preaches to him in person.

11. **The bereaved mother and the pinch of mustard seed** [xx. 15 = 287]. The Buddha admonishes a mother who has sought a pinch of mustard seed as medicine for her dead child.

12. **The woman who was bereft of all her family** [xx. 16–17 = 288–289]. The Buddha admonishes a woman who has lost all the members of her family by death.

Book XXI. Miscellaneous, Pakiṇṇaka Vagga

1. **The Ascent of the Ganges** [xxi. 1 = 290]. Vesāli is devastated by famine, evil spirits, and pestilence. The Licchavi prince Mahāli requests the Buddha to visit the city and abate the plagues. The Buddha consents. King Bimbisāra prepares a road from Rājagaha to the Ganges, and escorts the Buddha in state to the bank of the river. The Buddha descends the Ganges. The Licchavi princes prepare a road from the Ganges to Vesāli, and escort the Buddha to their city, bestowing on him honors double those bestowed by the king. Sakka and the deities descend, and the evil spirits flee away. By direction of the Buddha, the Elder Ānanda recites the Jewel Sutta, and the plagues abate. The Buddha is honored by men, deities, and Nāgas. The Buddha ascends the Ganges, and is received by the king with honors double those rendered by the Licchavi princes. The king escorts the Buddha back to Rājagaha. The monks express amazement at the supernatural power of the Buddha. The Buddha tells them that the honors accorded him are the result of a slight offering which he made in a previous state of existence, and relates the following

1 a. **Story of the Past: The Brahman Saṁkha.** The Brahman Saṁkha had a son named Susīma who became a Private Buddha. When Susīma died, Saṁkha made offerings at his shrine. Saṁkha was the Future Buddha.

2. **"Not hatred for hatred"** [xxi. 2 = 291]. A girl eats the eggs of a hen. The hen conceives a grudge against her, and prays that she may be reborn as an ogress, able to devour the children of her enemy. The hen is reborn as a cat, the girl is reborn as a hen, and the cat eats the eggs of the hen. The hen is reborn as a leopardess, the cat is reborn as a doe, and the leopardess eats the young of the doe. In five hundred successive states of existence, they return hatred for hatred. Finally the girl who ate the eggs of a hen is reborn as a young woman of Sāvatthi, and the hen is reborn as an ogress. The ogress devours two children of the young woman, and is about to seize the third when the young woman seeks refuge in the monastery. The Buddha admonishes them to return good for evil.

3. **The monks who were given to vanities** [xxi. 3–4 = 292–293]. The monks of Bhaddiya were given to the wearing of all manner of ornamental shoes, and neglected their religious duties. The Buddha reproved them.

4. The monk who had killed his mother and father [xxi. 5–6 = 294–295]. The Buddha points out a monk who has killed his mother and father.

5. The youth and the demons [xxi. 7–12 = 296–301]. A youth wins victories in his sports and escapes from the power of a demon by meditating on the Buddha and ejaculating, "Praise be to the Buddha."

6. The Vajjian prince who became a monk [xxi. 13 = 302]. A Vajjian prince who became a monk hears festive music and becomes discontented.

7. Citta, the faithful layman [xxi. 14 = 303]. A jealous monk insults a faithful layman and is rebuked by the Buddha. The layman presents alms to the Buddha, and is rewarded by deities and men. [**Excerpt from v. 14.**]

8. Cullā Subhaddā the virtuous [xxi. 15 = 304]. Cullā Subhaddā, daughter of Anāthapiṇḍika, marries the son of Ugga, a sectarian. Anāthapiṇḍika presents his daughter with a dowry, gives her Ten Admonitions, and provides her with eight sponsors to clear her of such charges as may be brought against her. She enters her husband's city in state, winning the hearts of the citizens by her virtues and her charm. Her father-in-law entertains the Naked Ascetics, and invites her to do them reverence. Out of modesty she refuses, and her father-in-law directs her to be put out of the house. She summons her sponsors and explains the situation to them. Her mother-in-law asks her to describe her own monks, and she does so. Her mother-in-law asks to see her monks. So she invites the Buddha and his monks and entertains them. The Buddha expounds the Law, and Ugga is established in the Fruit of Conversion.

9. The solitary monk [xxi. 16 = 305]. The Buddha praises the life of solitude.

Book XXII. Hell, Niraya Vagga

1. Murder of Sundarī [xxii. 1 = 306]. The envious sectaries conspire with the wandering nun Sundarī to cast reproach upon the Buddha. In the evening, when the throngs are returning to the city from Jetavana, she walks in the direction of Jetavana, and when the people ask her where she is going, she replies that she is on her way to Jetavana to spend the night alone with the hermit Gotama in the Perfumed Chamber. Having spent the night in some monastery belonging to the sectaries, she walks back in the morning in full view of the throngs on their way to Jetavana. After a few days the sectaries suborn villains to kill Sundarī and throw her body on a heap of rubbish near the Perfumed Chamber. The sectaries then report to the king that Sundarī has disappeared, and tell him that they suspect the disciples of the Buddha of having murdered her in order to conceal their master's misdeeds. The king permits them to make a search for her body. They remove the body from the rubbish-heap and carry it into the city on a litter, proclaiming publicly that the disciples of the Buddha have murdered her. The inhabitants of the city revile the monks, and the monks report the matter to the Buddha. The Buddha discourses on the evil end of liars. The king sends out his men to investigate the murder. The murderers betray themselves in a tavern while under the influence of strong drink. The king's men arrest the murderers and arraign them before the king. The murderers confess their guilt and implicate the sectaries. The king orders the execution of the sectaries.

2. The skeleton-ghost [xxii. 2 = 307]. As Moggallāna is descending Mount Vulture Peak with Lakkhaṇa, Moggallāna suddenly smiles. Lakkhaṇa asks him why he smiles. Moggallāna replies that he will tell him as soon as they are in the presence of the Teacher. When they are in the presence of the Teacher, Lakkhaṇa repeats his question, and Moggallāna tells him that he saw a ghost in the form of a skeleton, a monk soaring through the air with his body all aflame, and other of their co-religionists, five in all, tormented with fire. The Teacher informs the monks that these men retired from the world in the dispensation of the Buddha Kassapa and failed to act according to their profession.

3. **Magic for meat** [**xxii.** 3 = 308]. The Buddha reproves some monks for praising each other as possessors of supernatural powers for the sake of the belly.

4. **The man whom women loved** [**xxii.** 4–5 = 309–310]. Anāthapiṇḍika's nephew Khema was such a handsome youth that all the women who saw him fell madly in love with him. He spent most of his time running after other men's wives. The king was unable to turn him from his evil ways, but the Buddha converted him.

4 a. **Story of the Past: Khema's Earnest Wish.** Khema's attractiveness to women was due to the fact that in a previous existence he made an Earnest Wish that all of the women who saw him might fall in love with him.

5. **The presumptuous monk** [**xxii.** 6–8 = 311–313]. A monk thoughtlessly breaks off a blade of grass. Troubled in mind, he consults a brother monk. The second monk makes light of the offense of the first monk, and deliberately seizes a clump of grass with both of his hands and pulls it up. The Buddha rebukes the presumptuous monk.

6. **The jealous woman** [**xxii.** 9 = 314]. A jealous woman's husband lies with a female servant. The jealous woman binds her rival hand and foot, cuts off her nose and ears, and shuts her up in an inner chamber. Then she goes with her husband to hear the Law. The female servant is released by relatives of the woman, goes to the monastery, and tells the Buddha what has happened. The Buddha discourses on the folly of evil deeds.

7. **Fortify yourself like a city** [**xxii.** 10 = 315]. The inhabitants of a frontier country are so busily engaged in fortifying their city that they find no opportunity to minister properly to some visiting monks. The monks relate their experiences to the Buddha, who admonishes them to fortify themselves like a city.

8. **Degrees of nakedness** [**xxii.** 11–12 = 316–317]. Some monks, seeing a company of Naked Ascetics of the Jain order (Nigaṇṭhas), express the opinion that the Nigaṇṭhas are superior to the Acelakas, since the Nigaṇṭhas wear at least a covering in front, while the Acelakas go entirely naked. The Nigaṇṭhas hasten to explain that their sole reason for wearing any covering is to keep the dust and dirt from falling into the vessels in which they receive their food.

9. **Children visit the Buddha** [**xxii.** 13–14 = 318–319]. The sectaries administer an oath to their children not to salute the monks or to enter their monastery. One day, as the children are playing outside of the Jetavana monastery, they become thirsty, and send the son of a lay disciple to the monastery for water. The layman's son goes to the monastery, salutes the Buddha, and tells him the circumstances of his visit. The Buddha tells him to send the other boys to the monastery for their drink. The boys all come and have their drink. The Buddha chooses a subject suited to their understanding, discourses to them, and establishes them in the Refuges. Eventually their parents also become disciples of the Buddha.

Book XXIII. The Elephant, Nāga Vagga

1. **The sectaries insult the Buddha** [**xxiii.** 1–3 = 320–322]. At the instigation of Māgandiyā, the sectaries follow the Buddha about and shout insulting epithets at him. Ānanda suggests that they flee to another city, but the Buddha rejects his suggestion and compares himself to an elephant that has entered the fray. [**Excerpt from ii. 1, part 6.**]

2. **The monk who had been an elephant-trainer** [**xxiii.** 4 = 323]. A monk who had once been an elephant-trainer, stands by the bank of a river, watching an elephant-tamer break in an elephant. Observing that the elephant-tamer is not succeeding

very well, the monk remarks to some of his fellow-monks that if the elephant-tamer would only wound the elephant in such and such a place, he could very quickly teach him the trick he wishes to teach him. The elephant-tamer hears the remark, follows the monk's suggestion, and soon compels the elephant to submit to his will. The monks report the incident to the Buddha. The Buddha rebukes him, telling him that he has all he can do to tame himself.

3. **The old Brahman and his sons** [xxiii. 5 = 324]. An old Brahman divides half of his wealth among his four sons when they marry. When the Brahman's wife dies, the sons induce the father to divide the remainder of his wealth among them. The Brahman's daughters-in-law drive him from the houses of his sons. At the suggestion of the Buddha the Brahman recites his troubles before the assembled Brahmans. The Brahmans threaten to kill the sons. The sons thereafter take proper care of their father. The Brahman makes an offering of thanksgiving to the Buddha. At the Brahman's suggestion his sons entertain the Buddha. The Buddha praises the Brahman's sons for their tender care of their father, and relates the following

3 a. **Story of the Past: Mātuposaka Nāgarāja Jātaka.** The elephant Dhanapāla refused to eat in captivity for love of his mother.

4. **On moderation in eating** [xxiii. 6 = 325]. King Pasenadi Kosala, suffering from over-indulgence in food, visits the Buddha. The Buddha admonishes the king on the evils of over-eating, and directs the king's nephew to recite a certain stanza before the king at meal-time. The king takes the hint, diminishes his food, and improves in health. [Excerpt from xv. 6.]

5. **The novice and the ogress** [xxiii. 7 = 326]. A model novice makes over the merit he acquires by intoning the Sacred Word to his mother and father. On attaining manhood, he becomes discontented, resolves to leave the Order, and goes to the house of his mother. His mother remonstrates with him, but to no avail. An ogress who was his mother in a previous state of existence, takes possession of him, and wrings his neck until he falls to the ground, writhing and foaming at the mouth. When he recovers his senses, his mother urges him to return to the Order, and this he does. The Buddha admonishes him to restrain his thoughts.

6. **An elephant sticks fast in the mud** [xxiii. 8 = 327]. An elephant sticks fast in the mud. His keeper shows himself to the elephant with his head arrayed as for battle, and causes the battle-drum to be beaten. The elephant immediately exerts himself to the utmost and extricates himself from the mud. The monks report the incident to the Buddha, who admonishes them to extricate themselves from the quagmire of the evil passions.

7. **An elephant waits upon the Buddha** [xxiii. 9–11 = 328–330]. The Buddha takes up his residence in the forest, and is waited upon by a noble elephant. Ānanda, accompanied by many disciples and monks, goes to the forest. The monks ask the Buddha whether he has not endured much hardship. The Buddha replies that he has been waited upon by a noble elephant, and remarks that whoever obtains such a companion may well live alone. [Excerpt from i. 5.]

8. **Māra tempts the Buddha** [xxiii. 12–14 = 331–333]. Māra tempts the Buddha to exercise sovereignty and to transmute matter into gold. The Buddha rebukes Māra and admonishes him.

Book XXIV. Thirst or Craving, Taṇhā Vagga

1. **Redfish** [xxiv. 1–4 = 334–337].

1 a. **Story of the Past: The insolent monk. The bandits.** A certain monk, drunk with the intoxication of great learning, and overcome by desire of gain, behaved in an insolent manner towards his fellows. The monk was reborn in the Avīci hell.

Five hundred bandits took upon themselves the precepts and were reborn in the World of the Gods.

1 b. Story of the Present: The fishermen, and the fish with a stinking breath. The insolent monk is reborn as a fish with scales of ruddy gold, but with a stinking breath. The bandits are reborn as fishermen. The fishermen inclose the fish in their net and take it to the king. The king takes it to the Buddha. The Buddha informs the king that because in a previous state of existence the fish preached the Word of the Buddha, therefore it has scales of ruddy gold, but because the fish was guilty of insolence, therefore it has a stinking breath. To confirm the faith of his hearers, the Buddha lets the fish tell its own story. The Buddha admonishes his hearers to walk in heedfulness.

2. The young sow [xxiv. 5–10 = 338–343]. A young woman passes through thirteen successive births. In one of these births she is a young sow. The Buddha relates her previous history. In her thirteenth birth she marries the minister of King Gāmaṇī the Wicked, retires from the world, and attains Arahatship.

3. The renegade monk [xxiv. 11 = 344]. A monk returns to the world and joins a pack of thieves. One day he is captured. As he is on his way to the place of execution, a certain Elder admonishes him to consider once more the Subject of Meditation which he formerly employed. The renegade monk applies himself to meditation and enters into the fourth trance. The executioners take their places around him, but he exhibits not the slightest sign of fear. The executioners report the matter to the king, who orders his release. The renegade monk, even as he lies on the red-hot spikes, attains Arahatship, and proceeds through the air to the Buddha.

4. The prison-house [xxiv. 12–13 = 345–346]. Visiting monks pass a prison house, and see criminals bound with fetters. Approaching the Buddha, they ask him whether there are any bonds stronger than the bonds with which the criminals are bound. The Buddha assures them that the Bond of Craving is a thousandfold stronger, and remarking that wise men of old broke this bond, relates the following

4 a. Story of the Past: Husband and wife. The Future Buddha was reborn as a poor man. Not knowing that his wife was pregnant, he asked her permission to retire from the world. His wife asked him not to do so until she should have given birth to her child. When the child was born, she asked him to wait until the child was weaned. While he waited, his wife conceived a second child. The Future Buddha thereupon left her, breaking the bond of attachment once and for all.

5. Beauty is but skin-deep [xxiv. 14 = 347]. Khemā, chief consort of King Bimbisāra, was exceedingly beautiful. She had heard it said that the Buddha found fault with beauty of form, and therefore avoided him. One day, after listening to songs in praise of Veḷuvana, she was seized with a desire to go thither. The Buddha created the form of a woman of surpassing beauty, and caused her to stand beside him with a fan in her hand. Khemā stood with her gaze riveted upon the woman. The Buddha caused the woman to pass through old age, disease, and death. Khemā was thus brought to a realization of the transitoriness of outward beauty.

6. The youth who married a female acrobat [xxiv. 15 = 348]. A treasurer's son falls in love with a female acrobat, and marries her. He joins a troupe of traveling acrobats and becomes an acrobat himself. One day, while he is performing in the city of Rājagaha, the Buddha and his monks enter the city. The Buddha preaches the Law to the acrobat, and the latter attains Arahatship. The Buddha relates to the monks the following

6 a. Story of the Past: A joke in earnest. A husband and his wife presented alms to an Elder, making an Earnest Wish. The Elder, perceiving that their wish would be fulfilled, smiled. The wife remarked, "The Elder must be an actor." The husband replied, "He must be indeed." Because of his reply, the husband traveled about with acrobats; because he gave alms, he attained Arahatship.

7. Young Archer the Wise [xxiv. 16–17 = 349–350]. A young woman falls in love with a young monk, and is so attentive to him that he becomes discontented. The monks report the matter to the Buddha, who reproves the young monk and relates the following

7 a. Story of the Past: Young Archer the Wise. The wisest man in India was once slain by a bandit through the treachery of his wife. The bandit took the wife of the wise man, but fearing treachery, forsook her. Sakka took the form of a jackal and put her to shame. The treacherous wife was the seductive young woman.

8. Māra seeks in vain to frighten Rāhula [xxiv. 18–19 = 351–352]. Rāhula lies down to sleep in front of the Perfumed Chamber. Māra takes the form of an elephant, encircles Rāhula's head with his trunk, and trumpets the Heron's Call.

9. The skeptical ascetic [xxiv. 20 = 353]. The Naked Ascetic Upaka meets the Buddha and asks him, "Who is your teacher?" The Buddha replies that he is himself the All-knowing One. Upaka neither doubts nor believes.

10. The Summum Bonum [xxiv. 21 = 354]. The deities raise four questions: "Which is the best of gifts, of flavors, of delights? Why is the destruction of Craving the thing of all other things supreme?" Neither the Four Great Kings nor Sakka can answer. The Buddha declares the Law to be the best of gifts, of flavors, of delights, and the destruction of Craving to be the thing of all other things supreme because it leads to the attainment of Arahatship.

11. Treasurer Childless [xxiv. 22 = 355]. A certain treasurer dies without issue, and the king removes his wealth to the royal precincts. The king tells the Buddha that the treasurer took no delight in the good things of life. The Buddha relates the following

11 a. Story of the Past: The niggardly treasurer. In a previous birth this treasurer caused alms to be given to a Private Buddha, but afterwards regretted his act. Therefore he was reborn as a treasurer, but took no delight in the good things of life. He killed his nephew for his money, and therefore never had any children.

12. The greater and the lesser gift [xxiv. 23–26 = 356–359]. When the Buddha ascends to the World of the Thirty-three and sits upon the Yellowstone Throne of Sakka, the deity Indaka sits on his right hand, and the deity Aṅkura on his left. Indaka obtains the greater glory because he once gave the monk Anuruddha a spoonful of his own food. Aṅkura, who once set up a row of braziers twelve leagues long and gave abundant alms, gave alms without discrimination, and therefore receives the lesser glory. The Buddha discourses on the importance of the exercise of discrimination in the giving of alms.

Book XXV. The Monk, Bhikkhu Vagga

1. Guard the doors of the senses [xxv. 1–2 = 360–361]. Five monks, each of whom guards one of the five doors of the senses, argue with each other as to which of the five doors is the most difficult to guard, and ask the Buddha to decide the argument. The Buddha admonishes them to guard all the doors of the senses, reminds them that because in a previous state of existence they failed to do so, they went to perdition, and relates the following

1 a. Story of the Past: Takkasilā Jātaka. Ogresses tempt five travelers with objects pleasing to the senses of sight and sound and smell and taste and touch. The travelers yield to the temptations and are eaten alive.

2. The goose-killing monk [xxv. 3 = 362]. The Buddha rebukes a monk for not scrupling to kill a goose, reminds him that wise men of old entertained scruples about matters of the slightest importance, and relates the following

2 a. Story of the Past: Kurudhamma Jātaka. In times past there was a drought in the kingdom of Kaliṅga, but rain a-plenty in the kingdom of Kuru. The king of Kaliṅga, thinking that if the state elephant of the king of Kuru were brought to his kingdom, rain would fall, sent for him. Still no rain fell. The king of Kaliṅga then concluded that if he kept the Kuru precepts rain would fall in his kingdom, and requested the king of Kuru and the other members of his household to inscribe these precepts on a golden plate. But the king of Kuru and his household hesitated for a long time to do this, because of undue scruples as to whether they had themselves kept the precepts inviolate. Finally, on receiving the assurance of the Brahmans that by nothing which they had done had they violated these precepts, they complied with the request of the king of Kaliṅga. The king of Kaliṅga took upon himself these precepts, and immediately rain fell in his kingdom.

3. The monk who failed to hold his tongue [xxv. 4 = 363]. The monk Kokālika reviles Elders Sāriputta and Moggallāna, and is reborn in the Lotus hell. The Buddha informs the monks that in a previous state of existence also he failed to keep his mouth shut, and went to perdition for it. So saying, he relates the following

3 a. Story of the Past: The talkative tortoise, Bahubhāṇi (Kacchapa) Jātaka. Two geese carry a tortoise through the air on a stick, the tortoise gripping the middle of the stick with his teeth. The tortoise opens his mouth to reply to a taunt, falls to the ground, and splits in two.

4. By righteousness men honor the Buddha [xxv. 5 = 364]. From the day when the Teacher announces that in four months he will pass into Nibbāna, many thousands of monks spend their time in attendance upon him. And gathering in little groups, they ask each other, "What are we to do?" But a certain monk named Dhammārāma resolves to strive the more earnestly for the attainment of Arahatship. Accordingly Dhammārāma goes about by himself, pondering the Law preached by the Teacher. The monks, misunderstanding his motive, tell the Teacher that Dhammārāma has no affection for him. The Teacher admonishes them as follows: "Every other monk should show his affection for me just as Dhammārāma has done. For they that honor me with perfumes and garlands, honor me not; but they that practice the Higher and the Lower Law, they alone truly honor me."

5. The traitor monk [xxv. 6–7 = 365–366]. A certain monk tarries with the monks belonging to the faction of Devadatta for several days. The Buddha reproves him, and relates the following

5 a. Story of the Past: Elephant Damsel-face, Mahilāmukha Jātaka. After listening to the conversation of thieves and murderers, a well-behaved elephant becomes unruly and kills his keepers. But after listening to the conversation of sages and Brahmans, he becomes well-behaved again. The elephant Damsel-face was the traitor monk.

6. The Brahman who gave the gifts of first-fruits [xxv. 8 = 367]. A Brahman, after giving the five gifts of first-fruits, gives the Buddha half of his meal. The Brahman's wife asks the Buddha what it is that makes a monk.

7. The conversion of a pack of thieves [xxv. 9–17 = 368–376]. The layman Soṇa becomes a monk, and recites the Sixteen Octads in the Perfumed Chamber. He is applauded by deities, Nāgas, and Supaṇṇas. His mother, informed by a deity that he has preached the Law before the Buddha, invites him to preach the Law to her. She causes a pavilion to be erected, and on the appointed day goes to the pavilion, sits down, and listens to her son as he preaches the Law. In her absence a pack of thieves enter her house by a tunnel. The leader of the thieves goes to the pavilion with orders to stand beside the woman and to kill her in case she sets out for the house.

A female slave who has been left in charge of the house, discovers the thieves, and goes to her mistress three times in succession and reports that thieves are robbing her house. The woman tells her slave that she does not wish to be interrupted, and directs her to return to the house and permit the thieves to take all they wish. The leader of the thieves is filled with remorse, goes to the house, and orders his companions to restore the woman's property. The thieves go to the pavilion, beg the woman's pardon, and retire from the world.

8. **The grass withereth, the flower fadeth** [xxv. 18 = 377]. Five hundred monks attain Arahatship by contemplating fading jasmine flowers.

9. **The monk whose mother was a lioness** [xxv. 19 = 378]. A certain monk conducted himself with such composure and dignity as to attract universal attention. The story went that he was the son of a lioness. Description of the tidy habits of lionesses.

10. **The monk and the ragged garment** [xxv. 20–21 = 379–380]. A monk who had been a plowman overcomes discontent and attains Arahatship by contemplating a ragged garment and a plow which he had used as a layman.

11. **"Whosoever beholds the Law, he beholds me"** [xxv. 22 = 381]. A certain monk was so fascinated by the Buddha's beauty of person that he spent all his time gazing at him. When the Buddha entered upon residence, he directed this monk to leave him. The monk was so affected by despondency that he decided to commit suicide. As he was about to throw himself from the top of a mountain, the Buddha appeared to him in a vision. Then and there the monk attained Arahatship.

12. **The novice and the dragon** [xxv. 23 = 382].

12 a. **Story of the Past: The poor man Annabhāra and the rich man Sumana.** In the dispensation of the Buddha Padumuttara, a youth gives alms, praying that some day he may become Foremost of those that possess Supernatural Vision. The Buddha predicts that his prayer will be fulfilled in the dispensation of the Buddha Gotama, and that his name will be Anuruddha. In the course of time this youth is reborn as a poor man Annabhāra, servant of a rich man Sumana. Annabhāra gives alms to a Private Buddha, praying that he may be released from the wretched life he leads, and that he may never again hear the word *is n't*. Sumana offers Annabhāra a thousand pieces of money if he will make over to him the merit of his gift. Annabhāra refuses the money, but at the same time makes over to Sumana the merit of his gift. Annabhāra straightway attains wealth and social position. In the dispensation of the Buddha Gotama, he is reborn as Anuruddha the Sakyan, youngest brother of Mahānāma the Sakyan.

12 b. **Story of the Present: Anuruddha retires from the world.** Six Sakyan princes, of whom Anuruddha is one, engage in a game of marbles, wagering a cake on the result. Anuruddha loses three times in succession, and sends to his mother for cakes. When his mother's store of cake is exhausted, she sends back word, "There is n't cake to send." Anuruddha, having never heard the word *is n't*, orders his man to fetch *is n't* cake. His mother sends him an empty dish, which the deities fill with celestial cakes. Anuruddha never learns the meaning of *is n't*, and so long as he remains a layman, lives altogether on celestial cakes. Mahānāma informs Anuruddha that as yet no member of their family has become a monk, and suggests that one of the two become a monk. Anuruddha replies that he has been so delicately nurtured that it is out of the question for him to think of enduring the hardships of the monastic life. Mahānāma then offers to become a monk if Anuruddha will take up farming. Anuruddha asks Mahānāma what he means by the word *farming*. (It would have been unreasonable to expect Anuruddha to know the meaning of the word *farming*, for he did not even know where food comes from. For example, Anuruddha, Bhaddiya, and Kimbila once engaged in a discussion of the question, "Where does food come from?"

Kimbila thought it came from the granary; Bhaddiya, from the kettle; while Anuruddha expressed the opinion that it came from the golden bowl.) In reply to Anuruddha's question, Mahānāma enumerates the various duties connected with the life of a farmer. Anuruddha decides that he would rather become a monk. So Anuruddha, together with five other Sakyan princes, becomes a monk. Subsequently he attains Supernatural Vision, and perceives that Sumana has been reborn as Culla Sumana, youngest son of the lay disciple Mahā Muṇḍa. **[Excerpt from i. 12 a.]**

12 c. **Story of the Present: The novice Sumana and the dragon.** Sumana becomes the novice of the Elder Anuruddha. The Elder sends the novice to Lake Anotatta for drinking-water. Paṇṇaka, king of the dragons and guardian of the lake, refuses to give the novice water, and covers the surface of the lake with his hood. The novice resolves to do battle with the dragon, and summons the deities to witness the contest. The novice descends from the sky in the form of Brahmā, tramples upon the hood of the dragon, forces his head down, and squeezes him with all his might. Having defeated the dragon, the novice fills a vessel with water and returns to the Elder. The dragon swears an oath either to split open the heart of the novice, or to pick him up by the heels and fling him over the Ganges. The dragon pursues the novice and tells the Elder that the novice has stolen water from him. The Elder, knowing this to be a falsehood, orders the dragon to beg the novice's pardon. The dragon begs the novice's pardon, and promises to bring him water whenever he needs it. Subsequently the novice brings water to the Buddha, and the Buddha praises him.

Book XXVI. The Brahman, Brāhmaṇa Vagga

1. **Brahman Great-Joy [xxvi. 1 = 383].** A certain Brahman was so pleased by a sermon of the Buddha that he thereafter gave food regularly to sixteen monks. He greeted these monks, one and all, with the title "Arahats." The monks were offended at this, and went no more to his house. The Brahman went to the Teacher with tears in his eyes, and told him that the monks came no more to his house. The Buddha inquired into the matter, and told the monks that the Brahman's form of address was only a way of expressing his superabundant joy.

2. **What are the "Two States"? [xxvi. 2 = 384].** On the occasion of the visit of thirty monks from foreign parts to the Buddha, Elder Sāriputta asks the Buddha what is meant by the expression "Two States."

3. **What is the "Far Shore"? [xxvi. 3 = 385].** Māra assumes a disguise, and asks the Buddha what is meant by the expression "Far Shore."

4. **What is a Brahman? [xxvi. 4 = 386].** A Brahman by birth and lineage, observing that the Buddha calls his disciples Brahmans, asks the Buddha why he does not apply the same title to him.

5. **The Buddhas shine both day and night [xxvi. 5 = 387].** Elder Ānanda gazes upon the radiance of the sun as the sun sets, of the moon as the moon rises, of King Pasenadi Kosala, of an Elder in trance, and of the Tathāgata. The Elder remarks to the Teacher that the glory of the Buddha transcends that of all others. The Teacher replies that the Buddha shines in splendor all the day and all the night.

6. **What is a monk? [xxvi. 6 = 388].** A Brahman who has retired from the world under a teacher other than the Buddha, asks the Buddha why he does not call him a monk.

7. **The patient subdues the violent [xxvi. 7–8 = 389–390].** A certain Brahman hears some of the disciples say that no matter what the provocation, Elder Sāriputta never gets angry. So at the first opportunity he steps up behind the Elder and strikes him with his fist. The Elder pays no attention to him. The Brahman is so amazed

at the Elder's patience that he begs his pardon and invites him to be his guest. The indignant disciples lie in wait for the Brahman, but the Elder explains matters to them and sends them on their way. The monks report the incident to the Buddha, who remarks that no real Brahman ever strikes another Brahman.

8. **Mahā Pajāpatī Gotamī receives the Precepts [xxvi. 9 = 391].** Mahā Pajāpatī Gotamī received the Eight Cardinal Precepts privately, before their public promulgation. The Exalted One alone was her teacher. Some of the nuns expressed dissatisfaction at this, and the Buddha reproved them.

9. **Reverence to whom reverence is due [xxvi. 10 = 392].** Sāriputta first heard the Law from the lips of Assaji, and ever afterwards showed his reverence for Assaji by extending his hands and turning his head in Assaji's direction. The monks complained to the Buddha that Sāriputta was reverencing the cardinal points, and the Buddha corrected them.

10. **What is a Brahman? [xxvi. 11 = 393].** A Brahman by birth and lineage remarks that the Buddha calls his disciples Brahmans, and asks him why he does not apply the same title to him.

11. **The trickster Brahman [xxvi. 12 = 394].** A certain Brahman would climb a tree, grasp a branch with his feet, swing himself head downwards like a bat, and demand pennies from passers-by, threatening to let go and kill himself and destroy the city if they refused to give. The monks reported his doings to the Buddha, who remarked that it was not the first time he had been a trickster and a thief, and related the following

11 a. **Story of the Past: The false ascetic and the king of the lizards.** A false ascetic received a portion of lizard meat, and became fast bound by the bonds of the craving of taste. Now the king of the lizards dwelt in an ant-hill near the hermit's hut, and was in the habit of calling upon the ascetic from time to time. On that particular day the ascetic resolved to kill the lizard, and went and lay down near the ant-hill with a stick concealed in his robes, pretending to be asleep. The king of the lizards approached the ascetic, but not liking his actions, wriggled off in the opposite direction. The ascetic threw his stick at him, but the lizard dodged the stick and went into the ant-hill. The king of the lizards then poked his head out of the ant-hill and reproached the false ascetic.

12. **Kisā Gotamī, Wearer of Refuse-rags [xxvi. 13 = 395].** Kisā Gotamī approaches the Buddha, but observing Sakka seated near the Buddha, turns back. Sakka asks the Buddha who it is, and the Buddha replies that it is Kisā Gotamī, foremost of the wearers of refuse-rags.

13. **What is a Brahman? [xxvi. 14 = 396].** A Brahman by birth and lineage remarks that the Buddha calls his disciples Brahmans, and asks him why he does not apply the same title to him.

14. **Uggasena the acrobat [xxvi. 15 = 397].** The monks ask Uggasena, the former acrobat, whether he was not afraid when he balanced himself on the top of his pole. When Uggasena answers in the negative, the monks doubt his word, but the Buddha corrects them.

15. **A tug of war [xxvi. 16 = 398].** Two Brahmans fall to arguing about the comparative strength of their oxen. To decide the dispute, they load their cart with sand and whip up their oxen. The cart stirs not an inch, but the straps and thongs break. The monks relate the occurrence to the Buddha.

16. **The patient subdues the insolent [xxvi. 17 = 399].** The wife of a certain Brahman was in the habit of ejaculating the praises of the Buddha whenever she stumbled. One day the Brahman became greatly provoked at his wife for so doing, and went to the Buddha, intending to argue with him. The Brahman asked the Buddha a question, and the Buddha converted him by his answer. Each of the Brahman's

three younger brothers abused the Buddha in turn, and the Buddha converted them all without so much as saying a word.

17. Sāriputta is reviled by his mother [xxvi. 18 = 400]. Sāriputta stops at the door of his mother's house, and his mother reviles him. Sāriputta answers never a word.

18. Are not the Arahats creatures of flesh and blood? [xxvi. 19 = 401]. After the rape of the nun Uppalavaṇṇā by a former suitor, the monks raise the question whether the Arahats are to be blamed for gratifying their passions. The Buddha admonishes them that sexual passion no more adheres to the Arahat than a drop of water to a lotus-leaf. [**Excerpt from v. 10.**]

19. A slave lays down his burden [xxvi. 20 = 402]. The slave of a certain Brahman runs away and joins the Order. The Buddha admonishes the Brahman that the slave has laid down his burden.

20. Khemā the Wise [xxvi. 21 = 403]. Khemā approaches the Buddha, but observing Sakka seated near the Buddha, turns back. Sakka asks the Buddha who she is.

21. The monk and the goddess [xxvi. 22 = 404]. A monk takes up his residence in a cave tenanted by a goddess. The goddess wishes to dislodge him, but not daring to tell him to depart, and finding no flaw in him, contrives to cast reproach upon him. The goddess takes possession of the body of the child of a female supporter of the monk, and refuses to release him until the monk and the mother have sprinkled the child with water in which the monk has bathed. The goddess then reproaches the monk with having performed the work of a physician. The monk rejoices over the inability of the goddess to find a flaw in his virtue.

22. The monk and the woman [xxvi. 23 = 405]. A woman quarrels with her husband, decides to return to her family, and sets out through the forest. Seeing a monk on his way through the forest, she follows him. The husband sets out after his wife, and seeing the monk, beats him soundly.

23. The four novices [xxvi. 24 = 406]. The wife of a certain Brahman prepares food, and directs her husband to go to the monastery and bring back with him four old Brahmans. The husband returns with four seven-year-old novices who have attained Arahatship. The Brahman's wife, much provoked, refuses to give them food, and sends her husband back to the monastery for some old Brahmans. The Brahman brings back Sāriputta, who, upon learning that the novices have received no food, refuses to eat, demands his bowl, and returns to the monastery. Moggallāna does the same. The Brahman then brings Sakka, disguised as an aged Brahman, but his wife complains that he is too old. So the Brahman and his wife drag Sakka out of the house by main force. But so soon as they turn to enter the house, there sits Sakka as before, waving his hands! Sakka having thus made known his identity, the Brahman's wife gives food to the novices and to Sakka, and then all five depart. The novices return to the monastery and relate their experiences.

24. Did Big Wayman yield to anger? [xxvi. 25 = 407]. The monks raise the question whether Big Wayman did not yield to anger in expelling his brother Little Wayman from the monastery. The Buddha explains that Big Wayman was actuated solely by reverence for the Law.

25. The force of habit [xxvi. 26 = 408]. A certain monk was in the habit of accosting everybody with the epithet commonly applied only to outcasts. The monks complained to the Buddha. The Buddha called before his mind the previous abodes of the accused monk, and informed his accusers that the monk had been reborn as a Brahman in five hundred successive states of existence, and that he used the epithet, not out of ill-will, but simply from the force of habit.

26. The monk who was accused of theft [xxvi. 27 = 409]. A monk finds a cloak lying on the ground, and taking it for a refuse-rag, carries it off. The owner accuses him of theft. The monk explains matters, and returning to the monastery, relates the incident to his brethren. His brethren make merry at his expense.

27. **Sāriputta is misunderstood [xxvi. 28 = 410].** Sāriputta orders that belated supplies of requisites for the young monks be sent to him. The monks accuse Sāriputta of craving worldly possessions. The Buddha assures them that Sāriputta is actuated solely by the desire that nothing be lost.

28. **Moggallāna is misunderstood [xxvi. 29 = 411].** [Identical with the preceding, save for the stanza.]

29. **Renounce both good and evil [xxvi. 30 = 412].** The monks express their admiration for the meritorious works of the novice Sīvali. The Buddha admonishes them that Sīvali has renounced both merit and demerit. **[Excerpt from vii. 9.]**

30. **Elder Moonlight [xxvi. 31 = 413].**

30 a. **Story of the Past: A forester presents a moon-disk.** In the dispensation of the Buddha Kassapa, a merchant visits a forester and gives him presents, receiving a cart-load of sandalwood in return. Later on the forester visits the merchant, brings him a supply of sandalwood, and receives in return a large amount of money. The merchant honors the relics of the Buddha with sandalwood powder, and the forester places a moon-disk of sandalwood (*candana*) within the shrine.

30 b. **Story of the Present: Brahman Moonlight.** In the dispensation of the present Buddha, the forester is reborn as a wealthy Brahman. From the circle of his navel there proceeds a light like that of the moon's disk, and he is therefore called Moonlight (*Candābha*). The Brahmans travel about the country with him, proclaiming to the people that whoever shall stroke the body of the Brahman shall receive such and such power and glory. Coming to Sāvatthi, the Brahmans fall to arguing with the disciples of the Buddha as to which of their respective masters possesses the greater supernatural power. The Brahmans suggest that both parties go to the monastery and settle the dispute then and there. When the Brahman Moonlight comes into the presence of the Buddha, the radiance from his navel disappears. When he retires from the presence of the Buddha, the radiance reappears. The Brahman asks the Buddha to teach him the charm he possesses. The Buddha promises to do so if the Brahman will enter the Order. The Brahman enters the Order and attains Arahatship.

31. **Seven years in the womb [xxvi. 32 = 414].** Suppavāsā carries an unborn child in her womb for seven years, and for seven days endures the agonies of child-birth. She exchanges friendly greetings with the Buddha, and gives birth to a healthy son, who is named Sīvali. Sīvali becomes a monk and attains Arahatship. The monks comment on the sufferings which Sīvali has endured.

32. **A courtezan tempts the monk Ocean of Beauty [xxvi. 33 = 415].** Ocean of Beauty, Sundarasamudda, renounces great wealth and becomes a monk. His mother weeps because of his retirement from the world, and a courtezan promises for a sum of money to seduce him. She buys a house in the street through which the monk makes his round for alms, and takes up her abode therein. She first presents food to the monk at the door, then invites him to sit on the veranda, then entices him within the house, and finally prevails upon him to climb to the top floor of the house with her. Having enticed him to the top floor of the house, she tempts him in the forty ways in which a woman tempts a man. At that moment the Buddha, seated within the Jetavana, forty-five leagues distant, smiles. Ānanda asks him why he smiles. The Buddha replies that he is watching a battle between a monk and a courtezan, and adds that the monk will win the battle. The Buddha appears to the monk in an apparition, and the monk attains Arahatship. The monks discuss the incident, and the Buddha informs them that it is not the first time Ocean of Beauty has

been bound by the bonds of the craving of taste. So saying, he relates the Vātamiga Jātaka.

33. **Jotika and Jaṭila** [xxvi. 34 = 416].

33 a. **Story of the Past: Jotika in his previous existence as Aparājita.** The younger of two brothers gives sap to a Private Buddha in behalf of himself and his older brother. The younger brother prays for three Attainments, the older brother for Arahatship. The younger brother is reborn in the dispensation of the Buddha Vipassī as Aparājita, the older brother as Sena. Sena bestows his wealth on Aparājita, retires from the world, and attains Arahatship. At Sena's suggestion Aparājita builds a Perfumed Chamber for the Buddha. The wood and bricks of which the Chamber is built are studded with the seven jewels, and the seven jewels are heaped up knee-deep both within and without the Chamber. Aparājita entertains the Buddha, and permits the people to carry away with them as many jewels as they can hold in their hands. A Brahman steals a magnificent jewel which has been laid at the feet of the Buddha, and Aparājita reports the theft to the Buddha. At the suggestion of the Buddha, Aparājita prays that neither kings nor thieves may have the power to deprive him of his property. Aparājita gives alms on a magnificent scale. Having performed these works of merit, he dies and is reborn at Rājagaha in a treasurer's household.

33 b. **Story of the Present: The treasurer Jotika.** On the day of his birth, weapons and jewels throughout the city flash fire, and the entire city is one blaze of light. He is therefore given the name Jotika. When Jotika reaches manhood, Sakka creates a magnificent palace for him. It is composed entirely of the seven jewels; at the four corners stand four urns of treasure; seven Yakkhas stand guard over the seven gates. The deities bring Jotika a wife from Uttarakuru. His wife brings with her a pint-pot of rice and three burning-glasses. This pint-pot of rice suffices to provide Jotika and his household and guests with food during the remainder of his life. The burning-glasses supply the place of fuel. Multitudes visit the palace and carry away treasure, but the contents of the urns of treasure suffer no diminution. King Bimbisāra, accompanied by his son Ajātasattu, visits Jotika. Ajātasattu resolves to seize Jotika's palace as soon as he becomes king. The king is amazed at the magnificence of the palace and at the immensity of Jotika's wealth.

33 c. **Story of the Present: The Elder Jaṭila.** A Vijjādhara flies into the apartment of a treasurer's daughter and has intercourse with her. The treasurer's daughter gives birth to a son, and causes him to be placed in a vessel and set adrift in the Ganges. He is rescued by two women bathing in the Ganges and adopted by one of them, who is a retainer of the Elder Mahā Kaccāna. His foster-mother brings him up with the intention of having him become a monk under the Elder. When the child was bathed on the day of his birth, his hair remained matted, and therefore he is given the name Jaṭila. When Jaṭila is old enough to walk, his foster-mother commits him to the care of the Elder Mahā Kaccāna. The Elder takes him to Takkasilā and commits him to the care of a lay supporter of his. Jaṭila sells in one day the goods which have been accumulating in the layman's house for twelve years. The layman is so pleased that he gives him his daughter in marriage and has a house built for him. As soon as Jaṭila sets foot on the threshold, there arises in the rear of the house a mountain of gold eighty cubits in height. The king, hearing of this, appoints him treasurer. Jaṭila has three sons, and when they reach manhood he conceives a desire to become a monk. Reflecting that if a treasurer's family can be found possessed of wealth equal to his own, his sons will permit him to retire from the world, Jaṭila orders his men to search throughout India for such a family. Jaṭila's men visit Treasurer Ram, see his golden rams, and report to their master. Jaṭila sends out his men again, telling them to find out whether there is another such family. Jaṭila's men come to Jotika's palace, carrying with them a blanket worth a hundred thousand pieces of money. Jotika buys

the blanket and presents it to a slave woman for a foot-cloth. Jaṭila's men return to their master and describe Jotika's wealth. Jaṭila asks permission of the king to retire from the world, and the king gives his permission. Jaṭila summons his three sons and orders each of them to remove a nugget of gold from the mountain of gold. His two oldest sons fail, but the youngest succeeds. Jaṭila then presents all of his wealth to his youngest son, retires from the world, and attains Arahatship.

33 d. **Story of the Past: The goldsmith and his three sons.** While the shrine of the Buddha Kassapa was being erected, an Elder solicited contributions from a goldsmith. The goldsmith and his wife were quarreling when the Elder stopped at the door, and the goldsmith retorted angrily, "Throw your Teacher into the water." Therefore in seven successive states of existence the goldsmith was cast into the water on the day of his birth. In the seventh state of existence he was reborn as Jaṭila. The goldsmith made reparation for his insult by offering three vessels filled with golden flowers at the shrine of the Buddha. His two oldest sons refused to assist him, but the youngest gladly consented. Therefore the mountain of gold came into existence solely for Jaṭila and his youngest son.

34. **Ajātasattu attacks Jotika's palace [xxvi. 34 = 416].** After Ajātasattu has killed his father and has become firmly established in his kingdom, he decides that the time has come for him to take the palace of the treasurer Jotika. So he arms himself for battle and sallies forth with his host. Seeing the reflection of himself and his army in the jeweled walls, he concludes that the treasurer has come forth to do battle, and therefore flees in terror to the monastery. There he meets the treasurer Jotika, who is keeping Fast-day. The treasurer declares to the king that a thousand kings could not deprive him of his palace against his will. The treasurer then challenges the king to remove the rings from his fingers. The king is unable to do so. The treasurer, depressed by the thought that the king would have robbed him of his property, retires from the world and attains Arahatship. Thereupon all of his wealth vanishes, and the deities conduct his wife back to Uttarakuru. The monks ask Jotika whether he has any more longing for his palace or his wife. Jotika replies in the negative.

35. **The monk who was once a mime [xxvi. 35 = 417].** The monks, seeing a mime going through his performance, ask a monk who had once been a mime whether he has any more longing for that sort of thing. The monk replies in the negative. The monks doubt his word.

36. **The monk who was once a mime [xxvi. 36 = 418].** [Identical with the preceding, save for the stanza.]

37. **The skull-tapper [xxvi. 37–38 = 419–420].** A certain Brahman could tell by tapping on the skull of a dead man in which of the states of existence the dead man had been reborn. The Brahmans clothed him in red robes and traveled about the country with him, proclaiming to the people his marvelous powers. Coming to Sāvatthi, the Brahmans fell to arguing with the disciples of the Buddha as to which of their respective masters possessed the greater supernatural power. The disciples suggested that both parties go to the monastery and settle the dispute then and there. The Buddha placed in a row five skulls: one each of men who had been reborn in hell, the animal world, the world of men, and heaven, and one skull belonging to a man who had attained Arahatship. The Brahman tapped on the first four skulls and answered correctly, but was unable to tell in which of the states of existence the fifth had been reborn. The Brahman asked the Buddha whether he knew, and the Buddha answered in the affirmative. The Brahman then asked the Buddha to teach him the charm. The Buddha promised to do so if the Brahman would enter the Order. The Brahman entered the Order and attained Arahatship.

38. **Husband and wife [xxvi. 39 = 421].** Visākha listens to a sermon, retires from the world, and attains the Fruit of the Third Path. Dissatisfied with the world,

he bestows all of his wealth on his wife Dhammadinnā, and becomes a monk. Dhammadinnā follows his example, becomes a nun, and attains Arahatship. Visākha questions her on the Three Paths and the Three Fruits, and then questions her on Arahatship. Dhammadinnā, knowing that Visākha has got beyond his depth, laughs and suggests that Visākha consult the Buddha.

39. **Añgulimāla the fearless** [xxvi. 40 = 422]. On the occasion of the bestowal of the Gifts beyond Compare, a rogue elephant was placed beside Añgulimāla. The monks ask Añgulimāla whether he was afraid. Añgulimāla answers in the negative. The monks doubt his word. [Excerpt from xiii. 10.]

40. **It is the giver that makes the gift** [xxvi. 41 = 423]. The Buddha is attacked by rheumatism, and sends Elder Upavāṇa to the Brahman Devahita for hot water. The Brahman rejoices at the favor the Buddha has bestowed on him, fulfills his request, and asks the Buddha under what circumstances almsgiving yields abundant fruit. The Buddha replies that the value of a gift depends on the virtue of the giver.

BUDDHIST LEGENDS

Translated from the Dhamma-pada Commentary

TRANSLATION OF THE LEGENDS OF THE DHAMMAPADA COMMENTARY

Prologue[1]

Praise be unto him that is Highly Exalted, All-Holy, Supremely Enlightened.

I bow myself before the feet of the Supremely Enlightened, the All-Glorious. I honor his Good Law. I salute his Order.

Shrouded in darkness of error profound was the world, and he dwelt therein and beheld the ends thereof. With wonder-working power alight he lighted the lamp of the Good Law.

Skilled was he to know the true from the false in every matter. He, the Teacher, composed the Sentences of the Good Law, and moved with compassion, taught the pleasing Sentences of the Law, which yield increase of joy and satisfaction to gods and men alike.

"A subtile Commentary thereon has been handed down from generation to generation in the island of Ceylon. But because it is composed in the dialect of the island, it is of no profit or advantage to foreigners. It might perhaps conduce to the welfare of all mankind."

This was the wish expressed to me by Elder Kumāra Kassapa, self-conquered, living in tranquillity, steadfast in resolve. His earnest request was made to me because of his desire that the Good Law might endure.

Therefore I shall discard this dialect and its diffuse idiom and translate the work into the pleasing language of the Sacred Texts. Whatever in the Stanzas has not been made clear in the Stanzas themselves, whether in letter or in word, all that will I make clear. The rest I will also tell in Pāli, in accordance with the spirit of the Stanzas. Thus will I bring to the minds of the wise joy and satisfaction in matters both temporal and spiritual.

[1] See Introduction, § 5. Text: N i. 1–2.

BOOK I. PAIRS, YAMAKA VAGGA

I. 1. "IF THINE EYE OFFEND THEE, PLUCK IT OUT"[1]

1. Thought is of all things first, thought is of all things foremost, of thought are all things made.
If with thought corrupt a man speak or act,
Suffering follows him, even as a wheel follows the hoof of the beast of burden.

Where was this religious instruction given? At Sāvatthi. With reference to whom? Cakkhupāla the Elder.

At Sāvatthi, we are told, lived a householder named Great-Wealth, Mahā-Suvaṇṇa. He was rich, possessed of great wealth, possessed of ample means of enjoyment, but at the same time he was childless. One day, as he was on his way home from bathing at a ghat, he saw by the roadside a large forest tree with spreading branches. Thought he, "This tree must be tenanted by a powerful tree-spirit." So he caused the ground under the tree to be cleared, the tree itself to be inclosed with a wall, and sand to be spread within the inclosure. And having decked the tree with flags and banners, he made the following vow: "Should I obtain a son or a daughter, I will pay you great honor." Having so done, he went on his way.

Now in no long time his wife conceived a child in her womb. [4] So soon as his wife knew that she was with child, she informed her husband, and he performed the Protection of the Embryo for her. On the expiration of ten lunar months she gave birth to a son. Since the merchant obtained a son by protecting the tree, he named his son Protector, Pāla. After a time he obtained a second son. The younger son he named Protector junior, Culla Pāla, calling the older Protector senior, Mahā Pāla. When they reached manhood, their parents obtained wives for them. After a time the mother and father died, leaving the entire estate to be administered by the two sons.

At this time the Teacher, having set in motion the glorious Wheel of the Law, after journeying from place to place, took up his residence at Jetavana, a monastery erected by the wealthy merchant Anātha-

[1] Derived from this story are *Thera-Gāthā Commentary*, xcv, and Rogers, *Buddhaghosha's Parables*, i, pp. 1–11. Text: N i. 3–24.

piṇḍika at a cost of fifty-four crores of treasure. While in residence at Jetavana, he established the multitude in the Way to Heaven and the Way to Deliverance. (For the Tathāgata kept residence during but a single rainy season at the monastery erected by twice eighty thousand families of kinsmen, eighty on his mother's side, eighty on his father's. At Jetavana monastery, erected by Anāthapiṇḍika, he kept residence during nineteen rainy seasons; at Pubbārāma, erected by Visākhā at a cost of twenty-seven crores, he kept residence during six rainy seasons. Thus, by reason of the great merit of these two families, he kept residence near Savātthi during twenty-five rainy seasons.)

Anāthapiṇḍika and Visākhā, the eminent female lay disciple, went regularly twice every day to wait upon the Tathāgata. Knowing that the young novices would expect alms from them, they never went empty-handed. Before breakfast [5] they took food, both hard and soft; after breakfast they took the five medicaments and the eight beverages. Moreover, in their residences seats were always prepared for two thousand monks. Whoever wished food or drink or medicine was immediately provided with just what he wished.

Not a single day had Anāthapiṇḍika asked the Teacher a question. Anāthapiṇḍika, we are told, refrained from asking questions by reason of his excessive love for the Teacher. He thought to himself, "The Tathāgata is a delicate Buddha, a delicate prince. Were the Teacher, because of the thought, 'This householder is my supporter,' to preach the Law to me, he would grow weary." Therefore he asked the Teacher no questions. But so soon as Anāthapiṇḍika took his seat, the Teacher thought to himself, "This merchant protects me where I have no need to be protected. For I spent four Incalculables and a hundred thousand cycles of time in addition fulfilling the Perfections. My own gloriously adorned head have I cut off; my eyes have I torn out; my heart's flesh have I uprooted; both son and wife, dear to me as life, have I renounced, solely that I might preach the Law to others. This man protects me where I have no need to be protected." And straightway he preached a sermon on the Law.

At this time seventy million people dwelt in Sāvatthi. Of these, fifty million became Noble Disciples after hearing the discourse of the Teacher, but twenty million remained unconverted. The Noble Disciples had two duties: before breakfast they gave alms; after breakfast, bearing perfumes and garlands in their hands, with servants bearing garments, medicaments, and beverages, they went to hear the Law.

Now one day Mahā Pāla saw the Noble Disciples going to the monastery with perfumes and garlands in their hands. [6] When he saw them, he asked, "Where is this great throng going?" "To hear the Law." "I will go too," said he. So he went, paid obeisance to the Teacher, and sat down in the outer circle of the congregation.

Now when the Buddhas preach the Law, they have regard to the predispositions of their hearers for the Refuges, the Moral Precepts, and Retirement from the World. Thus they always preach the Law with reference to the disposition of mind of each individual. When, therefore, the Teacher preached the Law on that day, he had regard to Mahā Pāla's predispositions. And he preached in orderly sequence, expounding one subject after another; to wit, Almsgiving, the Moral Precepts, Heaven, the evil consequences and folly and defilement of Sensual Pleasures, and the blessings of Retirement from the World.

Mahā Pāla the householder listened Thought he, "When a man goes to the next world, neither sons nor daughters nor riches follow him; nay, even his own body goes not with him. Of what profit is it for me to live the house-life? I will become a monk." So at the end of the discourse he approached the Teacher and asked to be received into the Order. The Teacher asked him, "Have you no kinsman of whom it is proper that you should ask leave?" "Why yes, Reverend Sir, I have a younger brother." "Well then, ask him." To this Mahā Pāla agreed, and said, "Very well." So he paid obeisance to the Teacher and went home. Summoning his younger brother, he said to him,

"Dear brother, whatever wealth is in this house, whether animate or inanimate, all this I give into your hands; take possession thereof." "But you, master?" "I shall enter the Order under the Teacher." "What say you, dear brother? When my mother died, I gained in you as it were a mother; when my father died, as it were a father. Your house contains great wealth. Surely you can do works of merit even though you live the house-life. [7] Do not so." "Dear brother, after hearing the Teacher preach the Law, I can no longer live the life of a householder. For the Teacher preached a Law lovely in its beginning, its middle, and its end, and established precisely and exactly the Three Characteristics of existing things: Impermanence, Suffering, and Absence of Individuality. I cannot fulfill the Law amid the cares of the household life; I must enter the Order, dear brother." "Dear brother, now you are young. Wait until you are old, and then enter the Order." "Dear brother, in the case of an old man, even hands and feet are disobedient and answer not to his will; how much more so his kinsmen? No, I will not do as you say; I will fulfill the duties of a monk.

> Hands and feet weakened by old age are disobedient;
> How shall he whose strength is impaired fulfill the Law?

Dear brother, I shall enter the Order despite all considerations to the contrary."

In spite of his brother's lamentations Mahā Pāla went to the Teacher and asked to be admitted to the Order. He was admitted and professed and spent five rainy seasons in residence with teachers and preceptors. When he had completed his fifth residence and celebrated the terminal festival, he approached the Teacher, paid obeisance to him, and asked, "Reverend Sir, how many Duties are there in this religion?" "Two Duties only, monk: the Duty of Study and the Duty of Contemplation." "Reverend Sir, what is meant by the Duty of Study, and what is meant by the Duty of Contemplation?" "The Duty of Study necessitates gaining a knowledge of the Word of the Buddha in a manner conformable to one's understanding, the mastery of one or two Nikāyas, or indeed of the whole Tipiṭaka, bearing it in mind, reciting it, teaching it. [8] On the other hand the Duty of Contemplation, which leads to Arahatship, involves frugal living, satisfaction with a remote lodging, fixing firmly in one's mind the idea of decay and death, and the development of Spiritual Insight by persistent effort." "Reverend Sir, since I became a monk in old age, I shall not be able to fulfill the Duty of Study. But I can fulfill the Duty of Contemplation; teach me a Formula of Meditation."

So the Teacher taught him a Formula of Meditation leading to Arahatship. Then he paid obeisance to the Teacher, sought monks to accompany him, and having obtained sixty, departed with them. When he had proceeded a distance of twenty leagues, he arrived at a larger border-village, and accompanied by his retinue, entered the village for alms. The inhabitants, observing that the monks were faithful in the performance of their duties, were favorably disposed to them, provided them with seats, and served them with savory food. Then they inquired, "Reverend Sirs, whither go the noble monks?" "Lay brethren, to a suitable retreat." Then the wise villagers knew within themselves, "The reverend monks seek lodgings wherein to spend the rainy season."

Said they, "If the noble monks would reside here during these three months, we would abide steadfast in the Refuges and receive the Moral Precepts." The monks, thinking to themselves, "Through these families we shall effect escape from the round of existences," gave their consent. The villagers, having obtained the consent of the monks, proceeded to erect a monastery, building night-quarters and day-quarters, and when it was finished, presented it to the monks. The monks resorted regularly to that village only for alms. And a certain physician came to them and offered his services, saying, "Reverend Sirs, where many reside, disease is inevitable. Should sickness arise, pray send me word, and I will prescribe remedies for you."

When the monks entered upon residence on the first day of the rainy season, the Elder, addressing them, asked this question, [9] "Brethren, in how many Postures will you spend these three months?" "In all Four Postures, Reverend Sir." "But, brethren, is this proper? Assuredly we must be heedful, for it was from the living Buddha that we received our Formula of Meditation on coming hither; and the favor of the Buddhas may not be won by double-dealing, but only by the manifestation of upright intent. Four States of Suffering await whoso is heedless, that he may enter therein as into his own habitation. Therefore, brethren, be heedful." "But you, Reverend Sir?" "I shall spend the time in the Three Postures; I shall not stretch out my back, brethren." "Very well, Reverend Sir. Be heedful."

At the end of the first month the Elder, who allowed himself no sleep, began to suffer from an affection of the eyes. Streams of tears trickled from his eyes, as streams of water from a broken jar. All night long he devoted himself to meditation, and with the coming of dawn entered his cell and sat down. When it was time for the monks to go the rounds for alms, they came to the Elder and said to him, "Reverend Sir, it is time for us to go the rounds for alms." "Very well, brethren; take bowl and robe." Having thus directed them to take their own bowls and robes, he himself set out. The monks observed that his eyes were running and asked him, "What is the matter, Reverend Sir?" "The wind cuts my eyes, brethren." "Were we not offered the services of a physician, Reverend Sir? We will inform him." "Very well, [10] brethren."

They informed the physician, who prepared an ointment and sent it to the Elder. The Elder applied the ointment to his nose, remaining seated as he did so, and then entered the village. The physician, seeing him, said to him, "Reverend Sir, I am informed that the wind hurts your reverence's eyes." "That is true, lay disciple." "Reverend Sir, did you apply to your nose an ointment which I prepared and sent you?" "Yes, lay disciple." "How do you feel now?" "The pain continues just the same, lay disciple." The physician thought to himself, "The ointment which I sent him should have cured him with only one application. How is it that he is not cured?" So he asked the Elder, "Were you seated when you applied the ointment, or were you lying down?" The Elder remained silent. Though the physician repeated the question several times, he answered not a word. The physician thought to himself, "I will go to the monastery and have a look at his cell." So he dismissed the Elder, saying to him, "That will do, Reverend Sir." And going to the monastery, he inspected the Elder's cell. Seeing only a place to walk and a place to sit down, but no place to lie down, he asked the Elder, "Reverend Sir, were you seated when you applied the ointment, or were you lying down?" The Elder remained silent. "Reverend Sir, do not act in this way; the duties of a religious can be performed only so long as the body is properly cared for. Were you lying down when you applied the ointment?" After the physician had repeated the question several times, the Elder replied, "Go your way, brother; I will take counsel and decide the matter for myself."

Now the Elder had no kinsmen or blood-relatives there. With whom, therefore, was he to take counsel? Therefore he took counsel with his own person, saying, [11] "Come now, brother Pālita, tell me this, Will you regard your eyes or the Religion of the Buddha? For in the round of existences without conceivable beginning, there is no counting the number of times you have been without eyes. But while unnumbered hundreds of Buddhas and thousands of Buddhas have passed, your experience does not cover the period of even a single Buddha. Now in this rainy season you resolved not to lie down for three months. Therefore let your eyes perish or decay. Keep only the Law of the Buddha, not your eyes." And admonishing his own physical body, he uttered the following Stanzas,

> My eyes perish, my ears perish, so also my body,
> All that has to do with my body perishes;
> Why, Pālita, continue heedless?

My eyes wear out, my ears wear out, so also my body,
All that has to do with my body wears out;
Why, Pālita, continue heedless?

My eyes decay, my ears decay, so also my body,
All that has to do with my body decays;
Why, Pālita, continue heedless? [12]

Having thus admonished himself in three Stanzas, he applied the ointment to his nose, remaining seated as before, and then entered the village for alms. The physician, seeing him, asked him, "Reverend Sir, have you applied the ointment to your nose?" "Yes, lay disciple." "How do you feel?" "The pain continues just the same, lay disciple." "Reverend Sir, were you seated when you applied the ointment, or were you lying down?" The Elder remained silent. The physician repeated the question several times, but the Elder answered never a word. Then the physician said to him, "You are not doing as you ought for your own good. Henceforth do not say, 'So and So prepared ointment for me' and I will not say, 'I prepared ointment for you.'"

Given up by the physician, the Elder went to the monastery. Said he, "Monk, though you have been given up by the physician, do not give up your Posture."

You are given up as incurable, you are abandoned by your physician.
Destined to the King of Death, why, Pālita, are you heedless?

Having admonished himself in this Stanza, he resumed his meditations. At the end of the middle watch his eyes and his Depravities were blotted out simultaneously, and he became an Arahat dwelling in the bliss of Spiritual Insight. He entered his cell and sat down. When the time came for the monks to go the rounds for alms, they came to the Elder and said to him, "Reverend Sir, it is time for us to go the rounds for alms." "Is it time, brethren?" "Yes, Reverend Sir." "Well then, go your way." "But you, Reverend Sir?" "The sight of my eyes is gone, brethren." They looked at his eyes, and their own eyes filled with tears. "Do not worry, Reverend Sir; [13] we will look after you," said they to the Elder, comforting him. And having performed the various duties required of them, they entered the village for alms.

Not seeing the Elder, people asked the monks, "Brethren, where is our noble Elder?" When they learned what had happened, they sent rice-porridge to him. Afterwards, taking food, they went in person, paid obeisance to the Elder, and rolling on the ground before his feet, poured out their lamentations. Then they comforted him, saying, "We will care for you, Reverend Sir; do not worry," and went their way. From that time on they sent rice-porridge regularly to the monastery.

The Elder constantly admonished the other sixty monks, and they carried out his admonitions so faithfully that at the next Pavāraṇā all of them became Arahats possessed of the Supernatural Faculties. At the end of the rainy season, desiring to see the Teacher, they said to the Elder, "Reverend Sir, we desire to see the Teacher." When the Elder heard their request, he thought to himself, "I am weak, and on the way is a forest haunted by evil spirits. If I go with them, all will become weary and will be unable to obtain alms. I will send them on ahead."

So he said to them, "Brethren, you go on ahead." "But you, Reverend Sir?" "I am weak, and on the way is a forest haunted by evil spirits. If I go with you, you will all become weary; therefore you go on ahead." "Do not so, Reverend Sir; we will go only with you." "Brethren, please do not do so; if you do so, it will displease me. When my younger brother sees you and asks after me, tell him that [14] I have lost the sight of my eyes, and he will send someone to guide my steps. Greet in my name the Possessor of the Ten Forces and the eighty Chief Elders." So saying, he dismissed them.

They begged the Elder to pardon them for their insistence, and entered the village for alms. The villagers provided them with seats, presented them with alms, and asked them, "Reverend Sirs, may we know why the noble monks are leaving?" "Yes, lay disciples, we desire to see the Teacher." The villagers repeatedly begged the monks to remain, but finding that they were firm in their determination to go, accompanied them on their way weeping, and then turned back.

After journeying from place to place, the monks arrived at Jetavana and greeted the Teacher and the eighty Chief Elders in the name of the Elder. Having so done, they entered for alms the street where lived the Elder's younger brother. The householder recognized them, received them cordially, provided them with seats, and asked them, "Where is my dear brother the Elder?" They told him what had happened. Flinging himself at their feet, he rolled on the ground and wept.

Then he asked them, "Now, brethren, what is to be done?" "The Elder wishes to have someone come from here, that he may return with him." "Brethren, here is my sister's son Pālita. Send him." "It will never do to send him, for there is danger by the way. We might, however, send him, after first receiving him into the Order." "Do so and send him, brethren." So they received him into the Order and for a fortnight instructed him in such matters as the proper manner of putting on the robe. Then, showing him the way, they sent him forth.

After journeying from place to place, he arrived at the village. Seeing an old man at the village gate, he asked him, "Is there a forest hermitage near this village?" "There is, Reverend Sir." "Who lives there?" "An Elder named Pālita, Reverend Sir." "Show me the way there." "Who are you, Reverend Sir?" "I am the son of the Elder's sister." So the old man took him and [15] led him to the hermitage. He paid obeisance to the Elder and for a fortnight performed the major and minor duties for him, ministering to him faithfully. Then he said to him, "Reverend Sir, the householder my mother's brother desires to have you come to him. Let us go thither." "Very well, take hold of my staff." Taking hold of the staff by the tip, he entered the village with the Elder. The villagers provided the Elder with a seat and asked him, "Reverend Sir, may we know your purpose in going?" "Yes, lay disciples, I am going to pay my respects to the Teacher." The villagers sought by all means in their power to persuade them to remain, but failing in their efforts, escorted them part of the way, and then turned back weeping.

When the novice had gone part of the way with the Elder, holding the tip of the Elder's staff, he arrived at a forest village named Kaṭṭhanagara, near which the Elder formerly resided. As the novice came out of the village, he heard in the forest the voice of a woman singing away as she gathered firewood. As he listened to her song, he fell in love with her voice. (There is no sound to be compared with a woman's voice for power to thrill man's whole frame. Therefore said the Exalted One, "Monks, I know of no other single sound which so completely takes possession of the heart of a man as this, monks; namely, a woman's voice." [1])

The novice, fascinated by her voice, let go his hold of the Elder's staff. Said he, "Wait just a moment, Reverend Sir; I have some business." So saying, [16] he went in the direction of the woman. When she saw him, she became silent. The novice violated the law of

[1] *Aṅguttara*, i. 1.

chastity with her. The Elder thought to himself, "Just now I heard the sound of someone singing, and it was none other than a woman's voice. The novice tarries; he must have violated the law of chastity." When the novice had finished his business, he returned to the Elder and said, "Come, Reverend Sir, let us be off." But the Elder asked him, "Novice, have you committed sin?" The novice remained silent, and though questioned repeatedly, answered never a word. Then said the Elder to him, "A sinner like you can never hold the tip of my staff."

The novice, overwhelmed with remorse, removed his yellow robes, clothed himself in the garb of a householder, and said, "Reverend Sir, before I was a novice; now I have become a layman again. It was not through faith that I became a monk, but because I feared the dangers of the journey. Come, let us be off." The Elder replied, "An evildoer is an evildoer, be he layman or be he novice. While you were a novice, you were unable to keep the law of chastity. Will you be a better man for having become a layman? A sinner like you can never hold the tip of my staff." "Reverend Sir, the road is infested with evil spirits and you are blind. How can you remain here?" The Elder answered, "Brother, don't worry about that. No matter whether I lie down right here and die, or wander hither and thither, with you I will never go." So saying, he pronounced the following Stanzas,

> Alas! I have lost the sight of my eyes; a weary way have I come;
> I will lie down and go no farther; with a simpleton no fellowship may be. [17]
>
> Alas! I have lost the sight of my eyes; a weary way have I come;
> I shall die; I will go no farther; with a simpleton no fellowship may be.

When the novice heard this, he was overwhelmed with remorse. And he cried out, "A grievous sin indeed have I committed, a deed of violence and impropriety!" And wringing his hands and weeping, he plunged into the forest and made off.

By the power of the Elder's virtue the Yellowstone Throne of Sakka king of gods, sixty leagues long, fifty leagues wide, fifteen leagues thick, of the color of the Jayasumana flower, which has a way of lowering itself when Sakka sits down and of rising again when he stands up, manifested signs of heat. "Who, pray, can be seeking to thrust me from my seat?" thought Sakka. Surveying the world with Supernatural Vision, he saw the Elder. Therefore said those of old time,

The king of gods, possessing a thousand eyes, purified the Divine Eye;
This sin-abhorring Pāla purified his life.

The king of the gods, possessing a thousand eyes, purified the Divine Eye;
This Pāla, reverer of the Law, sat delighting in Religion.

Then this thought occurred to him, "Should I fail to go to the assistance of such a sin-abhorring, Law-revering Elder, my head is likely to split into seven pieces. I will go to him." And so

The king of the gods, possessed of a thousand eyes, bearing majestic sway over the gods,
In a single instant approaching, approached Cakkhupāla. [18]

Accordingly Sakka approached the Elder. When he was quite near him, he shuffled his feet. "Who is there?" asked the Elder. "It is I, Reverend Sir, a traveler." "Where are you going, lay disciple?" "To Sāvatthi, Reverend Sir." "Continue your journey, brother." "But, Reverend Sir, where is your reverence going?" "I am going there too." "Well then, let us go together, Reverend Sir." "I am weak, brother. If you go with me, you will be delayed." "I have no urgent business. Besides, if I go with you, I can avail myself of one of the ten ways and means of acquiring merit. Let us go together, Reverend Sir."

The Elder thought to himself, "This is without doubt some pious man." So he said to him, "Very well, take hold of the tip of my staff, lay brother." Sakka did so. And Sakka shortened the distance so that they arrived at Jetavana at eventide. The Elder, hearing the noise of trumpets, drums, and other instruments of music, asked, "Where is that noise?" "At Sāvatthi, Reverend Sir." "Lay brother, when I came here before, we were a long time in coming." "I know a short cut, Reverend Sir." At that moment the Elder perceived within himself, "This is no human being; it must be a divinity."

The king of gods, possessing a thousand eyes, bearing majestic sway over the gods,
Shortening the distance, came quickly to Sāvatthi.

Sakka conducted the Elder to a hut of leaves and grass which his younger brother had made for his express use, [19] seated him on a couch, and then, disguising himself as a dear friend of the younger brother, went to summon him. "Friend Pāla!" he called out. "What is it, friend?" "Do you know that the Elder has arrived?" "No; is it true that the Elder has arrived?" "Yes, friend, I have just returned from the hermitage, and saw the Elder seated in the hut of leaves and grass you built for him." So saying, he departed.

The householder went to the hermitage. When he saw the Elder, he flung himself at his feet, rolled on the ground, and wept. Then he said, "I knew this would happen, Reverend Sir. It was for this reason that I withheld from you my permission to become a monk." After talking with him for some time, he freed two slave-boys, had the Elder receive them into the Order, and committed him to their care, saying, "Bring rice-porridge and other kinds of food from the village and minister to the Elder." The novices ministered to the Elder, performing the major and minor duties faithfully.

Now one day a party of monks residing in foreign parts came to Jetavana to see the Teacher. After paying their respects to the Teacher and seeing the eighty Chief Elders, they made the rounds of the monastery. Coming to Cakkhupāla's retreat, they said to each other, "Let us see him too." So when evening came, they set out to visit him. Just at that moment a severe storm arose. So they turned back, saying, "It is now evening, and a storm has arisen. Therefore we will go and see him in the morning." The rain continued during the first watch, but ceased in the second. The Elder, a man of great energy, accustomed to walking, came down into the cloister in the last watch. Now at that time many insects had come out of the newly wet earth, [20] and as the Elder walked up and down, they perished in great numbers. The resident monks did not sweep betimes where the Elder walked. When the visiting monks arrived, saying, "We would see the place where the Elder resides," and saw the insects in the cloister, they asked, "Who was it that walked in this cloister?" "Our master, Reverend Sirs." They were offended and said, "See what the monk has done. When he had the sight of his eyes, he lay down and slept and did no sin. But now that he has lost his eyesight, saying to himself, 'I will take a walk,' he has destroyed these insects. 'That which is right I will do,' said he; but that which was not right he has done."

So they went and reported the matter to the Tathāgata, saying, "Reverend Sir, the Elder Cakkhupāla, saying to himself, 'I will take a walk,' has destroyed many insects." "But did you see him killing them?" "We did not, Reverend Sir." "Precisely as you did not see him, so also did he not see these insects. Monks, they that are freed from the Depravities have no thought of killing." "Reverend Sir, seeing that he was destined to become an Arahat, how was it that he became blind?" "Monks, it was by reason of his misdeed in a former existence." "Why, Reverend Sir, what did he do?" "Well then, monks, listen."

1 a. Story of the Past: The wicked physician and the woman[1]

In times long past, when the king of Kāsi reigned at Benāres, a certain physician went through towns and villages practicing his profession. Seeing a certain woman with weak eyes, he asked her, "What is the matter with you?" "My eyesight has failed." "I will prescribe for you." "Do so, master." "What will you give me?" "If you succeed in making my eyes well and strong again, I will become your slave, and my sons and daughters too." "Very well," said he. So he prescribed a remedy for her, and with a single application of the remedy her eyes became well and strong again. [21]

Upon this she thought, "I promised to become his slave, and my sons and daughters too. But he will not treat me kindly. Therefore I will deceive him." So when the physician came and asked her how she was getting on, she answered, "Before, my eyes pained me a little; but now they hurt me worse than ever." The physician thought, "This woman is deceiving me because she is unwilling to give me anything. I don't want her fee; now I will make her blind." So he went home and told his wife about the matter. His wife said nothing. Then he compounded an ointment, went to the woman's house, and directed her to rub it into her eyes. She did so, and her eyes went out like the flame of a lamp. That physician was Cakkhupāla. **End of Story of the Past.**

"Monks, the evil deed then committed by my son followed him ever after; for an evil deed follows the evildoer even as a wheel follows the hoof of the ox that bears the yoke." After relating this story, the King of Righteousness joined the connection, even as a king seals an edict with the royal seal after the clay has been affixed, and pronounced the following Stanza,

1. Thought is of all things first, thought is of all things foremost, of thought are all things made.
   If with thought corrupt a man speak or act,
   Suffering follows him, even as a wheel follows the hoof of the beast of burden.

[1] Cf. Story ix. 9 a, Physician, boys, and snake.

I. 2. WHY CRY FOR THE MOON? [1]

The Second Stanza also, beginning with the words, "Thought is of all things first," was recited in the same city, Sāvatthi, with reference to Maṭṭhakuṇḍali. [25]

At Sāvatthi, we are told, lived a Brahman named Never-Gave, Adinnapubbaka. He never gave anything to anybody, and that is why they called him Never-Gave, Adinnapubbaka. He had an only son who was his darling and delight. Now he desired to have a set of ornaments made for him. But knowing that in case he gave the commission to a goldsmith, he should have to pay him a fee, he beat out the gold himself, made him a pair of burnished earrings, and gave them to him. In this way his son received the name Burnished-Earrings, Maṭṭhakuṇḍali.

When his son was sixteen years old, he had an attack of jaundice. The mother looked at the boy and said, "Brahman, your son is sick; have him treated by a physician." "Wife, if I send for a physician, I shall have to pay him a fee in rice; you care nothing about the loss of my substance." "Well, Brahman, what are you going to do about it?" "I shall manage things in such a way as to lose none of my wealth." So he went to various physicians and asked, "What are you in the habit of prescribing for such and such an ailment?" They mentioned to him bark of trees and this or that.

So he procured these and prepared a remedy for his son. But in spite of all he did, his son's condition grew worse and worse, until finally he was past help. The Brahman, perceiving that his son was very weak, sent for a physician. The physician looked at the youth and said, "I have important business to attend to; send for some other physician and have him treat him." [26] Having thus refused to treat the boy, he turned and left the house. The Brahman realized

[1] Parallels: *Jātaka* 449: iv. 59–62; *Jātaka* 454: 85–87; *Vimāna-Vatthu Commentary*, vii. 9: 322–330 (cf. *Peta-Vatthu Commentary*, ii. 5: 92); Rogers, *Buddhaghosha's Parables*, ii, pp. 12–17. The author has evidently worked over *Jātaka* 449, both Introduction and Story of the Past, making one story out of two and expanding the original considerably. The Buddha's conversion of Maṭṭhakuṇḍali, a prominent feature of the *Dhammapada Commentary* story, is lacking in the *Jātaka* version. The *Vimāna-Vatthu Commentary* version is derived, not from the *Jātaka Book*, but from the *Dhammapada Commentary*. It is much briefer at the beginning and end; elsewhere more diffuse. *Vv. cm.*, 325^{3}–326^{13}, is word for word the same as *Dh. cm.*, i. 29–30. This story is referred to at *Milindapañha*, 350^{11-12}. Text: N i. 25–37.

that his son was at the point of death. Thought he, "All who come to see this youth will see the wealth in my house; therefore I will place him outside." So he carried his son out of the house and laid him down on the terrace.

On that day, very early in the morning, the Exalted One arose from a Trance of Great Compassion. And for the purpose of seeing those who had made their Earnest Wish under previous Buddhas, those the roots of whose merit were fully developed, brethren capable of conversion, he surveyed the universe with the Eye of a Buddha, spreading the Net of his Knowledge over the ten Cakkavāḷa Worlds. Straightway Maṭṭhakuṇḍali, lying outside on the terrace, appeared within the Net of his Knowledge. As soon as the Teacher saw him, he became aware that he had been removed from the house and laid there; and considering within himself, "Have I sufficient reason for going to him?" he saw the following:

"This youth will repose faith in me, will die, and will be reborn as a deity in the Heaven of the Thirty-three, in a golden mansion, with a retinue of a thousand celestial nymphs. The Brahman will burn his body and will go about the burning-ground weeping. The deity will survey his own person, three-quarters of a league in height, adorned with sixty cart-loads of ornaments, surrounded by a thousand celestial nymphs. And considering within himself, 'Through what merit have I attained this attainment of splendor?' he will perceive that he obtained it by reposing faith in me. Then he will say to himself, 'My father, who failed to provide medicine for me for fear of wasting his wealth, has now gone to the burning-ground and is weeping. I will effect a change in his attitude.' And provoked at his father, he will take the form of Maṭṭhakuṇḍali, will go [27] to a place not far from the burning-ground, and will fling himself on the ground and weep.

"The Brahman will ask him, 'Who are you?' He will reply, 'I am your son Maṭṭhakuṇḍali.' 'Where were you reborn?' 'In the World of the Thirty-three.' The Brahman will ask him, 'What deed of merit did you perform?' and Maṭṭhakuṇḍali will tell him that he was reborn in the World of the Thirty-three by reposing faith in me. Then the Brahman will ask me, 'Are there any that have been reborn in Heaven by reposing faith in you?' and I will reply to him, 'It is not so many hundreds or thousands or hundreds of thousands — there is no counting the number of them.' I will then recite a Stanza in the Dhammapada. At the conclusion of the Stanza eighty-four thousand living beings will obtain Comprehension of the Law, Maṭṭhakuṇḍali will receive the Fruit of Conversion, and so will Adinnapubbaka the Brahman. Thus through this noble youth many will obtain Comprehension of the Law."

Of all this the Teacher became aware. Accordingly, on the following day, having attended to his toilet, he surrounded himself with a large company of monks, entered Sāvatthi for alms, and in due course arrived at the house of the Brahman. At that moment Maṭṭhakuṇḍali was lying with face turned towards the house. The Teacher, observing that he did not see him, sent forth a ray of light. "What is that radiance?" asked the youth, turning over. Seeing the Teacher from where he lay, he said, "On account of a foolish father, I have been deprived of the privilege of approaching so excellent a Buddha, nor have I obtained the privilege either of waiting upon him or of giving him alms or of hearing the Law. Now I cannot even control the movements of my hands; there is nothing else I can do." So saying, he reposed faith in the Buddha. The Teacher said, "He has done enough," and departed.

As the Tathāgata receded from his range of vision, [28] he died with a believing heart, and as if awaking from sleep, was reborn in the World of the Gods in a golden mansion thirty leagues in extent. The Brahman burned the body of his son, and resorting to the burning-ground, abandoned himself entirely to lamentation. Every day he would go to the burning-ground and weep and say, "Where are you, my only son?"

The deity his former son surveyed his own glory and considered within himself, "By what deed of merit have I obtained this?" Perceiving that it was by reposing faith in the Teacher, he said to himself, "This Brahman failed to provide medicine for me when I was sick, but now goes to the burning-ground and weeps; I must effect a change in his attitude." Accordingly he took the form of Maṭṭhakuṇḍali, went to a place not far from the burning-ground, and stood wringing his hands and weeping. The Brahman saw him and thought to himself, "As for myself, I am weeping because of sorrow for my son; why is yonder youth weeping? I will ask him." So he asked him in the following Stanza,

> Richly adorned, wearing earrings of burnished gold,
> Bearing garlands, with protuberances of yellow sandal,
> You wring your hands and weep.
> Why are you afflicted in the midst of the forest?

Said the youth,

I have obtained a chariot-body,
Shining, of solid gold,
But I cannot find a pair of wheels for it;
Through grief over this I shall lose my life. [29]

Then said the Brahman to him,

Name wheels of gold, of precious stones,
Of copper, or of silver.
Name them to me, good youth,
And I will procure you a pair of wheels.

Hearing this, the youth thought to himself, "This Brahman failed to provide medicine for his son. But seeing that I look like his son, he says, 'I will procure wheels for your chariot, either of gold or of precious stones or of copper or of silver.' Very well! I will humble him." So he said, "How large a pair of wheels will you make for my chariot?" "As large as you wish." "I want the moon and the sun," said the youth. "Give them to me." By way of request

Said the youth to the Brahman, The moon and the sun are brothers twain.
My chariot is of solid gold; with such a pair of wheels it would shine.

The Brahman replied,

Youth, you are a simpleton to seek for what cannot be obtained.
I suppose you will die, for you will never obtain the moon and the sun.

But the youth said to him, "But which is the greater simpleton, he who weeps for what exists, or he who weeps for what does not exist?" [30]

They are seen that go and come;
The property of color is seen on both sides of the street;
But he that is dead and gone cannot be seen;
Which of us that weep here is the greater simpleton?

Hearing this, the Brahman came to the conclusion, "What this youth says is sensible." And he said to him,

Youth, what you say is quite true; it is I that am the greater simpleton of the two that weep;
Like a child crying for the moon, I desired a son that is dead and gone.

Having thus spoken, freed from sorrow by the words of the youth, the Brahman pronounced the following Stanzas in praise of the youth,

When I was all on fire, and the fire was as if fed with ghee,
You poured water on the fire, as it were, and extinguished all my grief.

You drew out the arrow that was in me, the sorrow that was in my heart;
Although I was dead with sorrow, you removed my sorrow for my son.

The arrow of my grief has been withdrawn, and I am tranquil and happy;
Having heard your words, youth, I sorrow no more, nor do I weep. [31]

Then the Brahman asked him, "Who are you?"

Are you a devatā or a gandhabba, or are you Sakka Purindada?
Who are you? whose son are you? how am I to know you?

The youth replied,

I am he for whom you lament, he for whom you weep,
Your son, whom you yourself burned in the burning-ground.
By the performance of a work of merit
I have attained the Society of the Thirty.

In these words the youth gave him the information he asked for. Then said the Brahman,

I never saw you give alms, either little or much, in your own home.
Nor did you so much as keep fast-day; by what work of merit did you attain the World of the Gods?

The youth replied,

As I lay in my own home, sick, afflicted, oppressed with a grievous ailment, my body weakened by disease,
I beheld the Buddha, free from passion, free from doubt, happy, of lofty wisdom.

With joyful mind and believing heart I did homage to the Tathāgata, with hands reverently clasped;
By the performance of this work of merit I attained the Society of the Thirty. [32]

As the youth spoke, the whole body of the Brahman was suffused with joy. And this joy he made known in the following Stanza,

Wonderful! marvelous! that such as this should be the fruit of a reverent salutation.
I too with joyful mind and believing heart seek refuge in the Buddha this very day.

Then said the youth,

This very day with believing heart seek refuge in the Buddha, the Law, and the Order;
Likewise take upon yourself the Five Precepts, and keep them unbroken and unimpaired;
Refrain from taking life, from this moment; take not that which is not given to you in this world;
Drink not strong drink; speak not falsely; be content with your own wife.

"Very well," said the Brahman, agreeing. And he pronounced the following Stanzas,

You desire my weal, yakkha; you desire my welfare, divinity;
I will obey your words; you are my teacher.

I seek refuge in the Buddha, and likewise in his incomparable Law,
And in the Order of the Prince of Men do I seek refuge.

From the taking of life do I refrain, from this moment; I abstain from taking that which is not given to me in this world;
I drink not strong drink; I speak not falsely; I am content with my own wife. [33]

Then said the deity to him, "Brahman, you have much wealth in your house. Approach the Teacher, give alms, listen to the Law, and ask him questions." So saying, he disappeared. The Brahman went home and said to his wife, "Wife, I shall invite the monk Gotama to my house and ask him questions; therefore prepare hospitality." Then he went to the monastery, and without saluting the Teacher or expressing any pleasure at seeing him, stood on one side and said, "Sir Gotama, consent for to-day to take a meal in my house with your company of monks." The Teacher consented. As soon as the Brahman received his consent, he returned home quickly and caused food, both hard and soft, to be prepared in his house.

The Teacher, accompanied by the Congregation of Monks, went to his house and sat down on the seat prepared for him. The Brahman waited upon him respectfully. A multitude of people assembled. We are told that when a man who holds false views invites the Tathāgata, two classes of people assemble. Those who hold false views assemble with the thought in their minds, "To-day we shall see the monk Gotama embarrassed by the questions that are asked him." Those who hold orthodox views assemble with the thought, "To-day we shall see the power of a Buddha and the grace of a Buddha."

Now when the Tathāgata had finished his meal, the Brahman approached him, seated himself on a low seat, and asked him the following question, "Sir Gotama, are there any that have been reborn in Heaven, without giving alms to you, without rendering honor to you, without hearing the Law, without keeping fast-day, solely by making an act of faith?" "Brahman, why do you ask me? Did not your own son Maṭṭhakuṇḍali tell you that he had been reborn in Heaven by reposing faith in me?" "When, Sir Gotama?" "Did you not go to the burning-ground to-day, and while you were weeping, see a youth near you wringing his hands and weeping? [34] And did you not say to him, 'Richly adorned, wearing earrings of burnished gold, bearing garlands, with protuberances of yellow sandal?'"

Continuing, the Teacher related in detail the conversation of the two and told the whole story of Maṭṭhakuṇḍali.

For this very reason the Teacher pronounced this Word of the Buddha, "Brahman, it is not a question of one hundred or two hundred — there is no counting the number of those who have been reborn in Heaven by reposing faith in me." The multitude were not free from doubt. The Teacher, perceiving that they were not free from doubt, commanded, "Let the deity Maṭṭhakuṇḍali come hither in his mansion." Thereupon Maṭṭhakuṇḍali drew near, three-quarters of a league in height, his person adorned with celestial adornments. Descending from his mansion, he paid obeisance to the Teacher and stood respectfully on one side. The Teacher asked him, "What work of merit did you perform to attain this glory?"

> Divinity, you who possess surpassing beauty,
> Illuminating all four quarters like the herb-star,
> I ask you, god of mighty power,
> What meritorious act did you perform in your human estate?

When the Teacher had completed this Stanza, the deity replied, "Reverend Sir, I obtained this glory by reposing faith in you." "You obtained it by reposing faith in me?" "Yes, Reverend Sir."

The populace surveyed the god and exclaimed, "Marvelous, indeed, are the powers of the Buddhas! the son of the Brahman Adinnapubbaka [35] obtained glory such as this simply by reposing faith in the Teacher, without doing a single other work of merit!" And they were filled with joy. Then the Teacher said to them, "Our thoughts are the source of all our actions, both good and bad, and by our thoughts are our actions controlled. For, like a shadow, an act done with thought of faith never leaves a man who goes to the World of the Gods or the world of men. Having related this story, the King of Truth joined the connection, and sealing, as it were, with the royal seal an edict to which the clay had been attached, pronounced the following Stanza,

> 2. Thought is of all things first, thought is of all things foremost, of thought are all things made.
> If with thought of faith a man speak or act,
> Happiness follows him, even as a shadow never fading.

I. 3. TISSA THE FAT [1]

He abused me. This religious instruction was given by the Teacher while he was in residence at Jetavana with reference to Elder Tissa. [37]

It seems that this Venerable Elder was the son of the sister of the father of the Exalted One. He was an old man when he retired from the world, and very fat. He enjoyed the gain and honor of the Buddhas; his clothes were always smooth from constant beating; he always sat in the center of the monastery in the Hall of State.

One day some visiting monks came to see the Tathāgata, and supposing Tissa to be some Great Elder, asked to be allowed the privilege of waiting upon him, offering among other things to rub his feet. Tissa remained silent. Thereupon a certain young monk asked him, "How many seasons have you kept residence?" "No seasons at all," replied Tissa; "I was an old man when I retired from the world." Said the young monk, "You wretched old monk, [38] you overestimate your own importance. Seeing before you, as you do, all these Great Elders, you are not even civil to them. To their offers to perform various services for you, you answer by silence. Moreover, you show not the slightest regret for your misconduct." So saying, he snapped his fingers. Recovering the pride of a member of the Warrior caste, Tissa asked them, "Whom did you come to see?" "We came to see the Teacher." "But with reference to me, you say to yourselves, 'Who is he?' I will extirpate your whole race." So saying, he went to the Teacher, weeping and sad and sorrowful.

The Teacher asked him, "Tissa, how is it that you come to me sad and sorrowful, with tears in your eyes, weeping?" The monks said to themselves, "If he goes alone, he may cause some trouble." So they went right with him, paid obeisance to the Teacher, and sat down respectfully on one side. Tissa answered the Teacher's question as follows, "Reverend Sir, these monks are abusing me." "But where were you sitting?" "In the center of the monastery in the Hall of State, Reverend Sir." "Did you see these monks when they came?" "Yes, Reverend Sir, I saw them." "Did you rise and go to meet them?" "No, Reverend Sir, I did not." "Did you offer to take their monastic utensils?" "No, Reverend Sir, I did not offer to take them."

[1] Derived from this story are *Thera-Gāthā Commentary*, xxxix, and Rogers, *Buddhaghosha's Parables*, iii, pp. 18–24. Cf. *Saṁyutta*, xxii. 84: iii. 106–109. Text: N i. 37–45.

"Did you offer to wait upon them and to provide them with water to drink?" "No, Reverend Sir, I did not offer to do either of these things." "Did you bring seats for them and rub their feet?" "I did not, Reverend Sir." "Tissa, you should have performed all these services for the old monks, for he who does not do this has no right to sit in the center of the monastery. You alone are to blame; ask pardon of these monks." "But they [39] abused me, Reverend Sir; I will not ask their pardon." "Tissa, do not act thus. You alone are to blame; ask their pardon." "I will not ask their pardon, Reverend Sir."

The monks said to the Teacher, "He is an obstinate monk, Reverend Sir." The Teacher replied, "Monks, this is not the first time he has proved obstinate; he was obstinate also in a previous state of existence." "We know all about his present obstinacy, Reverend Sir; but what did he do in a previous state of existence?" "Well then, monks, listen," said the Teacher. So saying, he told the following

3 a. Story of the Past: Devala and Nārada [1]

Once upon a time, when a certain king of Benāres reigned at Benāres, an ascetic named Devala, who had resided for eight months in the Himālaya country, desiring to reside near the city during the four months of the rains, returned from the Himālaya for salt and vinegar. Seeing two boys at the gate of the city, he asked them, "Where do monks who come to this city spend the night?" "In the potter's hall, Reverend Sir." So Devala went to the potter's hall, stopped at the door, and said, "If it is agreeable to you, Bhaggava, I should like to spend one night in your hall." The potter turned over the hall to him, saying, "I have no work going on in the hall at night, and the hall is a large one; spend the night here as you please, Reverend Sir."

No sooner had Devala entered the hall and sat down than another ascetic named Nārada, returning from the Himālaya, asked the potter for a night's lodging. The potter thought to himself, "The ascetic who arrived first may or may not be willing to spend the night with him; I will therefore relieve myself of responsibility." [40] So he said to the ascetic who had just arrived, "Reverend Sir, if the ascetic who arrived first approves, spend the night at his pleasure." So Nārada approached Devala and said, "Teacher, if it is agreeable to you, I should like to spend one night here." Devala replied, "The hall is a large one; therefore come in and spend the night on one side." So

[1] Cf. the story of Jātimanta and the Future Buddha in *Jātaka* 497: iv. 388–389.

Nārada went in and sat down behind the ascetic who had gone in before him. Both exchanged friendly greetings.

When it was bedtime, Nārada noted carefully the place where Devala lay and the position of the door, and then lay down. But when Devala lay down, instead of lying down in his proper place, he lay down directly across the doorway. The result was that when Nārada went out at night, he trod on Devala's matted locks. Thereupon Devala cried out, "Who is treading on my locks?" Nārada replied, "Teacher, it is I." "False ascetic," said Devala, "you come from the forest and tread on my locks." "Teacher, I did not know that you were lying here; pardon me." Nārada then went out, leaving Devala weeping as if his heart would break.

Devala thought to himself, "I will let him tread on me when he comes in also." So he turned around and lay down, placing his head where his feet had been before. When Nārada came in, he thought to himself, "The first time I injured the teacher; this time I will go in past his feet." The result was that, when Nārada entered, he trod on Devala's neck. Thereupon Devala cried out, "Who is that?" Nārada replied, "It is I, teacher." "False ascetic," said Devala, "the first time you trod on my locks; this time you tread on my neck. I will curse you." "Teacher, I am not to blame. I did not know that you were lying in this position. When I came in I thought to myself, 'The first time I injured the teacher; this time I will go in past his feet.' Pardon me." [41] "False ascetic, I will curse you." "Do not so, teacher." But Devala, paying no attention to what Nārada said, cursed him all the same, saying,

> The sun possesses a thousand rays and a hundred flames, is dispeller of darkness.
> When the sun rises on the morrow, may your head split into seven pieces.

Nārada said, "Teacher, I told you it was not my fault. But in spite of what I said, you have cursed me. Let the head of the guilty man split into seven pieces, not that of the innocent." Thereupon Nārada pronounced the following curse,

> The sun possesses a thousand rays and a hundred flames, is dispeller of darkness.
> When the sun rises on the morrow, may your head split into seven pieces.

Now Nārada possessed great supernatural power and could call to mind eighty cycles of time, forty cycles in the past and forty in the future. So considering, "On whom will the curse fall?" and perceiving that it would fall on his brother-ascetic, he felt compassion for him, and therefore put forth the power of his magic and prevented the sun from rising.

When the sun failed to rise, the citizens assembled before the gate of the king's palace and wailed, "Your majesty, the sun has not risen, and you are king. Make the sun rise for us." The king surveyed his own deeds, words, and thoughts, and seeing no impropriety, thought to himself, "What can be the cause?" Suspecting that it might be because of a quarrel of the monks, he inquired, "Are there any monks in this city?" "Your majesty, last evening there were some arrivals at the potter's hall." [42] The king immediately went there with torches carried before him, paid obeisance to Nārada, seated himself respectfully on one side, and said,

Nārada, the people of the Land of the Rose-Apple are unable to pursue their wonted occupations.
Why is the world overspread with darkness? Tell me in answer to my question.

Nārada told him the whole story. "For this reason," said he, "I was cursed by this ascetic. So I cursed him back, saying, 'I am not to blame; let the curse fall upon whichever of us is to blame.' But when I had cursed him, I considered within myself, 'Upon whom will the curse fall?' and perceived that, as soon as the sun rose, the head of my brother-ascetic would split into seven pieces. Therefore, out of pity for him, I am not permitting the sun to rise." "But, Reverend Sir, how can he escape destruction?" "He may escape destruction by begging my pardon."

"Well then," said the king to Devala, "beg his pardon." Devala replied, "Great king, this fellow trod on my matted locks and on my neck; I will not beg pardon of this false ascetic." "Beg his pardon, Reverend Sir; do not act thus." "Great king, I will not beg his pardon." "Your head will split into seven pieces." "Nevertheless I will not beg his pardon." "I am convinced that you will not beg his pardon of your own free will," said the king. Thereupon, taking him by the hands, feet, belly, and neck, the king compelled him to bow down before Nārada's feet. Nārada said, "Rise, teacher, I pardon you." Then said Nārada to the king, "Great king, since this ascetic does not ask pardon of his own free will, [43] take him to a certain lake not far from the city, put a lump of clay on top of his head, and make him stand in the water up to his neck."

The king did so. Then said Nārada to Devala, "Teacher, I will put forth my magical power and cause the sun to rise. At that moment duck in the water, rise in a different place, and go your way." As soon as the sun's rays touched the lump of clay, it split into seven pieces. Thereupon Devala ducked in the water, rose in a different place, and ran away. **End of Story of the Past.**

When the Teacher had given this religious instruction, he said, "Monks, at that time the king was Ānanda, Devala was Tissa, and Nārada was I myself; at that time also he was obstinate." Then he addressed the Elder Tissa as follows, "Tissa, if a monk allows himself to think, 'So and So abused me, So and So struck me, So and So defeated me, So and So robbed me of my goods,' his hatred never ceases. But if he does not cherish such thoughts, his hatred ceases." So saying, he pronounced the following Stanzas,

3. "He abused me, he struck me, he defeated me, he robbed me;"
If any cherish this thought, their hatred never ceases.

4. "He abused me, he struck me, he defeated me, he robbed me;"
If any cherish not this thought, their hatred ceases.

I. 4. "NOT HATRED FOR HATRED" [1]

For not by hatred. This religious instruction was given by the Teacher while he was in residence at Jetavana with reference to a certain barren woman. [45]

It appears that a certain householder's son, on the death of his father, did all the farm and household work by himself alone and took care of his mother to boot. Now his mother said to him, "Dear son, I will fetch you a young woman to wife." "Dear mother, speak not thus; my sole desire is to care for you so long as you shall live." "Dear son, you alone are doing all the farm and household work, and I am not satisfied to have it so; let me fetch you a young woman to wife." He protested time and again, and then held his peace.

The mother left the house, intending to go to a certain family and fetch home the daughter of that family. Her son asked her, "To what family are you going?" "To such and such a family." He would not let her go to the family she had in mind, but told her of a family he liked better. So she went to the family he fancied, selected a wife

[1] With this story cf. Stories xxi. 2 and x. 8 *a* and *Jātakas* 510 and 513. Text: N i. 45–53.

for her son, and having set the day, installed her in her son's house. The woman turned out to be barren.

Then said the mother to the son, "Son, you had me fetch you a wife you yourself selected. Now she turns out to be barren. Without children a family [46] dies out, and the line is not continued. Therefore let me fetch you another young woman to wife." "Enough said, dear mother," replied the son; but the mother repeated her request time and again. The barren wife heard the talk and thought to herself, "It is certain that sons cannot disobey the words of their mothers and fathers. Now if she fetches him a wife who is fruitful, they will treat me like a slave. Suppose I were to fetch him a young woman of my own selection?"

So the barren wife went to a certain family and selected a young woman for him. But she immediately encountered the opposition of the young woman's parents, who said to her, "Woman, what say you?" The barren wife replied, "I am a barren woman, and without children a family dies out. If your daughter gives birth to a son, she will be mistress of the family and the wealth thereof. Therefore give your daughter to me for my husband." She finally prevailed upon them to grant her request, and taking the young woman with her, installed her in her husband's house.

Then this thought occurred to her, "If my rival gives birth to a son or a daughter, she alone will be mistress of the household. I must see to it that she shall not give birth to a child." So the barren wife said to her rival, "As soon as you have conceived a child in your womb, pray let me know." "Very well," replied her rival. In accordance with her promise, as soon as she had conceived, she told her fellow-wife.

Now the barren wife was accustomed to give her rival a meal of rice-porridge regularly every day with her own hand. [47] So along with the food she gave her a drug to cause abortion. The result was that her rival had a miscarriage. Again the second time the fruitful wife conceived a child and informed the barren wife. And again her fellow-wife did as before and brought about a miscarriage.

The women who lived in the neighborhood asked the fruitful wife, "Is not your rival putting an obstacle in your way?" When she told them the facts, they said to her, "You foolish woman, why did you do this? This woman was afraid you would get the upper hand. So she mixed a preparation to bring about a miscarriage and gave it to you. Do not tell her again." Accordingly the third time the fruitful wife said nothing to her rival. But the barren wife, seeing her belly, said to her, "Why did you not tell me that you had conceived a child?" Said the fruitful wife, "It was you who brought me here, and twice you have caused me to suffer a miscarriage; why should I tell you?"

"Now I am lost," thought the barren wife. From that time on she watched to catch her rival off her guard. When the babe in the womb was fully matured, she took advantage of an opportunity, mixed a drug, and gave it to her. But because the babe in her womb was fully mature, an abortion was out of the question, and the result was that the child lodged across the neck of the womb. Immediately the mother suffered acute pains and feared that her hour had come.

"You have killed me!" she cried. "It was you alone that brought me here; it was you alone that killed my three children. Now I also am going to die. When I have passed out of this existence, may I be reborn as an ogress able to devour your children." And having made this Earnest Wish, she died, [48] and was reborn in that very house as a cat. The husband seized the barren wife, and saying to her, "It was you who destroyed my family," beat her soundly with elbows, knees, and otherwise. As the result of the beating she received, she sickened and died, and was reborn in that very house as a hen.

So the fruitful wife was reborn as a cat, and the barren wife was reborn as a hen. The hen laid eggs, and the cat came and ate them. This happened three times. Said the hen, "Three times have you eaten my eggs, and now you are seeking an opportunity to eat me too. When I have passed out of this existence, may I be able to eat you and your offspring." And having made this Earnest Wish, she passed out of that existence, and was reborn as a leopardess. The cat was reborn as a doe.

So the barren wife, at the end of her existence as a hen, was reborn as a leopardess; and the fruitful wife, at the end of her existence as a cat, was reborn as a doe. Thrice the doe brought forth young, and thrice the leopardess went and devoured the doe's offspring. When the doe came to die, she said, "Thrice this beast has devoured my offspring, and now she purposes to devour me too. When I have passed out of this existence, may I be able to devour her and her offspring." And having made this Earnest Wish, she was reborn as an ogress. When the leopardess passed out of that existence, she was reborn at Sāvatthi as a young woman of station.

So the fruitful wife, at the end of her existence as a doe, was reborn as an ogress; and the barren wife, at the end of her existence as a leopardess, was reborn at Sāvatthi as a young woman of station. When the latter grew up, she was married and went to live with her husband's family in a little settlement near the gate of the city. After a time she gave birth to a son. The ogress disguised herself as a dear friend of the young woman and went to see her. "Where is my friend?" said the ogress. "In the inner room; she has just given birth to a child." "Did she give birth to a son or a daughter? I should like to see her." So saying, the ogress went in. While pretending to be looking at the child, she seized him, devoured him, and then went out. Again a second time she devoured a child of the young wife in the same way.

The third time the young wife was great with child she addressed her husband, "Husband, in this place an ogress has devoured two sons of mine and escaped. [49] This time I intend to go to the house of my parents to give birth to my child."

Now at this time that ogress was away doing her turn at drawing water. (For Vessavaṇa's ogresses take their turn at drawing water from lake Anotatta, passing it along from the source. At the expiration of four or five months they are released; the others die of exhaustion.) The moment the ogress was released from her turn at drawing water she went quickly to the young wife's house and inquired, "Where is my friend?" "Where you will not see her. There is an ogress that devours every child she bears in this house, and therefor, she has gone to the house of her parents." "She may go wherever she likes, but she will not escape from me." Spurred on by an impulse of hatred, the ogress dashed towards the city.

On the day appointed for the naming of the child the mother bathed him, gave him a name, and then said to her husband, "Husband, now we will go back to our own home." Accordingly she took the boy in her arms and set out with her husband along the path leading through the grounds of the monastery. When they reached the monastery pool, the young wife gave the boy to her husband and bathed in the pool. When she had finished her bath, her husband bathed in the pool. While the husband was bathing, the wife remained near, giving suck to her child.

Just then the ogress drew near. The young wife saw her coming and recognized her. Immediately she screamed with a loud voice, "Husband! husband! come quickly! come quickly! here is that ogress!" Not daring to wait until her husband came, [50] she turned and dashed into the monastery.

Now at this time the Teacher was preaching the Law in the midst of the congregation. The young wife laid her boy at the feet of the Tathāgata and said, "I give you this child; spare the life of my son." The deity Sumana, who resided in the embattled chamber over the gate, prevented the ogress from entering. The Teacher addressed the Elder Ānanda, saying, "Go, Ānanda, summon that ogress within." The Elder summoned her within. The young wife said, "Here she comes, Reverend Sir." Said the Teacher, "Let her come; make no noise."

When the ogress came and stood before him, the Teacher said, "Why have you so done? Had you not come face to face with a Buddha like me, you would have cherished hatred towards each other for an aeon, like the Snake and the Mongoos,[1] who trembled and quaked with enmity, like the Crows and the Owls.[2] Why do you return hatred for hatred? Hatred is quenched by love, not by hatred." And when he had thus spoken, he pronounced the following Stanza,

> 5. For not by hatred are hatreds ever quenched here in this world.
> By love rather are they quenched. This is an eternal law. [51]

At the conclusion of the Stanza the ogress was established in the Fruit of Conversion.

The Teacher said to the woman, "Give your child to this ogress." "I am afraid to, Reverend Sir." "Fear not. You have no reason to be alarmed because of her." The young wife gave her child to the ogress. The ogress kissed and caressed him, gave him back again to his mother, and began to weep. The Teacher asked her, "Why do you weep?" "Reverend Sir, in the past I have managed somehow or other to get a living, but I have never had enough to eat. Now how am I to live?" Then the Teacher comforted her, saying, "Do not worry." And turning to the mother, he said, [52] "Take this ogress home with you, let her live in your own house, and feed her with the choicest rice-porridge."

So the young wife took the ogress home with her, lodged her on the central rafter of the hut, and fed her with the choicest rice-porridge. Now when the rice was threshed and the flail was raised, she feared that it would strike her head. So she said to her friend, "I shall not be able to live here any longer; lodge me elsewhere." She was lodged successively in the flail-hut, the water-chatty, the bake-house, the store-room for nimbs, the dust-heap, and the village gate. But she refused

[1] *Panchatantra*, Book v, Frame-story. Harvard Oriental Series, xiv., p. 131.
[2] *Panchatantra*, Book iii, Frame-story, ibidem, p. 90.

to live in any of these places, saying, "Here the flail rises as if it would split my head in two; here boys empty out slops; here dogs lie down; here boys attend to nature's needs; here they throw away sweepings; here village boys practice fortune-telling." So they lodged her in a quiet place by herself outside of the village, and there they brought her the choicest rice-porridge.

The ogress said to her friend, "This year there will be abundance of rain; therefore plant your crops in a dry place. This year there will be a drought; therefore plant your crops in a moist place." Other people's crops were destroyed either by excessive moisture or by drought, but the crops of the young wife flourished above measure.

People asked the young wife, "Woman, your crops are destroyed neither by excessive moisture nor by drought. When you plant your crops, you seem to know in advance whether the season will be wet or dry. How is this?" The young wife replied, "I have a friend, an ogress, [53] who tells me whether the season will be wet or dry; and I plant my crops according to her directions on high or low ground. Don't you see? Every day the choicest rice-porridge and other kinds of food are carried out of our house; to her are they carried. Do you also carry the choicest rice-porridge and other kinds of food to her, and she will look after your crops also."

Straightway all the residents of the city rendered honor to her. On her part, from that time forth, she looked after the crops of all. And she received abundant gifts and a large retinue. Subsequently she established the Eight Ticket-foods, which are kept up even to this present day.

I. 5. THE QUARRELSOME MONKS OF KOSAMBI [1]

But others do not understand. This religious instruction was given by the Teacher while he was in residence at Jetavana with reference to the monks of Kosambi.

[1] Parallels: *Jātaka* 428: iii. 486–490; *Vinaya, Mahā Vagga*, x. 1–5: i. 337–357; *Udāna*, iv. 5: 41–42. The story of the quarrel among the monks is almost word for word the same as *Jātaka* 428, which in turn is derived from the *Vinaya*. The story of the Buddha's residence in Protected Forest with an elephant for his attendant is for the most part an elaboration of *Vinaya*, i. 350–357. The story of the monkey is an original touch of the redactor. The redactor follows the *Vinaya* account rather than that of the *Udāna*. Text: N i. 53–66.

5 a. Quarrel among the monks

For at Kosambi, in Ghosita monastery, resided two monks, each with a retinue of five hundred monks. Of the two monks, one was a student of the Discipline, the other a preacher of the Law. One day the preacher of the Law, after easing himself, left in a vessel what remained of the water in which he had washed in the bathroom and came out. Afterwards the student of the Discipline went [54] in and saw the water. When he came out, he asked his companion, "Brother, was it you that left the water?" "Yes, brother." "But do you not know that it is a sin so to do?" "Indeed I do not." "But, brother, it is a sin." "Well then, I will make satisfaction for it." "Of course, brother, if you did it unintentionally, inadvertently, it is no sin." Thus the preacher of the Law came to look upon the sin as no sin.

Notwithstanding, the student of the Discipline said to his own pupils, "This preacher of the Law, although he has committed sin, does not realize it." They, seeing the pupils of the preacher of the Law, said, "Your preceptor, although he has committed sin, does not realize it." The preacher's pupils went and informed their own preceptor. The preacher of the Law spoke thus, "This student of the Discipline said before, 'It's no sin.' Now he says, 'It *is* a sin.' He's a liar." The preacher's pupils went and said, "Your teacher is a liar." Thus did they foment a quarrel between the two. Then the student of the Discipline, seizing the opportunity, pronounced sentence of excommunication against the preacher of the Law for failing to recognize his sin. Thenceforth even the supporters who furnished them the Requisites formed two factions. Even the nuns receiving instruction, even the protecting deities; their friends and intimates, the deities who dwell in the sky; beginning with these and extending to the world of Brahmā, all beings, even the unconverted, formed two factions. The quarrel extended from the Realm of the Four Great Kings to the Heaven of the Gods Sublime.

Now a certain monk drew near the Tathāgata and told him that those who pronounced the sentence of excommunication held the view that the monk had been excommunicated according to law; [55] but that the partisans of the excommunicated monk held the view that he had been excommunicated contrary to law, and that the latter had gathered round in support of him, in spite of the fact that those who pronounced the sentence of excommunication forbade them to do so. Twice the Exalted One sent word, "Let them be united," and received the reply, "Venerable Sir, they refuse to be united." The third time he exclaimed, "The congregation of monks is rent asunder! The congregation of monks is rent asunder!" So saying, he went to them and pointed out to those who had pronounced sentence of excommunication the wrong involved in their act, and to those who had failed to recognize sin the wrong involved in theirs. Again he enjoined upon them the holding of fast-day and other ceremonies right there within the boundary, and laid down the rule that those who quarreled in refectories and elsewhere were to occupy separate seats in the refectory.

Hearing that they were quarreling again, he went to them, and beginning his discourse with the words, "Enough, monks! No quarreling!" he continued, "Monks, quarrels, strifes, contentions, disputes, — all these are unprofitable. For because of a quarrel even a tiny quail brought about the destruction of a noble elephant." And he told the Birth-Story of the Tiny Quail.[1] Continuing, he said: "Monks, be united; engage not in disputes. For because of a dispute many thousand quails lost their lives." And he told the Birth-Story of the Quails.[2]

But in spite of this they paid no attention to his words, and a certain heretical teacher, who wished the Tathāgata to be relieved of annoyance, said to him, "Reverend Sir, let the Exalted One, the Lord of Truth, remain at home. Reverend Sir, let the Exalted One live a life of inaction and ease in this present world. [56] We shall make ourselves notorious by our quarrels, strifes, contentions, and disputes." Thereupon the Tathāgata told the following Story of the Past:[3]

"Once upon a time, monks, Brahmadatta reigned at Benāres as king of Kāsi. Brahmadatta fought against Dīghati Kosala, took away his kingdom, and killed him while he was living in disguise. Dīghati's son, Prince Dīghāvu, although he knew that Brahmadatta was the murderer of his father, spared his life. Thenceforth they were at peace with each other. Such, monks, is said to have been the patience and gentleness of these kings who took scepter and sword. How much more, monks, should you, who have retired from the world under a Law and Discipline so well taught, let your light so shine in this world as to be known of men as patient and gentle." Thus did the Teacher admonish them.

[1] *Jātaka* 357: iii. 174–177.

[2] *Jātaka* 33: i. 208–210. Cf. *Panchatantra*, Book ii. Frame-story.

[3] For a translation of the complete version of this beautiful story, see *Sacred Books of the East*, xvii (Vinaya Texts), pp. 293–305.

But in spite of his admonition he was unable to reunite them. Thereupon, unhappy because of the crowded conditions under which he lived, he reflected, "Under present conditions I am crowded and jostled and live a life of discomfort. Moreover, these monks pay no attention to what I say. Suppose I were to retire from the haunts of men and live a life of solitude."

After making his round for alms in Kosambi, without bidding the Congregation of Monks farewell, he took his own bowl and robe, and went quite alone to the village of Bālaka, the salt-maker, where he discoursed to the Elder Bhagu on the solitary life; thence he went to Eastern Bamboo Deer-park, where he discoursed to the three youths of station on the bliss of the sweets of concord; [57] and from there he went to Pārileyyaka. There, at the foot of a beautiful Sāl-tree, in Protected Forest, near Pārileyyaka, the Exalted One spent the rainy season pleasantly, attended by the elephant Pārileyyaka.

When the lay brethren resident at Kosambi went to the monastery and failed to see the Teacher, they asked, "Reverend Sirs, where has the Teacher gone?" "To Pārileyyaka Forest." "For what reason?" "He strove to reunite us, but we would not be reunited." "Do you mean, Reverend Sirs, that after receiving admission as monks at the hands of the Teacher, you refused to agree when he asked you to do so?" "Precisely so, brethren." People said, "These monks, after receiving admission at the hands of the Teacher, were unwilling to patch up their differences when the Teacher asked them to do so. It's all their fault that we were unable to see the Teacher. To these monks, assuredly, we will neither give seats nor offer respectful salutations or other civilities." And from that time on they showed them not so much as a sign of civility.

The monks got so little food that they were nearly famished, and it required only a few days to bring them to a better state of mind. Then they confessed their sins, one to another, asked to be pardoned, and said, "Brethren, we are reconciled; be to us as before." "Reverend Sirs, have you begged the Teacher's pardon?" "No, we have n't, brethren." "Well then, beg the Teacher's pardon, and as soon as the Teacher has pardoned you, we will be to you as before." But as the rainy season was then at its height, they were unable to go to the Teacher and spent the rainy season very uncomfortably. The Teacher, however, spent the time pleasantly, attended by an elephant. For this elephant, of noble breed, left his herd [58] and entered the forest for the sole purpose of having a pleasant time. As it is said,

5 b. The Buddha, the elephant, and the monkey

"Here I live, crowded by elephants, female elephants, elephant calves, and young elephants. They have chewed off the tips of the grass I eat; they eat branch after branch I break down; they muddy the water I have to drink. Whenever I plunge into the water, or come up out of the water, the female elephants come and rub against my body. Suppose I were to retire from the herd and live all alone."

So then this noble elephant withdrew from the herd and drew near to Pārileyyaka, to Protected Forest, to the foot of the beautiful Sāl-tree; even to where the Exalted One was, thither did he draw near. And when he had drawn near and paid obeisance to the Exalted One, he looked all about for a broom. And seeing none, he smote with his foot the beautiful Sāl-tree below and hewed away with his trunk at the Sāl-tree above. And taking a branch, he then swept the ground.

Then he took a water-pot in his trunk and procured drinking-water. And as hot water was required, he prepared hot water. (How was that possible?) First he produced sparks with a fire-drill which he worked with his trunk; then he dropped sticks of wood on the sparks. Thus did he kindle a fire. In the fire he heated small stones; these he rolled along with a stick and dropped into a little depression in the rock. Then, lowering his trunk and finding the water hot enough, he went and made obeisance to the Teacher. The Teacher asked, "Is your water hot, Pārileyyaka?" and went there [59] and bathed. After that the elephant brought various kinds of wild fruits and presented them to the Teacher.

Now when the Teacher enters the village for alms, the elephant takes his bowl and robe, puts them on top of his head, and accompanies him. When the Teacher reaches the vicinity of the village, he bids the elephant bring him his bowl and robe, saying, "Pārileyyaka, farther than this you are not permitted to go. Fetch me my bowl and robe." The Teacher then enters the village, and the elephant stands right there until he returns. When the Teacher returns, the elephant advances to meet him, takes his bowl and robe just as he did before, deposits them in the Teacher's place of abode, pays him the usual courtesies, and fans him with the branch of a tree. At night, to ward off danger from beasts of prey, he takes a big club in his trunk, says to himself, "I'll protect the Teacher," and back and forth in the interstices of the forest he paces until sunrise. (From that time forth, we are told, that forest was called "Protected Forest.") When the sun rises, the elephant gives the Teacher water wherewith to bathe his face, and in the manner before related performs all of the other duties.

Now a monkey saw the elephant up and doing each day, performing the lesser duties for the Tathāgata, and he said to himself, "I'll do something too." One day, as he was running about, he happened to see some stick-honey free from flies. He broke the stick off, took the honey-comb, stick and all, broke off a plantain-leaf, placed the honey on the leaf, [60] and offered it to the Teacher. The Teacher took it. The monkey watched to see whether or not he would eat it. He observed that the Teacher, after taking the honey, sat down without eating. "What can be the matter?" thought he. He took hold of the stick by the tip, turned it over and over, carefully examining it as he did so, whereupon he discovered some insect's eggs. Having removed these gently, he again gave the honey to the Teacher. The Teacher ate it.

The monkey was so delighted that he leaped from one branch to another and danced about in great glee. But the branches he grasped and the branches he stepped on broke off. Down he fell on the stump of a tree and was impaled. So he died. And solely because of his faith in the Teacher he was reborn in the World of the Thirty-three in a golden mansion thirty leagues in measure, with a retinue of a thousand celestial nymphs.

It became known over all the Land of the Rose-apple that the Teacher was residing in Protected Forest, attended by a noble elephant.[1] From the city of Sāvatthi, Anāthapiṇḍika, Visākhā, the eminent female lay disciple, and other such great personages sent the following message to the Elder Ānanda,

"Reverend Sir, obtain for us the privilege of seeing the Teacher." Likewise five hundred monks residing abroad approached the Elder Ānanda at the close of the rainy season and made the following request, "It is a long time, Ānanda, since we have heard a discourse on the Law from the lips of the Exalted One. We should like, brother Ānanda, if you please, to have the privilege of hearing a discourse on the Law from the lips of the Exalted One."

So the Elder took those monks with him and went to Protected Forest. When he reached the forest, he thought to himself, "The

[1] Cf. Story xxiii. 7.

Tathāgata has resided in solitude for a period of three months. It is therefore not fitting that I should approach him all at once with so many monks as these." [61] Accordingly he left those monks outside and approached the Teacher quite alone. When the elephant Pārileyyaka saw the Elder, he took his staff and rushed forward. The Teacher looked around and said to the elephant, "Come back, Pārileyyaka; do not drive him away. He is a servitor of the Buddha." The elephant immediately threw away his staff and requested the privilege of taking the Elder's bowl and robe. The Elder refused. The elephant thought to himself, "If he is versed in the rules of etiquette, he will refrain from placing his monastic requisites on the stone slab where the Teacher is accustomed to sit." The Elder placed his bowl and robe on the ground. (For those who are versed in the rules of etiquette never place their own monastic requisites on the seat or bed of their spiritual superiors.) The Elder, after saluting the Teacher, seated himself on one side.

The Teacher asked him, "Did you come alone?" The Elder informed him that he had come with five hundred monks. "But where are they?" asked the Teacher. "I did not know how you would feel about it, and therefore I left them outside and came in alone." "Tell them to come in." The Elder did so. The Teacher exchanged friendly greetings with the monks. Then the monks said to the Teacher,

"Reverend Sir, the Exalted One is a delicate Buddha, a delicate prince. You must have endured much hardship, standing and sitting here alone as you have during these three months. For of course you had no one to perform the major and minor duties for you, no one to offer you water for bathing the face or to perform any of the other duties for you." The Teacher replied,

"Monks, the elephant Pārileyyaka performed all of these offices for me. For one who obtains such a companion as he may well live alone; did one fail to find such, [62] even so the life of solitude were better for him." So saying, he pronounced these three Stanzas in the Nāga Vagga,

328. Should one find a prudent companion to walk with, an upright man and steadfast,
Let one walk with him, joyful, mindful, overcoming all dangers.

329. Should one not find a prudent companion to walk with, an upright man and steadfast,
Then like a king renouncing the kingdom he has conquered, let one walk alone,
Like an elephant roaming at will in an elephant-forest.

330. The life of solitude is better; one cannot be friends with a simpleton;
Let a man live in solitude, and do no evil deeds,
Taking his ease, like an elephant roaming at will in an elephant-forest.

At the conclusion of the Stanzas the five hundred monks were established in Arahatship.

The Elder Ānanda then delivered the message sent by Anāthapiṇḍika and the rest, saying, "Reverend Sir, fifty million Noble Disciples headed by Anāthapiṇḍika desire your return." "Very well," said the Teacher, "take bowl and robe." Causing them to take bowl and robe, he set out. The elephant went and stood crosswise on the road. "Reverend Sir, what is the elephant doing?" "Monks, he desires to give alms to you. For a long time he has served me; it is not right to hurt his feelings. Turn back, monks!" The Teacher and the monks [63] turned back. The elephant entered the forest, gathered bananas and various other fruits, heaped them together, and on the following day gave them to the monks. The five hundred monks were unable to dispose of them all. When they had finished eating, the Teacher took bowl and robe and set out. The elephant, threading his way through the monks, went and stood crosswise in front of the Teacher.

"Reverend Sir, what is the elephant doing?" "Monks, having sped your parting, he desires to make me turn back." Said the Teacher to the elephant, "Pārileyyaka, I am going now, never to return. You cannot hope in this existence to enter into states of trance, or to attain Spiritual Insight, or the Paths, or the Fruits. Halt!" When the elephant heard that, he thrust his trunk into his mouth and retreated very slowly, weeping as he went. (Could he have made the Teacher turn back, he would have cared for him in the very same way to the end of his days.)

Now when the Teacher reached the vicinity of the village, he said, "Pārileyyaka, farther than this it is unsafe for you to go. The habitations of men are fraught with danger to you. Halt!" The elephant halted where he was and wept. As the Teacher slowly passed out of sight, he died of a broken heart. Through faith in the Teacher he was reborn in the World of the Thirty-three in a golden mansion thirty leagues in measure, with a retinue of a thousand celestial nymphs. God Pārileyyaka was his name.

The Teacher arrived in due course at Jetavana. The monks of Kosambi, [64] hearing of the Teacher's return to Sāvatthi, went thither to beg his pardon. The king of Kosala, hearing that the quarrelsome monks of Kosambi had come to Sāvatthi, approached the Teacher and said, "Reverend Sir, I'll not allow those monks to come into my country." "Great king, these monks are good men; only because of a dispute they had with each other they paid no attention to my words. Now they are coming to beg my pardon; let them come, great king." Anāthapiṇḍika also said, "I'll not allow those monks to enter the monastery." But the Teacher took issue with him as he had with the king, and he was silent.

Now when those monks reached Sāvatthi, the Exalted One gave orders that separate lodging should be prepared and given to them. The other monks neither sit nor stand in their company. One after another those who come ask the Teacher, "Where, Reverend Sir, are the quarrelsome monks of Kosambi?" The Teacher points them out, saying, "There they are!" "There they are! There they are!" One after another those who come point their fingers at them, until for shame they are unable to lift their heads. Then they threw themselves at the feet of the Exalted One and asked him to pardon them. Said the Teacher,

"Monks, grievous was the sin you committed when, after receiving admission as monks at the hands of a Buddha like me, in spite of my efforts to reconcile you, you refused to obey my words. Even wise men of old hearkened to the admonition of their mother and father under sentence of death, [65] disobeyed it not, even while their parents were being deprived of life, and afterwards established their sovereignty over two kingdoms." So saying, he related the Kosambika Jātaka once more, concluding as follows,

"Thus, monks, Prince Dighāvu, even while his mother and father were being deprived of life, disobeyed not their admonition and afterwards, obtaining Brahmadatta's daughter in marriage, bore sway over the two kingdoms of Kāsi and Kosala. You, however, disobeyed my words, and thereby committed a grievous sin." So saying, he pronounced the following Stanza,

> 6. But others do not understand that we must here control ourselves;
> Yet let them understand this, and straight dissensions cease. [66]

At the conclusion of the Stanza the assembled monks were established in the Fruit of Conversion.

I. 6. KĀḶA JUNIOR AND KĀḶA SENIOR [1]

Whoever lives looking for pleasure. This religious instruction was given by the Teacher while he was in residence near the city Setavya with reference to Kāḷa junior and Kāḷa senior, Culla Kāḷa and Mahā Kāḷa.

For Culla Kāḷa, Majjhima Kāḷa, and Mahā Kāḷa were three householders who lived in Setavya, and they were brothers. Culla Kāḷa and Mahā Kāḷa, the oldest and youngest respectively, used to travel abroad with their caravan of five hundred carts and bring home goods to sell, and Majjhima Kāḷa sold the goods they brought. Now on a certain occasion the two [67] brothers, taking wares of various kinds in their five hundred carts, set out for Sāvatthi, and halting between Sāvatthi and Jetavana, unharnessed their carts.

At eventide Mahā Kāḷa saw Noble Disciples, residents of Sāvatthi, with garlands and perfumes in their hands, going to hear the Law. "Where are they going?" he asked. Receiving the answer that they were going to hear the Law, he thought to himself, "I will go too." So he addressed his youngest brother, "Dear brother, keep watch over the carts; I am going to hear the Law." So saying, he went and paid obeisance to the Tathāgata and sat down in the outer circle of the congregation.

On that day the Teacher preached the Law in orderly sequence with reference to Mahā Kāḷa's disposition of mind, and quoting the Sutta on the Aggregate of Suffering, and other Suttas, discoursed on the sinfulness and folly and contamination of sensual pleasures. Mahā Kāḷa, after listening to the discourse, thought to himself, "So a man must needs leave al things behind him when he goes hence. When a man goes to the world beyond, neither wealth nor kinsmen can follow him. Why should I continue to live the life of a householder? I will become a monk." Accordingly, when the multitude had paid obeisance to the Teacher and departed, he requested the Teacher to receive him into the Order.

"Have you no kinsman of whom it is proper that you should ask permission?" inquired the Teacher. "I have a younger brother, Reverend Sir." "Ask his permission." "Very well, Reverend Sir." So Mahā Kāḷa went to Culla Kāḷa and said to him, "Dear brother,

[1] Derived from this story are *Thera-Gāthā Commentary*, cxxxvi, and Rogers, *Buddhaghosha's Parables*, iv, pp. 25–31. Text: N i. 66–77.

receive all this wealth." [68] "But you, brother?" "I intend to retire from the world under the Teacher." Culla Kāḷa used all manner of arguments to dissuade his brother from carrying out his intention, but in vain. Finally he said to him, "Very well, master; do as you wish." So Mahā Kāḷa went and became a monk under the Teacher. Culla Kāḷa likewise became a monk. But the thought in Culla Kāḷa's mind was, "After a time I will return to the world and take my brother with me."

Somewhat later Mahā Kāḷa made his full profession, and approaching the Teacher, asked him, "How many duties are there in this Religion?" The Teacher informed him that there were two. Said Mahā Kāḷa, "Reverend Sir, since I became a monk in old age, I shall not be able to fulfill the Duty of Study, but I can fulfill the Duty of Contemplation." So he had the Teacher instruct him in the Pure Practice of a Burning-grounder, which leads to Arahatship. At the end of the first watch, when everyone else was asleep, he went to the burning-ground; and at dawn, before anyone else had risen, he returned to the monastery.

Now the keeper of the burning-ground, a certain woman named Kāḷī, whose duty was to burn the bodies of the dead, saw the Elder as he stood up and sat down and walked about. And she thought to herself, "Who can this be that comes here? I will find out about him." But she was unable to find out what she wished to find out about him. So one night she lighted a lamp in the hut of the burning-ground, and taking son and daughter with her, hid herself on one side of the burning-ground. When she saw the Elder approach, she approached him, paid obeisance to him, and asked him, "Reverend Sir, does our noble monk reside in this place?" "Yes, lay sister." "Reverend Sir, [69] those that reside in a burning-ground have certain rules to observe." The Elder did not say, "Do you think I shall observe any rules of your telling?" Instead he said, "What ought I to do, lay sister?"

Said the keeper of the burning-ground, "Reverend Sir, they that reside in a burning-ground are bound to declare the fact to the keepers of the burning-ground, to the Chief Elder at the monastery, and to the village headman." "Why?" "Thieves who commit depredations, when pursued by lawful owners of property, frequently flee to a burning-ground and leave their spoils there; then the owners come and threaten residents of the burning-ground with harm. But if the authorities are duly informed, they can avert trouble by saying,

'We know for a fact that this reverend monk has resided here for such and such a length of time; he is no thief.' For this reason you are bound to declare your intention to the authorities I have mentioned."

Mahā Kāḷa then asked, "Is there anything else I ought to do?" "Reverend Sir, so long as your reverence resides in a burning-ground, you must abstain from fish, flesh, sesame, flour, oil, and molasses. You must not sleep by day. You must not be slothful. You must live with high resolve, exerting all the powers of your will, avoiding double-dealing and deceit. At eventide, when all are asleep, you must leave the monastery and come here; at dawn, before any have risen, you must return to the monastery.

"In case, Reverend Sir, while you reside in this burning-ground, you succeed in reaching the goal of the Religious Life, and they bring a dead body here and cast it away, I will place it on the funeral pyre, and rendering the usual honors with perfumes and garlands, I will perform the funeral rites over the body. If you do not succeed, I will light the pyre, drag the body along with a stake, [70] throw it outside, chop it to pieces with an axe, throw the pieces into the fire, and burn it." The Elder said to her, "Very well, woman. But in case you should see a corpse which you think would afford me a suitable Subject of Meditation on Material Form, be good enough to tell me." "Very well," said she, promising him to do so.

In accordance with his intention the Elder Mahā Kāḷa performed his meditations in the burning-ground. The Elder Culla Kāḷa, however, busy and active, thinking always of the house-life, remembering son and wife, said to himself, "It is an excessively difficult task my brother is engaged in."

Now a certain young woman of station was attacked by a disease, and the very moment the disease attacked her, she died, at eventide, without a sign of withering or weariness. In the evening her kinsfolk and friends brought her body to the burning-ground, with firewood, oil, and other requisites, and said to the keeper of the burning-ground, "Burn this body." And paying the keeper the usual fee, they turned the body over to her and departed. When the keeper of the burning-ground removed the woman's dress and beheld her beautiful golden-hued body, she straightway thought to herself, "This corpse is a suitable Subject of Meditation to show to his reverence." So she went to the Elder, paid obeisance to him, and said, "I have a remarkably good Subject of Meditation; pray look at it, Reverend Sir."

"Very well," said the Elder. So he went and caused the dress which covered the corpse to be removed, and surveyed the body from the soles of the feet to the tips of the hair. Then he said, [71] "Throw this beautiful golden-hued body into the fire, and so soon as the tongues of fire have laid hold of it, please tell me." So saying, he went to his own place and sat down.

The keeper of the burning-ground did as she was told and went and informed the Elder. The Elder came and surveyed the body. Where the flames had touched the flesh, the color of her body was like that of a mottled cow; the feet stuck out and hung down; the hands were curled back; the forehead was without skin. The Elder thought to himself, "This body, which but now caused those who looked thereon to forget the Sacred Word, has but now attained decay, has but now attained death." And going to his night-quarters, he sat down, discerning clearly Decay and Death.

Impermanent are all existing things. It is their nature to come into existence and to decay.
They come into existence and perish. It is well when they have ceased to be.[1]

Having recited this Stanza, Mahā Kaḷa developed Spiritual Insight and attained Arahatship, together with the Supernatural Faculties.

When Mahā Kāḷa attained Arahatship, the Teacher, surrounded by the Congregation of Monks, traveling from place to place, arrived at Setavya and entered the Siṁsapā forest. Culla Kāḷa's wives, hearing that the Teacher had arrived, thought to themselves, "Now we shall recover our husband." So they sent and invited the Teacher. Now when a visit is expected from the Buddhas, it is customary to prepare a seat in a place which is not circumscribed, and in order to insure that this shall be done, it is customary for a single monk to go in advance and give warning. For the Seat of the Buddhas must be set in the midst, [72] on the right of the Buddha must be placed the seat of the Elder Sāriputta, on his left that of the Elder Mahā Moggallāna, and next to these on both sides must be arranged the seats for the Congregation of Monks. Therefore the Elder Mahā Kāḷa, standing in the place where the bowls and robes were kept, sent forth Culla Kāḷa, saying, "You go in advance and give warning to arrange the seats."

From the moment the members of the household caught sight of Culla Kāḷa, they made a jest of him, putting the low seats at the ends

[1] *Dīgha*, ii. 157 $^{8-9}$.

where the Elders of the Assembly were to sit, and the high seats where the novices were to sit. Culla Kāḷa said to them, "Do not arrange the seats thus; do not put the low seats above and the high seats below." But the women, pretending not to hear him, said, "What are you doing here, walking about? What right have you to give orders about the arrangement of the seats? By whose leave did you become a monk? Who made a monk of you? What made you come here?"

And having thus made a mock of him, they tore off his under and upper garments, clothed him with white garments instead, placed a garland-coil on his head, and packed him off, saying, "Go fetch the Teacher; we will arrange the seats." Now those who have been monks but a short time, and have returned to the world before keeping a single residence, are without a sense of shame. Therefore Culla Kāḷa, free from any anxiety on the score of his clothing, went to the Teacher, paid obeisance to him, and taking with him the Congregation of Monks presided over by the Buddha, returned.

When the Congregation of Monks had finished their meal, Mahā Kāḷa's wives thought to themselves, "Culla Kāḷa's wives recovered their husband; let us also recover ours." [73] Accordingly they invited the Teacher for the following day. But on this occasion a different monk came to arrange the seats, and so Mahā Kāḷa's wives failed of an opportunity to embarrass him. When they had seated the Congregation of Monks presided over by the Buddha, they presented them with food. Now Culla Kāḷa had two wives, Majjhima Kāḷa had four, and Mahā Kāḷa had eight. Those of the monks who desired to eat sat down and ate their meal; those who desired to go out arose and went out. The Teacher sat down and ate his meal. When he had finished his meal, those women said to him, "Reverend Sir, Mahā Kāḷa will pronounce the formula of thanksgiving and then return; you go on ahead." The Teacher said, "Very well," and went on ahead.

When the Teacher reached the village gate, the Congregation of Monks were offended and said, "What a thing for the Teacher to do! Did he do it wittingly or unwittingly? Yesterday Culla Kāḷa came in advance, and that was the end of his monastic life. But to-day a different monk came in advance, and nothing of the sort happened." The Teacher sent Mahā Kāḷa back and continued on his way. Said the monks, "The monk Mahā Kāḷa is virtuous and upright. Will they put an end to his monastic life?"

Hearing their words, the Teacher stopped and asked them, "What is it you are saying, monks?" When they told him, he said, "But, monks, you do not think that Mahā Kāḷa is like Culla Kāḷa?" "Yes, Reverend Sir; Culla Kāḷa has two wives, but Mahā Kāḷa has eight. If his eight wives gather about him and seize him, what can he do, Reverend Sir?" Said the Teacher, "Monks, do not speak thus. Culla Kāḷa lives a busy and active life and allows his thoughts to dwell on many pleasing objects. My son [74] Mahā Kāḷa, on the other hand, does not live looking for pleasure, but is immovable, like a mountain of solid rock." So saying, he pronounced the following Stanzas,

7. Whoever lives looking for pleasure, exercising no restraint over his senses,
Immoderate in his enjoyments, indolent, inert,
Him Māra overpowers, even as the wind overpowers a tree of little strength.

8. Whoever lives looking not for pleasure, exercising restraint over his senses,
Moderate in his enjoyments, endowed with faith, exerting the power of his will,
Him Māra does not overpower, even as the wind does not overpower a mountain of rock. [77]

Mahā Kāḷa's former wives surrounded him and said to him, "By whose leave did you become a monk? Will you now become a householder?" Having said this and much more to the same effect, they sought to strip him of his yellow robes. But the Elder, divining their intention, rose from the seat where he had been sitting and flew upwards by his supernatural power, rending the peak of the pagoda asunder. And having soared through the air, he descended to the ground as the Teacher spoke the concluding words of the Stanzas, praising the golden body of the Teacher and paying obeisance at the feet of the Tathāgata.

I. 7. DEVADATTA WEARS AN UNBECOMING ROBE [1]

Whoever, not free from impurity. This religious instruction was given by the Teacher while he was in residence at Jetavana with reference to Devadatta's assumption of the yellow robe at Rājagaha.

For on a certain occasion the two Chief Disciples, each with a retinue of five hundred monks, took leave of the Teacher and went from Jetavana to Rājagaha. The residents of Rājagaha united by twos and threes and in larger groups and gave alms in accordance with the custom of giving alms to visitors. Now one day Venerable Sāriputta

[1] Cf. *Jātaka* 221: ii. 196–199. Text: N i. 77–83.

said, in making the Address of Thanksgiving, [78] "Lay brethren, one man himself gives alms, but does not urge another to give; that man receives in succeeding states of existence the blessing of wealth, but not the blessing of a retinue. Another man urges his neighbor to give, but does not himself give; that man receives in succeeding states of existence the blessing of a retinue, but not the blessing of wealth. Another man neither himself gives alms nor urges others to give; in succeeding states of existence that man receives not so much as a bellyful of sour rice-gruel, but is forlorn and destitute. Yet another both himself gives alms and urges his neighbor to give; that man in succeeding states of existence, in a hundred states of existence, in a thousand states of existence, in a hundred thousand states of existence, receives both the blessing of wealth and the blessing of a retinue." Thus did Venerable Sāriputta preach the Law.

A certain wise man heard him and thought to himself, "Sir, the preaching of the Law is indeed a wonderful thing; well has the means of happiness been expounded. It behooves me to do works of merit productive of these two Attainments." So he invited the Elder to take a meal with him, saying, "Reverend Sir, accept my hospitality for to-morrow." "How many monks have you need of, lay disciple?" "But how many monks are there in your retinue, Reverend Sir?" "A thousand, lay disciple." "Bring all your monks with you to-morrow and accept my hospitality, Reverend Sir." The Elder accepted the invitation.

The lay disciple went through the street of the city urging others to give alms, saying, "Men and women, I have invited a thousand monks. How many monks will you be able to provide with food? how many will you?" The people promised to provide food, each according to his means, saying, [79] "We will give to ten; we will give to twenty; we will give to a hundred." The lay disciple then directed them to bring their offerings to one place, saying, "Well then, let us assemble in one place and cook the food as one body. All of you bring together in one place the sesame, rice, ghee, molasses, and other articles of food."

Now a certain householder presented a perfumed yellow robe worth a hundred thousand pieces of money, saying, "If your combined alms prove insufficient, sell this and devote the proceeds to supplying the deficiency; if they are sufficient, you may give it to whatever monk you please." The combined offerings proved sufficient for the householder's purpose; there was nothing lacking. The lay disciple therefore said to the men, "Honorable Sirs, this yellow robe, given by a certain householder for such and such a purpose, is superfluous. To whom shall we give it?"

Some said, "Let us give it to the Elder Sāriputta." Others said, "The Elder Sāriputta has a way of coming and going when the crops are ripe. But Devadatta is our constant companion, both on festival days and on ordinary days, and is ever ready like a water-pot. Let us give it to him." After a long discussion it was decided by a majority of four to give the robe to Devadatta. So they gave the robe to Devadatta. Devadatta cut it in two, fashioned it, dyed it, put one part on as an undergarment and the other as an upper garment, and wore it as he walked about. When they saw him wearing his new robe, they said, "This robe does not become Devadatta, but does become the Elder Sāriputta. Devadatta is going about wearing under and upper garments which do not become him." [80]

Now a certain monk who lived in foreign parts came from Rājagaha to Sāvatthi, and when he had paid obeisance to the Teacher and expressed his pleasure at seeing him, the Teacher asked him about the well-being of the two Chief Disciples. The monk thereupon told him the whole episode of the robe from beginning to end. Said the Teacher, "Monks, this is not the first time Devadatta has worn robes unbecoming to him; in a previous state of existence also he wore robes which did not become him." So saying, he related the following

7 a. Story of the Past: The elephant-hunter and the noble elephant

Once upon a time, when Brahmadatta ruled at Benāres, there dwelt at Benāres a certain elephant-hunter who made a living by killing elephants and marketing their tusks, claws, entrails, and solid flesh. Now in a certain forest several thousand elephants found pasture. One day, when they went to the forest, they saw some Private Buddhas. From that day, both going and coming, they fell down on their knees before the Private Buddhas before proceeding on their way.

One day the elephant-hunter saw their actions. Thought he, "It is only with great difficulty that I can kill these beasts. But every time they come and go they pay obeisance to the Private Buddhas. What is it they see that makes them pay obeisance?" Coming to the conclusion that it was the yellow robe, he thought to himself, "I too ought to get a yellow robe immediately." So he went to a pool used by a certain Private Buddha, and while the latter was bathing and his robes lay on the bank, stole his robes. Then he went and sat down on the path by which the elephants came and went, with a spear in his hand and the robe drawn over his head. The elephants saw him, and taking him for a Private Buddha, paid obeisance to him, and then went their way. The elephant which came last of all he killed with a thrust of his spear. And taking the tusks and other parts which were of value and burying the rest of the dead animal in the ground, he departed. [81]

Later on the Future Buddha, who had been reborn as an elephant, became the leader of the elephants and the lord of the herd. At that time also the elephant-hunter was pursuing the same tactics as before. The Great Being observed the diminution of his retinue and asked, "Where do these elephants go that this herd has become so small?" "That we do not know, master." The Great Being thought to himself, "Wherever they go, they must not go without my permission." Then the suspicion entered his mind, "The fellow who sits in a certain place with a yellow robe drawn over his head must be causing the trouble; he will bear watching."

So the leader of the herd sent the other elephants on ahead and brought up the rear himself, walking very slowly. When the rest of the elephants had paid obeisance and passed on, the elephant-hunter saw the Great Being approach, whereupon he gathered his robe together and threw his spear. The Great Being fixed his attention as he approached, and stepping backwards, avoided the spear. "This is the man who killed my elephants," thought the Great Being, and forthwith sprang forwards to seize him. But the elephant-hunter jumped behind a certain tree and crouched down. Thought the Great Being, "I will encircle both the hunter and the tree with my trunk, seize the hunter, and dash him to the ground." Just at that moment the hunter removed the yellow robe and allowed the elephant to see it. When the Great Being saw it, he thought to himself, "If I offend against this man, the reverence which thousands of Buddhas, Private Buddhas, and Arahats feel towards me will of necessity be lost." Therefore he kept his patience. Then he asked the hunter, "Was it you that killed all these kinsmen of mine?" "Yes, master," replied the hunter. "Why did you do so wicked a deed? You have put on robes which become those who are free from the passions, but which are unbecoming to you. In doing such a deed as this, you have committed a grievous sin." So saying, he rebuked him again for the last time, saying, [82]

Whoever, not free from impurity, lacking self-restraint and truth,
Puts on the yellow robe, he is not worthy of the yellow robe.

Whoever is free from impurity, firmly established in the moral precepts,
Possessed of self-restraint and truth, he is worthy of the yellow robe.

"Unbecoming is the deed you have done," said he.

When the Teacher had ended this lesson, he identified the characters in the Jātaka as follows, "At that time the elephant-hunter was Devadatta, and the noble elephant who rebuked him was I myself. Monks, this is not the first time Devadatta has worn a robe which was unbecoming to him; he did the same thing in a previous state of existence also." So saying, he pronounced the following Stanzas,

9. Whoever, not free from impurity, lacking self-restraint and truth,
Puts on the yellow robe, he is not worthy of the yellow robe.

10. Whoever is free from impurity, firmly established in the moral precepts,
Possessed of self-restraint and truth, he is worthy of the yellow robe.

I. 8. THE CHIEF DISCIPLES [1]

They who think to find the truth in falsehood. [83] This religious instruction was given by the Teacher while he was in residence at Veḷuvana, and it was with reference to the announcement made by the Chief Disciples of Sañjaya's refusal to go to the Teacher. From first to last the story is as follows:

8 a. Life of the Buddha

Four Incalculables and a hundred thousand cycles of time in the past our Teacher was born as a Brahman prince in the city of Amaravatī, and his name was Sumedha. After acquiring proficiency in all the arts, he renounced wealth amounting to countless millions which he inherited on the death of his mother and father, retired from the world, adopted the life of an anchorite, took up his residence in the Himālaya country, and there won for himself by Ecstatic Meditation the Supernatural Powers. Now it came to pass on a certain day that

[1] 8 a is a brief outline of *Nidānakathā*, *Jātaka*, i. 2^{13}–85^{24}: translated by Rhys Davids, *Buddhist Birth Stories*, pp. 2–119. 8 b is derived from *Vinaya*, *Mahā Vagga*, i. 23–24. 4: i. 39^{23}–43^{7}. Cf. Hardy, *Manual of Buddhism*, pp. 200–203. With 8 f (*Dh. cm.*, i. 100^{17}–104^{21}) cf. *Khuddaka Pāṭha Commentary*, 202^{4}–206^{6}, and *Peta Vatthu Commentary*, 19^{22}–23^{16}. *Peta Vatthu Commentary* is here almost word for word the same as *Khuddaka Pāṭha Commentary*. Text: N i. 83–114.

Dīpaṅkara, Master of the Ten Forces, set out from Sudassana monastery to go to the city Ramma, and the populace came forth to clear the way. As Sumedha came flying through the air on that day, he observed that a road was being cleared. Therefore selecting for himself a portion of the road which had not yet been cleared, when the Teacher approached, he made of himself a bridge for him, spread his mantle of antelope skin in the mud, laid himself thereon, and said, "Let not the Teacher with his company of disciples tread upon the mud. Let him rather tread upon me; so let him proceed upon his journey."

When the Teacher beheld Sumedha, he said, "Yonder prince is a nascent Buddha; four Incalculables and a hundred thousand cycles of time hence [84] he will become a Buddha named Gotama." Thus did the Teacher Dīpaṅkara prophesy regarding the Brahman prince Sumedha. After Dīpaṅkara came the following Buddhas: Koṇḍañña, Maṅgala, Sumana, Revata, Sobhita, Anomadassī, Paduma, Nārada, Padumuttara, Sumedha, Sujāta, Piyadassī, Atthadassī, Dhammadassī, Siddhattha, Tissa, Phussa, Vipassī, Sikhī, Vessabhū, Kakusandha, Koṇāgamana, and Kassapa. One after another these twenty-four Buddhas arose in the world and enlightened the world, and from each of them the Brahman prince Sumedha received the prophecy that he should one day become a Buddha. Now after Sumedha had fulfilled the Ten Perfections and the Ten Minor Perfections and the Ten Major Perfections, making in all Thirty Perfections, he was reborn as Vessantara; and in his existence as Vessantara he bestowed mighty alms which caused the earth to quake, and in that existence also he renounced both son and wife. When the term of life allotted to him was come to an end, he was reborn in the Heaven of the Tusita gods; and when he had remained in this state of existence during the term of life allotted to him, the deities of the Ten Thousand Worlds assembled together and thus addressed him,

> The time is come, mighty hero; descend into the womb of your mother;
> Rescue the worlds of men and gods; discover the Region of the Deathless.

Thereupon he made the Five Great Observations, and passing from that state of existence, received a new existence in the royal household of the Sākiyas. In this royal household he was brought up amid great splendor and in the course of time attained auspicious youth. He spent his youth in three mansions appropriate to the three seasons of the year, enjoying splendor and majesty of sovereignty comparable to the splendor of the World of the Gods. In the course of time it came to pass that, as he proceeded on three successive days to the garden to amuse himself, he beheld the Three Heavenly Messengers; namely, a man worn out by old age, a man afflicted with disease, and a dead man. [85] On each of the three days he returned to his palace, overcome with emotion.

On the fourth day he beheld a man who had retired from the world and adopted the life of a monk. "It were well for me to retire from the world and adopt the life of a monk," said he, conceiving a desire for the religious life; and with this thought in mind, he proceeded to the garden and spent the entire day sitting on the bank of the royal pool. While he sat there, the god Vissakamma approached him, disguised as a barber, and dressed him in rich apparel and adorned him with all manner of adornments. There also he received the message that a son had been born to him, Prince Rāhula; and realizing the strength of affection for a son, he reflected, "I must straightway break this bond, lest it become too strong for me." In the evening, as he entered the city, Kisā Gotamī, daughter of his father's sister, pronounced the following Stanza,

> Happy indeed is that mother, happy indeed is that father,
> Happy indeed is that wife whose husband is such a one as he.

When he heard Kisā Gotamī pronounce this Stanza, he said, "This woman has taught me where true happiness is to be found;" and taking off a string of pearls, he sent it to her as a present. Having entered his own residence, he lay down on the royal couch, and as he lay there beheld the disgusting appearance of the nautch-girls asleep. Heartsick he roused his courtier Channa, caused his steed Kanthaka to be brought to him, mounted Kanthaka, and taking Channa with him as his companion, and surrounded by the deities of the Ten Thousand Worlds, he went forth and made the Great Retirement. Proceeding to the bank of the river Anomā, he retired from the world and adopted the life of a monk.

Having adopted the life of a monk, he proceeded to Rājagaha and went about the city receiving alms. Then he retired to Paṇḍava mountain and seated himself in Paṇḍava mountain cave. While he was sitting there, the king of Magadha came to him and offered to bestow his kingdom upon him, but this offer of the king he straightway refused. He promised the king, however, to visit his kingdom so soon as he should attain Omniscience. Then he approached Āḷāra and Uddaka; but after following their system of discipline, failed to win the Attainment which distinguishes one who has attained Arahatship. Thereafter, for a period of six years, he engaged in the Great Struggle.

Early in the morning on the day of full moon of the month Visākhā [86] he ate rice-porridge presented to him by Sujātā, caused his golden bowl to float on the river Nerañjarā, and spent the day in Mahāvana Grove in the various degrees of Ecstatic Meditation. In the evening he listened to the praise of his noble qualities bestowed upon him by Kāla, King of the Dragons, ascended the Throne of Wisdom, received the bundles of grass presented to him by Sotthiya, scattered the grass before him, and formed the following resolution, "I will not abandon this posture until I have ceased utterly to care for the things of this world and my heart has thus rid itself of the Depravities."

Thereupon he sat down facing the east, and before the sun had set overcame the host of Māra. In the first watch he acquired the knowledge of previous states of existence; in the second watch he acquired the knowledge of the vanishing of creatures from one state of existence and of their reappearance in another; at the conclusion of the last watch he acquired the knowledge of the Causes of Existence, fathoming the depths of Omniscience and acquiring the Ten Forces, the Four Subjects of Confidence, and all of the Noble Qualities. For seven weeks he remained on the Throne of Wisdom; in the eighth week he seated himself under the Goatherd's Banyan-tree and meditated upon the depths of the Law, finally arriving at misgivings as to his ability to preach the Law to others.

Straightway Sahampati Brahmā, accompanied by the retinue of the Ten Thousand Worlds with which Mahā Brahmā is wont to be accompanied, approached him and requested him to preach the Law to others. Surveying the world with the eye of a Buddha, he acceded to Brahmā's request. "To whom, pray, shall I first preach the Law?" thought he. Surveying the world, he became aware of the death of Āḷāra and Uddaka. But remembering the devoted services of the Five Monks, he arose from his seat [87] and went to Kāsipura, meeting Upaka by the way and talking with him.

On the day of full moon of the month Āsāḷha he arrived at Isipatana in the Deerpark, at the place of residence of the Five Monks; and when the Five Monks addressed him improperly, he instructed them how properly to address him. Then he set in motion the Wheel of the Law, giving to drink of the Deathless to a hundred and eighty millions of angels, but above all to the monk Aññā-Koṇḍañña. Having set in motion the glorious Wheel of the Law, on the fifth day of the half-month he established all those monks in Arahatship. On the same day also he perceived that the noble youth Yasa possessed the dispositions requisite for Conversion; and when the noble youth Yasa left his house in disgust at what he saw during the night, he saw him and summoned him and made a monk of him, saying, "Come, Yasa!" In that same night also he caused him to attain the Fruit of Conversion, and on the following day caused him to attain Arahatship. Afterwards he made monks of his fifty-four companions, employing the formula, "Come, monks!" And having made monks of them, he caused them to attain Arahatship.

There were thus sixty-one Arahats in the world. Having kept residence during the season of the rains, and having celebrated the terminal festival, he sent out the sixty monks into all the world, saying, "Go forth, monks, preaching and teaching." He himself proceeded to Uruvelā, on the way thither, in Kappāsika grove, instructing the Thirty Youths known as the Bhaddavaggiyas. Of these the least attained the Fruit of Conversion and the greatest attained the Fruit of the Third Path. All these youths he received into the Order with the single formula, "Come, monks!" And when he had so done, he sent them out into all the world. Arriving at Uruvelā, he performed three thousand five hundred miracles [88] and converted Uruvela-Kassapa, Nadī-Kassapa, and Gayā-Kassapa. These were three brothers, ascetics who wore matted hair, with a following of a thousand disciples. These ascetics he instructed in the Law. And when he had so done, he received them into the Order with the single formula, "Come, monks!" Seating them at Gayāsīsa, he established them in Arahatship by preaching the Fire Sermon; then, attended by a thousand Arahats, he went to Laṭṭhivana Garden near the city of Rājagaha, intending to redeem the promise he had given to King Bimbisāra.

"The Teacher has arrived," went forth the cry. Hearing the report, King Bimbisāra approached with twelve nahutas of Brahman householders, and to him the Buddha preached the Law in a pleasing manner, establishing the king and eleven nahutas of Brahmans in the Fruit of Conversion and one nahuta of Brahmans in the Refuges. On the following day he listened to the praise of his noble qualities by Sakka king of the gods disguised as a Brahman youth, and then entered the city of Rājagaha. Having eaten his meal in the royal residence, he accepted the gift of Veḷuvana monastery and took up his residence there. And there it was that Sāriputta and Moggallāna came to him.

8 b. Life of Upatissa (Sāriputta) and Kolita (Moggallāna)

Before the Buddha appeared in the world, there were two Brahman villages not far from Rājagaha named Upatissa village and Kolita village. One day a Brahman's wife named Rūpasārī, who lived in Upatissa village, conceived a child in her womb; and on the same day a Brahman's wife named Moggalī, who lived in Kolita village, likewise conceived a child in her womb. We are told that for seven generations these two families had been firmly knit and bound together in the bonds of friendship; they performed the Protection of the Embryo for the two expectant mothers on the same day. On the expiration of ten lunar months, both women gave birth to sons.

On the day appointed for the naming of the children, they gave the name Upatissa to the son of the Brahman woman whose name was Sārī, because he was the son of the principal family in Upatissa village; [89] to the other boy, because he was the son of the principal family in Kolita village, they gave the name Kolita. As they grew up, both boys attained the highest proficiency in all the arts and sciences. Whenever the youth Upatissa went to the river or the garden to disport himself, five hundred golden litters accompanied him; five hundred chariots drawn by thoroughbreds accompanied the youth Kolita. The two youths had retinues of five hundred boys apiece.

Now there is a festival celebrated every year in Rājagaha which goes by the name of Mountain-top festival. A couch for the two youths was set up in one place, and the two youths sat together and witnessed the passing show. When there was occasion to laugh, they laughed; when there was occasion to weep, they wept; when it was time to give alms, they gave alms. In this way they witnessed the festivities for several days. But one day, when they had grown wiser, there was no laugh when they might have laughed, as on preceding days, there were no tears when they might have wept, and when their alms were sought they gave no alms.

The following thought, we are told, occurred to the two youths, "Why should we look at this? Before a hundred years have passed, all these people will have gone hence and will no more be seen. It behooves us rather to seek the Way of Release." And taking this thought to heart, they sat down. Then Kolita said to Upatissa, "Friend Upatissa, you do not appear to be pleased and delighted as on previous days. Nay rather, you are afflicted with melancholy. What is in your mind?" "Friend Kolita, I sit thinking, 'There is no lasting satisfaction in looking upon these folk; [90] this is all unprofitable; it behooves me rather to seek the Way of Release for myself.' But why are you melancholy?" Kolita said the same thing. When Upatissa discovered that Kolita's thoughts were one with his own, he said, "Both of us have had a happy thought. It behooves us both to seek the Way of Release and to retire from the world together. Under what teacher shall we retire from the world?"

Now at this time a wandering ascetic named Sañjaya entered the city of Rājagaha, accompanied by a large retinue of wandering ascetics. "We will retire from the world and become monks under Sañjaya," said Upatissa and Kolita. So they dismissed five hundred retainers, saying to them, "Take the litters and the chariots and go," and together with the remaining five hundred, retired from the world and became monks under Sañjaya. From the day when these two youths retired from the world and became monks under Sañjaya, Sañjaya reached the pinnacle of gain and renown. In but a few days they had passed the bounds of Sañjaya's teaching. Therefore they asked him, "Teacher, is this all the religious truth you know, or is there something more besides?" "This is all there is; you know all."

Upatissa and Kolita thought to themselves, "If this is the case, it is profitless for us to remain pupils of this teacher any longer. The Way of Release we retired from the world to seek for, we certainly cannot obtain from this teacher. But the Land of the Rose-apple is an extensive country. Let us journey through villages, market-towns, and royal cities. We shall surely find some teacher who will expound to us the Way of Release." From that time forth, wherever they heard there was a learned monk or Brahman, they went to him and held converse with him. The questions Upatissa and Kolita asked, the others [91] were not able to answer; but every question the others asked, Upatissa and Kolita answered. In this manner they traveled all over the Land of the Rose-apple; then they retraced their steps and returned to their own homes again. Before they separated, Upatissa said to Kolita, "Friend Kolita, whichever of us first attains the Deathless is to inform the other." Having made this agreement, they separated.

While they were living under this agreement, the Teacher, after traveling from place to place as has been related above, arrived at Rājagaha, accepted the gift of Veḷuvana monastery, and took up his residence at Veḷuvana. Now after the Teacher had sent forth the sixty-one Arahats to proclaim the virtues of the Three Jewels, saying, "Go forth, monks, preaching and teaching," one of the Band of Five, the Great Elder Assaji, turned back, came to Rājagaha, and on the following day, early in the morning, taking his bowl and his robe, entered Rājagaha for alms. On the same day, early in the morning, the wandering ascetic Upatissa ate his breakfast, and proceeding to the hermitage of the wandering ascetics, saw the Elder. When he saw him, he thought to himself, "Never before have I seen a monk like this monk. He must be one of those monks who have attained Arahatship in this world, or who have entered upon the path leading to Arahatship. Suppose I were to approach this monk and ask him, 'For whose sake, brother, have you retired from the world? And who is your teacher? And whose doctrine do you profess?'" Then this thought occurred to him, "It is not the proper time to ask this monk questions, for he is going from house to house for alms. Suppose I were to follow close in the footsteps of this monk, as those are wont to do who seek some favor?"

Therefore, observing that the monk had received a portion of alms and was on his way to a certain place, and perceiving that he desired to sit down, [92] he placed his own monk's stool on the ground and offered it to him; and when the monk had finished his meal, offered him water from his own water-pot. Having thus performed the duties of a pupil to a teacher, he exchanged pleasant greetings with the Elder after the meal was over and said to him, "Calm and serene, brother, are your organs of sense; clean and clear is the hue of your skin. For whose sake, brother, did you retire from the world? And who is your teacher? And whose doctrine do you profess?"

The Elder thought to himself, "These wandering ascetics are hostile to the religion I profess; therefore I will show this monk the profundity of our religion." But first he explained that he was himself a mere novice, saying, "Brother, I am as yet a mere novice; no long time have I been a monk; but recently did I approach this Doctrine and Discipline; just now I shall not be able to expound the Law at length." Thought the wandering ascetic, "I am Upatissa; say much or little according to your ability; I will undertake to fathom the meaning in a hundred ways or a thousand ways." Therefore he said,

Say little or much; tell me the substance only;
I have need of the substance only; why utter many words?

In response the Elder pronounced the first line of the Stanza,

Of all things that proceed from a cause, of these the cause the Tathāgata hath told.

So soon as the wandering ascetic heard the first line, he was established in the Fruit of Conversion, perfect in a thousand ways. [93] So soon as he was established in the Fruit of Conversion, the Elder completed the second line,

And also how these cease to be, this too the mighty monk hath told.

But after he had attained the Fruit of Conversion, the Higher Excellence failed to appear. Therefore he considered, "There must be a reason for this," and said to the Elder, "Do not carry your teaching of the Law any further; let this suffice. Where does our Teacher reside?" "At Veḷuvana, brother." "Well then, Reverend Sir, you go on ahead. I have a friend, and he and I made the following agreement with each other, 'Whichever of us first attains the Deathless is to inform the other.' I wish first to redeem this promise. I will bring my friend with me and go to the Teacher, following the same path you take." So saying, Upatissa prostrated himself before the feet of the Elder with the Five Rests, walked thrice around him sunwise, and then took leave of him and went to meet the leader of the wandering ascetics.

The wandering ascetic Kolita saw him approaching from afar and said to himself, "To-day my friend's face has a hue not as on other days; it must be that he has attained the Deathless." Therefore he asked him at once whether he had attained the Deathless. Upatissa said in reply, "Yes, brother, I have attained the Deathless." So saying, he pronounced the same Stanza Assaji had pronounced. At the conclusion of the Stanza Kolita was established in the Fruit of Conversion. Thereupon Kolita said, "Friend, where does our Teacher reside?" "At Veḷuvana, friend. So I was informed by our teacher the Elder Assaji." "Well then, friend, let us go; let us see the Teacher."

Now it was a distinguishing trait of the Elder Sāriputta that he always held a teacher in profound respect. Therefore said he to his friend, "Friend, let us inform our teacher, the wandering ascetic Sañjaya, that we have attained the Deathless. [94] Thus will his mind be awakened, and he will comprehend. But should he fail to comprehend, he will at any rate believe what we say to be true; and so soon as he has listened to the preaching of the Buddhas, he will attain the Path and the Fruit." Accordingly the two wandering ascetics went to Sañjaya. When Sañjaya saw them, he asked, "Friends, did you succeed in finding anyone able to show you the Way to the Deathless?" "Yes, teacher, such a one have we found. The Buddha has appeared in the world, the Law has appeared, the Order has appeared. You, sir, are walking in vain unreality. Come, sir, let us go to the Teacher." "You may go; I cannot go." "For what reason?" "In the past I have gone about as a teacher of the multitude. For me to become a pupil again would be as absurd as for a chatty to go to the well. I shall not be able to live the life of a pupil."

"Do not act thus, teacher." "Never mind, friends, you may go, but I cannot go." "Teacher, from the moment of the Buddha's appearance in the world the populace will take perfumes, garlands, and so forth in their hands and will go and do honor to him alone. Let us also go there. What do you intend to do?" "Friends, which are more numerous in this world, the stupid or the wise?" "Teacher, the stupid are many, the wise are few." "Well then, friends, let the wise men go to the wise monk Gotama, and let the stupid come to stupid me. [95] You may go, but I shall not go." "You will become a famous man, teacher!" said his two former pupils, and departed. As they departed, Sañjaya's congregation broke up; at that instant the grove was empty. When Sañjaya saw that the grove was empty, he vomited hot blood. Five hundred wandering ascetics accompanied the two on their journey a little way. Of these, two hundred and fifty remained loyal to Sañjaya and turned back; the other two hundred and fifty wandering ascetics the two received as their own pupils and took with them to Veḷuvana.

As the Teacher sat in the midst of the fourfold congregation preaching the Law, he saw the two wandering ascetics approaching from afar. Straightway he addressed the monks, "Monks, here come two friends, Kolita and Upatissa. They will become my pair of disciples, my chief and noble pair." The two wandering ascetics paid obeisance to the Teacher, sat down respectfully on one side, and spoke thus to the Teacher, "Reverend Sir, we should like to receive admission to the Order at the hands of the Exalted One; we should like to make our full profession." Said the Exalted One, "Come, monks! The Law has been well taught. Lead the holy life, to the end that all suffering may be utterly done away." Instantly they became possessed of bowls and robes created by supernatural power, and became as it were Elders of a hundred years' residence.

By the acts of the company of his disciples the Teacher caused the preaching of the Law constantly to increase. With the exception of the two Chief Disciples all attained Arahatship. The two Chief Disciples, however, did not complete the meditations leading to the Three Higher Paths. (What was the reason for this? It was because of the magnitude of the Perfection of Knowledge of Chief Disciples.)

Now Venerable Moggallāna the Great, [96] residing near the village Kallavāḷa in the kingdom of Magadha, fell into sloth and torpor on the seventh day after the day of his reception into the Order. But aroused by the Teacher, he shook off sloth and torpor, and applying himself to the Formula of Meditation on the Elements given him by the Tathāgata, completed the meditations leading to the Three Higher Paths and attained the goal of the Perfection of Knowledge of Chief Disciples.

As for the Elder Sāriputta, he spent the fortnight following his reception into the Order with the Teacher, residing at Sūkarakhata Cave near the same city Rājagaha. Having heard an exposition of the Vedanāpariggaha Suttanta by his own sister's son, the wandering monk Dīghanakha, he applied his mind to the Sutta, and like a man who eats rice boiled for another man, attained the goal of the Perfection of Knowledge of Chief Disciples.

(Surely the Venerable Sāriputta is a man of great intelligence. Why, then, does he require a longer time than Moggallāna the Great to attain the goal of the Perfection of Knowledge of Chief Disciples? Because the preliminaries are so elaborate. We must understand that the case is analogous to that of a king, who, when he wishes to set out on a journey, is obliged to make great preparations, such as caparisoning riding-elephants. On the other hand a poor man, no matter where he may wish to go, immediately goes there without more ado.)

On the very day when Sāriputta and Moggallāna were received into the Order, as the shadows of evening lengthened, the Teacher gathered his disciples together at Veḷuvana, assigned the place of Chief Disciples to the newcomers, and then recited the Pātimokkha. The monks were offended and said, "The Teacher shows favoritism in bestowing this distinction. In bestowing the place of Chief Disciples, he ought to give the preference to those who were the first to retire from the world; namely, the Band of Five. If he disregard their claims, he ought to give the preference to the Elder Yasa and his Fifty-four Companions. If he disregard their claims, [97] he ought to give the preference to the Thirty Youths. If he disregard their claims, he ought to give the preference to the Three Brothers, Uruvela-Kassapa, Nadī-Kassapa, and Gayā-Kassapa. In rejecting the prior claims of all these monks and giving the place of Chief Disciples to those who retired from the world last of all, the Teacher shows favoritism."

The Teacher asked them, "Monks, what is the subject you are discussing?" When they told him, he said, "Monks, I show no favoritism in bestowing this distinction. On the contrary I bestow on these monks and on all others that for which each has made his Earnest Wish. For Añña-Koṇḍañña gave the first fruits of a certain crop nine times, but in so doing did not make an Earnest Wish for the place of Chief Disciple. On the contrary, in bestowing his gift, he made the Earnest Wish that he might be the first to win the foremost estate of all; namely, Arahatship." "When was that, Reverend Sir?" "Listen, monks." "Yes, Reverend Sir." Thereupon the Exalted One related the following

8 c. Story of the Past: Kāḷa junior and Kāḷa senior

Monks, ninety-one cycles of time in the past the Exalted Vipassī appeared in the world. At that time two brothers, Mahā Kāḷa and Cūḷa Kāḷa, both of them householders, caused a great field to be planted with rice. One day Cūḷa Kāḷa went to the rice-field, hulled a kernel of rice, and ate it, and found it unusually sweet. Shortly afterwards he desired to make a gift of unripe rice to the Congregation of Monks presided over by the Buddha. So he went to his older brother and said to him, "Brother, let us have unripe rice hulled and cooked in a manner suitable for the Buddhas, and let us bestow the same in alms." "What say you, brother? No one has ever yet had unripe rice hulled and given in alms, nor is anyone likely to do such a thing in the future; don't spoil the crop."

The younger brother repeated his suggestion several times. [98] Finally the older brother said, "Very well, divide the field into two parts. Do not touch my portion, but do whatever you like in your own portion of the field." "Very well," said Cūḷa Kāḷa. So he divided the field into two parts, hired a large number of men for manual labor, caused grains of unripe rice to be hulled, had it cooked in rich milk, adding ghee, honey, and sugar, and presented the rice thus prepared to the Congregation of Monks presided over by the Buddha, saying at the conclusion of the meal, "Reverend Sir, by virtue of this my gift of first-fruits may I be the first to win the foremost estate of all; namely, Arahatship." "So be it," said the Teacher, returning thanks.

When he went back to the field and looked at it again, he saw that the entire field was filled with heads of growing rice, bound together, as it were, in sheaves. At this sight he experienced the five kinds of joy. Thought he, "I am indeed fortunate." When the rice was in the ear, he gave first-fruits of rice in the ear. In association with the residents of the village he bestowed the first-fruits of the crop. When the rice was reaped, he gave the first-fruits of the reaping; when it was in the sheaf, the first-fruits of the sheaves; when it was in the shock, the first-fruits of the shocks; when it was in the rick, the first-fruits of the ricks; when it was threshed, the first-fruits of the threshing-floor; when it was ground, the first-fruits of the flour; when it was measured, the first-fruits of the measuring; when it was put away in the storehouse, the first-fruits of the store. Thus he bestowed the first-fruits of a single crop nine times. Whatever he took away was made up, and he had a bumper harvest. Goodness keeps him who keeps it. Therefore said the Exalted One, [99]

Righteousness truly keeps him who keeps righteousness; righteous living brings happiness.
Herein is the advantage of living righteously, that he who walks righteously will never go to a state of suffering.

Thus, in the dispensation of the Supremely Enlightened Vipassī, did Aññā-Koṇḍañña bestow the gift of first fruits nine times, making the Earnest Wish to be the first to attain the foremost of all estates. Likewise in the dispensation of the Buddha Padumuttara, a hundred thousand cycles of time in the past, in the city Haṁsavatī, he gave mighty gifts, and falling at the feet of that Exalted Buddha, made the Earnest Wish to be the first to attain the foremost of all estates; namely, Arahatship. Thus I bestowed on him only that for which he made his Earnest Wish. I show no favoritism in bestowing distinction.

8 d. Story of the Past: Yasa and fifty-four companions

Reverend Sir, what work of merit did the fifty-five noble youths led by Yasa perform?——They too made an Earnest Wish for Arahatship at the feet of a certain Buddha and did many works of merit. Subsequently, but before the present Buddha had appeared in the world, they became friends, banded themselves together for the performance of works of merit, and devoted themselves to the care of the corpses of paupers. One day, seeing the dead body of a pregnant woman, they carried the body to the cemetery for the purpose of burning it. To Yasa and four of his companions was assigned the duty of burning the corpse; the rest returned and entered the village.

As the youth Yasa burned the body, piercing it with stakes and turning it over and over, he grasped the thought of the Impurity of the Body. This thought he communicated to his four companions also, saying, "Behold, brethren, this body. Here and there the skin has burst open; it resembles nothing so much as the skin of a mottled cow. It is impure, stinking, [100] repulsive." Straightway his four companions also grasped the thought of the Impurity of the Body. In their turn these five companions went to the village and informed the rest of their friends. As for Yasa, he went home and informed his mother and father and wife, and they all developed the thought of Impurity. This is the work of merit these youths performed in a previous state of existence. And because of this very work of merit, consciousness of the Impurity of the Body arose within Yasa's mind in the women's apartments. And thus, because they had acquired the faculties requisite thereto, all of them developed Specific Attainment. Therefore these youths also obtained precisely that for which they made their Earnest Wish. I show no favoritism in bestowing distinction.

8 e. Story of the Past: Thirty noble youths

But, Reverend Sir, what work of merit did the thirty noble youths perform?——They also made an Earnest Wish for Arahatship at the feet of previous Buddhas and performed works of merit. Subsequently, but before the present Buddha appeared in the world, they were reborn as thirty evildoers; but hearing the admonition addressed to Tuṇḍila, they kept the Five Precepts for sixty thousand years. Thus these men also obtained only that for which they made their Earnest Wish. I show no favoritism in bestowing distinction.

8 f. Story of the Past: Three brothers Kassapa

But, Reverend Sir, what work of merit was performed by the three brothers Kassapa: Uruvela-Kassapa, Nadī-Kassapa, and Gayā-Kassapa?——They also performed works of merit, making an Earnest Wish to attain Arahatship. Ninety-two cycles of time in the past, two

Buddhas appeared in the world at the same time, Tissa and Phussa; Phussa's father was King Mahinda. When Phussa attained Enlightenment, the king's youngest son became his Chief Disciple, and the son of the house-priest became his Second Disciple. The king went to the Teacher and said, "My oldest son is the Buddha, my youngest son is Chief Disciple, and the son of my house-priest is Second Disciple." And looking upon the three, he said, "My very own is the Buddha, my very own is the Law, my very own is the Order." And thrice he breathed forth the Solemn Utterance, "Praise be unto Him that is Highly Exalted, All-Worthy, Supremely Enlightened." Then he prostrated himself before the feet of the Teacher and said, **[101]** "Reverend Sir, now, at the end of a life lasting ninety thousand years, it is time, as it were, for me to sit down and close my eyes in slumber. So long as I live, go not to the door of others' houses, but receive the Four Requisites from me alone." Having thus obtained the Teacher's consent, the king thereafter ministered to him regularly.

Now the king had three other sons besides, the eldest of whom had a retinue of five hundred soldiers, the middlemost three, and the youngest two. One day they sought permission of their father to entertain their brother, the Buddha Phussa, but failed to obtain it. This happened many times. Shortly afterwards an insurrection broke out on the frontier, and they were sent to suppress it. Succeeding in restoring order on the frontier, they returned to their father. Their father embraced them, kissed their heads, and said to them, "Dear sons, I grant you whatever you desire." "Very well, your majesty," said they, accepting his offer. When, after a few days, their father again said, "Dear sons, I grant you whatever you desire," they replied, "Your majesty, we desire naught else but only this, that henceforth we may entertain our brother; grant us this boon." "I will not grant you this boon, dear sons." "If you are unwilling to grant us this privilege permanently, then grant it to us for seven years." "That will I not, dear sons." "Well then, grant us the privilege for six years, or five, or four, or three, or two years, or for one year; or for seven months, or six, or five, or four, or three, or two months, or for one month." "That will I not, dear sons." "Well then, your majesty, make it one month for each of us; grant us this privilege for three months in all." "Very well, dear sons; then entertain your brother for three months."

Now all three brothers had a single treasurer and a single steward, the latter of whom had a retinue of twelve nahutas of serving-men.

The three brothers summoned the treasurer and the steward [102] and said to them, "During the coming three months we shall take upon ourselves the Ten Precepts, put on yellow robes, and reside with the Teacher. In our absence it will be your duty to administer the alms; every day you are to provide all the food, both hard and soft, for ninety thousand monks and a thousand soldiers. From henceforth we shall have nothing at all to say." So the three brothers took their retinue of a thousand men, took upon themselves the Ten Precepts, put on yellow robes, and began residence in the monastery.

The treasurer and the steward joined forces and performed the duty of almsgiving by turns, taking provisions from the storehouses of the three brothers and bestowing them in alms. But when the children of the serving-men cried for rice-porridge and other kinds of food, the treasurer and the steward would give them what they cried for, even before the Congregation of Monks arrived. The result was that the Congregation of Monks received only what was left over at the end of a meal, and not a fresh supply of food at all. Finally the treasurer and the steward became so greedy that they would take food, and pretending that they were going to give it to the children, eat it themselves. The mere sight of the pleasing food they were unable to resist. They and their associates numbered eighty-four thousand men. Because they ate food which it was their duty to give to the Congregation of Monks, when they died and their bodies were dissolved, they were reborn in the World of Ghosts.

When the three brothers and their thousand men died, they were reborn in the World of the Gods and spent ninety-two cycles of time in passing from one celestial world to another. Thus did those three brothers perform works of merit at that time, making the Earnest Wish to attain Arahatship. What they received was only that for which they made their Earnest Wish. I show no favoritism in giving what I give. (Now at that time [103] their steward was Bimbisāra, their treasurer was the lay disciple Visākha, and the three royal princes were the three ascetics of the matted locks.)

Their serving-men, reborn at that time among the ghosts, after passing from one state of existence to another, both good and evil, were reborn in this present world-cycle in the World of the Ghosts for the space of four Buddha-intervals. In this present world-cycle they approached first of all the Exalted Kakusandha, whose term of life was forty thousand years, and asked him, "Tell us when we shall obtain something to eat." He replied, "You will receive nothing to eat in my time; but after me the great earth will be elevated a league, and the Buddha Koṇāgamana will appear; you had best ask him." They waited all that time, and when the Buddha Koṇāgamana appeared, asked him. He replied, "You will receive nothing to eat in my time; but after me the great earth will be elevated a league, and the Buddha Kassapa will appear; you had best ask him." They waited all that time, and when the Buddha Kassapa appeared, asked him. He replied, "You will receive nothing to eat in my time; but after me the great earth will be elevated a league, and the Buddha Gotama will appear. At that time your kinsman Bimbisāra will be king; he will give alms to the Teacher and will make over to you the merit acquired by that act; at that time you will receive something to eat."

The length of the period intervening between two Buddhas was to them as the morrow. When the Tathāgata appeared in the world and King Bimbisāra gave alms on the first day and they failed to receive the fruit thereof, they waited until it was night, and then made a fearful noise and showed themselves to the king. When the king went to Veḷuvana on the following day, [104] he related the incident to the Tathāgata. Said the Teacher, "Great king, ninety-two cycles of time in the past, in the dispensation of the Buddha Phussa, these ghosts were kinsmen of yours. They ate food which it was their duty to give to the Congregation of Monks, and because of this were reborn in the World of Ghosts. Passing through the round of existences, they asked the Buddhas Kakusandha, Koṇāgamana, and Kassapa when they should obtain food, and the Buddhas told them this and that. All this time they desired greatly to receive your alms; and the reason why they acted as they did last night was that, when you gave alms, they failed to receive the fruit thereof." "But, Reverend Sir, in case I were to give alms now, would they receive the fruit thereof?" "Yes, great king."

On the following day the king invited the Congregation of Monks presided over by the Buddha, bestowed abundant offerings, and said, "Reverend Sir, henceforth may celestial food and drink be the portion of these ghosts." And when he had thus transferred to the ghosts the merit of his offering, they received celestial food and drink. On the following day the ghosts made their appearance naked. Said the king to the Buddha, "To-day, Reverend Sir, these ghosts made their appearance naked," and asked him what he should do. Said the Teacher, "Great king, you did not give them clothes." So on the following day the king presented robes to the Congregation of Monks presided over by the Buddha, saying, "Henceforth may they possess celestial raiment." And when he had thus made over to them the merit of his offering, instantly they became possessed of celestial raiment, whereupon they put off their ghostly forms and took on the forms of celestial beings. When the Teacher returned thanks, he said, "Without the walls they stand," reciting the extra-mural formula. At the conclusion of his words of thanksgiving eighty-four thousand living beings obtained Comprehension of the Law. Thus did the Teacher expound the Law, relating the story of the three brothers of the matted locks.

8 g. Story of the Past: Sarada and Sirivaḍḍha

But, Reverend Sir, what work of merit did the Chief Disciples perform?——They made their Earnest Wish to attain the station of Chief Disciples. For an Incalculable of cycles of time and a hundred thousand cycles of time additional in the past, Sāriputta was reborn in the family of a Brahman of great wealth, and his name was Prince Sarada. Moggallāna [105] was reborn in the family of a householder of great wealth, and his name was Householder Sirivaḍḍha. The two youths were friends from the time when they played in the dirt together.

Prince Sarada came into a large family-inheritance on the death of his father. One day, when he was alone by himself, he thought, "I have certain knowledge of the life of this world only; I know nothing of the life of the world beyond. All they that are born are certain to die. I ought to retire from the world, enter some Order, and seek the Way of Release." Therefore he approached his friend and said, "Friend Sirivaḍḍha, it is my intention to retire from the world and seek the Way of Release. Can you, or can you not, retire from the world with me?" "Friend, I cannot retire from the world; you alone retire from the world." Prince Sarada thought to himself, "No one ever yet went to the world beyond with companions or kinsmen or friends. What one does, he must do by himself."

Accordingly he threw open the doors of his treasure-house and bestowed abundant alms on paupers and travelers and beggars. Having so done, he retired to the foot of a certain mountain and adopted the life of an anchorite. First one, then two, then three, then many others followed his example in adopting the monastic life. Finally there were seventy-four thousand ascetics with matted locks. Sarada acquired the Five Supernatural Faculties and the Eight Higher Attainments, and taught those ascetics of the matted locks the processes necessary to the practice of Ecstatic Meditation. All of them acquired the Five Supernatural Faculties and the Eight Higher Attainments.

At this time the Buddha Anomadassī appeared in the world. His city was Candavatī. His father was Yasavanta, of the Warrior caste, and his mother was Lady Yasodharā. His Bo-tree was the ajjuna-tree. Nisabha and Anoma were his Chief Disciples, Varuṇa was his supporter, and Sundarā and Sumanā were his principal female lay disciples. His term of life was a hundred thousand years, his stature [106] was fifty-eight cubits, and the radiance from his body flashed twelve leagues. He had a retinue of a hundred thousand monks. One day at dawn, arising from a Trance of Great Compassion, he surveyed the world and beheld the ascetic Sarada. Thereupon he became aware of the following, "To-day, through my approaching the ascetic Sarada, there will be mighty preaching of the Law. Sarada will make his Wish for the place of Chief Disciple, and his friend, Householder Sirivaḍḍha, will make his Wish for the place of Second Disciple. At the conclusion of the discourse the seventy-four thousand ascetics with matted locks who compose his retinue will attain Arahatship. Therefore it behooves me to go there." Accordingly, taking his own bowl and robe, saying not a word to anyone else, proceeding in solitude like a lion, he commanded, "Let Sarada know that I am the Buddha." And while the ascetic Sarada's pupils were absent seeking various kinds of fruits, he descended from the sky and alighted on the earth before Sarada's very eyes.

When the ascetic Sarada beheld the supernatural power of the Buddha and the perfection of form of the Buddha, he pondered in his mind the memorial verses relating to the characteristics of a great man. And he said to himself, "One endowed with these marks, if he lives the house-life, is a King, a Universal Monarch. Living the life of retirement, he is one who has rolled back the veil of passion, an Omniscient Buddha. This man is without doubt a Buddha." Therefore he advanced to meet him, paid obeisance to him with the Five Rests, prepared a seat and offered it to him. The Exalted One seated himself in the seat prepared for him, and the ascetic Sarada, selecting a seat appropriate to himself, sat down respectfully on one side.

At that moment the seventy-four thousand ascetics of the matted locks, who had been absent gathering various kinds of sweet and juicy fruits, returned to their teacher. Seeing the Buddha seated and their own teacher seated near him, they said, [107] "Teacher, we used to go about this world thinking to ourselves, 'There is no one greater than you.' But as for this man, we are certain that he is greater than you." "Friends, what say you? Do you mean to compare a grain of mustard seed to Mount Sineru, sixty-eight thousand leagues high? Little sons, do not compare me to an Omniscient Buddha." Then those ascetics thought to themselves, "Were this an insignificant man, our teacher would not use such a comparison as this. How great indeed must this man be!" And forthwith they fell before his feet and prostrated themselves before him.

Then their teacher said to them, "Friends, we have here no offering suitable to present to the Buddhas, and the Teacher has come here at a time when we usually go the rounds for alms; let us give him gifts according to our ability. Fetch hither all manner of fruits that are choicest." And having thus caused them to fetch fruits, he washed his hands and himself placed the fruits in the bowl of the Tathāgata. The moment the Teacher touched the fruits which were brought, the deities imparted a celestial flavor to them. The ascetic Sarada also himself filtered water and presented it to the Teacher. After the meal was over, while the Teacher still remained seated, Sarada summoned all of his pupils, and sitting down, discoursed pleasantly with the Teacher.

Thought the Teacher to himself, "Let the two Chief Disciples approach, together with the Congregation of Monks." Straightway those two ascetics with their retinue of a hundred thousand Arahats approached, paid obeisance to the Teacher, and sat down respectfully on one side. Then the ascetic Sarada [108] addressed his pupils as follows, "Friends, the seat wherein sit the Buddhas is low, and there is no seat for the hundred thousand monks. To-day you should render high honor to the Buddha. Fetch from the foot of the mountain flowers possessing bright colors and sweet perfumes."

There is a saying, "Time occupied in talk is wasted; inconceivable is the range of magical power possessed by one endowed with supernatural power;" and so it was in this case. In but an instant those ascetics brought back flowers possessing bright colors and sweet perfumes and arranged a cushion of flowers a league long for the Buddhas. Then they arranged a cushion of flowers three gāvutas long for the two Chief Disciples. The cushions for the rest of the monks were half a league long or less; those for the novices were an usabha long. It is not permissible to ask the question, "How could seats of such great size be arranged in this hermitage?" This was made possible by the power of magic. When the seats had thus been made ready, the ascetic Sarada took his stand before the Tathāgata, and raising his clasped hands in an attitude of reverent salutation, said, "Reverend Sir, ascend this bed of flowers to my everlasting welfare and salvation." Therefore it is said,

He gathered together various flowers and perfumes,
Prepared a bed of flowers, and spoke these words,

"Here, mighty hero, have I prepared a seat suitable for you.
Sit down on this bed of flowers, and render my heart tranquil.

"For seven nights and days the Buddha sat upon my bed of flowers,
Rendering my heart tranquil, gladdening the world of men and the Worlds of the Gods."

While the Teacher sat thus, the two Chief Disciples with the rest of the monks [109] sat each in the seat which had been prepared for him. The ascetic Sarada, taking a great flower-parasol, held it over the head of the Tathāgata. Said the Teacher, "May this honor rendered to me by the ascetics of the matted locks yield rich fruit." And straightway he entered into a state of trance, attaining the Attainment of Cessation. Observing that the Teacher had attained the Attainment of Cessation, the two Chief Disciples likewise entered into a state of trance and attained the Attainment of Cessation. For seven days the Teacher sat there, enjoying the bliss of the Attainment of Cessation. When it was time to seek food, Sarada's pupils went into the forest and ate wild fruits and other varieties of fruits. The rest of the time they stood holding out their hands in an attitude of reverent salutation before the Buddhas. The ascetic Sarada, however, went not to seek food, but for seven days continuously held the flower-parasol over the Buddha, experiencing thereby intense joy and pleasure.

When the Teacher arose from trance, he said to his Chief Disciple the Elder Nisabha, who sat on his right hand, "Nisabha, return thanks to the ascetics who have honored us with flowers and seats." Thereupon the Elder, like a mighty warrior who has just received high distinction at the hands of a Universal Monarch, his heart filled with joy, manifesting the Perfection of Knowledge capable of attainment by a disciple, began the address of thanksgiving for the flowers and seats. At the end of the discourse the Buddha addressed the Second Disciple as follows, "Do you also preach the Law to the monks." Thereupon the Elder Anoma, pondering the Tipiṭaka, the Word of the Buddhas, preached the Law. But although the two Chief Disciples preached the Law, not a single monk present attained Comprehension of the Law. Then the Teacher, manifesting the infinite power of a Buddha, began to preach the Law, with the result that at the conclusion of his discourse all seventy-four thousand ascetics of the matted locks attained Arahatship, with the sole exception of the ascetic Sarada. Then the Teacher stretched forth his hand and said to them, "Come, monks!" Instantly their hair and beard disappeared, and the Eight Requisites were attached to their persons.

Do you ask, "Why did not the ascetic Sarada attain Arahatship?" It was because his mind was distracted. We are told that when he seated himself in the seat of the Second Disciple of the Buddhas, [110] and the Chief Disciple, manifesting the Perfection of Knowledge of a disciple, preached the Law, at the very moment when he began to listen to the preaching of the Law by the Chief Disciple, the following thought arose in his mind, "Oh that at some time in the future, in the dispensation of a Buddha who shall arise hereafter, I might receive the burden which this disciple has received! Because of this thought, we are told, he was unable to attain the Path and the Fruit.

Sarada, however, paid obeisance to the Tathāgata, and standing face to face with him, said, "Reverend Sir, what is the title in your Religion borne by the monk who sits in the seat next to you?" "He it is that follows me in setting in motion the Wheel of the Law which I have set in motion; he it is that has reached the pinnacle of the Perfection of Knowledge capable of attainment by a disciple; he it is that has grasped the Sixteen Forms of Knowledge; he it is that is therefore called in my Religion Chief Disciple." "Reverend Sir, here for seven days have I stood holding the flower-parasol over you, thereby rendering honor to you. As the fruit of this work of merit, I do not wish for a second existence as Sakka or Brahmā. But at some time in the future may I become the Chief Disciple of a certain Buddha, even as is this present Elder Nisabha."

When Sarada had made this Earnest Wish, the Teacher considered within himself, "Will the Wish of this man be fulfilled?" Therefore he sent forth his perception into the future, and surveying the ages of the future, he passed before his mind a period of incalculable length and a hundred thousand cycles of time in addition; whereupon he saw that his Wish would be fulfilled. So when the Teacher saw that his Wish would be fulfilled, he said to the ascetic Sarada, "This Earnest Wish of yours will not be in vain. For at the end of a period of incalculable length and a hundred thousand cycles of time in addition, Gotama Buddha will appear in the world. His mother will be Lady Mahā Māyā, his father will be King Suddhodana, his son will be Rāhula, his servitor will be Ānanda, and his Second Disciple will be Moggallāna. And you will be his Chief Disciple, the Captain of the Faith, and your name will be Sāriputta." [111]

When the Teacher had thus predicted the future of the ascetic, he preached the Law, and then, surrounded by his company of monks, flew up into the air and departed. The ascetic Sarada sought out the pupils and elders and sent the following message to his friend, Householder Sirivaḍḍha, "Reverend Sirs, say to my friend, 'Your friend the ascetic Sarada fell down before the feet of the Buddha Anomadassī and made his Earnest Wish for the place of Chief Disciple under the dispensation of the Buddha Gotama, who shall hereafter arise in the world. Do you make your Earnest Wish for the place of Second Disciple.'" And when he had thus spoken, he preceded the Elders by a different route and went and stood at the door of Sirivaḍḍha's residence.

When Sirivaḍḍha saw him he said, "At last, after a long absence, my noble friend has returned." And straightway he seated his friend in a seat, and having seated himself in a lower seat, asked him, "But, Reverend Sir, have you no pupils and attendants?" "Yes, my friend, the Buddha Anomadassī came to our hermitage, and we did him honor to the extent of our power. The Teacher preached the Law to all, and at the conclusion of his discourse all the members of our community excepting me attained Arahatship and entered the Order. When I saw the Chief Disciple of the Teacher, the Elder Nisabha, I made my Earnest Wish for the place of Chief Disciple under the dispensation of the Buddha Gotama, who shall hereafter arise in the world. Do you also make your Earnest Wish for the place of Second Disciple under his dispensation." "But, Reverend Sir, I am not on terms of familiar acquaintance with the Buddhas." "I will assume the burden of talking with the Buddhas; you prepare a Great Resolve."

When Sirivaḍḍha heard his words, he adorned a space eight karīsas in extent before the door of his residence with the respect due to a king, sprinkled sand, [112] scattered flowers of five kinds, including lāja flowers, caused a pavilion to be erected with a thatch of blue lotuses, caused the Seat of the Buddha to be made ready, and seats for the monks also to be prepared. And having caused abundant offerings and gifts to be prepared, he directed the ascetic Sarada to invite the Buddhas. So the ascetic Sarada took the Congregation of Monks presided over by the Buddha and went with them to Sarada's residence. Sarada advanced to meet them, took the bowl from the hand of the Tathāgata, conducted them into the pavilion, seated the Congregation of Monks on the seats prepared for them, offered them Water of Donation, and provided them with the choicest food.

At the conclusion of the meal, having clothed the Congregation of Monks with robes of great price, he said to the Teacher, "Reverend Sir, it was for the purpose of gaining no mean place that this entertainment was undertaken. Show your gracious compassion by remaining here in this manner for a period of seven days." The Teacher condescended to remain. For seven days Sirivaḍḍha bestowed abundant offerings in this manner. At the end of his almsgiving he paid obeisance to the Teacher, and standing before him with hands clasped in an attitude of reverent salutation, said, "Reverend Sir, my friend the ascetic Sarada made his Earnest Wish to become Chief Disciple of a certain Teacher. May I also become the Second Disciple of that same Teacher."

The Teacher looked into the future, and beholding the fulfillment of his Earnest Wish, made the following prophecy, "At the end of a period of incalculable length and a hundred thousand cycles of time in addition, you will become the Second Disciple of Gotama Buddha." Hearing this prophecy of the Buddhas, Sirivaḍḍha was filled with joy and satisfaction. The Teacher returned thanks for the offering of food, and then, surrounded by the company of monks, returned to the monastery. This, monks, was the Earnest Wish made by my sons at that time. They have received precisely that for which they made their Earnest Wish. When I give, I give without respect of persons. **End of Stories of the Past.** [113]

When the Teacher had thus spoken, the two Chief Disciples paid obeisance to the Exalted One and said, "Reverend Sir, when we were yet householders, we went to see the festivities of Mountain-top;" and then told the entire story of the events which had recently taken place, to their attainment of the Fruit of Conversion at the hands of the Elder Assaji. Then they said, "Reverend Sir, we went to our teacher, desiring to lead him to your feet, and pointed out to him the shallowness of his own views, and dwelt upon the advantages of his coming here. But he said to us, 'For me to try to live the life of a pupil now would be as absurd as for a chatty to go to the well. I shall not be able to live the life of a pupil.' We replied, 'Teacher, the populace will now take perfumes, garlands, and so forth in their hands, and will go to do honor to the Teacher alone. What do you intend to do?' Said he, 'Which are the more numerous in this world, the stupid or the wise?' We replied, 'Teacher, the stupid are many; the wise are few.' 'Well then,' said he, 'let the wise men go to the wise monk Gotama, and let the stupid come to stupid me. As for you, go where you like.' With these words, Reverend Sir, did he refuse to come hither."

When the Teacher heard this, he said, "Monks, by reason of the false views which he holds, Sañjaya has mistaken falsehood for truth and truth for falsehood. But you, by reason of your own wisdom, have rightly discerned that which is true in its truth and that which is false in its falsity, and you have done wisely to reject that which is false and accept that which is true." So saying, he pronounced the following Stanzas,

11. They who think to find the truth in falsehood, they who discern but falsehood in the truth,
They never attain the goal of truth, but abide in the pasture-ground of error. [114]

12. They who have rightly discerned the true in its truth and the false in its falsity,
They attain the goal of truth and abide in the pasture-ground of right thinking.

I. 9. NANDA THE ELDER[1]

Even as rain breaks through an ill-thatched house. This religious instruction was given by the Teacher while he was in residence at Jetavana with reference to Venerable Nanda. [115]

9 a. Nanda becomes a monk in spite of himself

For after the Teacher had set in motion the glorious Wheel of the Law, he retired to Rājagaha and took up his residence at Veḷuvana. Thereupon his father, the great king Suddhodana, sent ten ambassadors to him, one after the other, each with a retinue of a thousand men, saying to them, "Fetch my son hither and show him to me

[1] 9 a follows *Nidānakathā*, *Jātaka*, i. 85^{24}–92^{14}, frequently word for word. 9 b is almost word for word the same as *Udāna*, iii. 2: 21^{18}–24^{13}. Parallel to 9 b is *Jātaka* 182: ii. 92–94. 9 c is entirely different from the Story of the Past in *Jātaka* 182. Cf. also Hardy, *Manual of Buddhism*, pp. 203–212; Chavannes, *Cinq cents Contes et Apologues*, 409: iii. 87–94; *Thera-Gāthā Commentary*, cxxxix; *Añguttara Commentary* on *Etadagga Vagga*, *Story of Nanda;* and Winternitz, *History of Buddhist Literature*, p. 207.

before my face." After nine ambassadors had gone thither, attained Arahatship, and failed to return, Elder Kāḷa Udāyi went thither and attained Arahatship. And knowing that it was the proper time for the Teacher to go, he described the beauties of the journey and conducted the Teacher with his retinue of twenty thousand Arahats to Kapilapura. And there, in the company of his kinsfolk, the Teacher, taking a shower of rain for his text, related the Vessantara Jātaka.[1] On the following day he entered the city for alms. By the recitation of the Stanza, "A man should exert himself and should not live the life of Heedlessness,"[2] he established his father in the Fruit of Conversion; and by the recitation of the Stanza, "A man should live righteously,"[3] he established Mahā Pajāpatī in the Fruit of Conversion and his father in the Fruit of the Second Path. And at the end of the meal, with reference to the praise bestowed on him by the Mother of Rāhula, he related the Canda Kinnara Jātaka.[4]

On the following day, while the ceremonies of Prince Nanda's sprinkling, house-warming, and marriage were in progress, the Teacher entered the house for alms, placed his bowl in Prince Nanda's hands, and wished him good luck. Then, rising from his seat, he departed without taking his bowl from the hands of the Prince. Out of reverence for the Tathāgata, Prince Nanda did not dare say, "Reverend Sir, receive your bowl," but thought within himself, "He will take his bowl at the head of the stairs." But even when the Teacher reached the head of the stairs, he did not take his bowl. Thought Nanda, "He will take his bowl at the foot of the stairs." But the Teacher did not take his bowl even there. [116] Thought Nanda, "He will take his bowl in the palace court." But the Teacher did not take his bowl even there. Prince Nanda desired greatly to return to his bride, and followed the Teacher much against his own will. But so great was his reverence for the Teacher that he did not dare say, "Receive your bowl," but continued to follow the Teacher, thinking to himself, "He will take his bowl here! he will take his bowl there! he will take his bowl there!"

At that moment they brought word to his bride Belle-of-the-Country, Janapada-Kalyāṇī, "My lady, the Exalted One has taken Prince Nanda away with him; it is his purpose to deprive you of him." Thereupon Janapada-Kalyāṇī, with tears streaming down her face and hair half-combed, ran after Prince Nanda as fast as she could

[1] *Jātaka* 547: vi. 479–593. Cf. Story xiii. 2. [2] *Dhammapada*, 168.
[3] *Dhammapada*, 169. [4] *Jātaka* 485: iv. 282–288.

and said to him, "Noble sir, please return immediately." Her words caused a quaver in Nanda's heart; but the Teacher, without so much as taking his bowl, led him to the monastery and said to him, "Nanda, would you like to become a monk?" So great was Prince Nanda's reverence for the Buddha that he refrained from saying, "I do not wish to become a monk," and said instead, "Yes, I should like to become a monk." Said the Teacher, "Well then, make a monk of Nanda." Thus it happened that on the third day after the Teacher's arrival at Kapilapura he caused Nanda to be made a monk.

On the seventh day the Mother of Rāhula adorned Prince Rāhula and sent him to the Exalted One, saying, "Dear son, go look upon this monk, possessed of a retinue of twenty thousand monks, possessed of a body of the hue of gold, possessed of the beauty of form of Mahā Brahmā. This monk is your father. To him once belonged great stores of treasure. From the time of his Great Retirement we have not seen him. Ask him for this your inheritance, saying, 'Dear father, I am a royal prince, and so soon as I shall receive the ceremonial sprinkling, I shall become a Universal Monarch. I have need of wealth; bestow wealth upon me; for to a son belongs the wealth which formerly belonged to his father.' "

Accordingly Prince Rāhula went to the Exalted One. The moment he saw him he conceived a warm affection for his father, and his heart rejoiced within him. And he said, "Monk, pleasant is your shadow," **[117]** and said much else befitting his own station. When the Exalted One had finished his meal, he pronounced the words of thanksgiving, arose from his seat, and departed. Prince Rāhula followed in the footsteps of the Exalted One, saying, "Monk, give me my inheritance; monk, give me my inheritance." The Exalted One did not repel the Prince; even the attendants were unable to prevent the Prince from accompanying the Exalted One. In this manner the Prince accompanied the Exalted One to the Grove. Then the thought occurred to the Exalted One, "The paternal inheritance which this youth seeks inevitably brings destruction in its train. Behold, I will bestow upon him the Sevenfold Noble Inheritance which I received at the foot of the Bo-tree; I will make him master of an inheritance which transcends the world."

Therefore the Exalted One addressed Venerable Sāriputta, "Well then, Sāriputta, make a monk of Prince Rāhula." When, however, Prince Rāhula had been received into the Order, the king his grandfather was afflicted with great sorrow. Unable to endure his sorrow, he made known his sorrow to the Exalted One and made the following request of him, "It were well, Reverend Sir, did the noble monks not receive into the Order any youth without the permission of his mother and father." The Exalted One granted him this request. Again one day, as the Exalted One sat in the royal palace after breakfast, the king, sitting respectfully at one side, said to the Exalted One, "Reverend Sir, while you were practicing your austerities, a certain deity approached me and said to me, 'Your son is dead.' But I refused to believe him and replied, 'My son will not die until he attains Enlightenment.'" Said the Exalted One, "Now will you believe? In a previous existence also, when a deity showed you bones and said to you, 'Your son is dead,' you refused to believe." And with reference to this incident he related the Mahā Dhammapāla Jātaka.[1] At the conclusion of the story the king was established in the Fruit of the Third Path.

9 b. Nanda and the celestial nymphs

When the Exalted One had thus established his father in the Three Fruits, [118] he returned once more to Rājagaha, accompanied by the Congregation of Monks. Now he had promised Anāthapiṇḍika to visit Sāvatthi, so soon as the great monastery of Jetavana should be completed, and receiving word shortly afterwards that the monastery had been completed, he went to Jetavana and took up his residence there. While the Teacher was thus residing at Jetavana, Venerable Nanda, becoming discontented, told his troubles to the monks, saying, "Brethren, I am dissatisfied. I am now living the Religious Life, but I cannot endure to live the Religious Life any longer. I intend to abandon the higher precepts and to return to the lower life, the life of a layman."

The Exalted One, hearing of this incident, sent for Venerable Nanda and said this to him, "Nanda, is the report true that you spoke as follows to a large company of monks, 'Brethren, I am dissatisfied; I am now living the Religious Life, but I cannot endure to live the Religious Life any longer; I intend to abandon the higher precepts and to return to the lower life, the life of a layman'?" "It is quite true, Reverend Sir." "But, Nanda, why are you dissatisfied with the Religious Life you are now living? Why cannot you endure to live the Religious Life any longer? Why do you intend to abandon the higher precepts and

[1] *Jātaka* 447: iv. 50–55.

to return to the lower life, the life of a layman?" "Reverend Sir, when I left my house, my noble wife Janapada-Kalyāṇī, with hair half-combed, took leave of me, saying, 'Noble sir, please return immediately.' Reverend Sir, it is because I keep remembering her that I am dissatisfied with the religious life I am now living; that I cannot endure to live the religious life any longer; that I intend to abandon the higher precepts and to return to the lower life, the life of a layman."

Then the Exalted One took Venerable Nanda by the arm, and by the power of his magic conducted him to the World of the Thirty-three. On the way the Exalted One pointed out to Venerable Nanda in a certain burnt field, seated on a burnt stump, a greedy monkey which had lost her ears and nose and tail in a fire. When they reached the World of the Thirty-three, he pointed out five hundred pink-footed celestial nymphs who came to wait upon Sakka, king of the gods. [119] And when the Exalted One had shown Venerable Nanda these two sights, he asked him this question, "Nanda, which do you regard as being the more beautiful and fair to look upon and handsome, your noble wife Janapada-Kalyāṇī or these five hundred pink-footed celestial nymphs?"

"Reverend Sir," replied Nanda, "as far inferior as this greedy monkey which has lost her ears and nose and tail is to Janapada-Kalyāṇī, even so far inferior, Reverend Sir, is my noble wife Janapada-Kalyāṇī to these five hundred pink-footed celestial nymphs. In comparison with these nymphs my noble wife does not come into the count; she does not come within a fraction of them, she does not come within a fraction of a fraction of them; on the contrary, these five hundred pink-footed celestial nymphs are infinitely more beautiful and fair to look upon and handsome."

"Cheer up, Nanda!" replied the Exalted One. "I guarantee that you will win these five hundred pink-footed celestial nymphs." Said Venerable Nanda, "If, Reverend Sir, the Exalted One guarantees that I shall win these five hundred pink-footed celestial nymphs, in that case, Reverend Sir, I shall take the greatest pleasure in living the exalted life of a religious." Then the Exalted One, taking Venerable Nanda with him, disappeared from the World of the Thirty-three and reappeared at Jetavana. Now it was not long before the monks heard the following report, "It appears that it is in the hope of winning celestial nymphs that Venerable Nanda, brother of the Exalted One, son of his mother's sister, is living the religious life; it appears that the Exalted One has guaranteed that he shall win five hundred pink-footed celestial nymphs."

As a result Venerable Nanda's fellow-monks treated him as a hireling and as one bought with a price. And they addressed him accordingly, saying, "It appears that Venerable Nanda is a hireling; it appears that Venerable Nanda is one bought with a price. It appears that it is in the hope of winning celestial nymphs that he is living the religious life; it appears that the Exalted One has guaranteed that he shall win five hundred pink-footed celestial nymphs."

Now Venerable Nanda, [120] although his fellow-monks despised him, were ashamed of him, and tormented him by calling him "hireling" and "bought with a price," nevertheless, living in solitude, withdrawn from the world, heedful, ardent, resolute, in no long time, even in this life, himself abode in the knowledge, realization, and attainment of that supreme goal of the religious life for the sake of which goodly youths retire once and for all from the house-life to the houseless life. This did he know: "Birth is at an end, lived is the holy life, duty is done: I am no more for this world." And there was yet another Venerable Elder numbered among the Arahats.

Now a certain deity came by night to the Teacher, illuminating the whole Jetavana; and bowing to the Teacher, thus addressed him, "Reverend Sir, Venerable Nanda, son of the sister of the mother of the Exalted One, by extinction of the Depravities, even in this life, himself abides in the knowledge, realization, and attainment of freedom from the Depravities, emancipation of the heart, emancipation of the intellect. And there arose within the Exalted One also knowledge of the following, "By extinction of the Depravities, Nanda, even in this life, himself abides in the knowledge, realization, and attainment of freedom from the Depravities, emancipation of the heart, emancipation of the intellect."

In the course of the same night Venerable Nanda also approached the Exalted One, bowed to him, and spoke as follows, "Reverend Sir, I release the Exalted One from the promise which he made when he, the Exalted One, guaranteed that I should win five hundred pink-footed celestial nymphs." The Exalted One replied, "Nanda, I myself grasped your mind with my own mind and saw, 'By extinction of the Depravities, Nanda, [121] even in this life, himself abides in the knowledge, realization, and attainment of freedom from the Depravities, emancipation of the heart, emancipation of the intellect.' Likewise a deity informed me of the fact, saying, 'By extinction of the Depravities, Nanda, even in this life, himself abides in the knowledge, realization, and attainment of freedom from the Depravities, emancipation of the heart, emancipation of the intellect.' When, therefore, Nanda, you ceased to cling to the things of the world, and your heart was released from the Depravities, at that moment I was released from that promise." Then the Exalted One, knowing the true inwardness of this matter, breathed forth the following Solemn Utterance,

> He that has crossed over the mud and crushed the thorn of lust,
> He that has destroyed delusion, such a man is unmoved, whether
> in pleasure or in pain.

Now one day the monks approached Venerable Nanda and asked him, "Brother Nanda, aforetime you said, 'I am dissatisfied.' Do you say the same thing now?" "Brethren, I am in no wise inclined to the life of a layman." When the monks heard his answer, they said, "Venerable Nanda says that which is not true, utters falsehood. On former days he used to say, 'I am dissatisfied,' but now says, 'I am in no wise inclined to the life of a layman." And forthwith they went and reported the matter to the Exalted One. The Exalted One replied, "Monks, in former days Nanda's personality was like an ill-thatched house, but now it has come to be like a well-thatched house. From the day he saw the celestial nymphs, he has striven to reach the goal of a monk's labors, [122] and now he has reached it." So saying, he pronounced the following Stanzas,

> 13. Even as rain breaks through an ill-thatched house,
> So lust breaks through an ill-trained mind.
>
> 14. Even as rain breaks not through a well-thatched house,
> So lust breaks not through a well-trained mind.

The monks began to discuss the incident in the Hall of Truth: "Brethren, the Buddhas are marvelous! Venerable Nanda became dissatisfied with the Religious Life all because of Janapada-Kalyāṇī; but the Teacher, employing celestial nymphs as a lure, won him to complete obedience." The Teacher came in and asked them, "Monks, what is it you are sitting here now talking about?" When they told him, he said, "Monks, [123] this is not the first time Nanda has been won to obedience by the lure of the opposite sex; the same thing happened in a previous existence also." So saying, he related the following

9 c. Story of the Past: Kappaṭa and the donkey

Once upon a time, when Brahmadatta reigned in Benāres, there dwelt at Benāres a merchant named Kappaṭa. Now Kappaṭa had a donkey which used to carry loads of pottery for him, and every day he used to go a journey of seven leagues. On a certain occasion Kappaṭa loaded his donkey down with a load of pottery and took him to Takkasilā. While he was engaged in disposing of his wares, he allowed the donkey to run loose. As the donkey wandered along the bank of a ditch, he saw a female of his species and straightway went up to her. She gave him a friendly greeting and said to him, "Where have you come from?" "From Benāres." "On what errand?" "On business." "How big a load do you carry?" "A big load of pottery." "How many leagues do you travel, carrying a big load like that?" "Seven leagues." "In the various places you visit, is there anyone to rub your feet and your back?" "No." "If that's the case, you must have a mighty hard time."

(Of course animals have no one to rub their feet and their back; she said this merely to join bonds of love between them.)

As the result of her talk, the donkey became dissatisfied. After the merchant had disposed of his wares, he returned to the donkey and said to him, "Come, Jack, let's be off." "Go yourself; I won't go." [124] Over and over again the merchant tried with gentle words to persuade him to go; and when, in spite of his efforts, the donkey remained balky, he vented abuse upon him. Finally he thought to himself, "I know a way to make him go," and pronounced the following Stanza,

> I will make a goad for you, with a sixteen-inch thorn;
> I will cut your body to shreds; know this, donkey.

When the donkey heard that, he said, "In that case I shall know just what to do to you." So saying, he pronounced the following Stanza,

> You say you will make a goad for me, with a sixteen-inch thorn. Very well!
> In that case I will plant my fore feet, let fly with my hind feet,
> And knock out your teeth; know that, Kappaṭa.

When the merchant heard that, he thought to himself, "What can be the reason for his talking thus?" The merchant looked this way and that, and finally his eyes fell upon the female. "Ah!" thought the merchant to himself, "she must have taught him these tricks. I will say to the donkey, 'I will bring you home a mate like that.' Thus, by employing the lure of the opposite sex, I will make him go." Accordingly he pronounced the following Stanza,

A four-footed female, with face like mother-of-pearl, possessed of all the marks of beauty,
Will I bring to you to be your mate; know that, donkey.

When the donkey heard that, his heart rejoiced, and he replied with the following Stanza,

So "a four-footed female, with face like mother-of-pearl, possessed of all the marks of beauty,"
You will bring to me to be my mate; in that case, Kappaṭa,
Whereas hitherto I have traveled seven leagues a day, hereafter, I will travel fourteen leagues. [125]

"Well then," said Kappaṭa, "come!" And taking the donkey with him, he went back to the place where he had left the cart.

After a few days the donkey said to him, "Did n't you say to me, 'I will bring you a mate'?" The merchant replied, "Yes, I said just that, and I will not break my word; I will bring you home a mate. But I will provide food only for you. It may or may not be enough for both you and your mate, but that is a matter for you alone to decide. After you both have lived together, foals will be born to you. The food I shall give you may or may not be enough for both you and your mate and your foals too, but that is a matter for you alone to decide." As the merchant spoke these words, the donkey lost his desire.

When the Teacher had ended his lesson, he concluded the Jātaka as follows, "At that time, monks, the female donkey was Janapada-Kalyāṇī, the male donkey was Nanda, and the merchant was I myself. In former times, too, Nanda was won to obedience by the lure of the female sex."

I. 10. CUNDA THE PORK-BUTCHER [1]

Here he suffers. This religious instruction was given by the Teacher while he was in residence at Veḷuvana with reference to Cunda the pork-butcher.

The story goes that for fifty-five years Cunda made his living by killing pigs which he then either used for food or marketed. In time

[1] Text: N i. 125–129.

of famine he would go to the country with his cart filled with rice, [126] and return with it filled with shotes bought in villages for a mere pint-pot or two of rice apiece. Back of his house he had a plot of ground fenced off as a sort of pigsty, and there he kept his pigs, feeding them all kinds of shrubs and excrement.

Whenever he wanted to kill a pig, he would fasten the pig securely to a post and pound him with a square club to make his flesh swell plump and tender. Then, forcing open the pig's jaws and inserting a little wedge in his mouth, he would pour down his throat boiling hot water from a copper boiler. The hot water would penetrate the pig's belly, loosening the excrement, and would pass out through the anus, carrying boiling hot excrement with it. So long as there was even a little excrement left in the pig's belly, the water would come out stained and turbid; but as soon as the pig's belly was clean, the water would come out pure and clear.

The rest of the water he would pour over the pig's back, and the water would peel off the black skin as it ran off. Then he would singe off the bristles with a torch. Finally, he would cut off the pig's head with a sharp sword. As the blood gushed forth, he would catch it in a dish; then he would roast the pig, basting it with the blood he had caught. Then he would sit down with his son and his wife and eat the pig. Whatever meat was left over, he would sell. In this way he made a living for fifty-five years. Although the Teacher was in residence at a neighboring monastery, not on a single day did Cunda do him honor by offering him so much as a handful of flowers or a spoonful of rice, nor did he do a single work of merit besides.

One day he was attacked by a malady, [127] and while he yet remained alive, the fire of the Great Hell of Avīci uprose before him. (The fire of Avīci is a consuming torment able to destroy the eyes of one who stands a hundred leagues away and looks at it. Indeed, it has been described[1] in this wise, "For ever and ever it shoots forth its flames continually a hundred leagues in all directions." Moreover, the Elder Nāgasena[2] employed the following simile to show how much more intense is its heat than that of ordinary fire, "Great king, reflect that a rock even as big as a pagoda goes to destruction in the fire of Hell in but an instant. However, living beings who are reborn there, through the effect of their past deeds, suffer not destruction, but are as though they reposed in their mothers' wombs.")

[1] *Añguttara*, iii. 35: i. 142.

[2] *Milindapañha*, 67$^{7-8}$, $^{21-23}$.

When the torment of the Great Hell of Avīci uprose before the pork-butcher Cunda, his mode of behavior was altered in correspondence with his past deeds. Even as he remained within his house, he began to grunt like a pig and to crawl about on his hands and knees, first to the front of the house and then to the rear. The men of his household overpowered him and gagged him. But in spite of all they did (since it is impossible for anyone to prevent a man's past deeds from bearing fruit), he kept crawling back and forth, grunting like a pig continually.

Not a person was able to sleep in the seven houses round about. The members of his own household, terrified by the fear of death, unable otherwise to prevent him from going out, barricaded the doors of the house that he might not be able to go out, but might be confined within. Having so done, they surrounded the house and stood on guard. Back and forth for seven days crawled Cunda within his house, suffering the torment of Hell, grunting and squealing like a pig. Having thus crawled about for a period of seven days, he died on the seventh day and was reborn in the Great Hell of Avīci. (The Great Hell of Avīci is to be described in the terms of the Devadūta Suttanta.[1])

Some monks who passed the door of his house [128] heard the noise, and thinking it was merely the noise of the grunting and squealing of pigs, went on to the monastery, seated themselves in the presence of the Teacher, and said to him, "Reverend Sir, for seven days the door of Cunda the pork-butcher's house has been closed, and for seven days the killing of pigs has gone on; doubtless he intends to give some entertainment. Think, Reverend Sir, how many pigs he has killed! Evidently he has not a single thought of loving-kindness and lacks utterly the sentiment of compassion. So cruel and savage a being has never been known before."

Said the Teacher, "Monks, he has not been killing pigs these seven days. Retribution in harmony with his past deeds has overtaken him. Even while he yet remained alive, the torment of the Great Hell of Avīci uprose before him. By reason of this torment he crawled hither and thither in his house for seven days, grunting and squealing like a pig. To-day he died, and was reborn in the Avīci hell." When the Teacher had thus spoken, the monks said, "Reverend Sir, having suffered thus here in this world, he went again to a place of suffering

[1] *Majjhima*, 130: iii. 178–187; cf. *Aṅguttara*, i. 138–142 (translated by Warren, *Buddhism in Translations*, pp. 255–259).

and was there reborn." "Yes, monks," replied the Teacher. "He that is heedless, be he layman or monk, suffers in both places equally." So saying, he pronounced the following Stanza,

15. Here he suffers; after death he suffers: the evildoer suffers in both places.
He suffers, he is afflicted, seeing the impurity of his own past deeds.

I. 11. THE RIGHTEOUS LAY BROTHER [1]

Here he rejoices. This religious instruction was given by the Teacher while he was in residence at Jetavana with reference to a righteous lay brother. [129]

At Sāvatthi, we are told, lived five hundred righteous lay brethren, each with a retinue of five hundred lay brethren. The senior layman had seven sons and seven daughters. Each of these sons gave regularly ticket-porridge, ticket-food, food of the waning moon, food of the new moon, invitation-food, fast-day food, visitors' food, and food of the season of the rains. All of them were "later born," so that the layman and his wife and fourteen children maintained sixteen forms of alms. And the layman, virtuous, upright, together with son and wife, took delight in the distribution of alms.

After a time the layman was attacked by a disease, and his vital forces began to decay. [130] Desiring to hear the Law, he sent word to the Teacher, "Send me eight or sixteen monks." The Teacher sent them, and they straightway went and gathered around his bed and sat down on seats prepared for them. "Reverend Sirs," said the layman, "it will be difficult for me to see you, for I am weak; rehearse me but a single Sutta." "Which Sutta would you like to hear, lay brother?" "The Satipaṭṭhāna Sutta,[2] common to all the Buddhas." Accordingly they began to rehearse the Sutta, beginning with the words, "There is this one Way, monks, this one Path which leads to the Salvation of living beings."

At that moment, from the Six Worlds of the Gods, approached six chariots a hundred and fifty leagues long, drawn by a thousand Sindh horses, adorned with all the adornments. In each chariot stood a deity, and each deity spoke and said, "Permit us to convey you to our celestial world." And they spoke again and said, "Even as one shatters a clay vessel and replaces it with a vessel of gold, even so are

[1] Text: N i. 129–132.

[2] *Dīgha*, 22; *Majjhima*, 10.

living beings reborn to take their pleasure in our celestial world." The lay disciple, unwilling to be interrupted in listening to the Law, said, "Wait! wait!" The monks, thinking that he was speaking to them, ceased their recitation of the Law. His sons and daughters cried out, "Formerly our father could never hear enough of the Law. But now, after summoning the monks and directing them to rehearse the Law, he stops them himself. After all, there is no man who does not fear death." The monks said to each other, "This is no time for us to remain." And forthwith they arose and departed.

After a time the layman recovered his attention and asked his sons, "Why do you weep?" "Dear father," said they, "you sent for the monks, and even as you listened to the Law, you yourself stopped them from rehearsing the Law. We weep to think, 'After all, there is no man who does not fear death.'" [131] "But where are the noble monks?" "They said to each other, 'This is no time for us to remain.' And forthwith they arose from their seats and departed." "Dear sons, I was not speaking to the noble monks." "With whom, then, were you talking, dear father?" "From the Six Worlds of the Gods six deities approached in six magnificently adorned chariots, and standing in their chariots poised in the air, they said to me, 'Take your pleasure in our celestial world; take your pleasure in our celestial world.' I was talking with them." "Dear father, where are the chariots? We do not see them." "Have I any wreaths of flowers?" "Yes, dear father." "Which celestial world is the most delightful?" "Dear father, the most delightful is the World of the Tusita gods, the abode of the mothers and fathers of the Buddhas and of all the Future Buddhas." "Well then, throw a wreath of flowers and say, 'Let this wreath of flowers cling to the chariot which came from the World of the Tusita gods.'"

Accordingly the children of the layman threw the wreath of flowers, and it clung to the pole of the chariot and hung suspended in the air. The populace saw the wreath of flowers suspended in the air, but did not see the chariot. Said the lay disciple, "Do you see this wreath of flowers?" "Yes, we see it." "This wreath hangs suspended from the chariot which came from the World of the Tusita gods. I am going to the World of the Tusita gods; be not disturbed. If you desire to be reborn with me, do works of merit even as I have done." And when he had thus spoken, he died and set foot in the chariot. Immediately he was reborn as a deity three-quarters of a league in stature, adorned with sixty cartloads of ornaments. A retinue of a thousand celestial nymphs attended him, and a golden mansion twenty-five leagues in extent became visible.

When those monks reached the monastery, the Teacher asked them, "Monks, did the lay disciple hearken to the recitation of the Law?" "Yes, Reverend Sir. But in the midst of the recitation he cried out, 'Wait! wait!' and stopped us. Then his sons and daughters began to weep, [132] whereupon we said to each other, 'This is no time for us to remain,' and arose from our seats and departed." "Monks, he was not talking to you. From the Six Worlds of the Gods six deities approached in six magnificently adorned chariots, and they summoned that lay disciple to go with them; but the lay disciple, unwilling that the recitation of the Law should be interrupted, spoke to them." "Is that true, Reverend Sir?" "That is true, monks." "Reverend Sir, where was he reborn just now?" "In the World of the Tusita gods, monks."

"Reverend Sir, but recently he lived here among his kinsfolk rejoicing, and just now he went again to a place of rejoicing and was there reborn." "Yes, monks. They that are heedful, be they laymen or monks, rejoice in both places equally." So saying, he pronounced the following Stanza,

16. Here he rejoices; after death he rejoices: he that has done good works rejoices in both places.
He rejoices, he rejoices exceedingly, seeing the purity of his own past deeds.

I. 12. DEVADATTA'S CAREER [1]

Here he suffers. [133] This religious instruction was given by the Teacher while in residence at Jetavana with reference to Devadatta. The story of Devadatta, from the time he became a monk to the time the earth opened and swallowed him up, is related in all the Jātakas.[2] The following is a synopsis of the story:

12 a. Retirement from the world of the six princes

While the Teacher was in residence at Anūpiya Mango-grove, which lies near Anūpiya, a market-town of the Mallas, eighty thousand

[1] i. 12 is for the most part derived from *Vinaya, Culla Vagga,* vii. 1–4. With i. 12 a, cf. xxv. 12 b. With i. 12 b, cf. Hardy, *Manual of Buddhism,* pp. 326–333, 337–340. Text: N i. 133–150.

[2] See *Jātakas* 542: vi. 129–131; 533: v. 333–337; 466: iv. 158–159; 404: iii. 355–358.

kinsmen one day recognized on him the Characteristics of a Tathāgata, and eighty thousand youths asserted, "Let him be a king or a Buddha, he will spend his days surrounded by a retinue of Warrior-princes." After all but six of these youths had retired from the world and become monks, the company of princes, observing that the six Sakyan princes, King Bhaddiya, Anuruddha, Ānanda, Bhagu, Kimbila, and Devadatta, had not yet retired from the world, discussed the matter as follows, "We admit only our own sons to the Order. But of course these six Sakyan princes are not kinsmen of the Buddha. For this reason, doubtless, they have not retired from the world and become monks." Now one day the Sakyan prince Mahānāma approached Anuruddha and said, "Friend, there isn't one of our family who has become a monk. You become a monk and I will follow your example."

Now Anuruddha is said to have been brought up in such softness and luxury that he had never heard the word *isn't* before. For example, one day these six Sakyan princes engaged in a game of marbles. Anuruddha staked cakes on the result, proved a loser, and sent home for cakes. His mother prepared cakes and sent them. [134] The princes ate the cakes and resumed their play. Anuruddha lost repeatedly. Three times in all his mother sent him cakes. The fourth time she sent back word, "There isn't cake to send. Now Anuruddha had never before heard the word *isn't*. Therefore, supposing that this must be a variety of cake, he sent the man back, saying to him, "Fetch me some *isn't* cakes. When his mother received the message, "Then, my lady, send me some *isn't* cakes," she thought to herself, "My son has never heard the word *isn't* before. By this means, however, I can teach him the meaning of it." So she took an empty golden bowl, covered it with another golden bowl, and sent it to her son.

The guardian deities of the city thought, "When Anuruddha the Sakyan was Annabhāra, he gave food that was his own portion to the Private Buddha Upariṭṭha, making the Earnest Wish, 'May I never hear the word *isn't;* may I never know where food comes from.' Now if he sees the empty bowl, we shall never be able to enter the assembly of the gods; it may even happen that our heads will split into seven pieces." So they filled the bowl with celestial cakes. As soon as the bowl was set down on the round platter uncovered, the fragrance of the cakes permeated the entire city. Moreover, the moment a morsel of cake was placed in the mouth, it thrilled the seven thousand nerves of taste. Anuruddha thought to himself, "My mother does not love me; all this time she has never fried this *isn't* cake for me. [135] From this time forth I shall eat no other kind of cake." So he went home and asked his mother, "Mother, do you love me or do you not?" "My dear son, even as the eye is dear to one who possesses but one eye, and even as the heart, so are you exceedingly dear to me." "Then, dear mother, why is it that all this time you have not fried *isn't* cake for me?" Said the mother to her little page, "Boy, is there nothing in the bowl?" "My lady, the plate is filled to overflowing with cakes, and with such cakes as I have never seen before." The mother thought to herself, "It must be that my son has acquired great merit; it must be that he has made an Earnest Wish; deities must have filled the plate with cakes and sent them." Said the son to the mother, "Dear mother, from this time forth I will eat no other kind of cake than this; henceforth, I pray you, fry *isn't* cake alone for me." From that time forth, whenever her son said, "I should like some cakes to eat," she would send a bowl absolutely empty, covered with another bowl. So long as he continued to live at home, during all that time deities sent him celestial cakes. Since Anuruddha was so unsophisticated as all this, how could he be expected to know the meaning of the expression *becoming a monk?*

For this reason, therefore, he asked his brother, "What is this *becoming a monk?*" His brother replied, "The life of a monk involves cutting off the hair and beard, sleeping with indifference whether in a thorn-brake or in a fine bed, and going the rounds for alms." Anuruddha replied, "Brother, I am exceedingly delicate; I shall never be able [136] to become a monk." "Very well, my dear brother, then learn farming and live the life of a householder. But at least one of us must become a monk." Then said Anuruddha, "What is this *farming?*"

How could you expect a youth to know the meaning of the word *farming* who did not know where food comes from? For example, on a certain day a discussion arose among the three princes Kimbila, Bhaddiya, and Anuruddha as to where food comes from. Kimbila said, "It comes from the barn." Bhaddiya said to him, "You do not know where food comes from; it comes from the boiler." Anuruddha said, "Both of you together do not know where food comes from. It comes from a golden bowl with jeweled knob."

We are told that one day Kimbila saw rice being removed from a barn, and immediately formed the opinion, "These grains of rice were produced in the barn." Likewise one day Bhaddiya saw food being taken out of a boiler, and formed the opinion, "It was produced in the boiler." Anuruddha, however, had never seen men pounding rice or boiling it or taking it out of the boiler, but had seen it only after it had been taken out of the boiler and set before him. So Anuruddha formed the opinion, "When one desires to eat, food makes its appearance in a golden bowl." Such was the ignorance of all three princes as to where food comes from.

Now when Anuruddha asked the question, "What is this *farming?*" he received the following answer, "First the field must be plowed, and after that such and such other things must be done, and these things must be done year after year." Said he to himself, "When will the duties connected with farming ever come to an end? When shall we ever have time to enjoy our possessions in peace?" And because it seemed to him that the duties connected with farming would never come to an end and never cease, he said to his brother, "Well then, if this is the case, you may live the life of a householder. But as for me, I have no use for it." Accordingly he approached his mother [137] and said to her, "Mother, give me your permission; I wish to become a monk."

Thrice Anuruddha requested his mother to give him permission to become a monk, and thrice she refused to do so. Finally she said to him, "If your friend King Bhaddiya will become a monk, then you may become a monk with him." Accordingly he approached his friend Bhaddiya and said to him, "Friend, whether I shall become a monk or not is conditional upon your becoming a monk." Anuruddha urged his friend Bhaddiya with every argument at his command to become a monk, and finally, on the seventh day, obtained Bhaddiya's promise to become a monk with him.

So six princes of the Warrior caste, Bhaddiya, king of the Sakyans, Anuruddha, Ānanda, Bhagu, Kimbila, and Devadatta, accompanied by Upāli the barber as seventh man, for seven days enjoyed celestial glory like gods, and then set out with fourfold array, as though on their way to a pleasure-garden. When they reached foreign territory, they turned back their army by royal command, and then entered foreign territory. There each of the six princes removed his own ornaments, made a bundle of them, and gave them to Upāli, saying, "Now, Upāli, turn back. All this wealth will suffice to provide you with means of livelihood." Upāli flung himself at their feet, rolled over and over on the ground, and wept bitterly. But not daring to disobey the order, he arose and turned back. When they parted, the forest wept, as it were, and the earth quaked, as it were.

When Upāli had gone a little way, he thought to himself, "Harsh and cruel are these Sakyans; they may kill me, thinking I have killed their brethren. These Sakyan princes have renounced all this splendor, have cast away these priceless ornaments like a mass of saliva, and intend to become monks; [138] why not I?" So saying, he untied the bundle, hung those ornaments on a tree, and said, "Let those who want them take them." Having so done, he went to the Sakyan princes, and when they asked him why he had turned back, told them the whole story.

So the six Sakyan princes took Upāli the barber with them, went to the Teacher, and said to him, "We, Reverend Sir, are proud Sakyans. This man has been a servitor of ours for a long time. Admit him to the Order first; to him first we will offer respectful salutations; so will our pride be humbled." Thus first did they cause Upāli the barber to be admitted to the Order, and after that entered the Order themselves.

Of the six Sakyan princes, Venerable Bhaddiya attained Threefold Knowledge in that very rainy season. Venerable Anuruddha attained Supernatural Vision, and after listening to the Sutta entitled "The Reflections of a Great Man," attained Arahatship. Venerable Ānanda was established in the Fruit of Conversion. Elder Bhagu and Elder Kimbila subsequently developed Spiritual Insight and attained Arahatship. Devadatta attained the lower grade of Magic Power.

After a time, while the Teacher was in residence at Kosambi, rich gain and honor accrued to the Tathāgata and his company of disciples. Men entered the monastery bearing in their hands robes, medicines, and other offerings and asked, "Where is the Teacher? Where is the Elder Sāriputta? Where is the Elder Moggallāna? Where is the Elder Kassapa? Where is the Elder Bhaddiya? Where is the Elder Anuruddha? Where is the Elder Ānanda? Where is the Elder Bhagu? Where is the Elder Kimbila?" So saying, they went about looking at the places where sat the eighty Chief Disciples.

12 b. Devadatta's wicked deeds

Since no one asked, "Where does the Elder Devadatta sit and stand?" Devadatta thought to himself, "I became a monk at the same time as these other monks. Even as they are men of the Warrior caste who have become monks, so also am I a man of the Warrior caste who have become a monk. [139] But whereas men bearing rich offerings seek out these monks, no one takes my name on his lips. With whom now can I make common cause? With whom can I ingratiate myself, that I may obtain gain and honor for myself?"

Then the following thought occurred to him, "This King Bimbisāra, on the day when he first saw the Buddha, became established in the Fruit of Conversion, together with eleven nahutas of men besides; I cannot make common cause with him. Neither can I make common cause with the king of Kosala. But this king's son Ajātasattu knows no one's good qualities or bad qualities; I will make common cause with him." Accordingly Devadatta departed from Kosambi to Rājagaha, transformed himself into a youth, put four snakes on his hands and feet, put one snake about his neck, coiled one snake about his head as a cushion-rest, placed one snake on one shoulder, and thus arrayed in a girdle of snakes, he descended from the air and seated himself in Ajātasattu's lap. Ajātasattu was frightened and said, "Who are you?" "I am Devadatta." In order to dispel Ajātasattu's fear, Devadatta changed his form, stood before Ajātasattu wearing the robe of a monk and carrying a monk's bowl, ingratiated himself with Ajātasattu, and obtained for himself gain and honor.

Overcome with the gain and honor he received, Devadatta thought to himself, "It is I who ought to be at the head of the Congregation of Monks." Once having allowed this evil thought to spring up in his breast, with the springing up of the evil thought Devadatta lost the power to work miracles. Now at this time the Teacher was preaching the Law to the Congregation at Veḷuvana monastery, and the king was among the Congregation. While the Exalted One was preaching the Law, Devadatta paid obeisance to him, and then rising from his seat, extended his hands in an attitude of reverent salutation and said, "Reverend Sir, the Exalted One is now worn out, stricken with years, and aged; let him live a pleasant life in this world, free from care. I will direct the Congregation of Monks; commit the Congregation of Monks to my hands." [140] The Teacher, instead of consenting to the arrangement suggested by Devadatta, refused his request and called him a lick-spittle. Therefore Devadatta was highly indignant, and now for the first time conceiving hatred towards the Teacher, departed. The Teacher caused public proclamation to be made concerning Devadatta at Rājagaha.

Devadatta thought to himself, "Now I have been rejected by the monk Gotama; now I will make trouble for him." With this thought in mind he approached Ajātasattu and said to him, "Youth, aforetime men were long-lived, but now they are short-lived. This makes it probable that you, being a prince, will soon die. Well then! You kill your father and become king, and I will kill the Exalted One and become Buddha." So when Ajātasattu was established in his kingdom, Devadatta hired men to kill the Tathāgata. But the men he hired attained the Fruit of Conversion and turned back. Then Devadatta himself climbed Vulture Peak and said to himself, "I alone will deprive the monk Gotama of life." So saying, he split off a piece of rock and hurled it down. But he succeeded only in drawing the Teacher's blood. Failing in this way also to kill him, he next dispatched the elephant Nālāgiri against the Teacher. When the elephant approached, the Elder Ānanda offered his own life in behalf of the Teacher and stood in the breach. The Teacher subdued the elephant, and then departed from the city and went to the monastery. After partaking of the offerings of food brought by countless thousands of lay disciples, he preached in due course to the residents of Rājagaha, one hundred and eighty millions in number, and eighty-four thousand living beings obtained Comprehension of the Law. Said the monks, "How noble is the Venerable Ānanda! When so mighty an elephant approached, he offered his own life **[141]** and stood in front of the Teacher." The Teacher, hearing the Elder praised in this wise, said, "Monks, this is not the first time he has renounced his life for my sake; he did the same thing in a previous state of existence." And in response to a request of the monks he related the Culla Haṁsa,[1] Mahā Haṁsa,[2] and Kakkaṭa [3] Jātakas.

Devadatta's wickedness did not by any means become so notorious from his having compassed the king's death nor from his hiring murderers to kill the Tathāgata nor from his splitting off the piece of rock, as it did from his letting loose the elephant Nālāgiri. For upon that, the people raised a tumult and said, "Devadatta alone had the king killed and hired murderers and cast down the rock. But now he has turned the elephant Nālāgiri loose. Behold what manner of evildoer the king has on his hands!" The king then, hearing the words of the populace, caused Devadatta's five hundred cooking-vessels to be removed and did not thereafter minister to his wants. Likewise the citizens did not so much as offer food to him when he came to their houses.

When he had thus lost gain and honor, he determined to live by

[1] *Jātaka* 533: v. 333–354.
[2] *Jātaka* 534: v. 354–382.
[3] *Jātaka* 267: ii. 341–345.

deceit. Therefore he approached the Teacher and made the Five Demands. But the Teacher rejected his demands, saying, "Enough, Devadatta! Whoever so desires, let him be a forest hermit." "Brethren, whose words are the nobler, the words of the Tathāgata or the words which I myself have uttered? Very well, Reverend Sir, all their life long monks should be forest-dwellers, beggars, wearers of rags from a dust-heap, living at the foot of a tree, eating neither fish nor flesh. Whosoever desires release from suffering, let him come with me." So saying, Devadatta departed. [142]

Some monks who had but recently retired from the world and who possessed little intelligence, hearing his words, said, "Devadatta spoke fair; let us join him." So they joined him. Thus Devadatta with his five hundred monks sought to persuade all manner of people, both hardened and believing, to accept the Five Points. And living by soliciting food from various families, he strove to create a schism in the Order. The Exalted One asked him, "Devadatta, is it true, as men say, that you are striving to create schism and heresy in the Order?" "It is true," replied Devadatta. Said the Teacher, "Devadatta, it is a grievous thing to create a schism in the Order." Continuing, the Teacher admonished him at length. But Devadatta paid no attention to the Teacher's words. He went forth, and seeing the Venerable Elder Ānanda going his round for alms in Rājagaha, said to him, "Brother Ānanda, from this day forth I shall keep Fast and Chapter apart from the Exalted One, apart from the Order." The Elder told the Exalted One. When the Teacher realized the fact, he was filled with righteous indignation and said to himself, "Devadatta is doing that which will be of no profit to him in the Worlds of the Gods and the world of men; that which will cause him to be tormented in the Avīci hell." And he reflected,

Easy to do are deeds that are evil, deeds that bring harm.
But the deed that brings welfare, the deed that is good, that truly is hard to do.

Having pronounced this Stanza, he then breathed forth the following Solemn Utterance,

Easy to do for the good is the good; the good for the evil man is hard.
Evil for the evil man is easy to do; evil for the noble is hard.[1]

On Fast-day, as Devadatta sat on one side with his own retinue, he said, "Let whoever approves of these Five Points take a ticket."

[1] *Udāna*, v. 8.

[143] Five hundred Licchavi princes, novices having little gratitude, took tickets. Devadatta took these monks with him and went to Gayāsīsa. When the Teacher heard that he had gone there, he sent forth the two Chief Disciples to bring those monks back. The Chief Disciples went there, instructed the monks by performing miracles and wonders, caused them to drink the Deathless, and returned through the air, bringing them with them.

Said Kokālika, "Rise, brother Devadatta; Sāriputta and Moggallāna have carried off your monks. Do you not remember my saying to you, 'Brother, trust not Sāriputta and Moggallāna'?" Said Devadatta, "Sāriputta and Moggallāna cherish evil desires, are under the control of evil desires." As he spoke thus, he struck the center of his heart with his knee, and straightway hot blood burst forth from his mouth.

When the monks saw Venerable Sāriputta, surrounded by his retinue of monks, soaring through the air, they said, "Reverend Sir, when Venerable Sāriputta went hence, he went with but a single companion; but now he is returning resplendent with a great retinue." Said the Teacher, "Monks, it is not the first time this has happened; when my son was reborn in the form of an animal, then also did he return to me resplendent." So saying, he recited the Lakkhaṇa Jātaka: [1]

All goes well with the virtuous, with those whose disposition is friendly.
Behold Lakkhaṇa returning at the head of a host of relatives;
Then look upon yonder Kāla without relatives. [144]

Again said the monks, "Reverend Sir, they say that Devadatta seats a Chief Disciple on either side of him and imitates you, saying, 'I will preach the Law with the grace of a Buddha.'" Said the Teacher, "Monks, this is not the first time he has so done; in a previous state of existence also he strove to imitate me, but was not able to do so.

Vīraka, have you seen a sweet-voiced bird
With neck like that of a peacock, my husband Saviṭṭhaka?

Because he tried to imitate a bird that walks both on water and on land,
Saviṭṭhaka became entangled in a sevāla-plant and died.

Supplying the rest of the story, the Teacher related the Vīraka Jātaka.[2] On succeeding days, with reference to the same subject, the Teacher related the Kandagalaka [3] and Virocana [4] Jātakas:

[1] *Jātaka* 11: i. 142–145.
[2] *Jātaka* 204: ii. 148–150.
[3] *Jātaka* 210: ii. 162–164.
[4] *Jātaka* 143: i. 490–493.

This garuḍa bird went through the woods pecking at trees whose branches were soft and rotten.
At last he came to an acacia-tree, whose wood is always sound, and broke his head. [145]

Your brains have run out, your head is split open,
All your ribs are broken; to-day you are a pretty sight!

Again one day, hearing the remark, "Devadatta was ungrateful," the Teacher related the Java Sakuṇa Jātaka:[1]

We did you what service we could.
King of beasts, we render homage to you.
May we obtain some favor from you.

Seeing that I hold you fast between my jaws, I who feed upon blood,
I whose nature is to kill, it is a great deal that you yet live.

Again with reference to Devadatta's going about for the purpose of slaying, he related the Kuruṅga Jātaka:[2]

It is well known to the antelope, that you let drop the fruit of the sepaṇṇi.
Let us go to another sepaṇṇi; your tree likes me not.

Again when the discussion took this turn, "Devadatta fell away both from gain and honor and from the high position of a monk," the Teacher said, "Monks, this is not the first time he has so fallen away; in a previous state of existence also he fell away." So saying, he related the Ubhatobhaṭṭha Jātaka:[3] [146]

Your eyes are put out, your garments are lost, in your own house there is strife;
Your business is ruined in both places, both on water and on land.

In this wise did the Teacher, while he was in residence at Rājagaha, relate many Jātakas about Devadatta. From Rājagaha he went to Sāvatthi, and took up his residence at Jetavana monastery.

Devadatta's sickness continued for nine months; at the last, desiring to see the Teacher, he said to his own disciples, "I desire to see the Teacher; make it possible for me to see him." They replied, "When you enjoyed good health, you walked at enmity with the Teacher; we will not lead you to him." Said Devadatta, "Do not destroy me; I have indeed conceived hatred towards the Teacher, but the Teacher has not cherished so much as the tip of a hair's hatred towards me." And in very truth

Towards the murderer Devadatta, towards the robber Aṅgulimāla,
Towards Dhanapāla and Rāhula, to each and all he manifested an even temper.

[1] *Jātaka* 308: iii. 25–27. [2] *Jātaka* 21: i. 173–174. [3] *Jātaka* 139: i. 482–484.

"Let me see the Exalted One," begged Devadatta again and again; so finally they laid him on a litter and started out with him. When the monks heard that Devadatta was approaching, they informed the Teacher of the fact, saying, "Reverend Sir, we hear that Devadatta is coming to see you." "Monks, he will not succeed in seeing me in this present existence." (It is said that from the moment monks make the Five Demands, they invariably fail to see the Buddhas again.) [147] "Reverend Sir, he has reached such and such a place; he has reached such and such a place." "Let him do as he likes; he will never succeed in seeing me again." "Reverend Sir, now he is only a league distant, now he is only half a league distant, now he is only a gāvuta distant, now he has reached the lotus-tank." "Even if he enters within the Jetavana, he will not succeed in seeing me."

Those who came with Devadatta set the litter down on the bank of the lotus-tank at the Jetavana and descended into the tank to bathe. Devadatta arose from his litter and sat down, resting both feet on the ground, whereupon his feet sank into the earth. By degrees he sank into the earth, first to the ankles, then to the knees, then to the hips, then to the breast, then to the neck. Finally, when his jaw-bone rested on the ground, he pronounced the following Stanza,

> With these bones, with these vital airs, I seek refuge in the Buddha,
> Preëminent among men, god of gods, charioteer of untamed humanity,
> All-seeing, endowed with the auspicious marks of a hundred virtues.

There is a tradition that when the Tathāgata saw that matters had gone thus far, he made a monk of Devadatta. And this he did because he became aware of the following, "If he shall remain a layman and not be received into the Order as a monk, inasmuch as he has been guilty of grievous crimes, it will be impossible for him to look forwards with confidence to future existence; but if he shall become a monk, no matter how grievous the crimes he has committed, it will be possible for him to look forwards with confidence to future existence." [148] (At the end of a hundred thousand cycles of time he will become a Private Buddha named Aṭṭhissara.)

When Devadatta had sunk into the earth, he was reborn in the Avīci hell. "Since he sinned against an unchanging Buddha, let him endure torture unchanging;" and such was the torture he suffered. When he had entered the Avīci hell, which is a hundred leagues in extent, his body became a hundred leagues in height. His head, as far as the outer ear, entered an iron skull; his feet, as far as the ankles, entered earth of iron. An iron stake as thick as the trunk of a palmyra-tree proceeded forth from the west wall of the iron shell, pierced the small of his back, came forth from his breast, and penetrated the east wall. Another iron stake proceeded forth from the south wall, pierced his right side, came forth from his left side, and penetrated the north wall. Another iron stake proceeded forth from the top of the iron skull, pierced his skull, came forth from his lower parts, and penetrated earth of iron. In this position, immovable, he suffers this mode of torture.

The monks began a discussion, saying, "All this distance came Devadatta, but failed to see the Teacher, and was swallowed up by the earth." Said the Teacher, "Monks, this was not the first time Devadatta sinned against me and was swallowed up by the earth; in a previous state of existence also he was swallowed up by the earth." And by way of illustrating the point, he told the story of an incident in his own previous existence as king of the elephants. He directed aright a man who had lost his way, allowed him to mount his own back, and carried him to a place of safety, only to have the man return to him three successive times and saw off first the tips of his tusks, then the middle, and then the roots. As the man passed out of sight of the Great Creature, he was swallowed up by the earth. [149]

The Teacher then completed the Sīlava Nāga Jātaka:[1]

> If one should give the whole earth to an ungrateful man,
> A man who is ever looking for an opportunity, it would not satisfy him.

The discussion reverting to the same subject again and again, in order to illustrate the swallowing up of Devadatta by the earth in his existence as Kalāburājā for an offense against himself in his existence as Khantivādi, he related the Khantivādi Jātaka.[2] Again, in order to illustrate the swallowing up of Devadatta by the earth in his existence as Mahāpatāparājā for an offense against himself in his existence as Culla Dhammapāla, he related the Culla Dhammapāla Jātaka.[3]

Now when Devadatta was swallowed up by the earth, the populace was pleased and delighted, and raising flags and banners and plantain-trees and setting up brimming jars, held high festival, saying, "His death is indeed our great gain." When the monks reported this incident to the Exalted One, the Exalted One said, "Monks, this is not the first time the populace has rejoiced at Devadatta's death;

[1] *Jātaka* 72: i. 319–322. [2] *Jātaka* 313: iii. 39–43. [3] *Jātaka* 358: iii. 177–182.

in times past also the populace rejoiced thereat." And when he had thus spoken, to illustrate the rejoicing of the populace at the death of King Piñgala of Benāres, a man who was hated by all the people for his harshness and cruelty, he related the Piñgala Jātaka:[1]

All the people suffered harm at the hands of Piñgala; so soon as he was dead they recovered confidence.
Was he of the yellow eyes dear to you? Why do you weep, porter? [150]

He of the yellow eyes was not dear to me; I fear to think of his return.
Now that he has gone hence, he may harm the king of death, and the king of death thus harmed may send him back again.

Finally the monks asked the Teacher, "Now, Reverend Sir, tell us where Devadatta was reborn." "Monks, he was reborn in the Avīci hell." "Reverend Sir, during his life here on earth he suffered, and when he went hence he was reborn in a place of suffering." "Yes, monks, they that abide in Heedlessness, be they monks or laymen, suffer in both places." So saying, he pronounced the following Stanza,

17. Here he suffers, after death he suffers; the evildoer suffers in both places.
He suffers to think, "I have done evil;" yet more does he suffer, gone to a place of suffering.

I. 13. LADY SUMANĀ[2]

Here he rejoices. This religious instruction was given by the Teacher while he was in residence at Jetavana with reference to Lady Sumanā. [151]

For every day two thousand monks take their meal in the house of Anāthapiṇḍika at Sāvatthi, and a like number in the house of the eminent female lay disciple Visākhā. Whoever desires to give alms at Sāvatthi, first seeks the good offices of these two lay disciples. Do you ask the reason for this? Suppose you are asked the question, "Has Anāthapiṇḍika or Visākhā given alms equal in amount to those which you have given?" and you answer, "They have not," you may dispense a hundred thousand pieces of money in alms, and in spite of this the monks will murmur dissatisfaction, saying, "What kind of alms are these?" The explanation is that both of these lay disciples understand thoroughly the tastes of the Congregation of Monks and

[1] *Jātaka* 240: ii. 239–242.
[2] Cf. the story of Kavi in *Manu*, ii. 150 (Lanman's *Sanskrit Reader*, 61[15]). Text: N i. 151–154.

know exactly what is the proper thing to do; therefore all who desire to give alms take them with them when they go. And thus it happens that they are unable to minister to the monks in person in their own houses.

Under these circumstances Visākhā, considering within herself, "Who shall stand in my place and minister to the Congregation of Monks?" seeing the daughter of her son, appointed her to represent her; and thenceforth Visākhā's granddaughter ministered to the Congregation of Monks in Visākhā's residence. Anāthapiṇḍika appointed his oldest daughter Mahā Subhaddā; the latter showed the monks the customary attentions, hearkened to the Law, and as a result obtained the Fruit of Conversion; afterwards she married and went to live with her husband's family. Then he appointed Cullā Subhaddā, who followed her older sister's example, obtaining the Fruit of Conversion, and afterwards marrying and going to live with the family of her husband. Finally he appointed his youngest daughter Sumanā. Sumanā obtained the Fruit of the Second Path, but remained unmarried. [152] Overwhelmed with disappointment at her failure to obtain a husband, she refused to eat, and desiring to see her father, sent for him.

Anāthapiṇḍika was in the refectory when he received his daughter's message, but immediately went to her and said, "What is it, dear daughter Sumanā?" Sumanā said to him, "What say you, dear youngest brother?" "You talk incoherently, dear daughter." "I am not talking incoherently, youngest brother." "Are you afraid, dear daughter?" "I am not afraid, youngest brother." She said no more, but died immediately.

Although the treasurer had obtained the Fruit of Conversion, he was unable to bear the grief that arose within him. Accordingly, when he had performed the funeral rites over his daughter's body, he went weeping to the Teacher. Said the Teacher, "Householder, how is it that you come to me sad and sorrowful, with tears in your eyes, weeping?" "Reverend Sir, my daughter Sumanā is dead." "Well, why do you weep? Is not death certain for all?" "I know that, Reverend Sir. But my daughter was so modest and so conscientious. What grieves me so much is the thought that when she died, she was unable to recover her right mind, but died raving incoherently."

"But what did your youngest daughter say, great treasurer?" "Reverend Sir, I addressed her as 'dear Sumanā,' and she replied, 'What say you, dear youngest brother?' Then I said to her, 'You talk incoherently, dear daughter.' 'I am not talking incoherently, youngest brother.' 'Are you afraid, dear daughter?' 'I am not afraid, youngest brother.' She said no more, but died immediately."

Said the Exalted One to Anāthapiṇḍika, "Great treasurer, your daughter did not talk incoherently." "But why did she speak thus?" "Solely because you *were* her youngest brother. [153] Householder, your daughter was old in the Paths and the Fruits, for while you have attained but the Fruit of Conversion, your daughter had attained the Fruit of the Second Path. Thus it was, because she was old in the Paths and the Fruits, that she spoke thus." "Was that the reason, Reverend Sir?" "That was the reason, householder."

"Where has she now been reborn, Reverend Sir?" "In the World of the Tusita gods, householder." "Reverend Sir, while my daughter remained here among her kinsfolk, she went about rejoicing, and when she went hence, she was reborn in the World of Joy." Then the Teacher said to him, "It is even so, householder. They that are heedful, be they lay folk or religious, rejoice both in this world and in the world beyond." So saying, he pronounced the following Stanza,

18. Here he rejoices, after death he rejoices: he that has done good works rejoices in both places.
He rejoices to think, "I have done good works;" yet more does he rejoice, gone to a world of bliss.

I. 14. TWO BRETHREN[1]

Though he utter much that is sensible. This religious instruction was given by the Teacher while he was in residence at Jetavana with reference to two fellow-monks. [154]

For at Sāvatthi lived two young men of station who were inseparable friends. On a certain occasion they went to the monastery, heard the Teacher preach the Law, renounced the pleasures of the world, yielded the breast to the Religion of the Buddha, and became monks. When they had kept residence for five years with preceptors and teachers, they approached the Teacher and asked about the Duties in his Religion. After listening to a detailed description of the Duty of Meditation and of the Duty of Study, one of them said, "Reverend Sir, since I became a monk in old age, I shall not be able to fulfill the Duty of Study, but I can fulfill the Duty of Meditation." So he had

[1] Text: N i. 154–159.

the Teacher instruct him in the Duty of Meditation as far as Arahatship, and after striving and struggling attained Arahatship, together with the Supernatural Faculties. But the other said, "I will fulfill the Duty of Study," acquired by degrees the Tipiṭaka, the Word of the Buddha, and wherever he went, preached the Law and intoned it. He went from place to place reciting the Law to five hundred monks, and was preceptor of eighteen large communities of monks.

Now a company of monks, having obtained a Formula of Meditation from the Teacher, went to the place of residence of the older monk, and by faithful observance of his admonitions attained Arahatship. Thereupon they paid obeisance to the Elder and said, "We desire to see the Teacher." [155] Said the Elder, "Go, brethren, greet in my name the Teacher, and likewise greet the eighty Chief Elders, and greet my fellow-elder, saying, 'Our Teacher greets you.'" So those monks went to the monastery and greeted the Teacher and the Elders, saying, "Reverend Sir, our teacher greets you." When they greeted their teacher's fellow-elder, he replied, "Who is he?" Said the monks, "He is your fellow-monk, Reverend Sir."

Said the younger monk, "But what have you learned from him? Of the Dīgha Nikāya and the other Nikāyas, have you learned a single Nikāya? Of the Three Piṭakas, have you learned a single Piṭaka?" And he thought to himself, "This monk does not know a single Stanza containing four verses. As soon as he became a monk, he took rags from a dust-heap, entered the forest, and gathered a great many pupils about him. When he returns, it behooves me to ask him some questions." Now somewhat later the older monk came to see the Teacher, and leaving his bowl and robe with his fellow-elder, went and greeted the Teacher and the eighty Chief Elders, afterwards returning to the place of residence of his fellow-elder. The younger monk showed him the customary attentions, provided him with a seat of the same size as his own, and then sat down, thinking to himself, "I will ask him a question."

At that moment the Teacher thought to himself, "Should this monk annoy this my son, he is likely to be reborn in Hell." So out of compassion for him, pretending to be going the rounds of the monastery, he went to the place where the two monks were sitting and sat down on the Seat of the Buddha already prepared. (For wherever the monks sit down, they first prepare the Seat of the Buddha, and not until they have so done do they themselves sit down. [156] Therefore the Teacher sat down on a seat already prepared for him.) And when he had sat down, he asked the monk who had taken upon himself the Duty of Study a question on the First Trance. When the younger monk had answered this question correctly, the Teacher, beginning with the Second Trance, asked him questions about the Eight Attainments and about Form and the Formless World, all of which he answered correctly. Then the Teacher asked him a question about the Path of Conversion, and he was unable to answer it. Thereupon the Teacher asked the monk who was an Arahat, and the latter immediately gave the correct answer.

"Well done, well done, monk!" said the Teacher, greatly pleased. The Teacher then asked questions about the remaining Paths in order. The monk who had taken upon himself the Duty of Study was unable to answer a single question, while the monk who had attained unto Arahatship answered every question he asked. On each of four occasions the Teacher bestowed applause on him. Hearing this, all the deities, from the gods of earth to the gods of the World of Brahmā, including Nāgas and Garuḍas, shouted their applause.

Hearing this applause, the pupils and fellow-residents of the younger monk were offended at the Teacher and said, "Why did the Teacher do this? He bestowed applause on each of four occasions on the old monk who knows nothing at all. But to our own teacher, who knows all the Sacred Word by heart and is at the head of five hundred monks, he gave no praise at all." The Teacher asked them, "Monks, what is it you are talking about?" When they told him, he said, "Monks, your own teacher is in my Religion like a man who tends cows for hire. But my son is like a master who enjoys the five products of the cow at his own good pleasure." So saying, he pronounced the following Stanzas, [157]

19. Though he utter much that is sensible, if the heedless man be not a doer of the word,
 He is like a cowherd counting the cows of others, and has no part in the Religious Life.

20. Though he utter little that is sensible, if a man live according to the Law,
 If he forsake lust and hatred and delusion, if he have right knowledge, if his heart is truly free,
 If he cling to naught in this world or in that which is to come, such a man has a share in the Religious Life.

BOOK II. HEEDFULNESS, APPAMĀDA VAGGA

II. 1. STORY-CYCLE OF KING UDENA OR UDAYANA[1]

Heedfulness is the Way to the Deathless. This religious instruction was given by the Teacher while he was in residence at Ghosita monastery near Kosambi, and it was with reference to the loss by death of the five hundred women led by Sāmāvatī and of Māgandiyā and her five hundred kinswomen. From beginning to end the story is as follows: [161]

Part 1. Birth and youthful career of Udena

Once upon a time King Allakappa ruled over the kingdom of Allakappa and King Veṭhadīpaka ruled over the kingdom of Veṭhadīpaka. They had been intimate friends since their boyhood-days and had received their education in the house of the same teacher. On the death of their fathers they raised the royal parasol and became rulers of kingdoms, each of which was ten leagues in extent.

As they met from time to time, and stood and sat and lay down to sleep together, and watched the multitudes being born into the world and dying again, they came to the conclusion, "When a man goes to the world beyond he can take nothing with him: [162] he must leave everything behind him when he goes thither; even his own body does not follow him; of what use to us is the life of the householder? Let us retire from the world."

Accordingly they resigned their kingdoms to son and wife, retired from the world, adopted the life of ascetics, and took up their residence in the Himālaya country. And they took counsel together, saying, "Although we have renounced our kingdoms and retired from the world, we shall encounter no difficulty in gaining a living; but if we reside together in the same place, our life will be quite unlike the life of ascetics; therefore let us live apart. You live on this mountain; I will live on that. Every fortnight, on fast-day, we will meet together." Then this thought occurred to them, "Under this arrange-

[1] For a discussion of the parallels to the Story-Cycle of Udena, see Introduction, § 11. See also Rogers, *Buddhaghosha's Parables*, v, pp. 32–60. Text: N i. 161–231.

ment neither of us will be in regular communication with the other; but in order that each of us may know whether the other is living or not, you light a fire on your mountain, and I will light a fire on mine." And this they did.

After a time the ascetic Veṭhadīpaka died and was reborn as a prince of deities of mighty power. A fortnight later Allakappa saw no fire on the mountain and knew that his comrade was dead. As soon as ever Veṭhadīpaka was reborn, he surveyed his own heavenly glory, considered the deeds of his former existence, reviewed the austerities he had performed from the day when he retired from the world, and said to himself, "I will go see my comrade." Accordingly he laid aside his form as a deity, disguised himself as a wayfarer, went to Allakappa, paid obeisance to him, and stood respectfully on one side.

Allakappa said to him, "Whence have you come?" [163] "I am a wayfarer, Reverend Sir; I have come a long distance. But, Reverend Sir, does your honor reside entirely alone in this place? Is there no one else here?" "I have a single comrade." "Where is he?" "He resides on that mountain; but as he failed to light a fire on fast-day, I know he must be dead." "Is that so, Reverend Sir?" "That is so, brother." "I am he, Reverend Sir." "Where were you reborn?" "Reverend Sir, I was reborn in the World of the Gods as a prince of deities of mighty power. I have returned to see your honor. Does your honorable self reside in this place undisturbed, or are you subject to some annoyance?" "Yes, brother, I am bothered to death by the elephants." "Reverend Sir, what do the elephants do to trouble you?" "They drop dung on the ground I have swept clean, and they stamp with their feet and kick up the dust. What with removing the dung and smoothing the ground, I am all worn out." "Well, would you like to keep them away?" "Yes, brother." "Well then, I will provide you with means whereby you can keep them away."

Accordingly Veṭhadīpaka gave Allakappa a lute to charm elephants with and likewise taught him spells for charming elephants. Now as he presented the lute to him, he showed him three strings and taught him three spells. "Strike this string," said he, "and utter this spell, and the elephants will turn and run away without so much as daring even to look at you; strike this string and utter this spell, and they will turn and run away, eyeing you at every step; strike this string and utter this spell, and the leader of the herd will come up and offer you his back. Now do as you like." With these words [164] he departed.

Thereafter the ascetic lived in peace, driving the elephants away by uttering the proper spell and striking the proper string.

At this time Parantapa was king of Kosambi. One day he was sitting out in the open air basking himself in the rays of the newly risen sun, and beside him sat his queen, great with child. The queen was wearing the king's cloak, a crimson blanket worth a hundred thousand pieces of money; and as she sat there conversing with the king she removed from the king's finger the royal signet, worth a hundred thousand pieces of money, and slipped it on her own.

Just at that moment a monster bird with a bill as big as an elephant's trunk came soaring through the air. Seeing the queen and mistaking her for a piece of meat, he spread his wings and swooped down. When the king heard the bird swoop down, he sprang to his feet and entered the royal palace. But the queen, because she was great with child and because she was of a timid nature, was unable to make haste. The bird pounced upon her, caught her up in the cage of his talons, and soared away with her into the air. (These birds are said to possess the strength of five elephants; they are therefore able to convey their victims through the air, settle wherever they wish, and devour their flesh.)

As the queen was being carried away by the bird, terrified though she was with the fear of death, she preserved her presence of mind and thought to herself, "Animals stand in great fear of the human voice. Therefore if I cry out, this bird will drop me the instant he hears the sound of my voice. But in that case I should accomplish only my own destruction and that of my unborn child. If, however, I wait until he settles somewhere and begins to eat, then I can make a noise and frighten him away." Through her own wisdom, therefore, she kept patience and endured.

Now there stood at that time in the Himālaya country a banyan-tree which, although of brief growth, had attained great size [165] and was like a pavilion in form; and to this tree that bird was accustomed to convey the carcasses of wild animals and eat them. To this very tree, therefore, the bird conveyed the queen, lodged her in a fork of the tree, and watched the path leading to the tree. (It is the nature of these birds, we are told, to watch the path leading to their tree.) At that moment the queen, thinking to herself, "Now is the time to frighten him away," raised both her hands, clapped them together and shouted, and frightened the bird away.

At sunset the pains of travail came upon her, and at the same time from all the four quarters of heaven arose a great storm. The delicate queen, half dead with suffering, with no one beside her to say to her, "Fear not, lady," slept not at all throughout the night. As the night grew bright, the clouds scattered, the dawn came, and her child was born at one and the same moment. Because the child was born at the time (*utu*) of a storm, at the time when she was upon a mountain, and at the time when the sun rose, she named her son Udena.

Not far from that tree was the place of residence of the ascetic Allakappa. Now on rainy days it was the custom of the ascetic not to go into the forest for fruits and berries, for fear of the cold. Instead he used to go to the foot of the tree and gather up the bones from which the birds had picked the flesh; then he would pound the bones, make broth of them, and drink the broth. On that very day, therefore, he went there to get bones. As he was picking up bones at the foot of the tree, [166] he heard the voice of a child in the branches above.

Looking up, he saw the queen. "Who are you?" said he. "I am a woman." "How did you get there?" "A monster bird brought me here." "Come down," said he. "Your honor, I am afraid to come down on account of difference of caste." "Of what caste are you?" "Of the Warrior caste." "I am also of the Warrior caste." "Well then, give me the password of the Warrior caste." He did so. "Well then, climb up and set down my boy." Finding a way to climb the tree on one side, he climbed up and took the boy in his arms; obeying the queen's behest not to touch her with his hand, he set the boy down; then the queen herself came down.

The ascetic conducted the queen along the path to his hermitage and cared for her tenderly without in any way violating his vow of chastity. He brought honey free from flies and gave it to her; he brought rice grown in his own field and prepared broth and gave it to her. Thus did he minister to her needs.

After a time she thought to herself, "For my part I know neither the way to come nor the way to go, nor can I repose absolute confidence even in this ascetic. Now if he were to leave us and go elsewhere, we should both perish right here. I must by some means seduce him to violate his vow of chastity, so that he will not abandon us. Accordingly she displayed herself before him with under and upper garments in disarray, and thus seduced him to violate his vow of chastity; thenceforth the two lived together.

One day, as the ascetic was observing a conjunction of a constellation with one of the lunar mansions, he saw the occultation of Parantapa's star. "My lady," said he, "Parantapa, king of Kosambi, is dead." [167] "Noble sir, why do you speak thus? Why do you bear ill-will against him?" "I bear him no ill-will, my lady. I say this because I have just seen the occultation of his star." She burst into tears. "Why do you weep?" he asked. Then she told him that Parantapa was her own husband. The ascetic replied, "Weep not, my lady; whoever is born is certain to die." "I know that, noble sir." "Then why do you weep?" "I weep, noble sir, because it pains me to think, 'To my son belongs the sovereignty by right of succession; had he been there, he would have raised the white parasol; now he has become one of the common herd.'" "Never mind, my lady; be not disturbed. If you desire that he shall receive the sovereignty, I will devise some means by which he shall receive it." Accordingly the ascetic gave the boy the lute to charm elephants with and likewise taught him the spells for charming elephants.

Now at that time many thousands of elephants came and sat at the foot of the banyan-tree. So the ascetic said to the boy, "Climb the tree before the elephants come, and when they come, utter this spell and strike this string, and they will all turn and run away, without even so much as daring to look at you; then descend and come to me." The boy did as he was told, and then went and told the ascetic. On the second day the ascetic said to him, "To-day utter this spell and strike this string, if you please, and they will turn and run away, eyeing you at every step." On that day also the boy did as he was told, and then went [168] and told the ascetic.

Then the ascetic addressed the mother, saying, "My lady, give your son his message and he will go hence and become king." So she addressed her son, saying, "You must say, 'I am the son of King Parantapa of Kosambi; a monster bird carried me off.' Then you must utter the names of the commander-in-chief and the other generals. If they still refuse to believe you, you must show them this blanket which was your father's cloak and this signet-ring which he wore on his finger." With these words she dismissed him.

The boy said to the ascetic, "Now what shall I do?" The ascetic replied, "Seat yourself on the lowest branch of the tree, utter this spell and strike this string, and the leader of the elephants will approach and offer you his back. Seat yourself on his back, go to your kingdom, and take the sovereignty." The boy did reverence to his parents, and following the instructions of the ascetic, seated himself on the back of the elephant and whispered in his ear, "I am the son of King

Parantapa of Kosambi. Get me and give me the sovereignty which I have inherited from my father." When the elephant heard that, he trumpeted, "Let many thousands of elephants assemble;" and many thousands of elephants assembled. Again a second time he trumpeted, "Let the old, weak elephants retire;" and the old, weak elephants retired. The third time he trumpeted, "Let those that are very young retire;" and they also retired.

So the boy went forth, surrounded by many thousands of warrior-elephants, and reaching a village on the frontier, proclaimed, "I am the son of the king; [169] let those who desire worldly prosperity come with me." Levying forces as he proceeded, he invested the city and sent the following message to the citizens, "Give me battle or the kingdom." The citizens answered, "We will give neither. Our queen was carried off by a monster bird when she was great with child, and we know not whether she is alive or dead. So long as we hear no news of her, we will give neither battle nor the kingdom." (At that time, we are told, the kingdom was handed down from father to son.) Thereupon the boy said, "I am her son." So saying, he uttered the names of the commander-in-chief and the other generals, and when they still refused to believe him, showed the blanket and the ring. They recognized the blanket and the ring, opened the gates, and sprinkled him king.

Part 2. Birth and youthful career of Ghosaka

Story of the Past: Kotūhalaka casts away his son

Once upon a time there was a famine in the kingdom of Ajita, and a man named Kotūhalaka, unable to get a living, took his young son Kāpi and his wife Kāḷi, and thinking, "I will go to Kosambi and get a living there," set out with provisions for the journey. (There are also those who say that he left his home because the people were dying of intestinal disease.) As they proceeded on their journey, their provisions gave out, and finally they were so overcome with hunger that they were not able to carry the boy. Thereupon the husband said to his wife, "Wife, if we live, we shall have another son. Let us cast this child away and continue our journey alone."

There is a proverb, "A mother's heart is tender," and so it was with this woman. She replied, "I could never cast away a living child." "Well, what shall we do?" "Carry him by turns." When the mother's turn came, she would lift the child like a wreath of flowers, clasp him to her breast, [170] or carry him on her hip, finally giving him back to his father. When the father took the child, no matter where he held him he suffered more intense pain than ever from hunger. Again and again he said to his wife, "Wife, if we live, we shall have another son. Let us cast this child away." But this the mother steadfastly refused to do.

Finally the child became so tired from being passed back and forth that he fell asleep in the arms of his father. When the father observed that he was asleep, allowing the mother to precede him, he went and laid the child on a couch of leaves under a bush, immediately resuming his journey. The mother turned, looked back, and not seeing the child, asked, "Husband, where is my son?" "I laid him down under a certain bush." "Husband, do not kill me. Without my son I cannot live. Bring my son back to me." And she smote upon her breast and wept. So the husband retraced his steps, recovered the child, and brought him back to her. (In consequence of having cast away his child on this one occasion, Kotūhalaka was himself cast away seven times in a later existence. Let no one regard an evil deed lightly, saying, "It is only a small matter.")

Continuing their journey, they came to the house of a certain herdsman. On that day, as it happened, one of the herdsman's cows had calved, and the herdsman was about to hold the customary festival in honor of the event. Now a certain Private Buddha was accustomed to take his meals in the house of the hersdman. The herdsman, after providing the Private Buddha with food, celebrated the cow-festival with an abundant supply of rice-porridge. When the herdsman saw the visitors, he asked them, "Whence have you come?" They told him the whole story, whereupon the tender-hearted youth took pity on them and saw to it that they were given rice-porridge with a plentiful supply of ghee. The wife said to the husband, "Husband, if only you can live, I can live. For a long time you have not had sufficient food. Now eat to your heart's content." So saying, she set the ghee and curds before him, eating only a little of the ghee herself. The husband ate heartily; but so intense was the hunger from which he had suffered during the preceding seven or eight days that he was unable to satisfy it.

When the herdsman had seen to it that they were provided with rice-porridge, [171] he began himself to eat. Now under the herdsman's stool lay a bitch he had raised, and as the herdsman sat there eating, he fed her with morsels of rice-porridge. Kotūhalaka watched him feed her and thought to himself, "Fortunate indeed is that bitch to get such food to eat!" Kotūhalaka was unable to digest the rice-porridge he had eaten, died during the night, and received a new existence in the womb of that very bitch.

His wife performed the funeral ceremonies over his body, and remaining in that very house, worked for hire. Receiving a pint-pot of rice, she cooked it and placed it in the bowl of the Private Buddha, saying, "May these grains of rice bring a reward to your servant." And she thought to herself, "It would be well for me to remain right here. The Private Buddha comes here regularly; and whether there be alms or not, I shall have the privilege of paying obeisance to him each day and of ministering to him. By so doing I shall obtain peace of mind and earn much merit." And she remained right there working for hire.

After six or seven months the bitch gave birth to a single pup. The herdsman reserved the milk of one cow for the pup, and in no long time he grew to be a fine big dog. When the Private Buddha ate his meal, he invariably gave him a portion of his rice; and because of this the dog became deeply attached to the Private Buddha.

Now the herdsman was accustomed to go regularly twice each day to wait upon the Private Buddha, and the dog always went with him. On the way was a lair of wild beasts, and the herdsman used to frighten the wild beasts away by striking bushes and ground with a stick and calling out three times, "Su! su!" One day he said to the Private Buddha, "Reverend Sir, in case at any time I should be unable to come, I will send this dog for you. Therefore if I send him, please understand that I wish you to come."

A few days later the herdsman found it inconvenient to go in person. He therefore sent the dog in his place, saying, "Boy, go bring his reverence back." At the mere word of the herdsman the dog started off. Where he had seen his master stop and strike bushes and ground, the dog also stopped and barked three times; and when he was sure that his barking had frightened away the wild beasts, he went on. [172] Early in the morning, having attended to nature's needs, he entered the hut of leaves and grass, went to the place where the Private Buddha sat, barked three times by way of announcing his arrival, and then lay down at one side. By this the Private Buddha knew that it was time for him to go, and therefore started out. The dog ran before him, barking constantly. From time to time the Private Buddha tested the dog by taking the wrong path; but every time he did so the dog, by standing across the path and barking, intimated to him to take the other path.

One day the Private Buddha took the wrong path, and when the dog tried to stop him, without turning back, he pushed away the dog with his foot and went on. The dog, perceiving that he did not intend to turn back, took the hem of his undergarment in his teeth and dragged him along until he brought him to the right path. Such was the strength of the affection of the dog for the Private Buddha.

Later on the Private Buddha's robe wore out. When the herdsman provided him with materials for a new set of robes, the Private Buddha said to him, "Brother, it is difficult for a person all alone to make a robe. I will go to a convenient place and have it made for me." "Make it right here, Reverend Sir." "No, brother, I cannot." "Well then, Reverend Sir, do not take up your residence far from here." The dog stood listening to every word they said. The Private Buddha said, "Wait a moment, brother." Thereupon, leaving the herdsman behind, he flew up into the air and departed in the direction of Gandhamādana.

When the dog saw him flying through the air, [173] he began to bark and howl, and he kept this up until the Private Buddha gradually faded from view, whereupon his heart broke. (Animals, they say, are straightforward and not given to deceit; men, however, think one thing in their heart, but say another with their lips. Therefore said the Exalted One to a monk, "The ways of men are past finding out, but the ways of the beasts are easy to discover.") So when the dog died, he was reborn, because of his straightforwardness and lack of deceit, in the World of the Thirty-three with a retinue of a thousand celestial nymphs, and there he enjoyed glory and bliss unspeakable. When he but whispered, his voice carried a distance of sixteen leagues; when he spoke in an ordinary tone, he could be heard all over the city of the gods, a city ten thousand leagues in extent. (Do you ask, "Of what was this the consequence?" It was because he barked and howled for love of the Private Buddha.)

Remaining in the World of the Thirty-three for no long time, he passed from that state of existence. (Deities pass from the World of the Gods through four causes: exhaustion of life, exhaustion of merit, exhaustion of food, and anger. He that has earned much merit is reborn in the World of the Gods, remains there during the term allotted to him, and is then reborn higher and higher. Thus he passes through "exhaustion of life." He that has earned little merit soon exhausts that merit, just as three or four pint-pots of rice tossed into a royal storehouse disappear; and he therefore soon dies. Thus he passes through "exhaustion of merit." Still a third, while enjoying the pleasures of sense, fails through confusion of memory to partake of food, and the strength of his body being thereby impaired, dies. Thus he passes through "exhaustion of food." A fourth, jealous of the glory of another, [174] becomes angry and dies. Thus he passes through "anger.")

Story of the Present: Ghosaka is cast away seven times

Ghosaka, while enjoying the pleasures of sense, became forgetful, passed, through exhaustion of food, from the World of the Thirty-three, and was conceived in the womb of a courtezan of Kosambi. On the day when the courtezan gave birth to the child, she asked her slave-woman, "What is it?" "A son, my lady." "Very well, put this boy into an old winnowing basket and cast him away on the dust-heap." Thus she caused him to be cast away. (Courtezans will bestow care on a daughter, but not on a son, for it is through a daughter that their line of business is maintained.) Crows and dogs surrounded the child and huddled about him; but in consequence of his barking and howling for love of the Private Buddha, not one dared to approach him.

At that moment a man came out and saw the crows and dogs all huddled together. "What does this mean?" thought he to himself, going nearer. When he saw the boy, he immediately took a fancy to him, and saying to himself, "I have gained a son," he picked the boy up and took him home with him.

Now the treasurer of Kosambi happened at that time to go to the royal palace. Seeing the house-priest returning from the royal residence, he asked him, "Teacher, have you observed a conjunction of a constellation with one of the lunar mansions to-day?" "Yes, great treasurer. What else have we to do?" "What will happen to the country?" "Only this: a boy has been born in this city to-day who will one day become the principal treasurer." As the treasurer's wife was at that time great with child, he immediately sent a messenger to his house, saying, "Go find out whether or not she has given birth to a child."

He received the answer that she had not yet given birth to a child. Therefore, as soon as he had seen the king, he went home quickly, summoned a slave-woman named Kāḷī, gave her a thousand pieces of money, [175] and said, "Go scour this city, find the boy that was born to-day, and bring him hither to me." While she was scouring the city, she came to the house where the child was and asked the mistress of the house, "When was this boy born?" "To-day." "Give him to me," said she, first offering a penny and gradually increasing the amount until finally, by offering a thousand pieces of money, she obtained him. Then she took him with her and presented him to the treasurer.

The treasurer gave him a home in his house, thinking to himself, "If a daughter is born to me, I will marry her to this boy and make him treasurer; but if a son is born to me, I will kill him." After a few days his wife gave birth to a son. Thereupon the treasurer thought to himself, "If only this foundling did not exist, my own son would obtain the post of treasurer. I had best kill him immediately." So he said to Kāḷī, "Carry this child to the cattle-pen, and when it is time for the cattle to come out, lay him across the doorway, and the cattle will trample him to death. Observe whether or not they trample him to death, and then come back and tell me."

She carried the child to the cattle-pen, and as soon as the door was opened, laid him across the doorway. Now at other times the leader of the herd, the bull, came out last of all; but on this particular day he came out first, inclosed the boy with his four feet, and stood stock still. Several hundred cows came out on either side of the bull, rubbing against his flanks as they passed. The herdsman thought to himself, "Hitherto this bull has always gone out last of all, but to-day he went out first and stood stock still in the doorway of the pen. What can this mean?" Going near, he saw the boy lying under the bull. Immediately taking a fancy to him, he said to himself, "I have gained a son," and picking him up, he carried him home.

Kāḷī went back to the treasurer and in answer to his question told him what had happened. Said the treasurer, "Go to the herdsman, give him these thousand pieces of money, and bring the child back to me again." So she brought the child back again and gave him to the treasurer. [176] Then he said to her, "Good Kāḷī, five hundred carts start from this city at dawn on a trading expedition. Take this child and lay him in the track of the wheels. Either the oxen will trample him under their feet or the wheels will crush him to death. Observe what happens to him, and then return to me."

She took the child and laid him down in the track of the wheels. The leader of the caravan came first; but when his oxen reached the place where the child lay, they threw off the yoke. Again and again the leader replaced the yoke and tried to drive the oxen forwards; but as often as he did so, they threw off the yoke and refused to move. He was still struggling with them when the sun rose. "Why have the oxen acted thus?" thought he. He looked at the road and saw the boy. "Oh, what a grievous wrong I have done!" thought he. His heart was filled with joy at the thought, "I have gained a son," and picking up the boy, he carried him off.

Kāḷī went back to the treasurer and in answer to his question told him what had happened. Said the treasurer, "Go to the caravan-leader, give him a thousand pieces of money, and bring the child back to me again." When she had so done, he said to her, "Now carry him to the burning-ground and lay him in the bushes. There he will either be eaten by dogs or attacked by demons, and he will die. As soon as you know whether or not he is dead, return to me."

She took the child, laid him in the bushes, and stood at one side. But neither dog nor crow nor demon dared to approach him. (Pray, if he had neither mother nor father nor brother nor other kinsman to protect him, what was it that did protect him? All that protected him was his howling for love of the Private Buddha in his former existence as a dog.)

Just then a goatherd passed on one side of the burning-ground, leading several thousand goats to pasture. A certain she-goat made her way into the bushes eating leaves and grass, and seeing the boy, knelt down and gave him suck. The goatherd called, "He! he!" but she did not come out. Thereupon he said to himself, "I will beat her with my stick and bring her out." So saying, he made his way into the bushes. [177] And there he saw the she-goat on her knees, giving suck to the boy. He immediately took a fancy to the boy, and saying to himself, "I have gained a son," picked him up and carried him off.

Kāḷī went back to the treasurer and in answer to his question told him what had happened. Said the treasurer, "Go to the goatherd, give him a thousand pieces of money, and bring the child back to me again." When she had so done, he said to her, "Good Kāḷī, take this child with you, climb the mountain that is known as Robbers' Cliff, and throw him down the precipice. He will strike against the sides of the ravine and be dashed to pieces when he reaches the bottom. As soon as you know whether or not he is dead, return to me."

She carried the child to Robbers' Cliff, and standing at the top of the mountain, threw him down. Now there grew along the mountain near that abyss a dense bamboo thicket, and the top of the mountain was covered with a thick growth of guñjā shrub. As the boy fell, he dropped into this bamboo thicket as into a coverlet of goat's hair. Now that very day the leader of the reed-makers had received a gift of bamboo and accompanied by his son, he had gone to chop that thicket down. As he began his work, the bamboo shook and the boy cried out. "That sounds like the voice of a boy," thought he. Climbing up on one side, he saw the boy. His heart was filled with joy at the thought, "I have gained a son," and picking up the boy, he carried him off.

Kāḷī went back to the treasurer and in answer to his question told him what had happened. Said the treasurer, "Go to the reed-maker, give him a thousand pieces of money, and bring the child back to me again." She did so. But in spite of the treasurer's attempts on his life, the child lived and thrived and grew to manhood. Ghosaka was his name. He was like a thorn in the eye of the treasurer, who could not look him straight in the face.

Thinking of a way to kill him, the treasurer went to a friend of his who was a potter and asked him, "When are you going to fire your bake-house?" "To-morrow." [178] "Well then, take these thousand pieces of money and do a job for me." "What is it, master?" "I have a single base-born son. I will send him to you. Take him into an inner room, chop him to pieces with a sharp axe, throw him into a chatty, and bake him in the bake-house. Here are a thousand pieces of money, to seal the bargain, as it were. But in addition I will reward you suitably later." "Very well," said the potter, consenting to the bargain.

On the following day the treasurer summoned Ghosaka and sent him to the potter, saying, "Yesterday I left an order with the potter to do a certain piece of work for me. Go say to him, 'Finish the job my father gave you yesterday.'" "Very well," said Ghosaka, and set out.

As Ghosaka was on his way to the potter's, the treasurer's other son, who was playing marbles with some boys, saw him. And calling to him, he asked, "Where are you going?" "I am carrying a message to the potter for father." "Let me go there. These boys have won a big stake from me. You win it back and give it to me." "I am afraid of father." "Do not fear, brother; I will carry that message. I have lost a big stake. You play until I return again, and win the stake back for me."

(We are told that Ghosaka was skillful at shooting marbles, and that for this reason his foster-brother was so insistent.)

So Ghosaka consented to let his foster-brother go in his place, saying, "Well then, go to the potter and say to him, 'Finish the job my father gave you yesterday.'" Thus it happened that the treasurer's own son carried the message to the potter. The potter killed him according to the letter of the directions he had received from the treasurer and threw his body into the bake-house. Ghosaka played marbles all day and went home in the evening. [179] "You have returned home, son?" queried the treasurer. Ghosaka then told him the reason why he had himself returned home and let his younger brother go to the potter.

"Woe is me!" cried the treasurer with a loud voice. He looked as though the blood had been drawn from his veins. He rushed to the potter, wringing his hands and wailing, "Oh, potter, do not kill me! do not kill me!" The potter saw him approaching in this wise and said to him, "Master, make no noise; the job is done." Thus was the treasurer overwhelmed with sorrow as with a mountain. Thus did he suffer great grief, even as do all who offend against those that are without offense. Therefore said the Exalted One,

137. Whosoever visits punishment on those that deserve not punishment,
Whosoever offends against those that are without offense,
Such an one will right quickly come to one of ten states:

138. He will incur cruel suffering, or infirmity, or injury of the body,
Or severe sickness, or loss of mind,

139. Or misfortune proceeding from the king, or a heavy accusation,
Or death of relatives, or loss of treasures,

140. Or else the fire of lightning will consume his houses;
Upon dissolution of the body such a fool will go to Hell. [180]

Now under these circumstances the treasurer was unable to look Ghosaka straight in the face. "How can I manage to kill him?" thought he. Finally he thought of a way. "I will send him to the superintendent of my hundred villages and order him to kill him," said he to himself. Accordingly he wrote the following letter to the superintendent, "This is my base-born son. Kill him and throw him into the cesspool. Let this be done, and I shall know how to reward my uncle properly." Then he said to his foster-son, "Dear Ghosaka, there is a superintendent over our hundred villages. Take this letter and give it to him." So saying, he fastened the letter to the hem of his garment. (Now Ghosaka did not know how to read and write, for ever since he was a boy the treasurer had striven, although without success, to kill him. Why, therefore, should he have taught him to read and write?) As Ghosaka set out with his own death-warrant fastened to the hem of his garment, he said to his father, "Father, I have no provisions for the journey." "You have no need of provisions for the journey. On the way, in such and such a village, lives a friend of mine who is a treasurer. Obtain your breakfast at his house, and then continue your journey." "Very well," said Ghosaka, and bowing to his father, set out on his journey.

When he arrived at the village, he inquired where the treasurer's house was, went there, and saw the treasurer's wife. "Whence have you come?" she inquired. "From the city," he replied. "Whose son are you?" "I am the son of your friend the treasurer, my lady." "Then you are Ghosaka." "Yes, my lady." She fell in love with him at first sight. Now the treasurer had a daughter about fifteen or sixteen years of age, and she was exceedingly beautiful and fair to look upon. In order to keep her safe and sound, her parents lodged her on the topmost floor of a seven-storied palace in an apartment of royal splendor, giving her a single slave-girl to run errands. [181] At that moment the treasurer's daughter sent this slave-girl to a shop. The treasurer's wife, seeing her, asked, "Where are you going?" "On an errand for your daughter, my lady." "Just come here a moment. Never mind the errand. Spread a seat for my son, bathe his feet, anoint them with oil, and then spread a couch for him. After you have done this, you may do your errand." The slave-girl did as she was told.

When she returned, the treasurer's daughter scolded her for her long absence. The slave-girl replied, "Be not angry with me. The treasurer's son Ghosaka has arrived, and I had to do this and that for him, besides going on an errand for you, before I returned." When the treasurer's daughter heard the name "treasurer's son Ghosaka," love suffused her body, cleaving her skin and penetrating the marrow of her bones.

(For she had been his wife in his former existence as Kotūhalaka and had given a pint-pot of rice to the Private Buddha. And through his supernatural power she had been reborn in the household of the treasurer. No wonder her old passion for him returned and overwhelmed her! Therefore said the Exalted One,

> Through previous association or present advantage,
> That love springs up like a lily in the water.)

The treasurer's daughter said to the slave-girl, "Girl, where is he?" "He is lying asleep on the couch." "Has he anything in his hand?" "There is a letter fastened to his garment." "What can be in this letter?" she thought. So while Ghosaka was asleep, and her mother and father were otherwise engaged, she came down without attracting their attention, detached the letter from his garment, took it with her, went into her room, closed the door, opened the window, and through her knowledge of writing read the letter. "Oh!" she exclaimed, "the simpleton is going about with his own death-warrant fastened to his garment. [182] Had I not seen it, he would surely have been killed."

So she tore up this letter and wrote another in the name of the treasurer as follows, "This is my son Ghosaka. Procure presents for him from my hundred villages. Prepare a festival in honor of his marriage with the daughter of this district-treasurer. Build him a two-storied house in the center of the village wherein he resides. Surround his house with a wall and with a guard of men, and so provide him with ample protection. Then send me a message, saying, 'I have done thus and so,' and I shall know how to reward my uncle properly." Having written the letter, she folded it up and fastened it to the hem of his garment.

After sleeping all day, Ghosaka arose, ate his meal, and went on his way. Early on the morning of the following day he arrived at that village and saw the superintendent performing his village duties. When the superintendent saw him, he asked him, "What is it, dear Ghosaka?" "My father has sent you a letter." "What is it about, dear Ghosaka? Bring it to me." He took the letter and read it, and then said with an exclamation of delight, "See, men, how my master loves me. He has sent me a message, saying, 'Prepare a festival in honor of my oldest son.' Bring wood and other building materials immediately." Having thus given orders to the householders, he caused a house of the kind described in the letter to be erected in the center of the village, had presents brought from the hundred villages, conducted the daughter of the district-treasurer thither, celebrated the marriage festival, and then sent word to the treasurer, saying, "I have done thus and so."

When the treasurer received the message, he said, "What I would do, that I do not; what I would not do, that I do." Disappointment over the failure of his latest plan, together with sorrow over the death of his own son, set him on fire within and produced diarrhea.

The treasurer's daughter gave orders, saying, "Should anyone come here from the treasurer, tell me before you tell the treasurer's son." [183] The treasurer said to himself, "At any rate I will not make this rascally son of mine heir to my property." With this thought in mind he said to a certain official, "Uncle, I wish to see my son. Send a servant and summon my son." "Very well," replied the official, and giving a certain man the letter, sent him away.

When the treasurer's daughter heard that the servant had arrived and was standing at the door, she sent for him and asked him, "What is it, my man?" "The treasurer is sick and wishes to see his son, and has therefore sent for him, my lady." "My man, is he strong or weak?" "He is still strong, my lady, and able to take nourishment." Without letting the treasurer's son know, she ordered that the man should be given lodging and expenses and said to him, "You may go when I send you. Remain here for the present."

Again the treasurer addressed the official, "Uncle, did you not send a messenger to my son?" "I did, master, but the man who went has not yet returned." "Well then, try again and send another." So the official sent another man, and the treasurer's daughter treated him just as she had the first. The treasurer's condition grew worse; one chamber-pot went in and another came out. Again the treasurer asked the official, "Uncle, did you not send a messenger to my son?" "I did, master, but the man who went has not yet returned." "Well then, try again and send another." So the official sent another man. When the third messenger arrived, the treasurer's daughter asked him the news. "The treasurer is a very sick man, my lady. He refuses to eat and is confined to his bed. One chamber-pot comes out and another goes in."

"Now it is time to go," thought the treasurer's daughter. So she said to the treasurer's son, "I learn that your father is sick." "Wife, what say you?" "It may be only a slight ailment, husband." "What is to be done now?" [184] "Let us take presents from his hundred villages and go see him." "Very well," said he. Having caused presents to be brought, he started out, conveying the presents in a cart. Then she said to him, "Your father is very weak. If we take all these presents, we shall be delayed on the way; send them back." Having sent all the presents back to their own house, she said to the treasurer's son, "Husband, please stand at your father's feet; I will stand beside his pillow." And as they entered the house, she gave orders to her own men, "Stand on guard both in the front of the house and in the rear." And when they had entered, the treasurer's son took his stand at his father's feet and his wife beside his pillow.

At that moment the treasurer was lying on his back and the official was rubbing his feet. The latter said to him, "Master, your son has arrived." "Where is he?" "Here he is, standing at your feet." When the treasurer saw his son, he sent for the receiver of his revenues and asked him, "How much wealth is there in my house?" "Master, of money alone there are four hundred millions; as for objects for employment and enjoyment, such as villages and fields and men and animals and wagons and carriages, such and such is the total." It was the treasurer's intention to say, "All of this wealth I do *not* give to my son Ghosaka." But instead of this he said, "I *do* give."

When the treasurer's daughter heard this, she thought to herself, "However, if this man should speak again, he might say something very different." Accordingly, pretending to be overcome with grief, she disheveled her hair, burst into tears, and said, "Dear father, do you really mean this? In spite of these words of yours, which we hear, we are indeed unfortunate." So saying, she fell on him, struck the middle of his breast with the crown of her head, and in order that he might not be able to speak again, rubbed the middle of his breast with the crown of her head, displaying at the same time signs of profound grief. At that very moment the treasurer died. [185]

They went and informed King Udena of his death. The king had the funeral ceremonies performed over his body and asked, "Has he any son or daughter?" "Your majesty, he has a son named Ghosaka; and, your majesty, he bestowed all his property on him before he died." Some time afterwards, the king sent for the treasurer's son. Now that day it rained, and there were pools of water here and there in the palace court. The treasurer's son set out to see the king. The king opened his window and watched him as he approached, noticing that as he crossed the palace court he leaped over the pools of water that stood in the court. When he reached the palace and paid obeisance to the king and stood before him, the king asked him, "Your name is Ghosaka?" "Yes, your majesty." The king comforted him, saying, "Do not grieve at the thought that your father is dead. I will give you alone your father's post as treasurer." Then he dismissed him, saying, "Now, dear Ghosaka, you may go," and stood and watched him as he left the palace.

Now whereas Ghosaka leaped over the water in approaching the palace, he walked through it on his return. The king sent orders for him to return from where he was and asked him, "Dear Ghosaka, is it a fact that whereas, in coming to me, you leaped over the water, on your return you walk through it?" "It is even so, your majesty. Then I was a boy and was fond of play, but now I have been promised a post of honor by your majesty. Therefore I must now lay aside my former ways and deport myself with modesty and dignity." On hearing this, the king thought to himself, "There is a wise man. I will give him the post immediately." Accordingly he gave him the wealth formerly possessed by his father and the post of treasurer, together with all the hundred villages. Then Ghosaka mounted his chariot and drove sunwise round the city. Every place he looked at quaked and trembled.

The treasurer's daughter sat talking with the slave-woman Kāḷī. [186] "Mother Kāḷī," said she, "it was through me that your son obtained all this worldly glory." "How is that, my lady?" "Why, this youth came to our house with his own death-warrant fastened to the hem of his garment. I tore up that letter and wrote another, ordering the celebration of a festival in honor of my marriage to him. In this way did I protect him all that time." "My lady, this is all you know about it. But as a matter of fact, from the time your husband was a little boy, the treasurer constantly sought to kill him, and though his attempts were unsuccessful, a large sum of money was spent solely for the purpose of accomplishing his death." "Kāḷī, the treasurer was indeed guilty of abominable crimes!"

Having performed his ceremonial circuit of the city, Ghosaka entered his house. Now when his wife saw him, she thought to herself, "It was through me that he obtained all this worldly glory," and laughed. The treasurer's son asked her, "Why do you laugh?" "For a certain reason." "Tell me the reason." She refused to do so. He drew his sword and said, "If you do not tell me, I will cut you in twain." Then she said, "I laughed to think that it was through me that you obtained all this worldly glory." "If what I possess was handed over to me by my father, where do you come in?" (We are told that during all that time Ghosaka knew nothing about the designs against his life, and that that was why he refused to believe what she said.) So she told him the whole story, saying, "When your father sent you forth bearing your own death-warrant, I did this and that and protected you."

"What you say is not true," replied Ghosaka, refusing to believe her. "I will ask Mother Kāḷī." So he asked the slave-woman, "Kāḷī, is what she says true?" "Yes, my lord. From the time you were a little boy your father sought constantly to kill you, and though his attempts were unsuccessful, a large sum of money was spent for the purpose of accomplishing your death. On seven occasions you had a narrow escape from death. Now, coming from the village of which he was headman, [187] you have obtained the post of treasurer, together with all the hundred villages."

When Ghosaka heard this, he thought to himself, "How great was my presumption! But since I have escaped from so terrible a death, I must no longer live the life of Heedlessness. Henceforth, therefore, I will live the life of Heedfulness." Accordingly he established alms for the blind and the poor, and employing his friend the householder as steward of his alms, he dispensed a thousand pieces of money daily.

Part 3. Birth and youthful career of Sāmāvatī

Now at this time there lived in the city of Bhaddavatī a treasurer named Bhaddavatiya, and he was a friend of the treasurer Ghosaka, although Ghosaka had never seen him. For the treasurer Ghosaka heard, from traders who came from the city of Bhaddavatī, of the wealth and age of the treasurer Bhaddavatiya, and desiring to be friends with him, sent him a present. Likewise the treasurer Bhaddavatiya heard, from traders who came from the city of Kosambi, of the wealth and age of the treasurer Ghosaka, and desiring to be friends with him, sent him a present. Thus, although neither had seen the other, they dwelt as friends.

After a time intestinal disease broke out in the house of the treasurer Bhaddavatiya. When this disease breaks out, the first to die are flies; afterwards, in regular order, insects, mice, domestic fowls, swine, cattle, slaves both female and male, and last of all the members of the household. Only those that break down the wall and flee, save their lives. Now at that time the treasurer Bhaddavatiya and his wife and daughter fled in this manner, and intending to seek the treasurer Ghosaka, [188] set out on the road to Kosambi. While they were still on their way, their provisions for the journey gave out, and their bodies became exhausted from exposure to wind and sun, and from hunger and thirst. Reaching Kosambi with difficulty, they bathed in a pool of water in a pleasant place and then entered a certain rest-house at the gate of the city.

Then the treasurer said to his wife, "Wife, those who travel in this way are not courteous even to a mother who has borne a child. Now I have a friend who, they say, dispenses a thousand pieces of money daily in alms to the blind, the poor, and other unfortunate persons. We will send our daughter there, have her bring us food, remain right here for a day or two and refresh our bodies, and then we will go and see my friend." "Very well, husband," she replied, and they took up their residence right there in the rest-house.

On the following day, when meal-time was announced and the blind, the poor, and other unfortunate persons went to obtain food, the mother and father sent forth their daughter, saying, "Daughter, go bring us food." So the daughter of a wealthy house, pride overcome with misfortune, hid her shame, took a bowl, and went with poor folk to procure food. "How many portions will you have?" she was asked. "Three," she replied. So they gave her three portions. She carried the food back to her parents, and the three sat down to eat together. The mother and daughter said to the treasurer, "Master, misfortune comes even to prominent families. Eat without regarding us and do not worry." After a good deal of urging, they prevailed upon him to eat. But after he had eaten, he was unable to digest his food, and when the sun rose, he died. The mother and daughter wept and wailed and lamented.

On the following day the young girl went the second time to procure food. "How many portions will you have?" [189] "Two." She carried the food back to her mother, and after a good deal of urging, prevailed upon her to eat. The mother yielded to her pleading and consented to eat, but died on that very day. The young girl, left alone to herself, wept and wailed and lamented over the misfortune that had come upon her. On the following day, suffering the pangs of hunger keenly, she went weeping in the company of beggars to procure food. "How many portions will you have, daughter?" "One," was her reply.

A householder named Mitta, remembering that she had received food for three days, said to her, "Perish, vile woman. To-day, at last, you have come to know the capacity of your belly." This daughter of a respectable family, modest and timid, felt as though she had received a sword-thrust in her bosom, or as though salt water had been sprinkled on a sore. She immediately replied, "What do you mean, sir?" "Day before yesterday you took three portions, yesterday two, to-day you take but one. To-day, then, you know the capacity of your belly." "Sir, do not think that I took these for myself." "Why then did you take them?" "Sir, day before yesterday we were three, yesterday we were two, to-day I am left alone." "How is that?" he inquired.

She then told him the whole story from the beginning. As he listened to her story, he was unable to control his tears, but was overcome by the power of the grief that arose within him. Finally he said to her, "My dear girl, if this is the case, do not worry. Hitherto you have been the daughter of the treasurer Bhaddavatiya, but from this day forth you shall be my very own daughter." And he kissed her on the head, conducted her to his own house, and adopted her as his own oldest daughter.

One day she heard loud and piercing screams in the refectory, whereupon she said to her foster-father, "Father, why do you not keep these people quiet when you dispense alms?" "It is impossible to do it, dear daughter." "Father, it is quite possible." "How would you do it, dear daughter?" "Father, [190] put a fence around the refectory and hang two gates through which the people may pass in and out, allowing only sufficient space for one person to pass through at a time. Then direct the people to pass in through one gate and out through the other. If you do this, they will receive their alms peaceably and quietly." When the householder had heard her plan he remarked, "A happy device, dear daughter," and did as she suggested. Now up to that time her name had been Sāmā, but through her construction of a fence (*vati*) she received the name Sāmāvatī. From that time on there was no more tumult in the refectory.

Now the treasurer Ghosaka had long been accustomed to hear this noise in the refectory and rather liked to hear it; for it always made him think, "That is the noise in my refectory." But after hearing no noise at all for two or three days, he asked the householder Mitta, who came one day to wait upon him, "Are alms being give to the blind, the poor, and other unfortunate persons?" "Yes, sir." "How then does it happen that for two or three days past I have not heard a sound?" "I have arranged matters so that the people now receive alms without making any noise." "Why didn't you do so before?" "I didn't know how, sir." "How did you happen to find a way just now?" "My daughter told me how to do it, sir." "Have you a daughter whom I have never seen?" Then the householder told him the whole story of the treasurer Bhaddavatiya, beginning with the outbreak of the plague and ending with his adoption of the young girl as his own oldest daughter.

Then said the treasurer to him, "If this is the case, why did you not tell me? My friend's daughter is my own daughter." So he sent for her and asked her, "Dear girl, are you the daughter of the treasurer?" "Yes, sir, I am." "Well then, do not worry; you are my own daughter." Then he kissed her on the head, gave her five hundred women for her retinue, and adopted her as his own oldest daughter.

One day a festival was proclaimed in this city. Now at this festival daughters of respectable families, who do not ordinarily go out, go on foot with their own retinue [191] and bathe in the river. Accordingly on that day Sāmāvatī also, accompanied by her five hundred women, went right through the palace court to bathe in the river. King Udena stood at his window and saw her. "Whose are those nautch-girls?" he inquired. "Nobody's nautch-girls, your majesty." "Then whose daughters are they?" "Your majesty, that is the daughter of the treasurer Bhaddavatiya, and her name is Sāmāvatī." Now the king fell in love with the girl the moment he saw her, and immediately sent word to the treasurer Ghosaka, "Send me the maiden they say is your daughter." "I will not send her, your majesty." "Do not act thus. Do as I ask and send her." "Your majesty, we householders do not give young girls, for fear people will say they are abused and maltreated." Angered by the treasurer's reply, the king caused the treasurer's house to be sealed and the treasurer and his wife to be seized and turned out of doors.

When Sāmāvatī returned after her bath and found no way of entering the house, she asked, "What does this mean, dear father?" "Dear daughter, the king sent for you; and when we refused to give you to him, he caused the house to be sealed and caused us to be turned out of doors." "Dear father, you made a great mistake. When one who is a king commands, you should not say, 'We do not give.' You should rather say, 'If you will take our daughter with her retinue, we will give her to you.'" "Very well, dear daughter. If that is your desire, I will do as you say." Accordingly Ghosaka sent a message to that effect to the king, and the king accepted his offer, saying, "Very well." Then the king conducted Sāmāvatī with her retinue to the royal palace, conferred the ceremonial sprinkling on her, and elevated her to the dignity of chief consort. The other women became her ladies-in-waiting.

Part 4. Winning of Vāsuladattā by Udena

Yet another of Udena's queen-consorts was Vāsuladattā, [192] daughter of Caṇḍa Pajjota, king of Ujjeni. One day, as Caṇḍa Pajjota was returning from his pleasure-garden, he surveyed his own splendor and asked, "Is there any other soever possessed of splendor like mine?" "Splendor such as it is, King Udena of Kosambi possesses exceeding great splendor." "Very well, let us take him captive." "It is impossible to capture him." "By employing some means or other, let us capture him all the same." "It is impossible, your majesty." "Why?" "He understands the art of charming elephants. By reciting spells and playing his elephant-charming lute, he either drives elephants away or captures them at his pleasure. No one possesses so many riding-elephants as he." "I suppose it is impossible for me to capture him." "If you are bent on doing it, have a wooden elephant made and turned loose near him. Let him hear of a good mount, be it elephant or horse, and he will go a long way for it. When he is close by, you can capture him." "A stratagem indeed!" exclaimed the king.

So the king had a mechanical elephant made of wood, wrapped about with strips of cloth and deftly painted, and turned it loose on the bank of a certain lake near the country of his enemy. Within the belly of the elephant sixty men walked back and forth; every now and then they loaded their shovels with elephant dung and dumped it out. A certain woodman saw the elephant, and thinking to himself, "Just the thing for our king!" went and told the king, "Your majesty, I saw a noble elephant, pure white even as the peak of Kelāsa, just the sort of elephant your majesty would like."

Udena mounted his elephant and set out, taking the woodman along as a guide and accompanied by his retinue. His approach was [193] observed by spies, who went and informed Caṇḍa Pajjota. The latter straightway dispatched armies on both flanks of his enemy, allowing the space between them to remain open. Udena, unaware of his enemy's approach, continued to pursue the elephant. He recited his spell and played his lute, but all to no purpose. The wooden elephant, driven with great speed by the men concealed within its belly, made as if it failed to hear the charm and continued its flight. The king, unable to overtake the elephant, mounted his horse. On and on sped the horse, galloping so rapidly that by degrees the army of the king was left far behind and the king was quite alone. Then Caṇḍa Pajjota's men, who were posted on both flanks, captured Udena and turned him over to their king. Udena's army, perceiving that their leader had fallen into the hands of the enemy, built a stockade just outside of Ujjeni and remained there.

Caṇḍa Pajjota, having thus captured Udena alive, clapped him into prison behind closed doors and kept wassail for three days. On the third day Udena asked his keepers, "Friends, where's your king?" "Carousing, for, says he, 'I've landed my enemy.'" "What does your king mean by acting like a woman? He has captured a royal adversary and surely ought either to release him or to kill him. He has brought humiliation upon us and is 'carousing'— indeed!" The keepers went and reported the incident to the king. The king came and asked, "Is it true that you said thus and thus?" "Yes, your majesty." "Very well, I will release you. They say you have such and such a charm; will you give it to me?" "Certainly I will give it to you; but when you receive it, will you pay me homage?" "I pay you homage? I'll not pay you homage." "Then I'll not give it to you." [194] "In that case I will have you executed." "Do so; you are lord of my body, not of my mind."

When the king heard Udena's defiant answer, he thought to himself, "How in the world can I get the charm? I have it. I'll have my daughter learn it from him, and then I'll learn it from her. It would never do to let anyone else learn a charm like this." So he said to Udena, "Will you divulge the charm to another, if the other will pay you homage?" "Yes, your majesty." "Well then, we have in our house a hunchbacked woman. She will sit behind a curtain; you remain outside and have her repeat the charm." "Be she hunchback or cripple, I will teach her the charm, provided she will pay me homage."

Then the king went to his daughter Vāsuladattā and said, "Dear daughter, there is a certain leper who knows a priceless charm. You sit behind a curtain, and he will remain outside and repeat it to you. You get it from him, for it would never do to let anyone else learn it, and then I will get it from you." After this sort, for fear of their making love, did Caṇḍa Pajjota feign that his daughter was a hunchback and Udena a leper. So Vāsuladattā seated herself behind a curtain, and Udena remained outside and caused her to repeat the charm.

One day Udena repeated the words of the charm over and over again to Vāsuladattā, but the latter was unable to reproduce it correctly. Thereupon Udena cried out, "Dunce of a hunchback, your lips are too thick and your cheeks too pudgy! I've a mind to beat your face in! Say it this way!" Vāsuladattā replied in anger, "Villain of a leper, [195] what do you mean by those words? Do you call such as I 'hunchback'?" Udena lifted the fringe of the curtain and asked, "Who are you?" Said the maiden, "I am Vāsuladattā, daughter of the king." "When your father spoke to me, he described you as a hunchback." "When he spoke to me, he made you out a leper." Both said, "He must have said it for fear of our making love." Then and there within the curtain they made love, and from that time on there was no learning charms or getting lessons. The king regularly asked his daughter, "Daughter, are you learning your lessons?" "Yes, father."

Now one day Udena said to Vāsuladattā, "My dear, a husband can do that which neither father nor mother nor brothers nor sisters can do. If you will save my life, I will give you a retinue of five hundred women and make you my chief consort." "If you will carry out your promise without fail, I will save your life." "My dear, I will do so without fail." "Very well, husband." So she went to her father, saluted him, and stood respectfully on one side. Her father asked her, "Daughter, is your task completed?" "Not quite completed, father." "What do you require, daughter?" "We must have at our disposal a door and a mount, father." "Why this request?" "Father, this is what my teacher says: 'In order to work the charm, a certain medicinal herb is necessary, and this must be obtained at night at a time indicated by the stars.' [196] Therefore whenever we are obliged to go out, whether it be early or late, we must have a door and a mount at our disposal." "Very well," said the king, giving his consent. They secured permission to use a certain door at any time they pleased.

Now the king was possessed of the five conveyances: a female elephant named Bhaddavatī, which could travel fifty leagues a day; a slave named Kāka, who could travel sixty leagues a day; two mares, Celakaṇṭhī and Muñjakesī, which could travel a hundred leagues a day; and an elephant named Nālāgiri, which could travel a hundred and twenty leagues a day.

Story of the Past: Caṇḍa Pajjota wins the five conveyances

It seems that before the appearance in the world of the present Buddha, the king had been the servitor of a certain ruler. Now one day as this ruler was returning from his bath outside of the city, a certain Private Buddha who had entered the city to receive alms came out with his bowl clean as it had been washed, having received not a single morsel of food by reason of the evil influence of Māra over all the residents of the city. Indeed when the Private Buddha reached the gate of the city, Māra approached him in disguise and asked him, "Reverend Sir, did you receive anything?" "But have you made it possible for me to receive anything?" "Well then, turn back and go in again. Now I will make it possible for you to receive alms." "I will not go back again." Had the Private Buddha returned, Māra would once more have taken possession of the bodies of all the residents of the city and would have subjected him to the embarrassment of hand-clapping and rude laughter.

Now when this ruler [197] saw the Private Buddha returning with his bowl clean as it had been washed, he asked him, "Reverend Sir, did you receive anything?" "I have gone my round and am coming out, brother." The ruler thought to himself, "His reverence does not answer the question I asked him, but tells me something I did not ask about. It must be that he failed to receive anything." The ruler looked at his bowl and saw that it was empty. Not knowing whether the food in his house was ready or not, and therefore, brave though he was, not daring to take his bowl, he said, "Wait a moment, Reverend Sir." So saying, he went home quickly and asked, "Is our food ready?" Receiving the answer that it was ready, he said to his servitor, "Friend, there is no one possessed of greater speed than you. Make the greatest possible speed, and when you reach his reverence, say to him, 'Reverend Sir, give me your bowl,' and then take his bowl and return to me."

At the mere word of his master the servitor set out, obtained the bowl, and brought it back. The ruler filled the bowl with his own food and said, "Convey this to his reverence with all speed. I make over to you the merit of this action." The servitor went quickly, gave the bowl to the Private Buddha, saluted him with the Five Rests, and said to him, "Reverend Sir, the time is short. I went and returned with the greatest possible speed. As the fruit of this speed, may I obtain the five conveyances able to travel fifty, sixty, a hundred, and a hundred and twenty leagues a day respectively. As I returned and went, my body was heated by the rays of the sun. As the fruit of this, in the various places where I shall be reborn, may I possess authority equal to the power of the rays of the sun. My master has made over to me the merit of this alms. In consequence of this [198] may I be a partaker of the Truth you have seen." The Private Buddha said, "So be it," and returned thanks in the following Stanzas,

> May all you've wished and prayed for come out well;
> May all your aspirations be fulfilled, even as the moon at the full.
> May all you've wished and prayed for come out well;
> May all your aspirations be fulfilled, as by the jewel Dew of Light.

This was the king's deed in a previous state of existence. He was now Caṇḍa Pajjota, and in consequence of this deed he came to possess these five conveyances. **End of Story of the Past.**

Now one day the king went out to amuse himself in the garden. "Now's the time to flee," thought Udena. So he filled several big leather sacks with gold and silver coins, placed the sacks on the back of the female elephant, assisted Vāsuladattā to mount, and away they went. The harem guards saw what was happening and went and told the king. The king sent out a force in pursuit. "Go quickly," said he. When Udena perceived that a force had set out in pursuit, he opened a sack of gold and scattered the coins along the way. His pursuers stopped to pick up the coins and then hurried along. Then he opened a sack of silver and scattered the coins along the way. While his pursuers delayed because of their greed for silver, [199] Udena reached his own stockade built without the city. When his men saw him coming, they surrounded him and escorted him back to Kosambi. When he arrived there, he sprinkled Vāsuladattā and raised her to the rank of chief consort.

Part 5. Rejection of Māgandiyā by the Buddha

Still another maiden who gained the dignity of chief consort of the king was Māgandiyā. She, we are told, was the daughter of the Brahman Māgandiya, who lived in the Kuru country, her mother also bore the name Māgandiyā, and her father's younger brother likewise bore the name Māgandiya. She was as beautiful as a celestial nymph. Now her father was unable to find a husband who was worthy of her; and although scions of all the great families in the country asked for her hand, her father sent them all away, reviling them and saying, "You are not worthy of my daughter."

Now one day, as the Teacher surveyed the world at early dawn, he perceived that the Brahman Māgandiya and his wife possessed the dispositions requisite for the attainment of the Fruit of the Third

Path. Therefore, taking his own bowl and robe, he went to a place just outside of a certain market-town, where the Brahman was tending the sacred fire. The Brahman surveyed the person of the Tathāgata, beholding in him the perfection of physical beauty, and thought to himself, "There is no other man in the whole world comparable to this man. I will give my daughter to this man to cherish and support." Accordingly he said to the Teacher, "Monk, I have a single daughter, and all this time I have not seen a man worthy of her. But you are suitable for her, and she is suitable for you. For you [200] ought to have a wife, and she ought to have a husband. I will give her to you. Wait right here until I come back." The Teacher said not a word, but remained silent.

The Brahman went home quickly and said to his wife, "Wife! wife! I saw a man who is worthy of our daughter. Hurry! hurry! Dress her in her beautiful garments." So the Brahman had his daughter dressed in her beautiful garments, and taking daughter and wife with him, went to the Teacher. The whole city was agitated. "All this time," said the people, "this man has said of every suitor, 'He is not suitable for my daughter,' and has refused to give her to anyone. But it is reported that he has said, 'To-day I saw a man who is suitable for my daughter.' What manner of man can he be? Let us go see him." So a great throng of people went out of the city with him.

Now when the Brahman set out with his daughter, the Teacher, instead of remaining in the place mentioned by the Brahman, moved away from that place and took his stand in another place, leaving a footprint. (When the Buddhas establish a footprint, it appears only in a trodden place and not elsewhere, and only those for whom it is established can see it. Let elephants or other wild animals tread upon a footprint of the Buddhas to render it invisible, or let a violent storm pour forth rain upon it, or let the roaring winds beat upon it, yet not one of them can obliterate it.)

Now the Brahman's wife said to the Brahman, "Where is this man?" The Brahman replied, "I said to him, 'Remain in this place.' Where can he possibly have gone?" He looked all about, and seeing his footprint, said, "Here is his [201] footprint." Now the Brahman's wife was familiar with the three Vedas, including the verses relating to signs. So she repeated the verses relating to signs, considering carefully the signs borne by the footprint before her. Finally she said, "Brahman, this is no footprint of one who follows the Five Lusts." So saying, she pronounced the following Stanza,

The footprint of a lustful man will be squatty;
That of a wicked man, violently pressed down;
Of one infatuate, the footprint will be shuffling;
This is the sort of footprint made by one who has rolled back the Veil of Passion.

Then said the Brahman to her, "Wife, you are always seeing crocodiles in the water-vessel and thieves hiding in the house. Be still." "Brahman, you may say what you like, but this is no footprint of one who follows the Five Lusts."

Just then the Brahman looked around and saw the Teacher. "There is the man!" said he. Thereupon the Brahman went to him and said, "Monk, I give you my daughter to cherish and support." The Teacher, instead of saying, "I have need of your daughter," or "I have no need of your daughter," said to him, "Brahman, I have something to say to you." "Say it, monk," replied the Brahman. Thereupon the Teacher told him how Māra had pursued him from the time of the Great Retirement to the time of the Session under the Goatherd's Banyan-tree, and how, when Māra seated himself under the Goatherd's Banyan-tree, overcome with sorrow at the thought, "Now this man has escaped from my power," Māra's daughters came to assuage their father's sorrow and endeavored to seduce him by appearing before him in the forms of women both young and old. [202] "At that time," said the Teacher,

Having seen Craving, Pining, and Lust,
I had no desire for the pleasures of love.
What is this body, filled with urine and dung?
I should not be willing to touch it, even with my foot.

At the conclusion of the Stanza the Brahman and his wife were established in the Fruit of the Third Path.

As for Māgandiyā, she said to herself, "If this man has no need of me, it is perfectly proper for him to say so, but he declares me to be full of urine and dung. Very well! By virtue of the fact that I possess birth, lineage, social position, wealth, and the charm of youth, I shall obtain a husband who is my equal, and then I shall know what ought to be done to the monk Gotama." And then and there she conceived hatred towards the Teacher.

(Did the Teacher know, or did he not know, that she had conceived hatred towards him? He knew. If he knew, why did he pronounce the Stanza? For the sake of the other two. For the Buddhas take no account of hatred directed against them, but preach the Law solely for the sake of those who are worthy to attain the Paths and the Fruits.)

Her mother and father took her and committed her to the charge of her uncle Culla Māgandiya, and then retired from the world and attained Arahatship. Culla Māgandiya thought to himself, [203] "My daughter is not suited to be the wife of a low person, but is suited to be the consort of a king." Accordingly he adorned her with all the adornments, took her with him to Kosambi, and presented her to King Udena, saying, "This jewel of a woman is worthy to become a consort of your majesty." When the king saw her, he fell deeply in love with her, conferred the ceremonial sprinkling upon her, provided her with a retinue of five hundred ladies-in-waiting, and raised her to the dignity of chief consort.

Thus the king had three chief consorts with a retinue of fifteen hundred nautch-girls.

Part 6. Death of Sāmāvatī and of Māgandiyā, and the explanation thereof

Treasurers, monks, and tree-spirit

Now at this time there were living in Kosambi three treasurers, Ghosaka, Kukkuṭa, and Pāvāriya. As the beginning of the rainy season drew near, these men saw five hundred ascetics who had returned from the Himālaya country going the round of the city for alms. With joyful hearts they provided them with seats, offered them food, and obtaining from them a promise to reside with them, they provided them with lodging in their own homes during the four months of the rains. Then, having obtained from them a promise to return and spend the following rainy season with them, they let them go. From that time forth, after the ascetics had resided for eight months in the Himālaya country, they kept residence during the four months of the rains with the three treasurers.

On a later occasion, as the ascetics were on their way back from the Himālaya country, they saw a certain great banyan-tree in a forest retreat and went and sat down at the foot of it. The oldest ascetic thought to himself, "The deity who resides in this tree cannot be mundane. There must be a deva-king of great power here. [204] How good it would be if he would give this band of ascetics water to drink!" Immediately the tree-spirit gave them water to drink. Then the ascetic thought of water to bathe in, and the spirit gave that also. Then he thought of food, and the spirit gave that also.

Then this thought occurred to the ascetic, "This deva-king gives us every single thing we think of. I wish we might see him." Immediately the spirit burst the trunk of the tree and showed himself. Thereupon they asked him, "Deva-king, you possess great power. What did you do to get it?" "Do not ask me, Reverend Sirs." "Deva-king, please tell us." But the spirit was exceedingly modest, for the reason that the work of merit he had performed was a very small one, and therefore he did not wish to tell. However, after a good deal of urging, he said, "Well then, listen," and told the following

Story of the Past: Tree-spirit's former deed

The tree-spirit, it appears, was once a poor man who sought and obtained work for hire from Anāthapiṇḍika and through him made a living. Now one fast-day Anāthapiṇḍika asked on his return from the monastery, "Has anyone told this laborer that to-day is fast-day?" "He has not been told, master." "Well then, cook him his supper." So they cooked him a measure of rice. Now the laborer had worked all day in the forest, and when he returned in the evening, he said, "I am hungry." But when the rice had been prepared and given to him, all of a sudden he refused to eat. "On other days," he thought to himself, "there is a great uproar in this house, 'Give me rice, give me sauce, give me curry;' but to-day all have lain down without making a sound, and they have prepared food for me alone. What can this mean?"

So he asked them, "Have the rest eaten?" "They have not eaten." "Why?" "In this house people eat no supper on fast-days; [205] all keep the fast. The great treasurer requires all to fast, even infants at the breast, first causing them to rinse their mouths and to eat the four sweet foods. A lamp of scented oil is lighted, and all, both young and old, retire to recite the Thirty-two Constituents of the Body. But we did not think it worth while to tell you it was fast-day, and therefore rice was cooked for you alone. Eat it." "If it is proper for me to begin the fast now, I should like to do so." "This is a matter for the treasurer to decide." "Well then, ask him." They went and asked the treasurer, and he replied as follows, "If he begins the fast now and rinses his mouth and takes upon himself the fast-day precepts, he will earn half the merit of keeping fast-day." When the laborer heard the answer, he began the fast.

Now the laborer had worked all day long and was hungry, and the result was that the humors of his body became disordered. He bound a girth about his body, and holding the end of the girth in his hand, he rolled over and over. When the treasurer learned of this, he took the four sweet foods and with torches borne before him went to the laborer and asked, "Friend, what is the matter?" "Master, the humors of my body are out of order." "Well then, get up and eat this medicinal food." "You eat it, master." "I am not sick. You eat it." "Master, as for keeping the fast, [206] I was not able to keep it all, but let me not be deprived of half." With these words the laborer refused to eat. "Do not act thus, friend," said the treasurer. But the laborer steadfastly refused to eat, and when the sun rose, he died even as a garland of flowers withers, and was reborn in that banyan-tree.

Treasurers, monks, and tree-spirit, concluded

Therefore the tree-spirit explained the matter as follows, "The treasurer was devoted to the Buddha, devoted to the Law, devoted to the Order; and it was through him, and in consequence of the merit I earned by keeping half of fast-day, that I obtained this power." When the five hundred ascetics heard the name "Buddha," they arose and stretched out their hands in an attitude of reverent supplication to the spirit and said, "Say 'Buddha.'" Three times they caused the spirit to confess his faith by repeating the formula, "I say 'Buddha.'" Then they breathed forth the solemn utterance, "This is an utterance difficult to obtain in this world," and said in conclusion, "Spirit, you have permitted us to hear a sound we have not heard for many hundred thousand cycles of time."

Then the pupils addressed their teacher as follows, "Well then, let us go to the Teacher." "Friends, we have three treasurers who are generous benefactors of ours. To-morrow we will receive food in their residence, tell them also what we have heard, and go. Give your consent, friends." Thereupon they gave their consent. On the following day the treasurers caused rice-porridge to be prepared and seats to be provided. And knowing that the ascetics would arrive on that day, they went forth and met them, escorted them to their residence, provided them with seats, and gave them food. When the ascetics had finished their meal, they said, "Great treasurers, we are going away." "Reverend Sirs, [207] did we not obtain from you a promise to reside with us during the four months of the rains? Where are you going now?"

"The Buddha has appeared in the world, the Law has appeared, the Order has appeared. We are therefore going to see the Teacher."

"But is it proper for you only to go to the Teacher?" "It is not forbidden to others also, friends." "Well then, Reverend Sirs, you wait, and we also will go as soon as we have made preparations." "If you wait to make preparations, we shall be delayed. Therefore we will go on ahead, and you may follow after." So they went on ahead, and seeing the Supremely Enlightened One, praised him, paid obeisance to him, and sat down respectfully on one side. Then the Teacher preached the Law to them in orderly sequence, and at the conclusion of his discourse all of them attained Arahatship, together with the Supernatural Faculties. Thereupon they asked to be received into the Order. "Come, monks!" said the Teacher. As soon as he spoke the word, they became full-fledged monks, possessed of bowls and robes created by magic.

Those three treasurers procured the requisites for alms, consisting of garments, coverlets, ghee, honey, molasses, and so forth, and conveying five hundred cartloads apiece, proceeded to Sāvatthi. On reaching Sāvatthi, they paid obeisance to the Teacher, listened to a discourse on the Law, and at the conclusion of the discourse were established in the Fruit of Conversion. For a fortnight they resided with the Teacher, bestowing alms, and then invited the Teacher to come to Kosambi. As the Teacher gave his promise, [208] he said, "The Tathāgatas delight in solitude." Said the treasurers, "Reverend Sir, as soon as we notify you by sending you a message, it will be proper for you to come." With these words they returned to Kosambi. The treasurer Ghosaka erected Ghosita monastery, the treasurer Kukkuṭa erected Kukkuṭa monastery, and the treasurer Pāvāriya erected Pāvāriya monastery.

When the treasurers had erected these three monasteries, they sent word to the Teacher to come and visit them. The Teacher, receiving their message, went there; whereupon they came forth to meet him, escorted him to the monasteries, and waited upon him by turns. The Teacher resided one day in each monastery and always went to receive alms at the door of the house of the particular treasurer in whose monastery he resided. Now these three treasurers had a servitor named Sumana, and he was a gardener. He said to the treasurers, "I have been a servitor of yours for a long time, and I should like to entertain the Teacher. Let me have the Teacher all to myself for just one day." "Well then," said they, "entertain him to-morrow." "Very well, masters," he replied, invited the Teacher, and made ready the usual honors.

Conversion of Sāmāvatī by Khujjuttarā

Now at that time King Udena was in the habit of giving Queen Sāmāvatī eight pieces of money every day to buy flowers with. A female slave of the queen named Khujjuttarā went regularly every day to the gardener Sumana and procured the flowers. When she came on that particular day, the gardener said to her, "I have invited the Teacher to be my guest and shall use my flowers to-day to honor the Teacher. You just wait, join with me in attendance on the Buddha, and listen to the Law. Then you may take with you the flowers that remain." [209] "Very well," said she, consenting to remain. Sumana waited upon the Congregation of Monks presided over by the Buddha and took his bowl that he might pronounce the words of thanksgiving. The Teacher began to pronounce the words of thanksgiving. Khujjuttarā listened to the discourse on the Law and became established in the Fruit of Conversion.

On previous days she had been in the habit of appropriating to her own use four pieces of money and of buying flowers with the other four; but on that day, spending all eight to buy flowers with, she returned with them. Sāmāvatī said to her, "My good woman, did the king give us twice as much money to-day to buy flowers with?" "No, my lady." "Then why so many flowers?" "On previous days I kept four pieces of money for myself and brought you only so many flowers as I could buy for four pieces of money." "Why didn't you take the money to-day?" "Because I heard the Supremely Enlightened discourse on the Law and acquired understanding of the Law."

The queen did not revile her and say, "You wretched slave, give me back the pieces of money you have stolen during all this time." Instead she said to her, "My good woman, you have drunk the Deathless. Give me thereof to drink also." "Well then," replied Khujjuttarā, "order that a bath be prepared for me." So the queen had her bathed with sixteen bowls of scented water and presented her with garments of fine cloth. One of these garments she caused her to put on as an undergarment, the other she caused to be thrown over her shoulder; then she had a seat prepared for her. Khujjuttarā thereupon sat down, took in her hand a painted fan, and addressing the five hundred women, preached the Law to them just as the Teacher had preached it. Then all of them paid obeisance to Khujjuttarā [210] and said, "Friend, from this day forth do no sinful deed, but be to us as a mother and a teacher. Go to the Teacher and listen to every discourse he preaches, and then come back and repeat it to us." And this she did so faithfully that later on she came to know the Tipiṭaka by heart. Indeed the Teacher assigned her preëminence, saying, "Preëminent among my female lay disciples who are learned in the Scriptures and able to expound the Law is Khujjuttarā."

Now those five hundred women said to her, "Woman, we should like to see the Teacher. Show him to us, that we may honor him with perfumes, garlands, and so forth." "My lady, it is a serious matter to live in a king's house. You have obtained access to it, but it is impossible for you to leave it." "Woman, do not destroy us. Let us see the Teacher." "Well then, make holes in the walls of your rooms large enough to look through. Then bring perfumes and garlands, and when the Teacher goes to the door of the house of the three treasurers, stand in your several places and look out and stretch forth your hands and pay obeisance to him and honor him." They followed her directions, and when the Teacher went and returned, they looked out and paid obeisance to him and honored him.

Māgandiyā's plot against Sāmāvatī and the Buddha

Now one day Māgandiyā came forth from her own mansion and walked along until she came to the place where those women lived. Seeing a hole in a room, she asked, "What is this?" The women, not knowing of the hatred she had conceived towards the Teacher, said, [211] "The Teacher has come to this city, and we stand here and look at the Teacher and honor him." "So the hermit Gotama has come to this city!" thought Māgandiyā. "Now I shall know what ought to be done to him. These women also are his supporters. I shall know what ought to be done to them also." So she said to the king, "Great king, Sāmāvatī and her followers are disloyal to you and in but a few days will take your life." The king replied, "They will do nothing of the sort," and refused to believe the charge. Even when the charge was repeated, he still refused to believe. When she made the charge the third time and he still refused to believe, she said to him, "If you do not believe me, great king, go to the place where they reside and judge for yourself." The king went there, and seeing the holes in the walls of the rooms, asked, "What does this mean?" When the matter was explained to him, he did not get angry, said not a word, but had the holes filled up and windows made with openings above in all the rooms. (Windows with openings above came in at this time, we are told.)

Unable to injure the women, Māgandiyā thought to herself, "At any rate I will do to the monk Gotama what ought to be done." So she bribed the citizens and said to them, "When the monk Gotama comes into the city and walks about, instigate slaves to revile him and abuse him and drive him out of the city." So heretics who did not believe in the Three Jewels followed the Teacher about when he entered the city and shouted at him, "You are a thief, [212] a simpleton, a fool, a camel, an ox, an ass, a denizen of hell, a beast, you have no hope of salvation, a state of punishment is all that you can look forward to." Thus they reviled and abused him with the Ten Terms of Abuse.

Venerable Ānanda heard this and said to the Teacher, "Reverend Sir, these citizens are reviling and abusing us. Let us go elsewhere." "Where shall we go, Ānanda?" "To some other city, Reverend Sir." "If men revile us there, where shall we go then, Ānanda?" "To yet another city, Reverend Sir." "If men revile us there, where shall we go then?" "To still another city, Reverend Sir." "Ānanda, one should not speak thus. Where a difficulty arises, right there should it be settled. Only under those circumstances is it permissible to go elsewhere. But who are reviling you, Ānanda?" "Reverend Sir, everyone is reviling us, slaves and all." "Ānanda, I am like an elephant that has entered the fray. Even as it is the duty of an elephant that has entered the fray to withstand the arrows which come from the four quarters, precisely so it is my duty to endure with patience the words spoken by many wicked men." So saying, he preached the Law with reference to himself by pronouncing the following three Stanzas in the Nāga Vagga,

320. Even as an elephant engaged in the fray withstands arrows shot from the bow,
So also must I bear abuse, for the multitude is wicked. [213]

321. It is a tamed elephant they lead to battle; it is a tamed elephant the king mounts;
It is the tamed that is best among men, he that endures abuse patiently.

322. Of surpassing excellence are mules which are tamed, and well-bred Sindh horses,
And great elephants of the jungle; but better yet is the man who has tamed
himself.

This discourse benefited the assembled multitude. When the Teacher had thus preached the Law, he said, "Ānanda, be not disturbed. These men will revile you for only seven days, and on the eighth day they will become silent. A difficulty encountered by the Buddhas lasts no longer than seven days."

When Māgandiyā had failed in her attempt to drive the Teacher out of the city by abusing him, she thought to herself, "Pray what can I do now?" Then the thought occurred to her, "These women are his supporters. I will destroy them." Accordingly one day, while King Udena was drinking strong drink and she was waiting upon him, she sent the following message to her uncle, "Let my uncle come with eight dead cocks and eight live cocks. Having arrived, let him stand at the top of the stairs and announce his arrival. When he hears the word 'Enter,' let him not enter, but send in first the eight live cocks and afterwards the others." And she gave a bribe to the page, saying, "Be sure to carry out my orders."

Māgandiya came and announced himself to the king. When, however, he heard the word "Enter," he said, "I will not enter the king's drinking-place." [214] Māgandiyā then sent her page, saying, "Boy, go to my uncle." He went, took the eight live cocks which Māgandiya gave him, carried them to the king, and said, "Your majesty, the house-priest has sent you a present." "A most excellent and dainty morsel!" said the king. "Now who will cook them?" Māgandiyā said, "Great king, the five hundred women led by Sāmāvatī have nothing to do. Send the cocks to them. Let them cook them and carry them to you." Accordingly the king sent them, saying to the page, "Go give these cocks to these women. Tell them not to intrust them to the hands of anyone else, but to kill them and cook them themselves." "Very well, your majesty," replied the page, and went and delivered the message. But the women refused to do the king's bidding, saying, "We do not take the life of any living creature." The page returned and so informed the king.

Māgandiyā said, "You see, great king? Now you shall find out whether or not they really take the life of living creatures. Your majesty, send word to them, 'Cook them and send them to the monk Gotama.'" So the king sent this message to them. But the page, while pretending to carry the live cocks to the women, in reality went and gave those cocks to the house-priest and carried the eight dead cocks to the women, saying, "Cook these cocks and send them to the Teacher." "This, to be sure, is our duty," said the women in reply, and going to meet him, they received the cocks. When the page returned to the king and the latter asked him, "What was the result, boy?" he gave the king the following report, "The moment I said to them, 'Cook these cocks and send them to the hermit Gotama,' they came to meet me and accepted them." "See, great king," said Māgandiyā, "they will not do it for the like of you. But you would not believe me when I said to you, 'Their inclination is towards another.'" But even when the king heard this, [215] he tolerated their conduct and remained silent. Māgandiyā thought to herself, "What shall I do now?"

Now at this time the king was accustomed to divide his time equally among his three consorts, Sāmāvatī, Vāsuladattā, and Māgandiyā, spending seven days by turns in the apartment of each. Māgandiyā, knowing that he would go on the morrow or on the day after to the apartment of Sāmāvatī, sent word to her uncle, "Send me a snake, first washing its fangs with a poisonous drug." He did as she told him to and sent her a snake. Now wherever the king went, he was accustomed to take with him his lute for charming elephants, and in the shell of this lute was a hole. Māgandiyā inserted the snake in the hole and stopped the hole with a bunch of flowers; for two or three days the snake remained within the lute.

On the day when the king was to go to Sāmāvatī's apartment, Māgandiyā asked him, "To whose apartment will you go to-day, your majesty?" "To Sāmāvatī's apartment." Said Māgandiyā, "Your majesty, to-day I had a bad dream; you must not go there." "I am going all the same." Three times she tried to dissuade him from going and failed. Finally she said, "In that case I will go too." In spite of the king's protests she went with him, saying, "Your majesty, I do not know what will happen to you."

The king, wearing garments, flowers, perfumes, and ornaments given him by Sāmāvatī and her followers, ate heartily, and then placed his lute by his pillow and lay down on the bed. Māgandiyā, pretending to be merely walking back and forth, removed the bunch of flowers from the opening in the lute; whereupon the snake, which had been without food for two or three days, glided from the opening, hissed, raised his hood, and coiled himself up on the top of the bed. [216] When Māgandiyā saw the snake, she screamed with a loud voice, "Oh, your majesty, there is a snake!" And she straightway abused the king, saying, "This stupid, unlucky king will not listen to anything I say to him. As for these shameless scoundrels, what do they not receive from the king? You will live happily just as soon as the king is dead, but so long as he lives, you will have a hard time. Your majesty, when I cried out to you, 'To-day I had a bad dream; you must not go to Sāmāvatī's apartment,' you would not listen to what I said."

When the king saw the snake, he was terrified with the fear of death, the fire of anger was kindled within him, and he said, "So this is the sort of thing they are capable of doing! What criminals they are! Yet I would not believe Māgandiyā when she told me of their evil nature. First they made holes in the walls of their own rooms and sat there; again, when I sent the cocks to them, they sent them back; to-day they have let a snake loose in my bed."

Sāmāvatī delivered the following admonition to her five hundred women, "Friends, we have no other refuge. Cherish precisely the same feelings towards the king and the queen as you do towards yourselves. Be not angry with anyone." The king took his horn-bow, which required a thousand men to string, twanged the bowstring, fitted a poisoned arrow to the string, and placing Sāmāvātī in front [217] and all the other women in single file behind her, shot an arrow at Sāmāvatī's breast. But through the supernatural power of her love the arrow turned back, and returning by the same path it had come, penetrated, as it were, the king's heart.

The king thought to himself, "The arrow I shot is capable of piercing even a rock, and there was nothing in the air to make it turn back. But it turned and came back by the same path it went. Indeed this senseless, lifeless arrow knows her goodness, but I, who am a human being, know it not." And throwing the bow away and stretching forth his hands in an attitude of reverent supplication, he knelt before Sāmāvatī's feet and pronounced the following Stanza,

> I am utterly confused and bewildered; all four quarters are confused in my mind.
> Protect me, Sāmāvatī, and be a refuge to me.

Sāmāvatī, hearing his words, instead of saying, "Very well, your majesty, seek refuge in me," said, "Great king, in whom I have sought refuge, in him do you also seek refuge."

Having thus spoken, Sāmāvatī, disciple of the Supremely Enlightened, said,

> Do not seek refuge in me! He in whom I have sought refuge,—
> He is the Buddha, great king, he is the Buddha Incomparable!
>
> Seek refuge in that Buddha, and do you be a refuge to me. [218]

The king said, "Now I am the more afraid," and pronounced the following Stanza,

> Now I am the more confused; all four quarters are confused in my mind.
> Protect me, Sāmāvatī, and be a refuge to me.

But she refused him precisely as before. Finally he said, "Well then, I seek refuge in you and in the Teacher, and I grant you a boon." "I accept the boon, great king," she replied.

The king approached the Teacher, sought refuge in him, invited him to accept his hospitality, and for seven days gave generous alms. Then, addressing Sāmāvatī, he said, "Rise and take your choice." Sāmāvatī replied, "Great king, I have no need of gold and silver, but grant me this boon. Arrange matters so that the Teacher may come here regularly with his five hundred monks, so that I may hear the Law." So the king paid obeisance to the Teacher and said, "Reverend Sir, come here regularly with your five hundred monks. Sāmāvatī and her attendants say they wish to hear the Law." The Teacher replied, "Great king, the Buddhas may not always go to one place; many desire their presence." "Well then, direct one monk to come." The Teacher directed Ānanda to go. So Ānanda went every day to the royal palace with five hundred monks, and those women every day provided the Elder with food and listened to the Law.

One day, after they had listened to the Elder's discourse on the Law, their hearts were filled with joy, and they rendered honor to the Elder by presenting him with five hundred yellow robes such as are worn over the shoulders, [219] each worth five hundred pieces of money. When the king saw that they had not a single garment left, he asked them, "Where are your yellow robes?" "We gave them to the Reverend Elder." "Did he take them all?" "Yes, he took them all." The king approached the Elder, paid obeisance to him, questioned him about the gift of the robes by the women, and learning that the women had given the robes and that the Elder had received them, asked, "Reverend Sir, there were a great many robes, were there not? What will you do with so many?" "I shall keep as many as we require for ourselves and send the rest to those whose robes are worn out, great king." "What will they do with their own worn-out robes?" "They will give them to those whose robes are in a still worse state of repair." "What will they do with their own worn-out robes?" "They will make bedspreads of them." "What will they do with the old bedspreads?" "They will make carpets of them." "What will they do with the old carpets?" "They will make foot-towels of them." "What will they do with the old foot-towels?" "They will cut them into small pieces, mix them with mortar, and use them to plaster walls with."

"Reverend Sir, although all these are given to your reverences, nothing is lost." "Quite so, great king." The king was so pleased that he caused five hundred more robes to be brought and placed at the Elder's feet.

(We are told that robes worth five hundred pieces of money [220] were presented to the Elder and laid at his feet in lots of a thousand, and that he received this number a hundred thousand times; that robes worth a thousand pieces of money were presented to the Elder and laid at his feet in lots of a thousand, and that he received this number a thousand times; that robes worth a hundred thousand pieces of money were presented to the Elder and laid at his feet in lots of a thousand, and that he received this number a hundred times. It is impossible to enumerate the number of robes he received by ones and twos and threes and fours and fives and tens. We are told that, upon the death of the Teacher, the Elder traveled all over the Land of the Rose-apple, presenting to the monks in all of the monasteries bowls and robes of his own.)

Burning of Sāmāvatī and punishment of Māgandiyā

Māgandiyā thought to herself, "Whatever I do turns out otherwise than I expect. What shall I do now?" Finally she decided on a plan. On her way to the garden to amuse herself, she sent the following message to her uncle, "Go to Sāmāvatī's palace, open the linen-closets and the oil-closets, soak pieces of cloth in the jars of oil, and wrap these cloths about the pillars. Then assemble all the women within the house, close the door, bar it from without, set fire to the house with torches, and then descend and go your way."

Māgandiya went up into the palace, [221] opened the closets, soaked garments in the oil-jars, and was just beginning to wrap them about the pillars when the women led by Sāmāvatī came up to him and said, "Why are you doing this, uncle?" "My ladies, the king desires these pillars to be strengthened, and has therefore given orders that they be wrapped in cloths soaked in oil. It is hard to understand why certain things should be done in a king's house and certain other things should not be done. I beg of you, my ladies, not to remain here with me." As soon as they had departed and entered their rooms at his suggestion, he closed the doors, barred them from without, set fire to first one cloth and then another, and descended.

Sāmāvatī delivered the following admonition to her followers, "It would not be an easy matter, even with the knowledge of a Buddha, to determine exactly the number of times our bodies have thus been burned with fire as we have passed from birth to rebirth in the round of existences which has no conceivable beginning. Therefore be heedful." As the fire consumed the house, the women applied themselves to meditation on the element of pain, with the result that some of them attained the Fruit of the Second Path, while others attained the Fruit of the Third Path. Therefore it is said [Udāna, vii. 10],

Now a large number of monks, returning from their alms-pilgrimage after breakfast, drew near to where the Exalted One was, and having drawn near, paid obeisance to the Exalted One and sat down reverently on one side. And as they sat there on one side, those monks said this to the Exalted One, "Here, Reverend Sir, while King Udena was in his pleasure-garden, the quarters of his women were consumed with fire, and five hundred women led by Sāmāvatī lost their lives. Reverend Sir, what will be the end, what will be the future state of these female lay disciples?"

"Monks, some of these female lay disciples [222] obtained the Fruit of Conversion, others obtained the Fruit of the Second Path, others obtained the Fruit of the Third Path. Monks, none of those female lay disciples failed to receive the fruit of their past deeds." And the Exalted One, clearly understanding the matter, breathed forth at that time the following Solemn Utterance,

Bound with the bond of delusion, the world appears to be good.
The simpleton, fettered by the conditions of being, enshrouded by darkness,
Thinks it eternal. But to him who really sees, there is naught.

So saying, he preached the Law, saying, "Monks, as living beings pass through the round of existences, they are not always heedful, and sometimes they commit sin. Therefore as they pass through the round of existences, they experience both pleasure and pain."

When the king heard the cry, "Sāmāvatī's house is on fire!" he went there quickly, but the house was burned before he could reach it. Having extinguished the flames, he sat down surrounded by his retinue of courtiers, overwhelmed with profound grief, and recalled to his mind the virtues of Sāmāvatī. "Who could have done this deed?" thought he. Coming to the conclusion that Māgandiyā was the author of the crime, he thought to himself, "If I frighten her by my questions, she will not tell me. Therefore I will employ craft and question her gently." [223]

Accordingly he said to his ministers, "Well, until this moment, no matter what I was engaged in or occupied with, I was apprehensive and suspicious; Sāmāvatī was ever seeking occasion to slay me. But now my mind will rest in peace, and I shall be able to lie down to sleep in security." "Who was it that did this deed, your majesty?" "Someone who really loved me must have done it." Now Māgandiyā happened to be standing near, and when she heard the king say this, she said, "None other than I could have done this. I alone did it. I sent word to my uncle and ordered him to do it." "Except you, there is not a living being who really loves me. I am delighted. I grant you a boon. Send for all of your relatives."

So Māgandiyā sent the following message to her relatives, "The king is pleased with me and has granted me a boon. Come immediately." The king rendered high honor to all those who came, insomuch that even persons who were in no way related to Māgandiyā, hearing about it, gave bribes and came and said, "We are relatives of Māgandiyā." When the king had them all in his hands, he caused pits to be dug waist-deep in the palace-court, set them therein, filled up the pits with earth, spread straw on top, and set the straw on fire. When the skin had been burned to a crisp, he caused the bodies to be plowed with an iron plow [224] and to be broken up into pieces and fragments. As for Māgandiyā, he had pieces of solid flesh ripped from various parts of her body with a sharp knife, and setting a vessel of oil on the brazier, he had them fried like cakes and made her eat them.

In the Hall of Truth the monks began to discuss matters, saying, "It is not right that a female lay disciple endowed with such faith should suffer such a death." The Teacher came in and asked them, "Monks, what is it you are sitting here now talking about?" When they told him, he said, "Monks, if you regard this existence alone, it is indeed highly improper and unjust that the five hundred women led by Sāmāvatī should suffer such a death. What they received, however, was in every way proper, considering the sin they committed in a previous existence." "Reverend Sir, what was the sin they committed in a previous existence? Pray tell us." Responding to their request, the Teacher related the following

Story of the Past: Sāmāvatī's attempt to burn a Private Buddha

Once upon a time, when Brahmadatta reigned in Benāres, there were eight Private Buddhas who regularly took their meals in the royal palace, and there were five hundred women who waited upon them. Seven of these Private Buddhas retired to the Himālaya, and the Private Buddha who remained sat down on the bank of the river where there was a tangle of grass, and entered into mystic meditation.

Now one day, after the Private Buddhas had departed, the king took those women [225] and went to sport in the water. When those women, who had sported there in the water all day, came out, they were stung with cold. Desiring to warm themselves, they said to each other, "Seek out some place where we can build a fire." As they walked back and forth, they saw the tangle of grass, and thinking it was no more than a heap of grass, they gathered round it and set it on fire. When the grass burned down and they saw the Private Buddha, they cried out, "We are lost! we are lost! The king's Private Buddha is burning up. If the king finds it out, he will kill everyone of us. Let us burn him well while we are about it." So all those women brought firewood from all directions and piled it on the Private Buddha until they had erected a great pyre. Then they poured oil on it, and saying to themselves, "Now he will burn," they departed.

Now in the beginning their act was a thoughtless one, and they were not bound thereby. But afterwards they committed a deliberate sin and were bound to suffer the consequences thereof. While the Private Buddha was absorbed in mystic meditation, they might have brought a hundred thousand cartloads of firewood and poured oil thereon, and they could not even have caused him to feel the heat. So on the seventh day the Private Buddha arose and went where he pleased. Because they committed this sin, those women were boiled for many hundreds of thousands of years in Hell, and because the fruit of that same evil deed was not yet exhausted, their houses were burned, and they were burned in their houses in a hundred successive states of existence in this very manner. This is the sin they committed in a previous state of existence.

When the Teacher had related this story, the monks asked him, "But, Reverend Sir, how did Khujjuttarā come to be a hunchback? How did she become so wise? How did she obtain the Fruit of Conversion? How [226] did she become an errand-girl?"

Story of the Past: Khujjuttarā's former deeds

Monks, while that same king was ruling in Benāres, there was a Private Buddha who was slightly hunchbacked. Now a certain serving-woman, throwing a blanket over her shoulder and taking a golden vessel in her hand, bent over so that she looked like a hunchback, and saying, "This is the way our Private Buddha walks," imitated his manner of walking. It was in consequence of this that she came to be a hunchback.

But on the first day she provided those Private Buddhas with seats in the royal palace, took their bowls, filled them with rice-porridge, and presented them to them. The Private Buddhas took the bowls of porridge, but they were so hot that they were obliged to shift them from one hand to the other. That woman, seeing what they were doing, presented to them eight ivory bracelets of her own, saying, "Use these bracelets as stands for your bowls." When they had so done, they looked at her, whereupon she said, "Reverend Sirs, we have no use for these bracelets. Accept them as a present from us before you go." The Private Buddhas took them with them to Nandamūla mountain-cave, and those bracelets are preserved there unimpaired to this day. As the result of this act of hers, she now knows the Tipiṭaka by heart and possesses profound wisdom. Likewise it was through waiting upon the Private Buddhas that she obtained the Fruit of Conversion. These were her deeds in the interval between two Buddhas.

In the dispensation of Kassapa, the Supremely Enlightened, a certain treasurer's daughter of Benāres took her mirror one day, as the shades of evening drew on, and sat down to adorn herself. Now a certain intimate friend of hers, [227] a nun freed from the Depravities, came to see her. For nuns freed from the Depravities like to visit the households of their supporters at eventide. But at that moment the treasurer's daughter happened to have no errand-girl with her. So she said to the nun, "I greet you, Reverend Lady. Just take that basket of ornaments and give it to me." The nun thought to herself, "If I do not take this basket and give it to her, she will take a dislike to me and will be reborn in Hell; but if I do give it to her, she will be reborn as the errand-girl of another. However, it is better to be the errand-girl of another than to suffer torment in Hell." So out of pity for her she took the basket and gave it to her. In consequence of this act she became the errand-girl of another. **Stories of the Past concluded.**

Again one day in the Hall of Truth the monks started a discussion. "Sāmāvatī and her five hundred women were burned with fire in their house; as for Māgandiyā and her kinswomen, a fire of straw was built over their bodies, and their bodies were torn asunder with iron plows, and Māgandiyā was boiled in boiling oil. Which of these are alive and which are dead?" The Teacher came in and asked, "Monks, what are you sitting here now talking about?" When they told him, he said to them, "Monks, they that are heedless, though they live a hundred years, yet are they dead. They that are heedful, be they dead or alive, yet are they alive. Māgandiyā, while she yet lived, was dead already. Sāmāvatī and her followers, though they be dead, yet are they alive. For, monks, the heedful never die." So saying, he pronounced the following Stanzas, [228]

21. Heedfulness is the Way to the Deathless; heedlessness is the way to death.
The heedful never die, but they that are heedless are, as it were, dead already.

22. Knowing this clearly, they that are advanced in heedfulness
Delight in heedfulness, and rejoice in the state of the Elect.

23. They that devote themselves to meditation, they that are persevering, they that put forth resolute effort,
They, the wise, attain Nibbāna, the highest bliss.

II. 2. THE VOICE OF A RICH MAN[1]

If a man exert himself. This religious instruction was given by the Teacher while he was in residence at Veḷuvana with reference to Kumbhaghosaka. [231]

For once upon a time the plague broke out at Rājagaha in the house of the principal treasurer of Rājagaha. When the plague breaks out, animals, from flies to cattle, are the first to die; after them, slaves; after them, the master and mistress of a household. So this disease attacked last of all the treasurer and his wife. As soon as they felt the first touch of the disease, they looked at their son, who stood near, and with eyes filled with tears said to him, "Dear son, as we know, when this disease breaks out, only those who break down the wall and flee succeed in saving their lives. Therefore have no consideration for us, but make your escape. Having thus saved your life, come back again, and in such and such a place you will find buried in the

[1] Text: N i. 231–239.

earth forty crores of treasure. Dig up the treasure and live on the money." [232] When the son heard his parents speak thus, he wept aloud, bade farewell to his mother and father, and terrified with the fear of death, broke down the wall and fled. Seeking refuge in a certain mountain jungle, he dwelt there for twelve years, and then returned.

Now since he was a mere boy when he went away, and when he returned his hair and beard had grown long, no one recognized him. A sign which his mother and father had given him enabled him to find the place where the treasure had been buried, and going there he discovered that the treasure had not been disturbed. But he thought to himself, "No one knows me here, and if I dig up this treasure and begin to spend it, they will say, 'A treasure has been dug up by a certain poor man,' and will seize me and subject me to annoyance. Suppose I were to work for hire and thus gain a living." So he dressed himself in rags and went through the servants' quarters, inquiring, "Is there anyone who has need of a servant?"

When the servants saw him, they said, "If you will do a certain piece of work for us, we will pay you for it in rice." "What kind of work is it, friends?" "To order and direct our work. You will be obliged to get up early in the morning and go the rounds of the workers and give orders to them, saying, 'Men, get up and bring out the carts and yoke the oxen; it is time for the elephants and horses to go to pasture. Women, you also get up and cook broth and rice.'" "Very well," said the rich man, accepting the task. So they gave him a house to live in, and he did his work faithfully every day.

Now one day King Bimbisāra, who could recognize anyone by the sound of his voice, heard his voice and straightway said, "That is the voice of some rich man." A certain female servant who stood near [233] thought to herself, "No matter what the king says, this is something I ought to investigate." Therefore she sent out a man, saying to him, "Just go and find out who this is." The messenger straightway went and looked at the man, and on his return made the following report, "That is a poor man who is a servant of servants." When the king heard his report, he said nothing; but on the second day and on the third day, hearing his voice, said precisely the same thing.

Every time the king made this remark the same thought occurred to that female servant, and again and again she sent a man to investigate. Every time she heard the report, "That is a poor man," she thought to herself, "Every time the king hears the report, 'That is a poor man,' he refuses to believe it, and keeps repeating, 'That is the voice of some rich man.' There must be a reason for this, and it is my duty to find out the real facts." Accordingly she said to the king, "Your majesty, give me a thousand pieces of money, and I will take my daughter and go to this man and bring this treasure to the royal palace."

The king caused a thousand pieces of money to be given to her. She took the money, caused her daughter to put on a soiled dress, and departed with her from the royal palace. Pretending that she was making a journey, she went to the servants' quarters, and entering a certain house, said to the mistress, "Woman, we are making a journey and should like to rest here for a day or two before we go on." "Woman, there are many persons living in this house, and it is out of the question for you to remain here. But Kumbhaghosaka's house is empty; go there." So she went there and said to Kumbhaghosaka, "Master, we are making a journey and should like to remain here a day or two." He refused her request, although she repeated it again and again. Finally she said, "Master, we will remain here to-day, just for one day, and early in the morning will continue our journey." So saying, she refused to depart.

So she took up her residence there. On the following day, when it was time for Kumbhaghosaka to go to the forest, she said to him, "Master, give me an allowance for food [234] before you go, and I will cook food for you." "Never mind about that," replied Kumbhaghosaka; "I will cook food all by myself and eat it." After she had urged him repeatedly, he gave her the allowance. As soon as she received it, she procured from a shop cooking-vessels and the purest of rice. Preparing the finest of boiled rice in the manner of cooking practiced in the king's household, and cooking with the greatest care three portions of sauce and curry, she presented the food to Kumbhaghosaka on his return from the forest.

When he had eaten his meal and his senses were dull, she said to him, "Master, we are tired and will remain here for a day or two." "Very well," said he, consenting to the arrangement. Likewise in the evening and on the following day she cooked savory food for him and gave it to him. When she perceived that his senses had become dull, she said to him, "Master, we will remain right here for a few days."

Thus she contrived to establish a residence in his house. One day she took a sharp knife and cut the cords of his mattress underneath at the bed-frame in several places. The result was that, when he returned and lay down on his bed, the mattress sank down. Said he, "How did this bed come to be cut in this fashion?" "Master, I cannot prevent the boys from coming here and jumping on it." "Woman, it is because of you that I have been subjected to this annoyance. Before you came, whenever I wished to go anywhere, I closed the door and went." "My friend, what shall I do? I cannot stop them." On three successive days she cut the mattress of his bed in this way, and when he became irritated and angry and rebuked her, she made the same answer.

Finally she cut all of the cords except one or two. [235] On that day, as soon as he lay down on the bed, the entire mattress fell to the ground, and he was doubled up with his head between his knees. Rising to his feet, he said, "What shall I do? Where shall I go now? I have no longer a bed on which I can lie." "Dear friend, what can I do? I cannot prevent the boys of the neighborhood from entering. Well, do not worry. Let me think where you might go at this time." And addressing her daughter, she said to her, "My dear daughter, make room for your brother to lie down." So her daughter lay down on one side of her bed and said to Kumbhaghosaka, "Master, come lie here." The mother also said to him, "Dear friend, go lie with your sister." Accordingly Kumbhaghosaka lay down on the same bed with the girl and that very night did the deed of kind with her. The young girl burst into tears. Her mother asked her, "Dear daughter, why are you weeping?" "Mother, such and such happened." "Well, what's to be done about it? You ought to have a husband, and he ought to have a wife." So she made Kumbhaghosaka her son-in-law, and thereafter Kumbhaghosaka and her daughter lived together.

After a few days she sent a message to the king, saying, "Cause the following proclamation to be made, 'Let those who dwell in the servants' quarters make holiday. Whoever does not make holiday in his house shall be visited with such and such punishment.'" The king did so. Kumbhaghosaka's mother-in-law said to Kumbhaghosaka, "Dear son, the king commands those who dwell in the servants' quarters to make holiday. What shall we do?" "Mother, I can barely get along on the wages I earn. What shall I do?" "Dear son, those who live in a house of their own can borrow money. [236] The king's command must not be disobeyed, but a debt can be paid off in some way or other. Go somewhere and get one or two pieces of money."

Kumbhaghosaka, much provoked, went to the spot where his forty crores of treasure were buried, removed but a single piece of money, and returned with it. His mother-in-law sent this piece of money to the king and paid the expenses of the holiday with a piece of money of her own. Again after a few days she sent the same message to the king. Again the king gave orders, "Let them make holiday. Those who do not shall be visited with such and such punishment." And again Kumbhaghosaka, under compulsion of his mother-in-law, who repeated the same suggestion she had previously made, went to his hidden store, removed three pieces of money, and brought and gave them to her. She sent these three pieces also to the king. After a few days more had passed, she sent yet another message to the king, saying, "Now let the king send some of his men and summon this man into his presence."

The king's men came and began a search for their man, inquiring, "Which man is Kumbhaghosaka?" When they saw Kumbhaghosaka, they said to him, "Come, sir, the king summons you." Kumbhaghosaka was frightened and was unwilling to go, saying, "The king does not know me," and much else. But the king's men overpowered him, and seizing him by the hands and feet, dragged him off. When his mother-in-law saw what they were doing, she reviled them, saying, "Rascally villains, you are not fit to lay hands on my son-in-law." Turning to Kumbhaghosaka, she said, "Go, my dear son; be not afraid. When I see the king, I will have him cut off the hands of those who seized you by the hands and feet." So saying, she took her daughter, and preceding the king's men, went to the royal palace. When she arrived at the palace, she changed her garments, adorned herself with all her adornments, and thus arrayed took her stand on one side.

The king's men came, pulling and dragging Kumbhaghosaka with them. Kumbhaghosaka paid obeisance to the king and took his stand before him. The king said to him, "You are Kumbhaghosaka?" "Yes, your majesty." "Why do you practice deceit in spending your great wealth?" [237] "Where is my great wealth, your majesty? I make a living by working for hire." "Do not act thus. Why do you deceive us?" "I am not deceiving you, your majesty. I have no wealth." Then the king showed him those pieces of money and asked him, "Whose are these pieces of money?" Kumbhaghosaka recognized the coins. Thought he, "Alas, I am lost! How did these pieces of money get into the hands of the king?" Looking about him, he saw those two women, adorned and bejeweled, standing at the door of the room. Thought he, "This is a deep-laid plot. These women must have been suborned by the king."

Then said the king to him, "Speak, sir. Why do you act thus?" "I have no protector, your majesty." "There does not exist a protector who is my equal." "Your majesty, it would be most agreeable to me if your majesty were my protector." "That am I, sir. How great is your wealth?" "Forty crores, your majesty." "What shall I send to convey your wealth hither?" "Carts, your majesty." So the king had several hundred carts yoked, and sent and had Kumbhaghosaka's wealth brought and heaped up in the palace court. Then he assembled the residents of Rājagaha and asked, "Is there anyone at all in this city that possesses so much wealth as this?" "There is not, your majesty." "What should be bestowed upon him?" "Honor, your majesty." So the king bestowed high honor upon him, appointed him to the post of treasurer, and gave him his daughter in marriage.

The king then took Kumbhaghosaka to the Teacher, paid obeisance to the Teacher, and said to him, "Reverend Sir, behold this man. For wisdom the like of him does not exist. Though he possesses forty crores of treasure, he gives no sign of being unduly elated, nor is he puffed up in his own conceit. As though he were a poor man, [238] he dressed himself in rags and worked for his living in the servants' quarter. In this way I came to know of him. And coming to know of him, I sent for him, made him admit his wealth, caused his wealth to be carried to the palace, appointed him to the post of treasurer, and gave him my daughter in marriage. So wise a man I never saw before."

Hearing this, the Teacher said, "If a man lives thus, great king, his life is a righteous life. But the deeds of thieves and other wicked men oppress them even in this world and afford them no happiness in the next. For if a man, when his wealth is exhausted, works for hire, his life is a righteous life. For such a man, exerting the power of his manhood, always mindful, pure in deeds and words and thoughts, circumspect of conduct through wisdom, exercising self-restraint in deeds and words and thoughts, leading a righteous life, never relaxing mindfulness, such a man goes from strength to strength." So saying, he pronounced the following Stanza,

24. If a man exert himself, if he be ever mindful, if his deeds be pure, if he be circumspect of conduct,
 If he control himself, if he live in accordance with the Law, if he be heedful, his glory ever increases.

II. 3. LITTLE WAYMAN [1]

By rousing himself, by heedfulness. This religious instruction was given by the Teacher while he was in residence at Veḷuvana with reference to Little Wayman the Elder. [239]

3 a. Birth of Little Wayman

We are told that the daughter of a rich merchant of Rājagaha, upon reaching the age of maturity, was provided by her mother and father with quarters on the topmost floor of a seven-storied palace and guarded with excessive care.[2] But in spite of this, maddened with the madness of youth and lusting for a man, [240] she did the deed of kind with her own slave. Frightened to think that others also might find out about her misconduct, she said to him, "It is out of the question for us to live here any longer. If my mother and father discover my misconduct, they will tear me limb from limb. Let us go live elsewhere."

So taking a few necessary things they could carry in the hand, they left the house by the principal door. "It matters little," said they, "where we go, so long as we go and live where others will know nothing about us." So saying, the two set out together. They took up their residence in a certain place and lived together, with the result that the young wife conceived a child in her womb. When her unborn child reached maturity, she took counsel with her husband, saying, "If I give birth to my child in a place far removed from kith and kin, it will bring suffering to both of us. There is but one place for us to go, and that is home to my parents." But her husband, fearing that, if he himself went there, he would be killed, kept postponing the day of their departure, saying, "We will go to-day; we will go to-morrow."

The young wife thought to herself, "This simpleton realizes the

[1] Parallels: *Jātaka* 4: i. 114–120; *Divyāvadāna*, xxxv: 483–515; Rogers, *Buddhaghosha's Parables*, vi, pp. 61–71; *Aṅguttara Commentary* on *Etadagga Vagga, Stories of Mahā Panthaka and Culla Panthaka.* 3 a and 3 b are almost word for word the same as the Introduction to *Jātaka* 4. 3 c is entirely different from the Story of the Past in the *Jātaka*. On *Divyāvadāna*, xxxv, see Introduction, § 12, paragraph 1. See also *Thera-Gāthā Commentary*, ccxxxi and ccxxxvi, and W. A. Clouston, *Popular Tales and Fictions*, ii, 317–321, together with the note on pp. 491–493. Text: N i. 239–255.

[2] Cf. the beginning of Stories viii. 3, viii. 12, and ix. 8.

enormity of his offense, and therefore dares not go. After all, a mother and a father are one's best friends. Let this fellow go or not; at any rate I intend to go." So while her husband was out of the house, she put the household utensils away, and informing her next-door neighbors that she was going home to her parents, she started out on the road. When her husband returned to the house and failed to see her, he inquired of the neighbors where she had gone. Hearing that she had gone home to her parents, he set out after her as fast as he could and overtook her on the road. And right there she gave birth to her child. "What is it, wife?" asked the husband. [241] "Husband, it is a son." "What shall we do now?" "That for which we intended to go home to my parents has happened by the way. Why, therefore, should we go there? Let us return to our own home."

Agreeing that this was the best plan, husband and wife returned to their own home. Since their son had been born by the way, they gave him the name Wayman. In no long time the young wife conceived a second child in her womb. (All is to be related in detail precisely as before.) Since this child also was born by the way, they gave him the name Little Wayman, calling the older son Big Wayman. Taking their two sons, they returned to their own place of residence.

While they were living there, Big Wayman heard other boys speak of their uncles and grandparents. So one day he asked his mother, "Mother, other boys speak of their grandfather and grandmother. Haven't we any relatives?" "Yes, my son. You have no relatives living here, but you have a grandfather, a rich merchant, living in Rājagaha, and we have many other relatives living there too." "Why don't we go there, mother?" The mother evaded telling her son why she did not go there. But the children repeated the question time and again. Finally she said to her husband, [242] "These children weary me excessively. Will my mother and father eat us alive when they see us? Come, why not let the children see the family of their grandparents?" "I should not dare meet them face to face, but I will escort you there." "Very well; some means must be found by which the children can see the family of their grandparents."

So mother and father took the children, and arriving at Rājagaha in due course, took up their residence in the hall of a certain woman near the gate of the city. Then the mother of the children sent word to her mother and father that she and her children had arrived. When her parents received this message, they said to each other, "As we have passed through the round of existences, we have not previously had a son or a daughter. But these two have grievously offended against us, and it is out of the question for them to stand in our sight. Let these two take as much money as they need and go and live in some pleasant place. However, let them send the children here." So the two took the money which was sent to them, and giving their children into the hands of the messengers who came, sent them to their grandparents. Thus it happened that the children were brought up in the home of their grandparents.

Of the two children, Little Wayman was still very young. Big Wayman, however, used to accompany his grandfather to hear the Possessor of the Ten Forces preach the Law. And as the result of his frequent visits to the Teacher, his heart inclined to retirement from the world. Accordingly he said to his grandfather, "If you would give me your permission, I should like to retire from the world." [243] "What say you, dear grandson? There is no one in the whole world whose retirement from the world would give me so much pleasure as your own. If you are able to do so, by all means retire from the world."

3 b. Little Wayman as a monk

Accordingly the grandfather took Big Wayman to the Teacher, who said, "Householder, you have won a boy?" "Yes, Reverend Sir, this is a grandson of mine who desires to become a monk under you." The Teacher bade a certain monk on his round for alms to receive the boy into the Order. The Elder assigned to him as a Subject of Meditation the first five of the Constituent Parts of the Body, and then received him into the Order. The youth learned by heart a considerable portion of the Word of the Buddha, kept residence during the season of the rains, made his full profession, and by diligently applying himself to meditation attained Arahatship.

As Big Wayman passed his time in the enjoyment of the bliss of Mystic Meditation, in the enjoyment of the bliss of the Fruit of the Path, he thought to himself, "Assuredly it is in the power of Little Wayman to experience this same bliss." Therefore he went to the treasurer his grandfather and said to him, "Great treasurer, if you will give your kind permission, I should like to receive Little Wayman into the Order." "By all means receive him into the Order, Reverend Sir." We are told that the treasurer was profoundly attached to the Religion of the Buddha, and that when asked, "Of which daughter of yours are these two children the sons?" he felt ashamed to say, "Of my daughter who ran away," and that for these two reasons he was only too glad to give them permission to retire from the world.

So the Elder Big Wayman received his brother Little Wayman into the Order [244] and established him in the Moral Precepts. But Little Wayman, once received into the Order, proved a dullard. Indeed in four months he was unable to learn by heart this single Stanza,

Even as the lotus, the red lotus, of fragrant perfume, appears at early morn full-blown, with fragrance unimpaired,
Behold the Buddha, resplendent as the blazing sun in the sky.

It seems that, in the dispensation of the Supremely Enlightened Kassapa, he possessed great wisdom, but that, after entering the religious life, he ridiculed and made fun of a certain monk who was a dullard, while the latter was trying to learn the Sacred Word; and that this monk, embarrassed by the ridicule to which he was subjected, was unable either to learn the passage by heart or even to repeat it. As the result of that act, Little Wayman was reborn as a dullard, and every sentence he learned put the preceding sentence out of his mind; indeed four months passed while he was striving to learn this one Stanza.

Thereupon Big Wayman said to his brother, "Little Wayman, it is not in your power to master this religion. In four months you have not been able to learn a single Stanza. How can you ever hope to reach the goal of the Religious Life? Leave the monastery at once." So saying, he expelled his brother from the Order. But Little Wayman was sincerely attached to the Religion of the Buddha, and the last thing in the world he wished to do was to leave the Order and return to the life of a householder.

Now at that time Jivaka Komārabhacca, taking an abundant supply of garlands and of various kinds of perfumes, went to his own mango-grove, rendered honor to the Teacher, listened to the Law, and then rising from his seat and paying obeisance to the Teacher, approached Big Wayman, who was steward of the Order, [245] and asked him, "Reverend Sir, how many monks are living with the Teacher?" "Five hundred." "To-morrow, Reverend Sir, bring the five hundred monks presided over by the Buddha and take a meal in our house." "The lay disciple Little Wayman is a dullard and has made no progress in the Law. I accept the invitation for all except him."

When Little Wayman heard that, he thought to himself, "The

Elder accepts an invitation for all these monks, but in accepting it, deliberately leaves me out. Beyond a doubt my brother's affection for me is gone. Of what profit to me any longer is this religion? I will return to the life of a householder and spend my days giving alms and doing other works of merit." So on the following day, very early in the morning, he set out with the intention of returning to the life of a householder. Very early in the morning also the Teacher surveyed the world, and seeing this incident, preceded Little Wayman to the gate and walked back and forth on the same road Little Wayman had taken.

As Little Wayman came along, he saw the Teacher, and approaching him, paid obeisance to him. Said the Teacher, "But, Little Wayman, where are you going at this hour of the day?" "Reverend Sir, my brother has expelled me from the Order, and therefore I intend to return to the world." "Little Wayman, it was at my hands that you received admission to the Order. Therefore when your brother expelled you, why did you not come to me? Come now, what have you to do with the life of a householder? You shall remain with me." So saying, the Teacher stroked him on the head with his hand, the palm of which was marked with the Wheel, and taking him with him, went and seated him over against the Perfumed Chamber. And creating by magic a perfectly clean cloth, he gave it to him, saying, "Little Wayman, remain right here, face towards the East, rub this cloth, and say as you do so, 'Removal of Impurity! Removal of Impurity!'" [246] Just then meal-time was announced, whereupon the Teacher, accompanied by the Congregation of Monks, went to the house of Jīvaka and sat down on the seat prepared for him.

Little Wayman sat down, facing the sun, and rubbed the cloth, saying as he did so, "Removal of Impurity! Removal of Impurity!" As he rubbed the piece of cloth, it became soiled. Thereupon he thought, "This piece of cloth was perfectly clean before. But through this body of mine it has lost its original character and has become soiled. 'Impermanent, indeed, are all existing things!'" And grasping the thought of decay and death, he developed Insight. The Teacher, knowing that Little Wayman's mind had attained Insight, said, "Little Wayman, think not that only a piece of cloth has become soiled and dyed with impurity. Indeed within you are lust, impurity, and other defilements; remove them." And sending forth a luminous image of himself, the Teacher, sitting before him, present in bodily form, as it were, pronounced the following Stanzas,

Lust, not dirt, is properly called impurity; to lust is correctly applied the term "impurity."
Monks should rid themselves of this form of impurity and live faithful to the religion of him who is devoid of impurity.

Hatred, not dirt, is properly called impurity; to hatred is correctly applied the term "impurity."
Monks should rid themselves of this form of impurity and live faithful to the religion of him who is devoid of hatred.

Delusion, not dirt, is properly called impurity; to delusion is correctly applied the term "impurity."
Monks should rid themselves of this form of impurity and live faithful to the religion of him who is devoid of delusion. [247]

At the conclusion of the Stanzas Little Wayman attained Arahatship, together with the Supernatural Faculties, and with the Supernatural Faculties also a knowledge of the Three Piṭakas.

It appears that in a previous state of existence he was a king. Once, while making a ceremonial circuit of the city, with sweat pouring down his forehead, he wiped his forehead with a clean cloth, whereupon the cloth became soiled. Thought he, "By reason of this body of mine a cloth so clean as this has lost its former character and become soiled. 'Impermanent, indeed, are all existing things!'" Thus did he acquire the concept of Impermanence. In consequence of this, in a later existence, Removal of Impurity became his salvation.

Jīvaka Komārabhacca offered Water of Donation to the Possessor of the Ten Forces. Said the Teacher, covering the bowl with his hand, "Jīvaka, are there no monks in the monastery?" Big Wayman replied, "No, Reverend Sir, there are no monks in the monastery." Said the Teacher, "But Jīvaka, there are!" "Very well," said Jīvaka, and sent a man to find out. Said he, "Go to the monastery and find out whether or not there are any monks there." At that moment Little Wayman said to himself, "My brother says, 'There are no monks in the monastery.' I will show him that there *are* monks in the monastery." And forthwith he filled the whole mango-grove with monks. Some of them were making robes, others were dyeing robes, others were repeating the Sacred Texts. Thus did Little Wayman create by supernatural power a thousand monks, each different from every other. So when Jīvaka's messenger saw the numerous monks, he returned and told Jīvaka, "Noble sir, the entire mango-grove is full of monks." And right there Elder [248]

Wayman, multiplying himself a thousand-fold,
Sat in the charming mango-grove until he was sent for.

Said the Teacher to the man, "Go to the monastery and say, 'The Teacher summons Little Wayman.'" The man went and said what he was told to say. Thereupon the cry went up from a thousand throats, "I am Little Wayman! I am Little Wayman!" The man returned and said, "Reverend Sir, they all say they are Little Wayman." Said the Teacher, "Well then, go and take by the hand the first man that says, 'I am Little Wayman,' and the rest will disappear." The man did so. Immediately the thousand monks disappeared. The Elder Little Wayman returned with the man who came for him.

At the end of the meal the Teacher addressed Jīvaka, "Jīvaka, take Little Wayman's bowl, and he will pronounce the words of thanksgiving for you." Jīvaka took his bowl. The Elder Little Wayman, like a young lion roaring a lion's roar, pronounced the words of thanksgiving, ranging through the whole of the Three Piṭakas. The Teacher arose from his seat, and surrounded by the Congregation of Monks, went to the monastery. After the monks had shown the Teacher the customary attentions, the Teacher, facing the Perfumed Chamber, admonished the Congregation of Monks with the Admonition of the Happy One, assigned a Subject of Meditation, dismissed the Congregation of Monks, and then, having entered the Perfumed Chamber, the fragrant, perfumed residence in which he resided, lay down lion-like on his right side.

Now at eventide the monks assembled from all quarters, and drawing as it were curtains of crimson blankets, [249] sat down and began to praise the virtues of the Teacher. "Brethren, Big Wayman, not understanding the disposition of Little Wayman, thinking merely, 'In four months this dullard has not been able to learn a single Stanza,' expelled him from the monastery. But the Supremely Enlightened, because he is King of Ultimate Truth, within the space of a single meal bestowed Arahatship upon him, and together with Arahatship the Supernatural Faculties, and with the Supernatural Faculties mastery of the Three Piṭakas. Oh, great is the power of the Buddhas!"

Now the Exalted One, knowing that they were discussing this matter in the Hall of Truth, thought to himself, "It is my duty to go to them this very moment." Accordingly he arose from the Seat of the Buddha, put on his gloriously dyed under and upper garments, girded himself as with lightning, and over his shoulders, like a crimson blanket, threw the great robe of the Happy One. And coming forth from his richly fragrant Perfumed Chamber, and walking with the stride of a noble elephant in rut, with the incomparable grace of a

Buddha, he proceeded to the Hall of Truth. And mounting the gloriously arrayed sublime Seat of the Buddha, and diffusing from his body the six-colored rays of a Buddha, even as the sun, newly risen on the top of Mount Yugandhara, agitates the inmost depths of the sea, he sat down in the center of the seat.

Now the moment the Supremely Enlightened One arrived, the Congregation of Monks ceased their talk, became silent. The Teacher surveyed the assemblage with soft, kind heart [250] and said, "This assemblage delights my heart beyond measure. Not a single hand is out of place, not a single foot is out of place; not a cough is to be heard, not a sneeze is to be heard; all these monks, reverent with reverence for the Buddha, subdued by the majesty of the Buddha, though I were to sit here for an aeon and not speak, would refrain from speaking first, would not so much as open their lips. I alone have the right to decide when it is proper to begin to speak. Therefore will I speak first."

Accordingly with sweet voice, a voice like that of Great Brahmā, he addressed the monks, "Monks, what is the subject of your conversation now, as you sit here all gathered together? What was the subject of the discussion which you so suddenly broke off?" When they told him, he said, "Monks, this is not the first time Little Wayman has proved a dullard. In a previous state of existence also he was a dullard. This is not the first time I have been his refuge. In a previous state of existence also I was his refuge. But in a previous state of existence I made him master of the wealth of this world. Just now I made him master of wealth that transcends this world." The monks desired to hear all about it. Responding to their requests, he related the following

3 c. Story of the Past: The world-renowned teacher, the young man, and the king of Benāres

Once upon a time a certain young man who lived in the city of Benāres went to Takkasilā for the purpose of acquiring the arts and became the pupil of a world-renowned teacher. He was by all odds the most helpful to the teacher of all the five hundred young men who were his pupils. All of his duties, such as bathing and perfuming the feet, he performed most faithfully. But he was such a dullard that he was not able to learn a single thing. The teacher thought, "This young man is most helpful to me; I will instruct him in the arts." But in spite of his best efforts he was unable to teach him a single thing. [251] When, after a long residence, the young man was unable to learn a single Stanza, he became discouraged, and resolving to return home, asked leave of the teacher.

The teacher thought to himself, "This young man is a devoted servitor of mine. I should like to make a learned man of him, but this I cannot do. However, I ought certainly to make him some return for the assistance he has rendered me. I will compose a certain charm for him and give it to him." So he took him to the forest and composed for him the charm, "You're rubbing! you're rubbing! Why are you rubbing? I know too!" And this charm he taught him, causing him to repeat it many hundred times. "Do you know it now?" asked the teacher. "Yes," replied the young man; "I know it now." Thought the teacher, "If a dullard by dint of hard labor once learns by heart a form of words, it will never leave him." And giving him money to defray the expenses of his journey, he dismissed him, saying, "Now go make your living by this charm. But in order that you may not forget it, keep repeating it over and over." When he arrived at Benāres, his mother said to herself, "My son has returned after acquiring the arts," and held high festival in his honor.

It happened just at this time that the king of Benāres made a careful examination of his thoughts, words, and deeds for the purpose of discovering whether he had been guilty of any fault. So far as he could see, he had been guilty of no impropriety. But he reflected, "A person never sees his own faults; it takes other persons to see them. I will make a tour of the city and listen to what others say about me. When people have eaten supper and have sat down, they gossip and talk about all sorts of things. If I am ruling unjustly, they will say, 'We are utterly ruined by the punishments, taxes, and other oppressions of our wicked king.' If, on the other hand, I am ruling justly, [252] they will comment on my good qualities, paying me many compliments and saying, 'Long life to our king!'" So at nightfall he put on a disguise and went about the city, walking close to the walls of their houses.

At that moment some tunnel-thieves began to dig a tunnel between two houses in order to enter two houses by the same tunnel. The king saw them and took his stand in the shadow of the house. Now in this house lived the young man who had just returned from Takkasilā with the charm. When the thieves had dug the tunnel, they entered the house and began to look over the goods in the house. Just then the young man woke up and began to repeat his charm, "You're rubbing! you're rubbing! Why are you rubbing? I know too!" When the thieves heard this, they exclaimed, "This man knows what we are up to. Now he will kill us." And forthwith, dropping even the clothes they had on, they fled in terror in the first direction that was handy. The king, seeing them fleeing and hearing the words of the young man as he repeated his charm, continued his tour of the city and then entered the royal residence.

When the night grew bright and the dawn came, the king summoned a certain man and said to him, "My man, go into such and such a street, and in a certain house, where a tunnel has been dug, you will find a young man who has just returned from Takkasilā after learning the various arts. Bring him to me." The man went and said to the young man, "The king summons you," and conducted him to the king. The king said to him, "Friend, are you the young man that has just returned from Takkasilā after learning the various arts?" "Yes, your majesty." "Give us this charm also." "Very well, your majesty. Sit down on the same seat with me and learn it." The king sat down on the same seat with him, learned the charm, [253] and then said to him, "Here is your fee as teacher," and gave him a thousand pieces of money.

Just at this time the commander-in-chief of the army said to the king's barber, "When do you expect to shave the king's beard?" "To-morrow or the day after." The commander-in-chief of the army gave the king's barber a thousand pieces of money and said to him, "I have something for you to do." "What is it, master?" "Go through the form of shaving the king's beard, but grind your razor very sharp and cut his windpipe. Then you shall be commander-in-chief of the army and I shall be king." "Very well," said the barber, agreeing to the bargain.

When the day came for the barber to shave the king's beard, he moistened the king's beard with scented water, sharpened his razor, and applied it to the king's cheek. Discovering that the razor was slightly dull, and realizing that he must cut the king's windpipe with a single stroke, he stepped aside and began to sharpen his razor again. At that moment the king remembered his charm and began to repeat it, saying, "You're rubbing! you're rubbing! Why are you rubbing? I know too! I know!" Beads of sweat stood out on the forehead of the barber. "The king knows all about this business," thought he. He flung his razor to the ground in terror and prostrated himself on his breast before the feet of the king.

Now kings know a thing or two; and the king of Benāres immediately said to the barber, "Scoundrel of a barber, you thought to yourself, 'The king doesn't know about this.'" "Spare my life, your majesty." "Very well; fear not. Tell me about it." "Your majesty, the commander-in-chief of the army gave me a thousand pieces of money, saying to me, 'Go through the form of shaving the king's beard, but cut his windpipe. Then I shall be king and you shall be commander-in-chief of the army.'"

The king thought to himself, "It is due to my teacher that my life was spared." [254] He sent for the commander-in-chief of the army and said to him, "Well, commander-in-chief, what is there that you have not received from me? Henceforth I can endure to look upon you no longer. Depart from my kingdom." With these words he banished him from the kingdom. Then he sent for the young man who had been his teacher and said to him, "Teacher, it is due to you that my life was spared." And when he had so said, he bestowed high honor upon him and made him commander-in-chief of his army. **End of Story of the Past.**

"At that time," said the Teacher, "the young man was Little Wayman, and the world-renowned teacher was the Teacher himself." Therefore when the Teacher had finished this Story of the Past, he said, "Monks, thus in a previous state of existence also Little Wayman was a dullard, and at that time also I became his refuge and established him in the possession of the wealth of this world." Again one day the monks began a discussion, "The Teacher indeed became a refuge to Little Wayman." Thereupon the Teacher related the Story of the Past found in the Culla-Seṭṭhi Jātaka.

A man who is wise and intelligent can elevate himself to high position in the world with but little wealth,
Even as by blowing a tiny flame one can start a great fire.

Having pronounced this Stanza, the Teacher said, "Monks, this is not the first time I have been a refuge to Little Wayman; in a previous state of existence also I was a refuge to him. But in a previous state of existence I made him master of the wealth of this world; just now I made him master of wealth that transcends the world. At that time the young pupil was Little Wayman and the young merchant was I myself." Thus did he identify the characters in the Jātaka.

Again one day in the Hall of Truth the monks began a discussion:

"Brethren, in four months Little Wayman was unable to learn by heart a Stanza of four verses; but because he never relaxed the powers of his will, [255] he became established in Arahatship and has just now become master of wealth that transcends this world." The Teacher came in and asked, "Monks, what is it that you are sitting here now talking about?" When they told him, he said, "Monks, a monk who exerts all the powers of his will in following the Precepts cannot fail to make himself master of wealth that transcends this world." So saying, he pronounced the following Stanza,

25. By rousing himself, by heedfulness, by controlling himself, by restraining himself,
A wise man may make for himself an island which the flood can never overwhelm.

II. 4. SIMPLETONS' HOLIDAY [1]

Simpletons are given to heedlessness. This religious instruction was given by the Teacher while he was in residence at Jetavana with reference to Simpletons' Holiday, Bālanakkhatta. [256]

For on a certain date there was a festival celebrated in Sāvatthi called Simpletons' Holiday, and on the occasion of this festival foolish, unintelligent folk used to smear their bodies with ashes and cow-dung and for a period of seven days go about uttering all manner of coarse talk. At this time people showed no respect for kinsfolk or friends or monks when they met them, but stood in the doorways and insulted them with coarse talk. Those who could not endure the coarse talk would pay the holiday-makers a half or a quarter or a penny, according to their means, and the holiday-makers would take the money and depart from their houses.

Now at this time there were in Sāvatthi five crores of Noble Disciples, and they sent word to the Teacher, "Reverend Sir, let the Exalted One refrain for a period of seven days from entering the city with the Congregation of Monks; let him instead remain at the monastery." And for a period of seven days the Noble Disciples caused food to be prepared for the Congregation of Monks at the monastery and sent it to them, but did not themselves leave their houses. On the eighth day, however, when the festival was at an end, they invited the Congregation of Monks to be their guests, escorted them into the city, and gave abundant offerings. And having seated themselves

[1] Text: N i. 256–258.

respectfully on one side, they said to the Teacher, "Reverend Sir, we have spent the past seven days most unpleasantly. Our ears had like to burst from hearing the coarse talk of foolish folk. [257] No one showed any respect for anybody else, and for this reason we did not permit you to enter the city. We ourselves did not go out of the house." The Teacher listened to what they said, and then replied, "After this manner do foolish, unintelligent men conduct themselves. But they that are intelligent preserve heedfulness as their greatest treasure, and by so doing at last attain the attainment of the Deathless, Great Nibbāna." So saying, he pronounced the following Stanzas,

26. Simpletons, folk of little intelligence, are given to heedlessness;
But the intelligent man preserves heedfulness as his greatest treasure.

27. Give not yourselves up to heedlessness; indulge not in lust and sensual pleasure;
For he that is heedful and practices meditation attains profound happiness.

II. 5. KASSAPA THE GREAT [1]

When the wise man banishes heedlessness by heedfulness. This religious instruction was given by the Teacher while he was in residence at Jetavana with reference to the Elder Mahā Kassapa. [258]

For on a certain day, while the Elder was in residence at Pipphali Cave, he made his round of Rājagaha for alms, and after he had returned from his round for alms and had eaten his breakfast, he sat down and developed Insight, surveying with Supernatural Vision all living beings, both heedless and heedful, in the water, on the earth, on the mountains, and elsewhere, both coming into existence and passing out of existence.

The Teacher, seated at Jetavana, [259] exercised Supernatural Vision and pondered within himself, "With what is my son Kassapa occupied to-day?" Straightway he became aware of the following, "He is contemplating the rising and falling of living beings." And he said, "Knowledge of the rising and falling of living beings may not be compassed even with the Knowledge of a Buddha. Living beings pass from one existence to another and obtain a new conception in a mother's womb without the knowledge of mother or father, and knowledge thereof may not be compassed. To know them is beyond your range, Kassapa, for your range is very slight. It comes within

[1] Text: N i. 258-260.

range of the Buddhas alone to know and to see in their totality the rising and falling of living beings." So saying, he sent forth a radiant image of himself, and as it were sitting down face to face with Kassapa, pronounced the following Stanza,

28. When the wise man banishes heedlessness by heedfulness,
He climbs the terrace of wisdom, and free from sorrow, looks upon the sorrowing folk of the world.
Steadfast, as though standing on a mountain-top, he gazes upon the simpletons standing on the ground below.

II. 6. TWO BRETHREN [1]

Heedful among the heedless. This religious instruction was given by the Teacher while he was in residence at Jetavana with reference to two brethren. [260]

It appears that these two monks obtained a Subject of Meditation from the Teacher and retired to a forest hermitage. Early in the morning one of them brought firewood, prepared the charcoal-dish, and during the first watch sat and chatted with the probationers and novices. The other, a heedful monk, engaged in meditation, thus admonished his friend, "Brother, do not act thus. For a monk that is heedless stand ready four states of suffering, as if they were his own house. The favor of the Buddhas may not be won by double-dealing." When the lazy monk paid no attention to his admonition, the zealous monk said, "This monk cannot endure to be spoken to." Having failed to spur his comrade to greater effort, the zealous monk, abiding in heedfulness, resumed his meditations. [261]

The slothful Elder, having warmed himself during the first watch, entered the monastery just as his friend, having finished his walk, entered his cell. Said the slothful monk to the zealous monk, "Slothful one, you entered the forest for the purpose of lying down and sleeping. Seeing that you obtained a Subject of Meditation from the Buddhas, ought you not rather to rise and devote yourself to the practice of meditation?" So saying, he entered his own place of residence, lay down, and went to sleep. But his friend, after walking up and down during the first watch and resting during the second watch, rose in the last watch and devoted himself to the practice of meditation. Living thus the life of heedfulness, in no long time he attained Arahatship,

[1] Text: N i. 260–263.

together with the Supernatural Faculties. The other monk, however, spent his time in utter heedlessness.

When the two monks had completed residence, they went to the Teacher, paid obeisance to him, and sat down respectfully on one side. The Teacher exchanged friendly greetings with them and queried, "I trust that you have lived the life of heedfulness and that you have devoted yourselves earnestly to the practice of meditation. I trust that you have reached the goal of the Religious Life." The heedless monk replied, "Reverend Sir, how can this monk be said to be heedful? From the time he left you he has done nothing but lie and sleep." "But *you*, monk?" "I, Reverend Sir, betimes in the morning brought firewood and prepared the charcoal-dish, and during the first watch I sat and warmed myself, but I did not spend my time sleeping." Then said the Teacher to the slothful monk, "You who have spent your time in heedlessness say, 'I am heedful.' You mistake heedlessness for heedfulness. [262] Compared with my son, you are like a decrepit hack; but he, compared with you, is like a racer." So saying, he pronounced the following Stanza,

> **29.** Heedful among the heedless, watchful among the sleeping,
> Even as a racer outstrips a hack, even so goes a wise man.

II. 7. HOW MAGHA BECAME SAKKA[1]

By heedfulness Maghavā attained leadership of the gods. This religious instruction was given by the Teacher while in residence at a summer-house near Vesāli with reference to Sakka king of gods. [263]

7 a. Story of the Present: Mahāli's question

For a Licchavi prince named Mahāli, who lived at Vesāli, hearing the Teacher recite the Suttanta entitled Sakka's Question, thought to himself, "The Supremely Enlightened has described the great glory of Sakka. Has the Teacher seen Sakka? or has he not seen Sakka? Is the Teacher acquainted with Sakka? or is he not acquainted with Sakka? I will ask him." So the Licchavi prince Mahāli drew near to where the Exalted One was, and having drawn near, saluted the Exalted One and sat down on one side. And having

[1] **7 a** is almost word for word the same as *Saṁyutta*, xi. 2. 3: i. 230–231. **7 b** is a free version of *Jātaka* 31: i. 198–206. Text: N i. 263–281.

sat down on one side, the Licchavi prince Mahāli spoke thus to the Exalted One, "Reverend Sir, has the Exalted One seen Sakka king of gods?" [264] "Yes, Mahāli, I have indeed seen Sakka king of gods." "Reverend Sir, it must certainly have been a counterfeit of Sakka; for, Reverend Sir, it is a difficult matter to see Sakka king of gods." "Nevertheless, Mahāli, I know Sakka; I know what qualities made him Sakka; I know by the cultivation of what qualities Sakka attained Sakkaship.

"Mahāli, in a previous state of existence Sakka king of gods was a human being, a prince named Magha; therefore is he called Maghavā. Mahāli, in a previous state of existence Sakka king of gods was a human being who in a previous state of existence gave gifts (*pure dānaṁ adāsi*); therefore is he called Purindada. Mahāli, in a previous state of existence Sakka king of gods was a human being, who gave alms assiduously (*sakkaccaṁ*); therefore is he called Sakka. Mahāli, in a previous state of existence Sakka king of gods was a human being who gave a dwelling-place (*āvasathaṁ*); therefore is he called Vāsava. Mahāli in a previous state of existenceSakka king of gods was a human being who could think of as many as a thousand things (*sahassaṁ atthaṁ*) in an instant; therefore is he called Sahassakkha. Mahāli, Sakka king of gods has an Asura maiden named Sujātā to wife; therefore is he called Sujampati. Mahāli, Sakka king of gods bears sway as lord and master over the Gods of the Thirty-three; therefore is he called King of Gods. Mahāli, Sakka king of gods in a previous state of existence as a human being took upon himself and fulfilled seven vows. Because he took upon himself and fulfilled these seven vows, Sakka [265] attained Sakkaship.

"Now what were the seven? 'So long as I live, may I be the support of my mother and father. So long as I live, may I honor my elders. So long as I live, may I speak gentle words. So long as I live, may I never give way to backbiting. So long as I live, may I live the life of a householder with heart free from taint of avarice, generous in renunciation of what is mine, with open hand, delighting in liberality, attentive to petitions, delighting in the distribution of alms. So long as I live, may I speak the truth. So long as I live, may I be free from anger. Should anger spring up within me, may I quickly suppress it.' Mahāli, Sakka king of gods in a previous state of existence took upon himself and fulfilled seven vows. Because he took upon himself and fulfilled these seven vows, Sakka attained Sakkaship."

If a man support his mother and father, if he honor his elders in the household,
If he be gentle and friendly in conversation, if he avoid backbiting,
If he steadfastly put away avarice, if he be truthful, if he suppress anger,
Such a man the Gods of the Thirty-three call a good man.

When the Teacher said, "This, Mahāli, was what Sakka did in his previous existence as Prince Magha," Mahāli, desiring to hear the whole story of his conduct, asked the Teacher, "Reverend Sir, how did Prince Magha conduct himself?" "Well then," said the Teacher, "listen." So saying, he related the following

7 b. Story of the Past: How Magha became Sakka

In times long past a prince named Magha lived in the village of Macala in the kingdom of Magadha. [266] One day he went to the place where the business of the village was carried on, removed with his foot the dust from the place where he stood, and having made a comfortable place for himself, stood there. Thereupon another struck him with his arm, pushed him aside, and took his place. But instead of becoming angry at the man, he made another comfortable place for himself and stood there. Thereupon another struck him with his arm, pushed him away, and took his place. But neither did he allow himself to become angry at this man; he merely made another comfortable place for himself and stood there. In like manner one man after another came out of his house, struck him with his arm, and pushed him away from the place which he had cleared for himself.

The prince thought to himself, "All these men appear to be pleased. Since this work of mine conduces to the happiness of men, it must be a meritorious work." So on the following day he took a spade and cleared a space as big as a threshing-floor, whereupon all the men came and stood there. In cold weather he built a fire to warm them, so that the place became a favorite resort for all. Then he thought to himself, "It behooves me to take upon myself the task of making the road smooth and even." So early in the morning he started out to make the road smooth and even, cutting down and removing all the branches of trees that needed to be removed. Thus did he spend his time.

Another man saw him and said to him, "Master, what are you doing?" He replied, "Master, I am treading the Path that leads to Heaven." "I also am your companion." "Be my companion, master; heaven is a pleasant place for many." [267] Seeing these two, a third man asked the same question, received the same answer, and joined them; then a fourth, then a fifth, until finally there were thirty-three.

All these men worked together with spades and axes and made the road smooth and even for a distance of one or two leagues. The village headman saw them and thought to himself, "These men are all following the wrong occupation. If they would only fetch fish and flesh from the forest, or indulge in strong drink, or do something else of the sort, I should make something by it." So he sent for them and asked them, "What is it you are doing?" "Treading the Path to Heaven, master." "That is no proper occupation for men living the lives of laymen. What you should do is to bring fish and flesh from the forest, indulge in strong drink, and have a general good time." But they refused to follow his suggestion, and the more he urged them, the more firmly they refused to do as he suggested.

Finally the village headman became angry. "I will destroy them," said he. So he went to the king and said to him, "Your majesty, I see a band of thieves going about committing depredations." The king replied, "Go catch them and bring them before me." So the village headman arrested the thirty-three youths and haled them before the king. Without instituting an inquiry into their conduct, the king gave the following order, "Cause them to be trampled to death by an elephant." Thereupon Magha admonished his companions as follows, "Friends, we have no refuge but love. Therefore let your hearts be tranquil. Cherish anger towards no one. Let your hearts be full of love for the king and the village headman and the elephant that tramples you under his feet." The thirty-three youths followed the admonition of their leader. Such was the power of their love that the elephant dared not approach them.

When the king heard of this, he said, [268] "If the elephant sees so many men, he will not venture to trample them under his feet. Have the men covered with heavy matting, and then order the elephant to trample them." So the village headman had the men covered with heavy matting and drove the elephant forwards to trample them. But when the elephant was yet a long way off, he turned round and went back. When the king heard what had happened, he thought to himself, "There must be some reason for this." So he caused the thirty-three youths to be brought before him and asked them, "Friends, is there anything which you have failed to receive at my hands?" "Your majesty, what do you mean?" "I am informed that you are a band of thieves and that you rove about the forest committing depredations." "Your majesty, who said that?" "Friends, the village headman so informed me."

"Your majesty, it is not true that we are thieves. The fact is, we are clearing a Path to Heaven for ourselves, and we do this and that. The village headman tried to persuade us to adopt an evil mode of life, and when we refused to follow his suggestions, he became angry at us and determined to destroy us. That is why he said this about us." "Friends, this animal knows your good qualities; but I, who am a man, was unable to discern them. Pardon me." So saying, the king made the village headman their slave, together with his children and wife, gave them a riding-elephant, and presented that village to them to do with as they saw fit. Thought the thirty-three youths, "Even in this life the advantage to be derived from the performance of works of merit is clearly to be seen." And mounting the elephant by turns, they rode about the village.

As they went about the village, they took counsel together, [269] saying, "It is our duty to perform yet more abundant works of merit. What shall we do?" Thereupon the following thought occurred to them, "Let us build at the crossing of the four highways a rest-house for the multitude, making it secure and strong." So they summoned a builder and ordered him to build a hall for them. And because desire for women had departed from them, they resolved to give women no share in the building of the hall.

Now there were four women living in Magha's house, Joy, Thoughtful, Goodness, and Wellborn. Goodness went secretly to the builder, gave him a bribe, and said to him, "Brother, give me the principal share in the building of this hall." "Very well," replied the builder, agreeing to her proposal. Accordingly he first marked a tree out of which to make a pinnacle, felled it, and laid it aside to season. Then he hewed it and planed it and bored it, and having fashioned it in the form of a pinnacle, carved the following inscription on it, "This is the Hall of Goodness." Having so done, he wrapped it in a cloth and laid it aside.

Now when he had completed the hall and the day came to erect the pinnacle, he said to the thirty-three youths, "Noble sirs, there is something we have forgotten." "What is it, sir?" "A pinnacle." "Let us procure one." "It is impossible to make one out of a freshly hewn tree. We should procure for a pinnacle a tree felled long ago and laid away to season." "What had we best do under the circumstances?" "If in anybody's house there is a completed pinnacle which has been laid away to season and which is for sale, [270] that is the thing for you to search for." So they searched everywhere, and finding what they wanted in the house of Goodness, offered her a thousand pieces of money for it. But they were unable to secure it for the price they offered. Said Goodness, "If you will give me a share in the building of the hall, I will give you the pinnacle." But they replied, "We have resolved to give women no share in the building of this hall." Thereupon the builder said to them, "Noble sirs, what are you doing? With the exception of the World of Brahmā, there is no place from which women are excluded. Take the pinnacle, for if you do, our work will speedily be finished." "Very well," said they. So they took the pinnacle and completed the hall. And they divided the hall into three parts, reserving one chamber for kings, another for the poor, and another for the sick.

Then the thirty-three youths built thirty-three seats, and having so done, gave the following orders to the elephant, "If a visitor comes and sits down in a seat, take him and lodge him in the house of whoever built and owns that seat. It then becomes the duty of the owner of that seat to see that his guest's feet and back are rubbed, to provide him with food both hard and soft, and with lodging; to perform for him, in fact, all the duties of hospitality." Accordingly, whenever a visitor came, the elephant would take him and conduct him to the house of the owner of the seat in which he had sat, and the owner of the seat would on that day perform for him all the duties of hospitality.

Magha planted an ebony-tree near the hall and built a stone seat at the foot of the ebony-tree. All those who entered the hall looked at the pinnacle, read the inscription, and said, "This is the Hall of Goodness." The names of the thirty-three youths did not appear.

Joy thought to herself, "The youths who built this hall resolved to deprive us of a share in the building thereof. [271] But Goodness by her own cleverness obtained a share. I also ought to do something. What can I do?" Thereupon the following thought occurred to her, "Those who come to the hall should be provided with water for drinking and water for bathing. I will have a place dug for a pool." Accordingly Joy caused a bathing-pool to be built.

Thoughtful thought to herself, "Goodness has given a pinnacle, and Joy has caused a swimming-pool to be built. What can I do?" Thereupon the following thought occurred to her, "After those who come to the hall have drunk water and bathed, they should be decked with garlands when they are ready to depart. I will cause a flower garden to be laid out." So Thoughtful caused a beautiful flower garden to be laid out. So many and so various were the flowers that grew therein that it was impossible for anyone to say, "Such and such a flower-bearing or fruit-bearing tree does not grow in this garden."

Now Wellborn thought to herself, "I am the daughter of the brother of the mother of Magha and likewise the wife of Magha. The merit of the work he has wrought accrues to me only, and the merit of the work I have wrought accrues to him only." Accordingly she did nothing but spend her time adorning herself.

Thus did Magha minister to his mother and father, honor his elders in the household, speak the truth, avoid harsh words, avoid back-biting, put away avarice, suppress anger. Even thus did he fulfill the Seven Precepts, as it is said: [272]

If a man support his mother and father, if he honor his elders in the household,
If he be gentle and friendly in conversation, if he avoid backbiting,
If he steadfastly put away avarice, if he be truthful, if he suppress anger,
Such a man the Gods of the Thirty-three call a good man.

Having attained so praiseworthy a state, Magha, upon reaching the end of the term of life allotted to him, was reborn in the World of the Thirty-three as Sakka king of gods. His companions were likewise reborn there. The builder was reborn god Vissakamma.

Now at that time there were Asuras dwelling in the World of the Thirty-three, and when they learned that new gods had been reborn there, they prepared celestial drink for them. But Sakka gave orders to his retinue that no one should drink thereof. The Asuras, however, drank freely and became intoxicated. Thereupon Sakka thought to himself, "Why should I share my kingdom with these deities?" Forthwith, giving a sign to his retinue, he caused them to pick up the Asuras by the heels and fling them into the Great Ocean. So the Asuras fell headlong into the Ocean. By the power of their merit there sprang up at the foot of Mount Sineru the Palace of the Asuras and the Tree that is called Pied Trumpet-flower.

When the conflict between the gods and the Asuras was over and the Asuras had been defeated, there came into existence the City of the Thirty-three. The distance from the eastern gate to the western gate was ten thousand leagues, and the distance from the southern gate to the northern gate was the same. Now this city was provided with a thousand gates and was adorned with gardens and pools, and in the midst thereof, [273] as the fruit of the building of the hall, there arose a palace called the Palace of Victory. Its height was seven hundred leagues, and it was decked with banners three hundred leagues long. On staffs of gold were banners of jewels, and on staffs of jewels were banners of gold; on staffs of coral were banners of pearls, and on staffs of pearls were banners of coral; on staffs of the seven precious stones were banners of the seven precious stones. Such was the palace that arose as the fruit of the building of the hall; a thousand leagues was its height, and it was composed of the seven precious stones.

As the result of the planting of the ebony-tree, there arose the Coral-tree, a hundred leagues in circumference. As the result of the building of the stone seat, there came into existence at the foot of the Coral-tree the Yellowstone throne, of a reddish yellow color like that of the jasmine flower, sixty leagues in length, fifty leagues in breadth, and fifteen leagues thick. When Sakka sits down on this throne, half its mass sinks into the ground; when he rises, it is all above ground. The elephant was reborn as god Erāvaṇa. There are no animals in the World of the Gods; so when he went into the garden to play, he would quit his form as a god and become the elephant Erāvaṇa, a hundred and fifty leagues in size. For the thirty-three youths, Erāvaṇa created thirty-three water-pots, each two or three quarters of a league around.

In the center of all, Erāvaṇa created for Sakka a water-pot called Beautiful. It was thirty leagues in circumference, and above it was a canopy, twelve leagues in size, made entirely of precious stones. [274] At regular intervals about the canopy there arose banners a league in length, made entirely of the seven precious stones. And from the lower edge of each banner depended a row of tinkling bells, which, when they were shaken by the gentle wind, gave forth sweet music like the mingled strains of the music of the five kinds of instruments or the singing of the celestial choir. In the center of the pavilion was prepared for Sakka a jeweled couch a league in length. There Sakka reclined in state. Erāvaṇa created thirty-three water-pots for the thirty-three gods. Each vessel bore seven tusks, each fifty leagues long; each tusk bore seven lotus-tanks; each lotus-tank bore seven lotus-plants; each lotus-plant bore seven flowers; each flower, seven leaves; and on each leaf danced seven celestial nymphs. Thus on all sides round about for a space of fifty leagues there were dancing-assemblies poised on elephants' tusks. Such was the glory in the enjoyment of which lived Sakka king of gods.

When Goodness died, she was also reborn there. And at the same time there came into existence Goodness, Moot-hall of the gods, nine hundred leagues in extent, than which exists no other place more charming. [275] Here, on the eighth day of the month, is preached the Law. Unto this day, when men behold a charming place, they say, "It is like Goodness, Moot-hall of the gods." When Joy died, she also was reborn there. And at the same time there came into existence a lotus-tank called Joy, five hundred leagues in extent. When Thoughtful died, she also was reborn there. And at the same time there came into existence Thoughtful's Creeper-grove, five hundred leagues in extent. Thither they conduct the gods whose prognostics have appeared, and walk rejoicing. But when Wellborn died, she was reborn as a crane in a certain mountain-cave.

Sakka surveyed his wives and considered within himself, "Goodness has been reborn here and likewise Joy and Thoughtful. Now where has Wellborn been reborn?" Perceiving that she had been reborn as a crane in a mountain-cave, he thought to himself, "Because she wrought no work of merit, the foolish girl has been reborn as an animal. It is my duty to have her perform some work of merit and bring her here." So saying, he laid aside his proper form, and assuming a disguise, he went to her and asked, "What are you doing here?" "But, master, who are you?" "I am your husband, Magha." "Where were you reborn, husband?" "I was reborn in the Heaven of the Thirty-three. Do you know where your companions were reborn?" "No, husband, I do not." "They also were reborn in the Heaven of the Thirty-three as my wives. Should you like to see your companions?" "How can I get there?" Said Sakka, "I will carry you thither."

Placing her in the palm of his hand, he carried her to the World of the Gods and set her free on the bank of the lotus-tank named Joy. Then he said to the other three, "Should you like to see your companion Wellborn?" "Sire, where is she?" [276] "On the bank of the lotus-tank named Joy." So the three went and looked at her. "Alas!" they cried out, "see what has been the result of the noble woman's spending her life in the adornment of self! Look now at her beak! Look at her feet! Look at her legs! She presents a beautiful appearance indeed!" Thus did they ridicule her. Having so done, they departed.

Sakka went once more to her and said, "Did you see your companions?" "Yes," replied Wellborn, "I saw them. They ridiculed me and then went their way. Take me back again." So Sakka took her back again, set her free in the water, and then asked her, "Did you see their celestial glory?" "Yes, Sire, I did." "You also should employ such means as will enable you to obtain rebirth there." "Sire, what shall I do?" "If I admonish you, will you keep my admonition?"

"Yes, Sire, I will keep your admonition." So Sakka taught her the Five Precepts. Having so done, he said to her, "Be zealous in keeping the Precepts," and departed.

Thenceforth she sought after and ate only such fish as had died a natural death. After a few days had passed, Sakka determined to test her. So he went, and taking the form of a fish, lay down on the surface of the sand, pretending to be dead. When she saw the fish, thinking that it was dead, she took it in her beak. Just as she was about to swallow the fish, it wriggled its tail. The instant she discovered the fish was alive she released it in the water. Sakka waited a little while, and then lay down before her on his back once more. Again thinking it was a dead fish, she took it in her beak. But just as she was about to swallow the fish, it moved the tip of its tail. The instant she saw the fish move its tail she knew it was alive, and therefore let it go. When Sakka had thus tested her three times and had satisfied himself that she was keeping the Precepts faithfully, he revealed his identity to her and said, "I came here for the purpose of testing you. You are keeping the Precepts faithfully. If you continue thus faithfully to keep them, [277] you will before long be reborn as one of my wives. Be heedful." So saying these words, he departed.

Thenceforth she used for food either fish that had died a natural death or none at all. After only a few days had passed, she shriveled up and died, and solely as the fruit of her virtuous conduct was reborn at Benāres as the daughter of a potter. When she was about fifteen or sixteen years old, Sakka considered within himself, "Where has she been reborn?" Perceiving that she had been reborn at Benāres as the daughter of a potter, he said to himself, "I ought now to go to her."

So filling a cart with the seven kinds of precious stones disguised as cucumbers, he drove into the city of Benāres. "Come, get cucumbers!" he cried, as he entered the street. But when people came to him with coins in their hands, he said, "I do not part with my cucumbers for a price." "On what terms do you part with them, then?" the people asked him. "I give them to the woman that keeps the Precepts," he replied. "Master, what do you mean by 'precepts'? Are they black or brown or of some other color?" "You don't even know what Precepts *are;* much less will you keep them. I will give my cucumbers to the woman who keeps the Precepts."

"Master, there is a potter's daughter who is always going about saying, 'I keep the Precepts.' Give them to her." The potter's daughter said to him, "Very well, master, give them to me." "Who are you?" "I am a maiden that has never failed to keep the Precepts." [278] "For you alone have I brought these," said Sakka. And driving his cart to her house, he presented to her, in the guise of cucumbers, celestial treasure which cannot be taken away by others. And making his identity known to her, he said, "Here is wealth sufficient for you to live on. Keep the Five Precepts unbroken." So saying, he departed.

At the end of her existence as a potter's daughter she was reborn in the World of the Asuras as the daughter of Vepacitti, king of Asuras, a bitter enemy of Sakka. Since she had kept the Precepts in two successive existences, she was fair of form, her skin was of a golden hue, and she was endowed with beauty and comeliness the like of which had never been seen. Vepacitti, king of Asuras, said to all the Asura princes who sought her in marriage, "You are not fit to marry my daughter." Having thus refused to give her in marriage to any of the Asura princes, he said, "My daughter shall choose for herself such a husband as she sees fit." So saying, he assembled the host of Asuras, and placing a garland of flowers in the hand of his daughter, said to her, "Choose for yourself a husband who suits you."

At that moment Sakka looked to see where she had been reborn. Perceiving what was taking place, he assumed the form of an aged Asura and went and stood in the outer circle of the assembled company. The daughter of Vepacitti looked this way and that. Suddenly, because in a previous state of existence she had lived with Sakka, she was overwhelmed as by a mighty torrent by the power of the love for him which sprang up within her. And crying out, "He is my husband!" she threw the garland of flowers over his head. Said the Asuras, "For a long time our king has been unable to find a husband suitable for his daughter. Now, however, he has found one. This fellow is old enough to be his daughter's grandfather." [279] And they departed, hanging their heads with shame.

Sakka took her by the hand, cried out, "I am Sakka," and flew up into the air. The Asuras exclaimed, "We have been fooled by Old Sakka," and started up in pursuit. Mātali the charioteer brought up the chariot called Chariot of Victory and stopped by the way. Thereupon Sakka assisted his bride to mount and set out for the City of the Gods. Now when they reached the Forest of the Silk-cotton Trees, the Garuḍa fledglings, hearing the sound of the chariot and fearing they would be crushed to death, cried out.

When Sakka heard their cries, he asked Mātali, "What are they that are crying?" "Garuḍa birds, Sire." "Why are they crying?" "They hear the sound of the chariot and fear they will be crushed to death." "Let not so numerous a host perish, crushed by the impact of the chariot, because of me alone. Cause the chariot to turn back." Thereupon Mātali gave the sign with the lash to the thousand Sindh horses and caused the chariot to turn back.

When the Asuras saw that the chariot had turned back, they said, "Old Sakka started out in flight from the city of the Asuras, but has just caused his chariot to turn back. Doubtless he has received reënforcements." And turning back, the Asuras entered the city of the Asuras by the same road by which they had come out and nevermore lifted up their heads. Sakka bore the Asura maiden Wellborn to the City of the Gods and installed her as the chief of twenty-five million celestial nymphs.

One day Wellborn asked Sakka for a boon, saying, "Great king, in this World of the Gods I have neither mother nor father nor brother nor sister; therefore pray take me with you wherever you go." **[280]** "Very well," replied Sakka, promising to do for her as she had asked. Thenceforth, when the tree that is called Pied Trumpet-flower blooms, the Asuras cry out, "Now is the time when our heavenly Coral-tree blooms," and straightway they sally forth to attack Sakka. Therefore Sakka posts a guard to defend the Nāgas in the sea below, and likewise affords protection to the Supaṇṇas and the Kumbhaṇḍas and the Yakkhas, and likewise to the Four Great Kings. And over all, for the purpose of averting disaster, he places before the gates of the City of the Gods images of Indra bearing the thunderbolt in his hands. When the Asuras, after defeating the Nāgas and the other supernatural beings approach the City of the Gods and see the images of Indra, they cry out, "Sakka has made a sally," and flee away. **End of Story of the Past.**

"Thus, Mahāli, Prince Magha adopted the way of Heedfulness. Because he was so heedful, he obtained such sovereignty so exalted and came to rule over the two Worlds of the Gods. Heedfulness is praised by the Buddhas and by others likewise. For it is through Heedfulness that all attain the Higher Attainments, both those that are of this world and those that transcend this world." So saying, he pronounced the following Stanza,

> 30. By heedfulness Maghavā attained leadership of the gods;
> All men praise heedfulness; heedlessness is ever reprobated.

II. 8. A MONK ATTAINS ARAHATSHIP [1]

A monk who delights in heedfulness. This religious instruction was given by the Teacher while he was in residence at Jetavana with reference to a certain monk. [281]

The story goes that this monk obtained from the Teacher a Subject of Meditation leading to Arahatship and retired to the forest. Although he strove and struggled with might and main, he was unable to attain Arahatship. Thereupon he said to himself, "I will ask the Teacher to give me a Subject of Meditation better suited to my needs." So he departed from his place of residence and set out to return to the Teacher. On the way he saw a great forest fire raging. Accordingly he climbed up to the top of a bald mountain and sat down. As he watched the fire consume the forest, [282] he concentrated his mind on the following thought, "Even as this fire advances, consuming all obstacles both great and small, so also ought I to advance, consuming all obstacles both great and small by the Fire of Knowledge of the Noble Path."

The Teacher, even as he sat in his Perfumed Chamber, became aware of the course of his thoughts and spoke as follows, "Monk, this is precisely true. Even as fire consumes all obstacles both great and small, so also is it necessary with the Fire of Knowledge to consume and utterly destroy all Attachments both small and great which arise within these living beings." And sending forth a luminous image of himself, present, as it were, sitting face to face with that monk, he pronounced the following Apparition-Stanza,

> 31. A monk who delights in heedfulness and views heedlessness with fear
> Advances like a fire, consuming Attachments both small and great. [283]

At the conclusion of the Stanza that monk, even as he sat there, consumed all the Attachments and attained Arahatship, together with the Supernatural Faculties. And straightway, soaring through the air, he approached the Teacher, praising and glorifying the golden body of the Tathāgata. And when he had done him homage, he departed.

[1] Text: N i. 281–283.

II. 9. TISSA OF THE MARKET-TOWN [1]

A monk who delights in heedfulness. This religious instruction was given by the Teacher while he was in residence at Jetavana with reference to Elder Tissa of the Market-town, Nigamavāsī Tissa. [283]

For a youth of station, born and reared in a certain market-town not far from Savātthi, retired from the world and became a monk in the Religion of the Teacher. On making his full profession, he became known as Tissa of the Market-town, or Nigama Tissa. He acquired the reputation of being frugal, contented, pure, resolute. He always made his rounds for alms in the village where his relatives resided. Although, in the neighboring city of Sāvatthi, Anāthapiṇḍika and other disciples were bestowing abundant offerings and Pasenadi Kosala was bestowing gifts beyond compare, he never went to Sāvatthi.

One day the monks began to talk about him and said to the Teacher, "This monk Nigama Tissa, busy and active, lives in intimate association with his kinsfolk. Although Anāthapiṇḍika and other disciples are bestowing abundant offerings and Pasenadi Kosala is bestowing Gifts beyond Compare, he never comes to Sāvatthi." [284] The Teacher had Nigama Tissa summoned and asked him, "Monk, is the report true that you are doing thus and so?" "Reverend Sir," replied Tissa, "it is not true that I live in intimate association with my relatives. I receive from these folk only so much food as I can eat. But after receiving so much food, whether coarse or fine, as is necessary to support me, I do not return to the monastery, thinking, 'Why seek food?' I do not live in intimate association with my relatives, Reverend Sir." The Teacher, knowing the disposition of the monk, applauded him, saying, "Well done, well done, monk!" and then addressed him as follows, "It is not at all strange, monk, that after obtaining such a Teacher as I, you should be frugal. For frugality is my disposition and my habit." And in response to a request of the monks he related the following

[1] The Story of the Past presents an interesting problem. *Dh. cm.*, i. 284^{12}–285^{8}, is almost word for word the same as *Jâtaka* 429: iii. 491^{4-20}. *Dh. cm.* then makes Sakka utter, not the first stanza of *Jâtaka* 429, but the first stanza of *Jātaka* 430, and refers the reader to the tenth *Nipâta* for the rest of the story. In Fausböll's edition the story occurs in the ninth *Nipāta*. But it has ten stanzas and doubtless stood in the tenth *Nipāta* of the recension of the *Jātaka Book*, to which the compiler of the *Dhammapada Commentary* had access. Text: N i. 283–286.

9 a. Story of the Past: Sakka and the parrot

Once upon a time several thousand parrots lived in a certain grove of fig-trees in the Himālaya country on the bank of the Ganges. One of them, the king-parrot, when the fruits of the tree in which he lived had withered away, ate whatever he found remaining, whether shoot or leaf or bark, drank water from the Ganges, and being very happy and contented, remained where he was. In fact he was so very happy and contented that the Abode of Sakka began to quake. Sakka considered the cause, and seeing the parrot, determined to put him to the test. Accordingly he employed his supernatural power and withered up the tree. Straightway the tree became a mere stump, full of holes and cracks. When the wind beat upon it, there came forth from the tree a hollow sound, and out of the holes and cracks came forth dust. [285] The parrot ate the dust, drank water from the Ganges, and going nowhere else, remained perched on the top of the fig-tree, recking naught of wind and sun.

When Sakka observed how very happy and contented the parrot was, he said to himself, "I will go to him, let him talk of the virtue of friendship, grant him his heart's desire, and cause the fig-tree to bear ambrosial fruit." Accordingly Sakka assumed the form of a royal goose, and preceded by Wellborn in the form of an Asura nymph, went to the grove of fig-trees, alighted on the branch of a certain tree not far off, and entered into conversation with the parrot by pronouncing the following Stanza,

> There are trees with green leaves, trees aplenty with abundant fruit.
> Why does the parrot's heart delight in a tree that is withered and hollow?

(The entire Jātaka is here to be related in detail, just as it occurs in the tenth Nipāta. The occasion there is different from what it is here, but everything else is the same.) [1] When the Teacher had given this religious instruction, he said, "At that time Sakka was Ānanda, and the parrot-king was I myself. Thus, monks, contentment is my disposition and my habit. It is, therefore, not at all strange that my son Nigamavāsī Tissa, because he was so happy and contented, obtained me for his teacher. Such a monk, because he has attained the

[1] The *Jātaka* goes on to say that the parrot replied, "This tree has been good to me in the past. Why should I forsake it now?" Thereupon Sakka caused the tree to bloom anew and to bear abundant fruit.

Paths and the Fruits, is not liable to fall away; nay rather he is nigh even unto Nibbāna." So saying, he pronounced the following Stanza,

> 32. A monk who delights in heedfulness and views heedlessness with fear,
> Is not liable to fall away, but is nigh even unto Nibbāna.

Published by

Facsimile Publisher
Ashok Vihar, Delhi-110052 (India)
Website: www.facsimilepublisher.com

Distributed by

Gyan Books Pvt. Ltd.
5, Ansari Road, Daryaganj, New Delhi-110002 (India)
E-mail: books@gyanbooks.com, Website: www.gyanbooks.com

2 222000 011765